MANAGING THE UNIONS

MANAGING THE UNIONS

*The Impact of Legislation on
Trade Unions' Behaviour*

ROGER UNDY,
PATRICIA FOSH,
HUW MORRIS,
PAUL SMITH,
RODERICK MARTIN

CLARENDON PRESS · OXFORD

1996

Oxford University Press, Walton Street, Oxford OX2 6DP
Oxford New York
Athens Auckland Bangkok Bombay
Calcutta Cape Town Dar es Salaam Delhi
Florence Hong Kong Istanbul Karachi
Kuala Lumpur Madras Madrid Melbourne
Mexico City Nairobi Paris Singapore
Taipei Tokyo Toronto
and associated companies in
Berlin Ibadan

Oxford is a trade mark of Oxford University Press

Published in the United States
by Oxford University Press Inc., New York

British Library Cataloguing in Publication Data
Data available

Library of Congress Cataloging in Publication Data
Managing the unions: the impact of legislation on trade unions'
behaviour/Roger Undy . . . [et al.].
Includes bibliographical references and index.
1. Industrial relations—Great Britain. 2. Trade-unions—Great
Britain. 3. Labor laws and legislation—Great Britain. I. Undy,
R. (Roger) HD8391.M2964 1996 331.88'00941—dc20 95–47073
ISBN 0–19–828919–7

1 3 5 7 9 10 8 6 4 2

Typeset by Cambrian Typesetters, Frimley, Surrey
Printed in Great Britain on acid-free paper by
Biddles Ltd., Guildford and King's Lynn

PREFACE

The research reported in *Managing the Unions* could not have been written without the extensive co-operation we have received from trade unionists, politicians, and others: we are extemely grateful for their co-operation in the project. In particular, we are indebted to the national and local union officials who participated in the major case studies. They were very generous in giving their time and provided access to a wealth of written material. Many of the insights we gained were provided in off-the-record interviews on controversial and contentious issues, both inside and outside the trade union movement.

The research project has extended over a decade. The period has witnessed major changes in Government policy and in union strategies, developed partly in reaction to Government policy. We have tried to show the interaction between Government policies and union responses within the context of broader changes in the position of trade unions, as Government policy has been only one influence. The study shows how trade unions have modified structures and processes to adapt to the political and economic pressures of the 1980s and 1990s.

Large-scale empirical social research is necessarily a team effort. *Managing the Unions* is no exception. All team members were involved in all stages of the project, but with different contributions at different stages. Initial fieldwork was done primarily by Huw Morris and Paul Smith, with contributions by Patricia Fosh and Roger Undy. Subsequent papers were written by all members of the team. The team members took responsibility for different chapters of the book, which was brought together by Roger Undy; the order of authors reflects a division of labour, not a measure of overall contribution. The authors are especially grateful to Doreen Hirons of Templeton College for her patient work in processing the numerous drafts which have finally led to the present work.

We are very grateful to the Economic and Social Research Council for funding the major part of the early research and to the Nuffield Foundation for financial assistance with the later stages of the project.

Responsibility for material in the book and for the opinions expressed rests with the authors collectively.

CONTENTS

FIGURES

TABLES

ABBREVIATIONS

AC	Central Confederation of Professional Associations (Denmark)
ACAS	Advisory, Conciliation and Arbitration Service
AEEU[1]	Amalgamated Engineering and Electrical Union
AEU[1]	Amalgamated Engineering Union
APEX	Association of Professional, Executive, Clerical and Computer Staff
ASLEF	Associated Society of Locomotive Engineers and Firemen
ASTMS	Association of Scientific, Technical and Managerial Staffs
AUEW[1]	Amalgamated Union of Engineering Workers
AUEW(E)[1]	Amalgamated Union of Engineering Workers (Engineering Section)
AUT	Association of University Teachers
BACM	British Association of Colliery Management
BAEA	British Actors Equity Association
Bakers or BFAWU	Bakers, Food and Allied Workers' Union
BALPA	British Airline Pilots Association
BIFU	Banking, Insurance and Finance Union
Boilermakers	Amalgamated Society of Boilermakers, Shipwrights, Blacksmiths and Structural Workers
BT	British Telecom
CBI	Confederation of British Industry
CEC	Central Executive Committee
Cmnd.	Command Paper
CO	Certification Officer
COHSE	Confederation of Health Service Employees
COOO	Workers' Commissions (Spain)
CPS	Centre for Policy Studies
CPSA	Civil and Public Services Association
CPTUBIA 1990	Code of Practice for Trade Union Ballots on Industrial Action 1990

CPTUBIA 1991	Code of Practice for Trade Union Ballots on Industrial Action 1991
CROTUM	Commissioner for the Rights of Trade Union Members
CSEU	Confederation of Shipbuilding and Engineering Unions
DA	*Dansk Arbrejdsgiverforening* (Denmark)
DE	Department of Employment
EA 1980	Employment Act 1980
EA 1982	Employment Act 1982
EA 1988	Employment Act 1988
EA 1990	Employment Act 1990
EEF	Engineering Employers' Federation
EETPU	Electrical, Electronic, Telecommunication and Plumbing Union
EG	*Employment Gazette*
EIRR	*European Industrial Relations Review*
EMA	Engineers' and Managers' Association
EPA 1975	Employment Protection Act 1975
EPI	Employment Policy Institute
Equity	British Actors' Equity Association
ERBS	Electoral Reform Ballot Services
ETU	Electrical Trades Union
ETUC	European Trade Union Confederation
EU	European Union
FBU	Fire Brigades Union
FDA	Association of First Division Civil Servants
FT	*Financial Times*
FTAT	Furniture, Timber and Allied Trades Union
FTF	Central Confederation of Salaried Employees (Denmark)
GB	Great Britain
GLC	Greater London Council
GMB[2]	Name given to the union formed by GMBATU (GMWU)-Apex merger
GMBATU[2]	General, Municipal, Boilermakers and Allied Trades Union

GMWU[2]	General and Municipal Workers' Union
GPMU	Graphical, Paper and Media Union
HCSA	Hospital Consultants and Specialists Association
HRM	Human Resource Management
HVA	Health Visitors' Association
ICR	*Industrial Court Reports*
IDS	Incomes Data Services
ILO	International Labour Organization
INEM	National Employment Institute (Spain)
INSERO	National Institute of Social Services (Spain)
IOD	Institute of Directors
IPA	Involvement and Participation Association
IPM	Institute of Personnel Management
IRA 1971	Industrial Relations Act 1971
IRLIB	*Industrial Relations Legal Information Bulletin*
IRLR	*Industrial Relations Law Reports*
IRS	Industrial Relations Services
IRSF	Inland Revenue Staff Federation
ISTC	Iron and Steel Trades Confederation
LO	*Landorganization* (Denmark)
LRD	*Labour Research*
LUL	London Underground Limited
MEP	Member of European Parliament
MSF	Manufacturing Science and Finance Union
NALGO	National and Local Government Officers' Association
NAPO	National Association of Probation Officers
NATFHE	National Association of Teachers in Further and Higher Education
NCU	National Communications Union
NEDO	National Economic Development Office
NGA	National Graphical Association '82
NIRC	National Industrial Relations Court
NOMIS	National On-Line Manpower Information System
NUGMW	National Union of General and Municipal Workers (also referred to as the GMWU)

NUJ	National Union of Journalists
NUM	National Union of Mineworkers
NUPE	National Union of Public Employees
NUR	National Union of Railwaymen
NUS	National Union of Seamen
NUT	National Union of Teachers
OECD	Organization for Economic Co-operation and Development
PEC	Principal Executive Committee
POA	Prison Officers' Association
POEU	Post Office Engineering Union
PSOE	Spanish Socialist Workers' Party
RMT	National Union of Rail, Maritime and Transport Workers
RPI	Retal Price Index
SLADE	Society of Lithographic, Artists, Designers, Engravers and Process Workers
SOGAT	Society of Graphical and Allied Trades '82
SPOA	Scottish Prison Officers Association
STE	Society of Telecom Executives
TASS	Technical, Administrative and Supervisory Section (of Amalgamated Union of Engineering Workers)
T&G or TGWU	Transport and General Workers' Union
TSSA	Transport Salaried Staffs' Association
TUA 1871	Trade Union Act 1871
TUA 1984	Trade Union Act 1984
TUC	Trades Union Congress
TUCC	Trade Union Coordinating Committee
TUFL	Trade Unions for Labour
TULR(C)A 1992	Trade Union and Labour Relations (Consolidation) Act 1992
TURERA 1993	Trade Union Reform and Employment Rights Act 1993
TWU	The Tobacco Workers' Union
UCATT	Union of Construction, Allied Trades and Technicians
UCW	Union of Communications Workers

UGT	General Workers Confederation (Spain)
UK	United Kingdom
UNISON	Name given to the union formed by the NALGO-NUPE-COHSE merger
USDAW	Union of Shop, Distributive and Allied Workers
WIRS	Workplace Industrial Relations Survey

1. The AEEU, AEU, AUEW, and AUEW(E) are all abbreviations used by the Engineering Union which changed its name in the period studied following amalgamations (see Technical Appendix). In order to avoid confusion we have generally used the abbreviation AEU.
2. The GMB, GMBATU, GMWU, G&M, and NUGMWU are all abbreviations used by the General and Municipal Union which changed its name in the period studied following amalgamations (see Technical Appendix). In order to avoid confusion we have generally used the abbreviation GMB.

CONTRIBUTORS

ROGER UNDY is Fellow in Industrial Relations and Director of the Oxford Institute for Employee Relations at Templeton College, Oxford, and Lecturer at the University of Oxford.

PATRICIA FOSH is Professor of Human Resource Management at Cardiff Business School, University of Wales, College of Cardiff.

HUW MORRIS is Principal Lecturer in the Industrial Relations/Personnel Management Department, Kingston University.

PAUL SMITH is Lecturer in Human Resource Management in the Department of Human Resource Management and Industrial Relations, Keele University.

RODERICK MARTIN is Professor of Organizational Behaviour and Director of Glasgow Business School, Department of Management Studies, Glasgow University.

1

THE SCOPE AND STRUCTURE OF THE STUDY

INTRODUCTION

All Conservative Governments holding office throughout the 1980s and in the first half of the 1990s sought to manage the unions. They attempted, by a variety of means, including legislation, to solve what they saw as the union problem. This was both an economic and a political priority. Reducing union power was perceived as economically essential for freeing the labour market, and hence rejuvenating the economy through the free play of market forces. Politically, unions were perceived as 'overmighty subjects' in need of reform. Reducing their political and industrial power was seen as popular with the electorate and an important factor in helping the Conservatives win successive general elections. Moreover, it was also an integral part of the new right's ideologically determined agenda (Wedderburn 1989).

A central plank of the programme of legislative reform was the legislation on union ballots. Through a series of Acts the Conservatives tried to establish a common template for decision-making on key union elections and the calling of industrial action. The main vehicle chosen for this purpose had become by 1994 the individual secret postal ballot. In this study we examine the origins of this legislation, its purpose, the manner in which unions adapted to it, and its actual effect on union behaviour. We also assess the effect of this legislation compared with the impact of other environmental factors and union leaders' own initiatives for change. In the remainder of this introductory chapter we describe briefly the scope and method of the research, outline the structure and content of the study—including the frameworks adopted for assembling and analysing the material—and summarily describe the remaining chapters.

SCOPE AND METHOD OF RESEARCH

The research began in 1987, but built on previous work by Undy and Martin (1984) which examined the effect of the balloting provisions in the

1980 Employment Act. There were five major elements to the research strategy. First, we conducted two surveys of the rule books of TUC-affiliated unions in 1987 and 1992 and compared and contrasted these with a similar survey conducted for the previous research in 1980–2 (see the Technical Appendix for a detailed commentary on the rule book analysis). Through this process we established the extent and nature of changes in rule which may have been associated with the legislation. Second, we interviewed national officers of twenty-four unions, covering three-quarters of TUC membership (the unions are listed in Table 3.3). This complemented the rule book survey and was designed to establish union practice in balloting for elections and industrial action. It also explored whether or not the rule changes previously identified were the product of the legislation. Third, detailed case studies were made of six of the twenty-four unions (see Table 1.1) and four industrial disputes in which these unions were or had been involved. The twenty-four unions themselves represented a wide range of contrasts in size, membership composition, systems of government, merger activity and the use of ballots in the early 1980s. Particular care was taken in choosing six to be the subject of in-depth studies. Following the analytical taxonomy provided by Undy *et al.* (1981), six relatively large unions—over 100,000 members—with a range of different government systems and types of membership were selected for the case studies. The six unions categorized according to the taxonomy are shown in Table 1.1.

In Table 1.1 the first four columns are concerned with different aspects of union government, i.e., moving from left to right, the existence of one or two channels of decision-making (normally a bargaining and a non-bargaining channel); whether or not the union is relatively centralized or decentralized in its non-bargaining channel; whether or not power is concentrated or diffused at the national level; and whether or not union government is subject to political factionalism—or similar divisions—at the national level. The remaining three columns describe the membership of the six unions according to its composition, growth/decline, and member-ship market; in this latter category the issue is whether or not it was sheltered from, or exposed to, inter-union competition for members. The sheltered/exposed categorization indicates that the unions concerned had some sections of their membership in both categories.

As can be seen from Table 1.1, we had a wide variety of different types of union government represented in our six case studies. Thus, from the combination of surveys, the study of balloting practice in twenty-four unions and the six in-depth case studies, we were able to assess both to what extent the legislation affected different types of unions' decision-making processes, and to what extent these different processes influenced the application of the legislation and its outcomes.

The fourth element in the research strategy was the study of four

TABLE 1.1 Summary of characteristics of case-study unions

	Single/Dual channel	Vertical dimension	Horizontal dimension	Government factions	Membership composition	Growth/ Decline	Membership market
AEU	single channel	devolved	diffused	party system	homogeneous	decline	sheltered and exposed
CPSA	dual channel	centralized	diffused	3-way faction/party	homogeneous	decline	sheltered
EETPU	single channel	centralized	concentrated	party system	homogeneous	decline/ merger	sheltered
GMB	intermediate	devolved	concentrated	no caucus system	heterogeneous	decline/ merger	sheltered and exposed
NCU	federated organization	federated/ centralized	diffused	party system	homogeneous	decline/ merger	sheltered
TGWU	dual channel	centralized	diffused	caucus system	heterogeneous	decline/ merger	sheltered and exposed

collective bargaining situations—British Telecommunications, Derwent-side District Council, Jaguar Cars, and 'National Engineering Company' (a major British-owned engineering firm in the Midlands). These cases included disputes involving one or more of the six case-study unions. They therefore enabled us to study the effect of the balloting legislation on collective bargaining and industrial action in practice.

The fifth element in the research strategy was interviews with representatives of parties and institutions interested in the balloting legislation. These included, amongst others, employers' associations, the Department of Employment, and all three political parties. Obviously, we also examined relevant documents, papers, and academic studies. The research thus relied on multiple sources of data. It combined both relatively hard data from rule book surveys and qualitative data from interviews. It relied extensively on examining the effect of the legislation in its context and appreciating the complex interaction between the different parties or actors and their institutions, as they came to terms with the legislation. The case studies were thus critically important for helping unravel the effects of the legislation compared with other factors on changes in the relevant areas of union behaviour.

STRUCTURE AND CONTENT OF THE STUDY

The structure and content of the study is presented diagrammatically below (Figure 1.1, A Qualified Contingency Model of Change). This framework places the union at the centre of a complex web of pressures for change and interprets the effect of these on the union's leadership through the use of an amended and extended version of Child *et al.*'s (1973) representative and administrative rationalities. It is a 'qualified' contingency model because it recognizes that, despite the imposition of a new legal framework, unions still had choices to make in responding to the various factors represented in the diagram as bearing down on the union. The leaders had to evaluate the importance of the various pressures and decide on their responses. This was not solely dictated by the context in which they operated, although this was clearly very important for determining the range of choices available.

The structure and content of the study will now be outlined by reference to the diagram, starting with the two outer arcs, working inwards, and concluding with an explanation of the three rationalities. The arrows represent the general direction of the different influences and the inter-action between them. The broader arrows emanating from the external environment, and the unions' decision-making systems, are intended to emphasize the overall importance of these factors in influencing union behaviour.

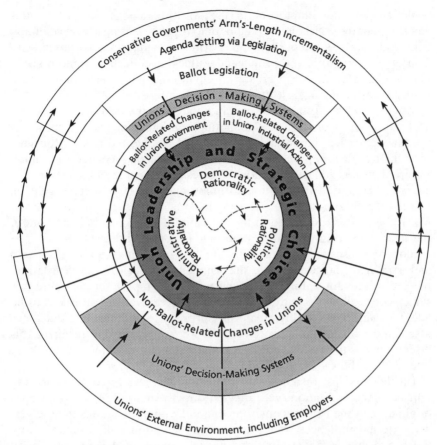

FIG. 1.1. Managing the unions: a qualified contingency model of change

The two outer areas—at the top, Conservative Governments' Arm's-Length Incrementalism: Agenda Setting via Legislation, and at the bottom, Unions' External Environment, including Employers (in which we include managers)—were closely connected. This interaction is indicated by the arrows. In this period the legislation and the external environment reinforced each other. The Conservatives' legislation was largely enabling, primarily relying for its application on the compliance of the unions or its enforcement by employers (or disaffected union members). The Government itself therefore stood above and at arms length from its actual application as it incrementally increased the legal regulation of the unions between 1980 and 1993. The wider environment—the economic, political, and social climate—served to weaken union resistance to the legislation, while encouraging employers to use, or threaten to use, it. In this environment the legislation served both to regulate certain aspects of union behaviour and to establish a much wider agenda. In association with Conservative rhetoric and propaganda attacking collectivism and praising individualism, it aimed to create an environment in which unions were perceived as acting against the wider public interest.

Moving inwards from the top arc in Figure 1.1, the next three layers, or arcs, show the Conservatives' balloting legislation emanating from the agenda-setting legislation and being filtered (the dotted arrows) through the unions' decision-making systems and affecting changes in union government and industrial action. The resulting degree of change in rule and practice varied from union to union and was largely contingent on unions' existing systems of decision-making. However, the manner in which the unions responded to the legislation (broad arrows in and out of the next inner ring) was also important for determining its effects. The unions' responses are illustrated by the next inner ring—union leadership and strategic choices. Given the enabling nature of the legislation, the procedures for enforcement, and unions' own preferences, there was some scope, albeit limited, for exercising choice over the processes to be adopted, and considerably greater opportunity to influence the outcomes associated with the new processes. As we will show, one result of this discretion was to produce outcomes which sometimes differed from those intended by the sponsors of the legislation.

The leaderships' responses to the legislation, and in consequence the impact of the legislation, was affected directly and indirectly by changes originating in the external environment and within the unions themselves. The external influences are represented in the bottom half of Figure 1.1 by the broad arrows penetrating directly into union leadership; the broad arrows filtering through the unions' decision-making systems; and the broad arrows directly producing non-ballot-related changes in the unions and subsequently feeding into the leadership. An example of the kind of factors involved can be made by reference to changes in employment. Changes in the size and composition of employment directly reduced union membership and indirectly reduced union income. As a consequence the leadership became more concerned with controlling and reducing the union's administrative costs, and thus made changes that directly affected union government and eventually fed back into the union's system of government and its democracy. For example, in cutting costs some unions opted to close offices, reorganize districts, and reduce the frequency of representative meetings—such as branch meetings. In some cases this led to more centralized decision-making. At the political level the loss of members and a reduction in income gave an added urgency to membership recruitment. This in turn raised the question of whether or not unions should adopt the politically controversial policy of offering employers single-union no-strike deals in exchange for sole recognition rights. Such developments affected union leaders' responses to the balloting legislation. For example, the threat of fines for non-compliance with the legislation was given added weight by the unions' financial fragility, while refusing to co-operate with strike ballots was not conducive to achieving single-union recognition agreements. Thus, an assessment of the effects of the balloting legislation on union behaviour cannot be achieved without recognizing that union leaders' responses were also contingent on other developments.

Similarly, in assessing the importance of the balloting legislation as an agent of change, it is important to set its effects on the outcomes associated with industrial action and union government against other factors also producing change in such aspects of union behaviour. For example, it would be naïve to assume that the marked fall in the number of strikes in the 1980s (see p. 219), as compared to the 1970s, was directly and solely due to unions complying with the balloting legislation on the calling of industrial action.[1] Clearly such factors as the level and rate of change of employment, the rate of inflation, increases in real wages and changes in the extent and levels of collective bargaining, all shown in Figure 1.1 as originating in a union's external environment, could be expected to influence the number of strikes called by a union, independent of changes in balloting processes.

Analogously, the extent to which union election results were determined by the type of ballot used also needs to be examined with reference to other developments. For example, changes in the choices offered in elections and the effect of increased campaigning for, and the organization of, votes may have an impact on outcomes. These kinds of considerations are represented in Figure 1.1 by both the arrows filtering through from the external environment to affect union leadership and its choices and the arrows on the curved lines linking non-ballot-related union change and ballot-related change. An example of this latter kind of non-ballot-related change would be the formation of a new and effective faction capable of fighting and winning union elections. As we will show later, this kind of development took place in the Manufacturing Science and Finance Union (MSF). The new faction had its roots in the internal political machinations that followed the formation of MSF by amalgamation and owed little to changes in the balloting process.

Finally, as illustrated in the centre of Figure 1.1, we analyse union leaders' responses to the balloting changes with reference to their strategic choices as interpreted through the rationalities framework. By strategic choice we do not necessarily mean that the leadership had formally adopted a consistent, cohesive, and integrated set of policies, although some unions were moving towards this position towards the mid-1990s. It is rather that, following Mintzberg (1987: 66–75), we 'read' their strategies from the patterns of relevant union responses to the legislation and related changes identified in our research. In other words we will be concerned with unions' realized strategies as discernable patterns of behaviour.

As regards 'rationalities' we have amended and extended the work of Child *et al*. (1973) regarding the tension within union organization between administrative and representative rationalities.[2] It is not our intention to suggest that union responses to legislation or other external developments were as precise or calculative as 'rationality' may be taken to indicate. Union leaders were presented with a restricted range of options. They were constrained by both the union's environment and union government and culture. Hence, their rationality was structured by events and organizational forms which, in the short run, they could not change. In this situation rationality is also taken to have both formal and substantive components. It is concerned with both means and ends. The leaders' responses to the balloting legislation and other factors were very much concerned with making adjustments to the means in order to safeguard the unions' abilities to achieve their ends. However, in the circumstances of the 1980s and 1990s the ends themselves were also subject to scrutiny and reassessment, particularly as regards organizational priorities.

As shown in Figure 1.1, we take the three rationalities as forming the union world and use them to analyse union leaders' strategic responses to the legislation in terms of their political, democratic, and administrative rationalities. Political rationality refers to the ultimate purpose and primary means of trade unions. It embraces both unions' ideological positions and their general approach to industrial relations. Means includes both political affiliation and their bargaining behaviour, for example co-operative or adversarial, when dealing with employers. Democratic rationality refers both to the unions' notions of democracy and the associated governmental systems. This covers such issues as the power relationship between full-time officials and lay activists and the centralization or decentralization of decision-making. Administrative rationality refers to the procedures designed to achieve the efficient management of the union. However, concern with efficiency in unions cannot be equated with the approach adopted in profit-maximizing or -satisficing organizations. Nevertheless, in the period under examination union leaders were generally very sensitive to issues which raised financial costs. Cost-cutting and the search for efficiency gains were important leadership concerns across most of the unions by the end of the period.

Thus, union leaders did not perceive or respond to the Conservative legislation, ostensibly designed to create a new form of individualized democratic rationality, solely in terms of its democratic purpose. They were also concerned to safeguard union political and administrative rationalities by, respectively, protecting the collective nature of the union and maintaining its organizational base. Hence, they sought to meet the demands made on their unions by the legislation and other hostile developments by limiting the perceived negative effects, using the legislation positively where possible and making changes in other fields to compensate for the difficulties it caused. Thus, we conclude the study of the balloting legislation by interpreting unions' responses and initiatives by reference to their strategic choices as shaped by the three rationalities at the centre of Figure 1.1.

THE REMAINING CHAPTERS

Following the above structure, we establish in Chapter 2 the external context in which the changes in unions examined in Chapters 3, 5, and 6 took place. In particular we examine the external developments which had most effect on the national level of union organization and specifically on union government. The role of Conservative Governments in instigating and encouraging such developments is central to this discussion, but the detail of its balloting legislation is reserved for Chapter 4. Chapter 3 explains and analyses a number of non-ballot-related changes in unions. It stresses the importance of the unexpected and marked reduction in union membership and density as a critical factor dominating much of union behaviour. Membership loss is seen as being a major cause, both direct and indirect (via mergers), of change in union structure and, consequently, union government. Hence, Chapters 2 and 3 provide the external and internal context of union organization before examining the balloting legislation and its effect on union behaviour.

Chapter 4 addresses directly the central topic of balloting legislation. It examines the wellsprings of the legislation before considering mandatory ballots for elections and industrial action. It demonstrates clearly the character of the Conservatives' incrementalist approach to legislation and how, over the period, the degree of intervention and regulation of union decision-making gradually became both more prescriptive and more extensive. Chapter 5 provides an assessment of the actual effect of this legislation on union elections and government. Changes in rule are examined before considering the legislative effect in practice. We show that there was, in rule and practice, extensive procedural compliance, but that the effect on electoral outcomes was much more problematic. In Chapter 6 we conduct a similar analytical exercise in respect of ballots and industrial action. In this case unions did not generally alter their rules to comply with the legislation. Instead they tended to use detailed and centrally prescribed regulations to ensure there was procedural compliance in practice. Again we raise questions about the effect on outcomes and consider how unions maintained their collective voice in the face of individualizing legislation. Chapter 7 completes this analysis by summarizing the findings in Chapters 5 and 6 and concludes by drawing the different strands of the study together under the umbrella of the three rationalities as discussed above. We show that leaders did have choices and they sought, with some success, to limit the damage threatened by the legislation before starting, at the end of the period, to respond to the challenge posed in a more strategic and positive manner.

In the final chapter we turn away from the British experience and consider its implications for other European countries. We compare and contrast the British approach to unions in the 1980s and early 1990s with that of the rest of the European Union. Our findings show that the other countries tended to work with the unions for economic recovery, rather than diminish their role by interventionist legislation. Thus the British unions' experience was and is likely to remain, at least in Europe, an exceptional case.

NOTES

1. In the Green Paper *Industrial Relations in the 1990s* (DE 1991: 1–5) the government recognized that a number of factors had affected the markedly reduced strike rate, while at the same time claiming that the law was of fundamental importance to the claimed and associated transformation of industrial relations.
2. The Child *et al.* (1973) framework was intended to facilitate the study of unions as complex organizations and to provide a guide for further empirical investigation of union behaviour. We found it very useful, as amended, for the latter purpose. In adopting and amending this approach we added the notion of political rationality and thus extended its application. However, we also limited its scope both by focusing on a particular type of change agent, i.e. the impact of balloting legislation on union behaviour, and by using it to analyse the leadership's strategic choices.

2

THE UNION CONTEXT

INTRODUCTION

In the period 1984–94, unions experienced marked changes in the context in which they operated. As Kessler and Bayliss (1992) and others have shown, unions, which reached the pinnacle of their influence and membership growth in 1979, suffered a series of adverse political and economic changes in the 1980s. Given the influence enjoyed by the unions in the 1970s these adverse developments came as a severe shock to the unions. Environmental changes produced a situation not previously experienced by the leaders of the major unions. Membership and influence both declined rapidly. Moreover, the unions' leaders were not prepared for such changes: they had no contingency plans to deal with such developments.

This chapter is not, however, primarily concerned with overall changes. We are not, for example, intending to explain the relationship between external changes and general developments on the shop-floor. Our more limited aim is to examine those key features of the environment most relevant to change in the national level of union organization and particularly in the structure and processes of union government.

The relative importance of the balloting legislation for union government can only be fully appreciated and evaluated alongside other factors also shaping such changes. Union leaders had choices to make in responding to Conservative legislation: such choices had to respond to other pressures as well as to Government legislation. In the area of union government specifically, decisions on various structures associated with mergers had a marked impact on union government. This chapter is concerned with the broader contextual influences which impacted on unions; the next chapter is concerned with relevant changes within the trade union movement.

In terms of Figure 1.1 presented on page 5, this chapter explores the factors represented in the interrelated upper and lower arcs. As suggested in the upper arc of the diagram, we see the Conservative Governments of the period as seeking to establish a particular political agenda through legislation and other means. This agenda conditioned the perceptions other key actors had of the role and legitimacy of trade unions. In this process it became an extremely powerful and indirect influence on union behaviour.

Following Lukes's (1974: 25) three-dimensional view of power, the agenda set by the Conservatives may be perceived as structuring the responses of all parties dealing, or interact'ₙ with trade unions. The agenda served to undermine the basic valuₐs of trade unionism by elevating individualism at the expense of collectivism. In this way it sought to discriminate against trade unions both politically and industrially. An iterative process of incremental and ever more restrictive anti-union legislation was at the centre of this approach. It was also accompanied by rhetorical denigration of trade unions. This rhetoric was an integral part of a process used to justify further rounds of restrictive legislation. The effect was therefore cumulative. The responses of union leaders—as of the public generally—were also conditioned by this cumulative process. Union leaders initially opted for resistance to change and made a series of *ad hoc* responses. In the late 1980s the damaging cumulative effect became more apparent and unions considered a more strategic response. We will examine such critically important environmental developments under the heading 'political climate'.

Unions also faced changes in the economic environment and in employers' policies (as noted in the lower arc of Figure 1.1). We include amongst economic factors changes in the labour market. In discussing employers' policies we examine the derecognition of unions and the introduction of Human Resource Management (HRM) and its associated techniques. Broadly, these developments again served to undermine the unions' organizational base. As we will show, unemployment and shifts in the level and composition of employment reduced the core territory traditionally organized by the large and predominantly manual unions. Thus, economic changes reinforced the negative influence of the political climate. In this situation the power balance shifted towards the employer and provided the opportunity for the introduction of new approaches and strategies, including HRM. Nevertheless, not all unions suffered equally from a deteriorating economic and employment environment and employers' new policies. Some unions were noticeably more exposed to, or sheltered from, the worst excesses of unemployment, compositional change, and anti-union employers. As a result unions differed in their responses to such developments. In general, it was the unions which experienced the most damage that moved to change their system of government. In many cases, this was driven by financial concerns, resulting from major membership loss. Political and economic factors and employers' policies are examined separately in this chapter for analytical purposes; but it was their combined and cumulative effects which helped shape union behaviour and led to changes in union government.

POLITICAL CLIMATE

The socially structured agenda aimed at the marginalization of the unions was primarily the product of three major changes in the political climate of the 1980s and early 1990s compared with the 1970s. These had important indirect and direct effects on union government. First, and most important, was the political dominance achieved by the Conservative Party. It was returned to power in four consecutive elections in 1979, 1983, 1987, and 1992. Over this period its free market economic policies and associated industrial relations legislation had a marked effect on union behaviour and internal organization. Second, and associated with the above, was the demise of tripartism. Third, as a corollary of the Conservatives' success, was the Labour Party's political weakness. The latter two developments also affected union organization, although to a lesser extent than the first. We will examine each of these factors in turn: the detail of the Conservatives' legislation will be explored in depth in Chapter 4.

The major environmental change directly affecting unions was engineered by successive Conservative Governments. Conservative administrations established a broadly consistent political and economic approach to unions which was held to justify and legitimize direct and extensive Government regulation of unions and their internal affairs. This system of regulation replaced the long established voluntary system of collective *laissez-faire*— although the system had already come under pressure in the 1970s from both Conservative and Labour Governments. The new approach was given special legitimation by the failure of the previous Labour Government to secure a continuing and viable 'Social Contract' with the unions in the later 1970s, so powerfully demonstrated by a series of strikes in the 'winter of discontent' in 1978–9 (McCarthy 1992: 37–9). The new system of union restrictions was presented as a vital and necessary part of the Conservative drive to create a deregulated and therefore free labour market. The fact that this itself involved an extreme form of regulation, compared with most western and industrialized societies,[1] did not deter the Conservatives. They introduced seven separate pieces of original legislation between 1980 and 1993 directly affecting trade unions. Each was used to tighten control over unions incrementally. Extensive restrictions on union freedom to organize and engage in industrial action and retain and recruit members were at the heart of this process. These restrictions included making unions vicariously liable for any industrial action by their members not previously sanctioned as required by the law; making unlawful all secondary action; outlawing the closed shop; repealing legislation supporting union rights for recognition and the extension of collective bargaining; and regulating the deduction of union subscriptions by employers (the 'check-off'). This process was accompanied by the private and public denigration of trade unions as the 'enemy within'[2] and as 'barriers to employment'.[3]

In the drive to make employees' terms and conditions of employment more responsive to the market, Conservative Governments also encouraged the decentralization of pay bargaining and the use of individualized performance-related pay systems (Kessler 1994: 469). They sought, by decentralization, to make bargaining outcomes adhere more closely to the demands of the local labour market. Further, by linking at least part, if not all, of pay settlements to the individual employee's performance, they tried to reduce the collectively determined element of pay. Thus, if the work-force could not be de-unionized and pay decollectivized it could, at least, be brought closer to the market and fragmented, if not atomized.

Government changes in the public sector, affecting both the nationalized industries and the non-trading public sector, also affected the political climate. The nationalized industries with obvious profit potential, such as BT and British Gas, were privatized early in the period—BT in 1984 and British Gas in 1986 (Marsh 1992: 187). The loss-making nationalized industries such as coal mining were prepared for denationalization by radical rationalization. Largely as a result of privatization and rationalization, employment in the nationalized industries fell from 1.85 million to 0.66 million between 1979–90 (Kessler and Bayliss 1992: 124).

The manner in which these policies were implemented also served to advance the Government's wider strategy towards trade unions. Two much-publicized and abortive strikes in the nationalized industries demonstrated to the unions the Conservative Government's power and resolve to execute the above policy. First, the Post Office Engineering Union's (POEU—later renamed the National Communications Union [NCU]) opposition to, and industrial action against, the privatization of BT served to demonstrate in 1983 the futility of industrial action judged by the Courts to be political. The Court of Appeal granted an interlocutory injunction to Mercury Communications (the new telecommunications company created to compete with BT) in 1983 on the grounds that the POEU action was not a trade dispute under the new narrow definition as provided by the Employment Act 1982 (Simpson 1986: 176–80). In essence the Court found that the dispute was called over the liberalization and privatization of BT. It therefore fell outside the newly narrowed immunity available to striking trade unions. This judgement showed clearly that a full-frontal assault on Government policy could not be sustained within the law.

Second, and much more importantly, the National Union of Mine-workers' (NUM) strike against pit closures in 1984–5 demonstrated the Government's resolve in the face of generally lawful industrial action. This year-long strike, which resulted in crushing defeat for the NUM, showed that the Government would go to extreme lengths to defeat any union opposing its public sector policies. Moreover, in defeating the NUM it defeated the 'vanguard of the proletariat'. For the NUM had, following its militant and successful action of the 1970s, persuaded the wider labour movement that it was almost invincible. As a consequence of its defeat, subsequent union resistance to the Government's policy on nationalized industries was very limited. When opposition did surface it tended to focus on more limited ends, such as achieving the best terms for redundancy or for transfer to the new employer, rather than outright opposition to the planned changes. For example, in 1994 in the face of Government plans for privatizing British Rail, the RMT directed its attention and the threat of industrial action towards securing good terms and conditions for members due to be transferred to Railtrack, one of the new rail businesses, and not directly against the scheme itself (*FT* 17.3.94).

In the public service and non-trading sector, outside the scope of privatization, the Government introduced substitute market mechanisms through a variety of means. Compulsory competitive tendering in local authorities (Walsh 1991); outsourcing across a range of services in all parts of the sector; market testing in central government; and the establishment of self-managing trusts in the NHS were all part of this process (Common *et al.* 1992). National pay negotiations with trade unions were seen as obstacles to the effective working of a market policy which aimed to produce market rates for the job. Hence, a number of changes were made to the process of pay determination. As in the civil service (Kessler and Bayliss 1992: 113), the emphasis was switched from treating employees fairly by comparison with similar workers in other sectors to paying a market rate which was seen as serving to recruit, retain, and motivate employees.

Unions in the public sector therefore faced either directly or indirectly a particularly determined and aggressive anti-union employer. Nevertheless, public sector unions in general, excluding the NUM, fared better in terms of membership growth than their counterparts in the more exposed parts of the private sector. In 1989, 69 per cent of public sector workers were unionized compared to 28 per cent in the private sector. Even among the recently privatized industries, unions sustained comparatively high levels of membership. For example, in water supply, privatized in 1989, 69 per cent of employees were still in a union in 1992 (*EG* 5.93: 193).

The financial pressures which were exerted on several private sector unions due to a very large loss of members were therefore absent from many, but not all, of the public sector unions. Hence the demands for an overhaul of their internal systems of organization to cut costs were generally less pressing in these unions. Nevertheless, the decentralization of bargaining, and the withdrawal of the Government's long-standing support for trade unions in the public sector, led public sector unions to consider the appropriateness of their internal organization. In many cases the structure and processes of government, particularly in the bargaining channel, was built around a highly formalized and centralized system of national negotiations. Moreover, local representation for grievances and other matters was for many public sector unions highly dependent on the employer providing generous time off, and other facilities, for lay representatives. In some unions there were few, if any, local full-time officials. Thus, although many public sector unions were less exposed than their counterparts in the private sector to external financial pressures, changes in the political environment exercised considerable pressure on public sector unions, causing them to reflect on the efficiency of their organizations and to search for new systems of government and representation, as with the NCU and the RMT organizing, respectively, in BT and British Rail.

The other two changes in the political climate noted above, the demise of tripartism and the failure of the Labour Party to win general elections, had less direct and significant impact on unions' systems of government than the overall policies and actions of the Conservative Government. However, the attack on tripartism and Labour's electoral failures contributed to the general atmosphere of anti-collectivism and anti-unionism. Both helped push trade unions on to the defensive, contributing to the pressures for a review of union strategy and internal structure.

In embracing free market economics the Conservatives clearly had little sympathy for previous Governments' consensual policies, which included involving unions in affairs of the state and seeking their co-operation in incomes policies (Buxton *et al.* 1994: 416–26). In the process of dismantling the tripartite system, trade union representatives were removed from Government bodies and quangos. This even extended in 1994 to removing the politically moderate General Secretary of the AEU from the Board of Governors of the Bank of England. The peak of the Conservative attack on tripartism was probably reached in 1992 when the Government abolished the National Economic Development Office (NEDO), created by a previous Conservative Government in 1962; abolition followed reduction in NEDO's activities in 1987 when its committees were cut and its status diminished by the Prime Minister's withdrawal from the Chair (Kessler and Bayliss 1992: 166).

The main effects of the changes in tripartism were felt by the TUC, not individual unions. The TUC, as the 'voice' of unionism to Government, clearly found its pressure-group role severely limited by the Conservative Government's opposition to any form of tripartism that appeared to give the trade unions a privileged position. As a consequence, the TUC found its member unions questioning the purpose of the TUC. Also, given their own financial problems, they questioned the value of their TUC subscriptions. Further, the Trade Union Reform and Employment Rights Act 1993 raised doubts about the TUC's traditional role in resolving inter-union disputes. The TUC's role in policing the 1939 Bridlington Agreement was undermined by the restrictions the 1993 Act placed on unions excluding or expelling union members.[4]

A corollary of Conservative electoral success was, self-evidently, the continued failure of the Labour Party in the four general elections held between 1979 and 1992. The effect of Labour's electoral defeats on the trade unions varied over the period. In the early 1980s trade unions had hoped and expected that the Labour Party would make a quick return to power in 1983. Following such a return the Labour Government was expected to repeal all Conservative union legislation. This was the optimistic phase. Again in the 1990s and in particular in 1992, hopes for a Labour victory were strongly held, but unions had begun to accept that trade union legislation would not be subject to total repeal by any incoming Labour Government.

In the optimistic phase, most unions resisted Government attempts at legislatively encouraged and subsequently enforced change in their systems of government. Moreover, they saw little need to reorganize on their own initiative, as the environment was expected to return to 'normal' when Labour was re-elected. Thus, as shown by Undy and Martin (1984: 173–6), most unions initially refused to accept money for postal ballots, as provided for by the 1980 Employment Act: a form of self-denial. Subsequently, following the 1984 Trade Union Act, refusal to conform became a much more costly exercise, as several unions found in resisting the legal requirement to hold a secret ballot on industrial action in 1984: the November 1984 dispute at Austin-Rover eventually resulted in the Transport & General Workers' Union (TGWU) being fined £200,000 (see below, p. 224). Within twelve months most unions, including the TGWU, were complying with the balloting legislation on industrial action. Union hopes of a future Labour Government winning an election, replacing the legislation, and, possibly, retrospectively repaying any fines were already receding.

The unions did not, however, lose faith in the Labour Party. Despite repeated electoral failures, union support for the Party remained solid. Following the requirements in the 1984 Trade Union Act for unions to secure a majority in secret ballots every ten years for the continuation or introduction of political funds (used by many unions to support the Labour Party), all the unions affected by the legislation balloted successfully for the retention of their funds. Thirty-seven unions balloted on this issue between May 1985 and March 1986. They all achieved substantial majorities in favour of their funds. In aggregate, 83 per cent of those voting supported the funds (Fatchett 1987: 121). The small number of unions that had reballoted before April 1994, as required under the ten-year rule, also voted to retain their funds. Thus the unions continued to finance the Labour Party. Over the period since 1979 their financial support continued to be very substantial: for example, the TGWU and GMB together provided some £40 million for the Labour Party in this period. The National Union of Public Employees (NUPE) also substantially increased its funding of the party. For some unions, the more repressive the Conservative legislation became, the more important it became to work for Labour's return to power. Nevertheless, the Labour Party's electoral failure helped convince unions that continued refusal to comply with those aspects of the Conservatives' legislation that carried sanctions was likely to prove financially costly.

To summarize, the Conservative Party's dominance of national politics throughout this period and its corollary, Labour's electoral failure, were the main environmental factors affecting change in union government. In addition to the crucial and central role played by the legislation, the Conservative Government's willingness to confront and defeat the NUM also served to demonstrate its resolve and ability to confront and defeat any trade union. As the Chancellor Nigel Lawson put it, it was a 'worthwhile investment' (Adeney and Lloyd 1986: 121). Further, the Government used its role as employer, and its opposition to tripartism, to foster a general anti-union climate in which unions could be politically and industrially marginalized. The failure of the Labour Party to win an election or limit the flow of anti-union legislation also served to convince the unions that continued non-compliance with the law was too costly. As the restrictive legislative framework was reinforced on a regular basis— new legislation approximately every two years—the overall political effect was cumulative and vitally important for exerting pressure for change in the trade unions.

ECONOMIC ENVIRONMENT AND THE LABOUR MARKET

Political and economic developments were closely associated during the period. However, three interrelated features of the economic context are particularly significant for their indirect effect on trade union organization. These are inflation, earnings, and the level and composition of employment. Changes in all three will be briefly described before commenting on their importance for prompting change in union government.

As noted by Kessler and Bayliss, there were three different periods of economic activity of relevance to industrial relations in the period 1982–90 (Kessler and Bayliss, 1992: 40). From 1982–6 there was a period of slow economic recovery following the recession of 1979–81. Between 1987–9 there was an economic boom, followed by a period of severe recession starting in 1990, with some signs of slow and hesitant recovery in employment in 1993–4. However, as Figure 2.1 shows, unemployment rose, despite a resumption of output growth, over the whole period between 1980 and 1986, reaching a peak of 3 million in 1986–7, before

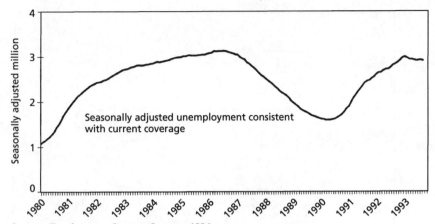

Source: *Employment Gazette*, January 1994.

FIG. 2.1. Claimant unemployment: United Kingdom 1980–93

falling temporarily below 2 million between 1987–90. It rose rapidly again from a low point in April 1990, reaching 2.8 million in 1993. This was 1.3 million above the April 1990 level. It should also be recognized that the above figures underestimated the growth in unemployment: changes in the methods used for calculating unemployment in this period resulted in a significant reduction in the numbers recognized as unemployed (EPI 1992, 1993).

The consumer prices indices (Figure 2.2) show that inflation fell from a high point of 20 per cent in 1980 to around 5 per cent in 1984. It then peaked in the boom years at 10 per cent in 1989–90, before falling to an historically low figure of 1.4 per cent in November 1993. Over the whole period 1979–90 the RPI increased by 130 per cent. Over the same period occupational earnings more than kept pace with inflation. Average earnings for all men increased by 192 per cent and for women by 220 per cent (Kessler and Bayliss 1992: 46). However, there were wide variations in the growth of earnings between occupations. The higher-paid employees benefited most, with the professional and related occupations experiencing an increase of 244 per cent for men and 253 per cent for women (ibid. 197). Manual employees and the low-paid, particularly in the public sector, fared much worse than other groups. The overall increase for manual groups was 155 per cent for men and 168 per cent for women (ibid. 97).

The composition of employment also changed radically. Changes in gender and status of employment (full-time or part-time) are shown in Figure 2.3 for the period 1983–93. It can be seen from Figure 2.3 that female employment grew much faster than male over this period, as did part-time, compared with full-time, employment. Over 2 million of the 3 million increase in employment between 1983 and 1990 was accounted

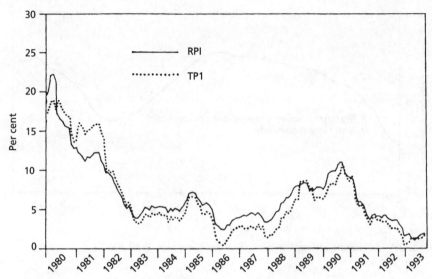

Source: *Employment Gazette*, January 1994.

FIG. 2.2. Consumer prices indices: increases over previous year

for by women. In the period 1981–92 part-time employment provided 1¼ million extra jobs and its share of employment rose from 19 per cent to 24 per cent.

There were also marked changes in the composition of employment by industry over the period from the early 1980s. As Figure 2.4 shows, there was a reduction of 2 million jobs in manufacturing between 1981 and 1993 and a growth of over 2 million in services over the same period. The resulting changes in the composition of employment are shown in Figure 2.5.

As clearly shown in Figure 2.5, apart from services there was a marked fall in employment in all sectors between 1981 and 1993. However, in the early 1990s recession almost 340,000 jobs were also lost in services between 1990 and December 1992. Nevertheless, this was still considerably fewer than lost by manufacturing, which declined by a further 820,000 jobs in the same period.

In parallel with the above movement towards part-time, female, and service industry employment, there were two further changes of importance to unions: first, a change in the occupational pattern of employment and, second, a reduction in the size of employing units. Regarding occupational changes, between 1984 and 1991 there was a marked increase in white-collar jobs and a sharp decline in blue-collar or manual jobs.

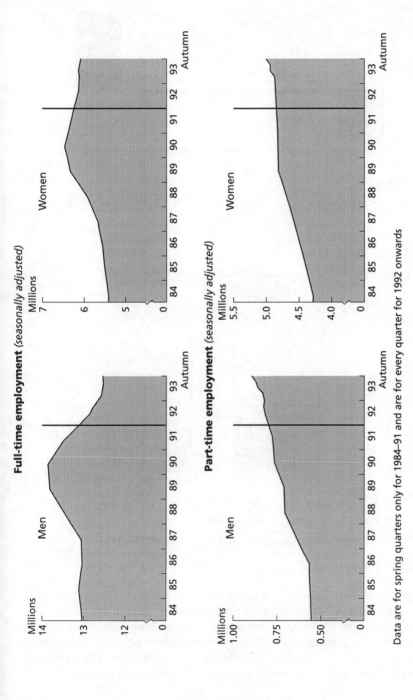

Source: *Labour Force Survey Quarterly Bulletin* no. 7, March 1994.

FIG. 2.3. Change in the type of unemployment: 1983 and 1993

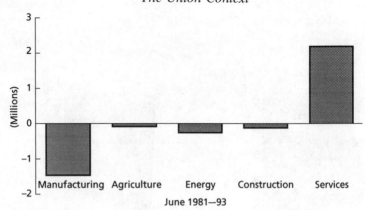

Source: NOMIS.

FIG. 2.4. Changes in the number of employees 1981–93: by industry GB

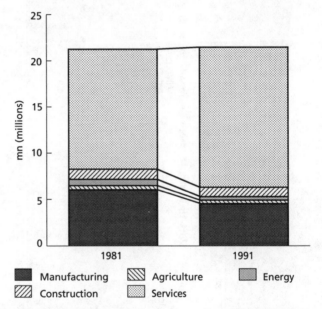

FIG. 2.5. Employees in employment by industry, June 1981–93 GB

Managerial and professional occupations (as broadly grouped in the 1991 labour force survey) increased by 25 per cent, clerical and related jobs by 11 per cent, and other non-manual occupations by 12.6 per cent. In contrast, craft and similar occupations dropped by 3 per cent and general labourers by 50 per cent. Over the same period the self-employed increased from 11 per cent to 13 per cent of total employment.

The size of the employing unit also declined during the 1980s. The most comprehensive survey of industrial relations conducted in this period recorded a decline in the mean size of workplaces from 118 employees in 1980 to 102 in 1990 (Millward *et al*. 1992: 16). In manufacturing the mean size fell from 185 employees in 1980 to 128 in 1990. Thus, between 1980 and the early 1990s there was a shift away from manual employment in large employing units towards white-collar work in smaller units and an increase in self-employment.

The economic and employment changes briefly noted above were all inimical to trade union organization. Even though, as we will show in the next chapter, there is no generally accepted comprehensive theory of union growth or decline, it is generally accepted that the above changes were damaging to trade union organization and specifically to the recruitment and retention of union members. Unemployment and the compositional changes reduced the actual and potential membership traditionally recruited by the leading general worker unions (the TGWU and GMB) and the former craft unions (the Amalgamated Engineering Union [AEU] and the Electrical, Electronic, Telecommunication and Plumbing Union [EETPU]), by reducing employment in their core job territories. The TGWU's General Secretary graphically described it in interview as a 'meltdown' in the labour market. Moreover, many of the new employment opportunities developed in industries and occupations notoriously difficult to unionize, even in times of economic boom. This was particularly so with the growth of employment in retailing. Further, the demise of many large employing units and the growth of smaller units shifted employment into units normally with lower levels of union density and more costly to organize. Finally, the growth in self-employment, part-time employment, and female employment produced more workers less likely to unionize compared with full-time employees. For example, in 1991 43 per cent of full-time male employees were unionized compared to 39 per cent full-time women, 22 per cent part-time employees, and 11 per cent of full-time self-employed (*EG* 1993a: 673–89).

Economic factors also combined to reduce union bargaining power. Historically high levels of unemployment for the greater part of the period reduced the likelihood that union members would risk their jobs by taking industrial action over pay. Further, the failure of the miners' year-long strike to prevent job losses strongly suggested that industrial action to save jobs could be counter-productive. More recently, in the early 1990s, high unemployment and low inflation combined to restrict further unions' bargaining power. The threat to jobs, and the knowledge that there would be little chance of gaining pay increases significantly above the very low rate of inflation, depressed militancy.

Such enforced moderation helped produce, by 1992, the UK's lowest strike activity for more than a century. Working days lost per 1,000 employees declined to 20 in 1992, compared with an average of 250 between 1983–92 (*EG*, 12.93: 545–51). In several interviews in 1993, leading national officials referred to the important role of the economic environment in reducing industrial action by noting their members' tendency 'to keep their heads down' in such circumstances. These economic factors also interacted with changes in the composition of employment to contribute to the reduction in union membership: an increase in membership in non-unionized territories is at least partly dependent on unions demonstrating their effectiveness in highly unionized areas. The defeat of the NUM, referred to above, and union failure to defend jobs in their traditional territories, no doubt reinforced the view that unions had little to offer the non-unionized. Similarly, the long-term increase in real earnings, with many of the less unionized groups gaining the greater increases, suggested that union membership did not necessarily lead to higher pay.

In so far as economic factors reduced trade union membership, they had marked direct and indirect effects on union organization. In particular the unions recruiting primarily, and often competitively, in the manufacturing sector—the TGWU, AEU, GMB, and the Manufacturing Science and Finance Union (MSF)—suffered from these developments. They all experienced a deterioration in their financial situation due to a marked loss of membership. Amongst others, the TGWU, AEU, and MSF all suffered major financial difficulties. The TGWU moved from a surplus of some £5 million on income over expenditure in 1986 to a loss of £12 million in 1991.[5] Thus, one of the main causes of union-instigated change in union government (including administration) in the early 1990s was the need 'to balance the books'.

Towards the end of the period, therefore, economic pressures bit deeply into unions' resources and raised questions about their effectiveness. In many large and predominantly private sector unions, financial difficulties were critically important factors causing the national leadership to introduce changes in union systems of government and administration. At the same time, some public sector unions were more sheltered from such economic pressures: changes made in these unions were thus more likely to be the product of mergers or political and legislative requirements.

To summarize and conclude concerning the economic aspects of the unions' environment between 1984–94: apart from a brief period between 1987–9, the economy acted as a significant constraint on union power throughout the period. Crucially, the level of unemployment remained historically high and the new jobs created were not readily unionized. This contributed to a significant continuing and largely unexpected membership decline. Loss of members and the associated financial difficulties had a particularly marked effect on unions' recruiting, primarily in manufacturing. It caused them to question their existing forms of organization, including their systems of government. In some cases, and towards the end of a very difficult economic period, this led to a radical review of the organization, including retrenchment and union mergers. As a consequence changes were also made in union government.

EMPLOYERS' POLICIES

The political and economic developments noted above had a notable impact on the balance of power between employer and union. The context in which unions organized post-1979 served to enhance the power of the employer and diminish that of the union. In these circumstances employers had much greater discretion in the choice and implementation of industrial relations policies than they had experienced in the preceding decade. Moreover, the Government's legislative programme depended extensively on employers and, to a much lesser extent, on union members and members of the public, for its implementation. In the latter two cases, but not the first, they could be aided in their actions by, respectively, the Commissioner for the Rights of Trade Union Members (1988 Employment Act) and the Commissioner for Protection Against Unlawful Industrial Action (1993 Trade Union Reform and Employment Rights Act).[6]

The provision of an economic and political context that gave employers the confidence and opportunity to exercise their rights under the legislation, particularly in respect of industrial action, was therefore central to the successful operation of the legislation. As argued above, the context served this purpose extremely well. Over the period, union leaders became more sensitive to threats of fines and ultimately sequestration (Wedderburn 1986: 705–12). Given the deterioration in the financial well-being of many of the larger unions by 1994, the threat of fines was an important consideration in determining how to respond to the legislation. Hence, unions took great care to comply with the law on industrial action in order to avoid the sanctions open to employers.

In this climate employers initiated a number of changes in the 1980s and early 1990s which directly and indirectly affected union organization, including union government. These involved, *inter alia*, the decentralization of collective bargaining, derecognition of trade unions, and the introduction of human resource management techniques.

The decentralization of bargaining initiated in the 1970s gathered pace throughout the latter part of the 1980s. Multi-employer bargaining declined significantly between 1984–90, as Table 2.1 reveals. Unions faced the dissolution of many national agreements, including 16 major agreements covering one million employees between 1985–90. However, as Table 2.1 also shows, multi-employer bargaining remained the most important level of pay determination in 1990 despite falling from 40 per

TABLE 2.1 Basis for most recent pay increase, all sectors, 1980, 1984, and 1990

	Manual employees			Non-manual employees		
	1980	1984	1990	1980	1984	1990
Result of collective bargaining	55	62	48	47	54	43
Most important level:						
Multi-employer	32	40	26	29	36	24
Single employer, multi-plant	12	13	13	11	13	15
Plant/establishment	9	7	6	4	4	3
Other answer	1	1	2	2	1	1
Not result of collective bargaining	44	38	52	53	46	57
Locus of decision about increase:						
Management at establishment	–	20	31	–	30	37
Management at higher level	–	11	15	–	15	17
National joint body	–	5	4	–	2	5
Wages Council	–	3	2	–	1	*
Not stated	–	1	*	–	*	*
Base: establishments with employees named in column heads						
Unweighted	1899	1853	1831	2034	2010	2058
Weighted	1823	1749	1697	1988	1985	1992

Source: Millward et al. (1992), 221.

cent to 26 per cent. Nevertheless, unions affected by these changes clearly needed to consider how they could reorganize their bargaining arrangements and representation in order to service the new lower-level negotiations.

Derecognition of trade unions increased over this period. As can be seen from Table 2.1, pay increases not determined by collective bargaining grew for manual employees from 38 per cent to 52 per cent, and for non-manuals from 46 per cent to 57 per cent, between 1984 and 1992. Millward (1994: 16–19), in a subsequent analysis of the causes of these changes, showed that a significant part was due to derecognition of unions in existing plants, as well as union failure to gain recognition in newly established plants. The most extensive derecognition took place in shipping, provincial newspapers, and national newspapers (Smith and Moreton, 1993: 106). However, it also occurred across a wide spread of other industries, including the derecognition of large groups of managers in British Rail and BT (Gall and McKay 1994). The unions facing derecognition searched for new means of organization capable of resisting or compensating for such developments. For the unions in printing and shipping the response involved union mergers and, as a consequence, changes in their systems of government, as we will show in the next chapter.

Human resource management (HRM) was more talked of, or written about, than implemented in this period. In essence HRM involved, in its more innovative form, a strategic approach to managing employees, a shift towards individualism and away from collectivism, and the introduction of a number of techniques aimed at gaining the commitment of newly empowered employees (Blyton and Turnbull 1992). The most comprehensive survey of management practice, rather than management rhetoric, found, in 1990, that the evidence for a growth in HRM pointed to a 'rather modest change and development, rather than a sea change' (Millward 1994: 127). The growth found in HRM practices was mainly 'confined to large, unionised enterprises' (ibid. 128). This, it was suggested, pointed towards its use as a means of reducing the role of unions as intermediaries between employer and management, rather than for increasing employees' involvement.

HRM may therefore be seen as a means of extending managerial control. As the Government sought to prevent unions from distorting the workings of the free market, so some managers sought to prevent what they saw as the unions' damaging restrictions on management control of the work process. Joint regulation was 'bad' and unilateral management regulation 'good'. The most likely and direct impact of such changes on trade unions was to raise questions about the relevance of union political rationality and associated forms of organization. In particular, the individualization of the employees' effort–reward bargain, mainly through the introduction of performance-related pay, challenged unions' basic collectivist values. A survey of derecognition cases cited the desire to introduce personal contracts and/or link pay to individual performance as a primary reason for derecognition (IDS 1992b: 11).

The threat that individualization of this kind posed for unions was widely recognized within the union movement. In the TGWU's 'Focus for the Future' and the MSF's paper 'MSF into the 21st Century' individualization was seen as a central issue. Both strategy papers discussed the kind of reorganization needed to cater for such developments. In contemplating putting more resources into individual representation, both unions also noted the demands which such a move would have on the services they would be expected to provide and the reorganization this would involve. For example, the MSF noted that the individualization of employment relationships required the union to 'adapt our services to these new circumstances and market them in new ways . . . this could include different levels of services for different levels of subscription' (MSF 1993: 8).

However, management does not necessarily use HRM as an overt or covert anti-union strategy. In certain circumstances union support for HRM, or some of its techniques, can help management legitimize its introduction and gain employee co-operation in its implementation. For example, the union could be expected to represent the collective view on such HRM issues as teamwork, joint consultation, flexible working, etc. and negotiate its introduction, rather than see it introduced unilaterally. This was indeed the case in the much-publicized and innovative 'New Deal' signed at Rover cars in 1992 (IRS 1992: 12–15). Under this agreement the leading unions involved, the TGWU and the AEU, negotiated an agreement guaranteeing a high degree of job security and no lay-offs in return for accepting a package of HRM changes. Thus, even if the survey material suggests that HRM is in general damaging for unions, case studies suggest that this is not necessarily the automatic outcome of managements adopting such policies, even in the hostile climate of the early 1990s.

To summarize: many employers had a clear and growing opportunity to marginalize unions in the period after 1979. Some clearly took this opportunity and in extreme cases derecognized trade unions. This policy was, however, still limited to a small minority of employers even in the 1990s. Many more employers chose to decentralize bargaining. Thus, unions which had traditionally organized themselves to deal with national multi-employer negotiating bodies faced the problem of reorganizing their bargaining structures to meet the needs of local negotiations. This clearly had implications for union government. The development and application of HRM policies was more limited. Although it was probably intended to lead to a further reduction in trade union influence in most companies in which it was developed, it was not always used for this purpose. Moreover, some unions were ready to adjust to the new management techniques and negotiate agreement to their introduction. In these instances, unions offered management their qualified support for those parts of HRM which they considered compatible with their own objectives. Indeed, in the early 1990s, a number of senior union leaders promoted the notion of industrial partnership and the advantages of co-operating in HRM-type initiatives (IPA 1993: 16).

SUMMARY AND CONCLUSIONS: UNIONS AND THE HOSTILE ENVIRONMENT

The political, economic, and employer context in which unions operated after 1979 reinforced the restrictive legal framework the Conservative Governments gradually established. It is not easy to unravel the specific effects of these developments. However, to the extent that the dominance of free market economics, the deregulation of the labour market, the revision of public sector industrial relations, and the near-destruction of the NUM were all the result of Conservative Government action, then the political context was the critical factor. These developments and the manner in which they were achieved established a political agenda that dominated the unions' environment. This continuous and consistent social structuring was cumulative. It served to make the marginalization of trade unions both politically and industrially respectable. Employers were thus given the encouragement and the power to execute a similar policy in the workplace and, when appropriate and necessary, sufficient confidence to use the anti-union legislation.

At the beginning of the period, following the influence they enjoyed in the 1970s, unions were rather complacent. There was an initial tendency to sit back and wait for the Labour Party to win a general election, repeal the legislation, and reverse the economic policies. Gradually, the scale of the changes taking place was recognized. Outright rejection of the legislation, particularly if it gave employers the right to bring court action against the unions, was discarded and more circumspect policies adopted. Unions also, in time, started to look to their own salvation. In the late 1980s or early 1990s, following further membership loss and the failure of Labour, yet again, to win a general election, comprehensive and radical proposals for change in union government began to emerge in some of the larger unions. They reviewed their systems of organization and attempted to shape their own environment. By these changes they sought to create a more favourable political climate and to reposition and reorganize themselves so as to respond more positively to the problems they faced. The next chapter now examines the changes which unions made largely in response to the threats posed by the above external developments.

NOTES

1. For an international comparison of legal intervention in union affairs which shows the extent of Britain's regulations as compared to other industrial societies, see Fosh *et al.* (1993b).
2. Mrs Thatcher used this phrase when Prime Minister while addressing the 1922 Committee on 19 July 1984.
3. 'Removing Barriers to Employment' was the title of the Department of Employment Green Paper (DE 1989a).
4. *IRLIB* 479 (Aug. 1993), commenting on TURERA 1993, noted that 'A further effect of the new law is to undermine the TUC's "Bridlington principles", in that a trade union will no longer be able to exclude would-be members solely on the grounds that their membership would break "Bridlington Principles" '. The new s. 174 of the Act, within certain restrictions, allowed an employee to join any union of their choice where more than one union organizes employees of a similar class. As a consequence, it was thought the TUC would find it more difficult to deal with and resolve claims of 'poaching' by competing member unions, because it could not order a union to return 'poached' members to the original unions without breaching the new Act.
5. See TGWU (1992a: 2) for a discussion of the union's financial difficulties.
6. See Chapter 4 for a discussion of the role of the two Commissioners.

3

CHANGING UNION BEHAVIOUR

INTRODUCTION

The industrial relations climate of the 1980s and early 1990s moved, as shown in the previous chapter, strongly against trade unions' interests, particularly towards the end of the period. Partly as a result of this development, many unions experienced significant and unexpected falls in membership. Following the rapid growth of union membership and union influence in the 1970s, the unions were not well prepared, either organizationally or financially, to deal with such marked changes in their fortunes. There had been little reason in the 1970s to develop contingency plans for the hostile environment of the next decade and, despite the increases in membership between 1969 and 1979, the unions' basic financial position in 1980 was not healthy. For, as Willman (1989) has shown, even in the halcyon days of the 1970s, income from membership subscriptions ran consistently below total expenditure. Unions were not therefore in a position to spend their way out of their difficulties even if they had known what new initiatives to fund. Moreover, the Conservative Government's attempts to marginalize the unions politically and industrially compounded their difficulties and helped to serve notice that they could not expect much, if any, help from external sources. Unions were therefore thrown back onto their own rather limited resources. Membership loss was in these circumstances both a major change and the trigger for further changes in union behaviour.

As illustrated in Figure 1.1 (p. 5), the non-ballot-related changes both affected and reflected leaderships' strategic choices and interacted with the balloting legislation to influence its effectiveness. Hence, before examining in detail in later chapters the balloting legislation and its effect on union elections and collective bargaining behaviour, we will consider some of the important non-ballot-related changes in unions which occurred over the same period. Given the severity of the impact of membership loss on other aspects of union behaviour, we first consider the closely related questions of membership, merger, and structure, before turning, second, to government. Issues of government include matters that affected, and in turn were affected by, both democratic and administrative rationalities. As we will show, changes in government generated tension between the two.

Third, and central to a union's political rationality, we consider changes in objectives and means. We will examine each of these areas of change and comment on their causes. In conclusion, the interrelationship between these different aspects of union behaviour, and the relative influence of the various factors promoting change, will be considered.

UNION MEMBERSHIP, MERGER, AND STRUCTURE

In the period of Conservative Government the number of unions and union members declined from the 1979 peak as shown in Table 3.1. In total, union membership fell by 28 per cent and the number of unions by 39 per cent. The TUC experienced a similar decline in its affiliation and membership. In 1979 the TUC had 112 affiliated unions and a membership of 12,128,078. By 1991 the number of affiliates was down to 74, a fall of 34 per cent, and its membership was 8,192,664, down by 32 per cent (see Table 3.2).

The 24 unions in our study (including the six in-depth case studies) experienced changes in membership over the period 1979–91 as shown in Table 3.3.

As this table shows, 20 of the 24 unions in our study suffered a loss of members between 1979 and 1991. The average loss per declining union was 30 per cent. The four unions gaining membership averaged an increase of

TABLE 3.1. Trade unions: numbers and membership, 1979–91

Year	Number of unions at end of year	Total membership at end of previous year (thousands)	Percentage change in membership since previous year
1979	453	13,289	+1.3
1980	438	12,947	−2.6
1981	414	12,106	−6.5
1982	408	11,593	−4.2
1983	394	11,236	−3.1
1984	375	10,994	−3.2
1985	370	10,821	−1.6
1986	335	10,539	−2.6
1987	330	10,475	−0.6
1988	315	10,376	−0.9
1989	309	10,158	−2.1
1990	287	9,947	−2.1
1991	275	9,585	−3.6

Source: *EG* 5.93: 191.

TABLE 3.2. TUC affiliated unions and membership, 1979–89

Year	Number of unions	Membership	Percentage change in membership since previous year
1979	112	12,128,078	
1980	109	12,172,508	+0.5
1981	108	11,601,413	−5.0
1982	105	11,005,984	−5.0
1983	102	10,512,157	−4.5
1984	98	10,082,144	−4.0
1985	91	9,855,204	−2.0
1986	88	9,585,729	−2.5
1987	87	9,243,297	−3.5
1988	88	9,126,911	−1.0
1989	78	8,652,318	−5.5
1990	76	8,416,832	−2.7
1991	74	8,192,664	−2.7

Source: TUC Congress Reports, 1979–91

17 per cent. Overall the 24 unions lost, in aggregate, 29 per cent of their 1979 membership. Thus, the general experience of the unions in our study of union practice was one of considerable membership loss. It was the exceptional union operating in the public—or recently privatized—sector that increased its membership: two of the unions with gains in 1989 recruited in the newly privatized BT and the other two recruited in the public sector. One of the unions enjoying a growth in membership, the NCU (23 per cent growth), was included in the case studies. However, it should be noted that the NCU secured a transfer of approximately 40,000 members from the CSPA in 1985 and that without this transfer it too would have experienced a marginal decline in membership. Also, as will be shown later, a number of other unions also mitigated their membership loss by merging in this period.

Aggregate union density also declined over the period 1979–91. Changes in density are not easily calculated.[1] However, there is no doubt that union density fell significantly throughout this period. Table 3.4 indicates the extent of the change in density in the UK between 1979 and 1987 (in this table the unemployed are included as members of the labour force used for calculating the percentage in trade unions). Using data from the 1989, 1990, and 1991 Labour Force Surveys, it has also been calculated that union density fell again to 38.8 per cent in spring 1989, 38.0 per cent by the following spring and to 33 per cent in 1991 (*EG* 1991: 342).

Changing Union Behaviour

TABLE 3.3. Trade unions in ballots study: membership change, 1979–91

	1979	1991	Percentage change
NUM	254,887	53,112	−79
*AEU	1,509,607	702,228	−53
TSSA	72,659	36,566	−50
NUR	180,000 ⎱	118,000[1]	−46
NUS	40,000 ⎰		
*CPSA	223,884	122,677	−45
NUT	290,740	169,007	−42
*TGWU	2,086,281	1,223,891	−41
UCATT	348,875	207,232	−41
BFAWU	44,221	35,206	−20
SOGAT	205,784	163,635	−20
IRSF	65,257	52,913	−19
NUPE	691,770	578,992	−16
*EETPU	420,000	366,650	−13
EMA	47,000	40,944	−13
ASLEF	21,446	18,850	−12
*GMB	967,153	933,425	−4
TASS	200,954 ⎱	653,000[2]	−3
ASTMS	471,000 ⎰		
NALGO	753,226	744,453	−1
NATFHE	70,652	73,796	4
STE	22,933	27,151	18
*NCU	125,723	154,783	23
FBU	41,533	51,638	24
Total	9,155,585	6,528,149	−29

*Case-study unions

[1] The figure for the NUR in 1991 is the combined membership of the NUR and NUS resulting from their merger in 1990 to form the RMT.
[2] The figure for the ASTMS in 1991 is the combined membership of the ASTMS and TASS resulting from their merger in 1988 to form the MSF.

The Workplace Industrial Relations Survey (WIRS) of 1990 also provides further information on changes in union density over the period 1984–90 (Millward *et al.* 1992). The survey found that union density declined from 58 per cent in 1984 to 48 per cent in 1990, with a more marked decline among manual than non-manual employees. One of the most striking features of the 1990 survey was that there was an increase in the proportion of workplaces with no members at all and a significant movement away from union membership across all workplaces in the

TABLE 3.4. Trade union density

	Per cent
1979	53
1980	52
1981	51
1982	49
1983	48
1984	46
1985	45
1986	43
1987	41

Source: Disney (1990).

trading sector (the traditionally highly unionized sector) across the period 1984–90. This decline in density was experienced in workplaces with both high and low densities of membership in 1984.

Various explanations or hypotheses have been advanced for the above decline in union membership and density. These explanations vary according to the following interrelated dimensions of the studies conducted. The research method, or dominant research method, predetermines the nature of the findings to a great extent. If the researchers seek to explain aggregated data and work top-down, rather than explore disaggregated data and work bottom-up, they will tend to one set of explanations rather than another. Top-down analysis lends itself to quantitative and deductive methods and bottom-up to qualitative and inductive methods of research. If those seeking to explain the cause of aggregated union growth work on data from the top down, they invariably use econometric modelling, select their data, test their correlations for significance, and then search, often imaginatively, for an explanation of the process which supports their findings. The result is that they almost always conclude that it is the external (i.e. external to the union as an institution) variables, which they managed to quantify in order to include them in their model, that caused the changes to occur (see Disney 1990). In contrast, the more qualitative researchers, such as ourselves, tend to focus on the interaction between external and internal variables within a particular union setting. As Lincoln and Gubba (1985) argued, this can lead to well-grounded and hence more credible and dependable theories concerning the process of change, but it limits the confidence with which these findings can be transferred and used to explain changes in the wider population or aggregated data.

The external and internal explanations for union growth have recently been re-examined by a number of academics seeking to advance understanding in this field of work by drawing on the hypotheses developed to explain the growth in the 1970s to also explain the decline of the 1980s. There have also been some attempts to explain union decline by developing a new set of variables or by significantly amending previous models. Also, the OECD (1991: 97–131) tested a number of hypotheses by reference to changes in union density across its member countries. The econometric modellers have continued to argue, often implicitly, that unions primarily, if not totally, 'receive' (Undy *et al.* 1981: 160–3) or lose members because of factors outside the union's control. In their models, unions are generally found to have played little part in determining growth or decline. Members—or potential members—are assumed to be indifferent as between unions. Unions therefore grow or decline in response to an undifferentiated demand for their services or lose members from a lack of demand. Employees' propensity to join a union may be found in these models to vary, *inter alia*, according to the level of employment, the composition of employment (gender, full-time/part-time workers, size of establishment, sector, geographic location, manual/non-manual workers, age of worker (Green 1992), the level of economic activity—primarily level of employment—inflation, and the real rate of wage increases (Disney 1990: 165–177). Political factors, and the employer's/manager's behaviour with regard to union membership, may also be said to influence union growth and decline. However, employers and managers are again assumed to be indifferent as between which unions they do or do not encourage or discourage in the recruitment of their employees.

We would see little grounds for disagreeing with Kelly (1989) that changes in employment composition have played a limited but significant role in reducing union membership in relatively closed industrial-type unions recruiting in the high-density territories of coal, steel, and rail in the early to mid-1980s. These unions have broadly sustained their high densities (coal 90 per cent; rail 94 per cent, and metal extraction and manufacture 64 per cent unionized) but still suffered a major loss of members due to the decline in employment in their territories. For reasons not satisfactorily explained by external factors alone, the compositional changes which increased employment in relatively low-density private service industries have also contributed to the reduction in aggregate union density. The Labour Force Survey (*EG* 6.91: 341–3) shows that in the largest single sector listed in 1989, i.e. the retailing of food, clothing, and household goods, only 17 per cent of the 2,206,220 employees were unionized. Similarly in hotels and catering, out of 939,209 employed only 11 per cent were unionized. A movement of workers, and therefore potential union members, to these traditionally low-density sectors has helped to reduce union membership. The OECD study (1991) further confirms that structural employment shifts have affected trends in unionization across its member countries, but that they do not alone account for the changes in union density experienced in these countries. Also, a study by Green (1992) calculates that the composition effect contributed approximately 30 per cent towards the fall in aggregate density between 1983 and 1989. The WIRS study of the period 1984–90 also helped place the effect of compositional change in context by concluding that 'changes in density within continuing workplaces appear to have been more important than compositional changes in the population of trading sector establishments in the overall decline in union membership' (Millward *et al.* 1992: 68).

A number of quantitative studies point towards the business cycle's having the major part to play in reducing union density. In the period of growing and high-level unemployment, between 1979 and 1986, the unemployment effect is claimed, when combined with real increases in wages, to account for a major part of the fall in union membership in this period. Kelly refers to a correlation of 0.72 between employment changes and union density for the period 1980–5, and Disney claims that 'a period of rising unemployment, high real-wage growth and a Conservative Government is sufficient to explain the decline in density' (Kelly 1989; Disney 1990: 168).

The above strong correlation between a number of economic and employment variables in the 1980s and the decline in union density suggests that external factors, and particularly the rise in unemployment, have in some manner not explainable by quantitative analysis reduced the propensity of workers to unionize. This is probably the result of some combination of economic and employment factors influencing the workers themselves directly, and indirectly affecting the employers' and managers' behaviour towards unionization and unions' ability to recruit. However, between 1986 and 1989 there was an increase of 1.4 million in employees in employment (*EG* 6.9: 340), yet, as can be seen from Table 2.2, the TUC's membership fell by 5.5 per cent in 1989 alone—the highest figure for four consecutive years of falling membership, i.e. −2.5 per cent in 1986, −3.5 per cent in 1987, and −1 per cent in 1988. This suggests either that there were new forces at work or the emphasis given to the importance of unemployment effects in the early part of the 1980s was misplaced.

Alternatively, it is suggested by some commentators (*EG* 6.91: 337–43) that the post-1986 decline in density is largely due to the compositional effect, as the increase in employment was predominantly in areas of low union density. This does not of itself explain why these areas have been and remain low union density. Moreover, when various authorities have attempted to quantify the impact of compositional effects they have tended to suggest that it accounts for considerably less than half of the loss of density in the period 1980–9.

A somewhat different explanation for the fall in union density, but with its origins in the same econometric system of analysis, is offered by

Freeman and Pelletier (1992). They conclude: 'the vast bulk of the observed decline in union density in the UK is due to the changed legal environment for industrial relations' (ibid. 165). Moreover, these changes are not the result of the legislation in general, but of those laws that 'directly impact on organizing (ibid. 148)'. Although recognizing that the authors give due recognition to the role of unions and the resources they may, or may not, direct to organizing, it is still difficult to accept their conclusions as a satisfactory explanation for the decline in union density. As we will show, the key balloting parts of the legislation operated in a complex manner and require careful analysis before pronouncing on their effects on both the processes and outcomes they sought to influence. Freeman and Pelletier's assumption that the far more limited legal attempts to reduce the union's ability to organize had the intended effect on union and management behaviour is justified neither by studies of the impact of the Labour Government's previous legislation on recognition and unionization (Bain and Price 1983: 19–20) nor by our findings on the working of the much more substantial and significant balloting legislation. Furthermore, it is necessary to distinguish between achieved and received union growth, and to recognize that the unions' ability to achieve growth is far more dependent in the UK on factors other than the law (Undy *et al.* 1981: 127–66).

The question of union growth and decline therefore requires an examination of why it is that the trade unions themselves have not acted more effectively to stem the outflow of members, or recruit more members. Trade unions have continued to supply the services required by potential new members and have achieved an increase in new members by their own actions in this period: without this recruitment activity they would have lost considerably more members. For example, USDAW recruited 118,000 new members in order to add 10,000 to its total. Further, USDAW actually increased the percentage of members entering the union each year in the late 1980s and 1990 as compared to the early 1980s, as Table 3.5 shows.

The TGWU recruited 220,438 members in 1985, 238,093 in 1986, 241,450 in 1987, and 244,910 in 1988. Despite this recruitment of 944,891 new members over four years, its membership fell over the same period by 177,702 members. Unions are therefore recruiting new members, whether by their own achievements, or by merely receiving them into membership due to external factors. What they are not doing is recruiting sufficient numbers to replace those leaving. This is despite a number of recruiting campaigns launched by individual unions, such as the GMB and 'Decision 84', which committed this previously restrictive-passive[2] union to a positive recruitment strategy and campaign. Also, the TGWU's 'Forward TGWU' (1988 and 1989 versions) gave a high priority to recruitment. This followed and superseded the TGWU's 'Link-Up' Campaign in 1987, which sought to

TABLE 3.5. USDAW: new members as
proportion of total

	Per cent
1980	29
1981	23
1982	22
1983	24
1984	27
1985	26
1987	28
1988	30
1989	31
1990	30

Source: Upchurch and Donnelly (1992).

consolidate the union's position in areas of existing strength while also extending into new areas of recruitment. Also, the TUC has co-ordinated and targeted some recruiting activities.

In a study of full-time officials' recruitment activities Kelly and Heery (1989) concluded that despite a developing national commitment to active recruitment by the national leadership of some general worker unions there were considerable constraints on recruiting in 'new job territories, where there is little tradition of union organization' (ibid. 210). Full-time officials were found to devote little time to this kind of recruitment activity, in comparison with their other responsibilities. These findings are particularly important when taken in conjunction with the adverse compositional effects of the 1980s and the manner in which unions achieved growth in the 1970s. In the 1970s, unions positively oriented towards recruitment achieved growth by projecting a particular union image, effective recruitment campaigns, provision of more local recruiting agents, and increased security of membership and other methods (Undy *et al*. 1981: 161–6). ASTMS, in particular, worked hard to project a particular national image for itself and its General Secretary Clive Jenkins, while in practice it was locally highly flexible and ready to adjust to meet the needs of its new members. A militant image and successful strikes also brought rapid immediate increases in membership for a number of other unions, as they demonstrated their ability to 'deliver the goods'.

Recruitment campaigns which targeted non-unionized groups in existing job territories were also markedly effective in the 1970s (ibid. 169). In some parts of the country, sole recognition agreements negotiated in new firms were important for achieving growth. Increased shop steward activity in the TGWU, previously dominated by its full-time officials, also assisted recruitment. Finally, membership was made more secure and some of the very high losses which occurred through not following up on initial recruitment were staunched, if not stopped, by the more extensive use of check-off and the increased use of the closed shop.

In the industrial relations climate of the 1980s and early 1990s many of these means of achieving growth were not available to the unions. The advances made by increasing security of membership were largely 'one-off' administrative changes which could not be repeated. Shop steward power and influence were relatively muted and shop steward activity generally reduced. Union image—underpinned by the traditional values associated with combination and collectivism—may have been blunted by the Conservative Government's promotion of individualism. Instead of strikes demonstrating union effectiveness, the most prominent strikes had the opposite effect. 'The goods', in terms of real wage increases, seemed available without recourse to industrial action. Moreover, having 'mopped up' many of the non-unionized workers in their own job territories, the full-time officials were incapable of pursuing, or reluctant to pursue, recruitment campaigns amongst the non-unionized groups in those industries previously shown as expanding, as work-force composition changed in the 1980s (Kelly and Heery 1989). Many unions also lacked the financial resources necessary to support the staff increases needed if more resources were to be put into direct recruiting in new territories. Finally, as we will show below, individual unions which could have been expected to pursue more vigorous recruitment campaigns became as much, if not more, concerned to increase their membership through mergers. Thus, in the circumstances of the 1980s and early 1990s, the means of achieving growth previously exploited by the expansionist unions of the 1970s were not generally appropriate for recruiting in the newly expanding job territories which were traditionally difficult to unionize.

In future studies of union growth and decline there may therefore be advantage in focusing attention on both received and achieved growth in the same research framework. The assumption that all potential members (and managers and employees) are indifferent as between unions should be abandoned. It should be accepted as a departure point for such research that unions may, to some degree, influence their own rate of growth and decline and in so doing affect aggregate growth and decline. Further, the often implicit assumption that the same exogenous factors affect all phases of growth and decline should also be questioned.[3] The research method used could probably be improved by examining flows of members in and out of unions and by assuming that different factors may affect the ability of unions to recruit and retain members within workplaces with different densities, i.e. at different phases of growth and decline. The relative importance of the different phases for union growth and decline should be considered. This may be represented diagrammatically as a progression, in either direction, through four quadrants or phases, as shown in Figure 3.1.

Figure 3.1 is intended to provide a framework for examining union growth at both the workplace and subsequently the aggregate level of analysis, by combining consideration of both achieved and received growth (and decline) at each of four interrelated phases of union organization or density. Each of the quadrants represents a phase of union development within the workplace. The levels of density allocated to each phase were

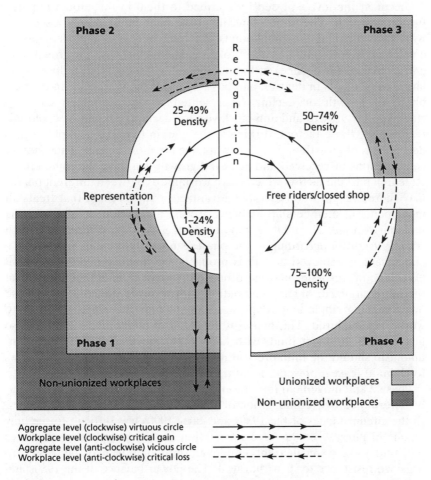

Fig. 3.1. Framework for research into union growth and decline

chosen rather arbitrarily. However, the underlying assumption is that there are some critical points in union growth and decline which, if achieved, may produce further significant changes in the level of density at the workplace. In the diagram these are: (1) between phases 1 and 2, representational rights, involving the union gaining or losing its right to represent its individual members in, for example, grievances and disciplinary procedures; (2) between phases 2 and 3, recognition rights, involving the union gaining or losing the right to bargain collectively on pay and related issues; (3) between 3 and 4, the power which the union may accrue (or lose) which enables it to 'mop up' free riders by exerting pressure for a *de facto* closed shop, or similar arrangements guaranteeing a very high level of union membership.

Whether or not these phases are interrelated and 'breakthrough' points do occur at the levels of density ascribed to them in this model requires further research. The notion that the phases may be so closely associated with each other at the breakpoints that relatively minor movements of employees (represented by the broken curves—clockwise for growth and anti-clockwise for decline) at the margin will subsequently produce much larger movements in density, and possibly move the workplace into a new phase of growth or decline (represented by the unbroken curves—clockwise for growth and anti-clockwise for decline), should be explored. If this is so, those factors working at the margin to move workplaces into new phases of growth and decline will have the most impact. Thus, not all combinations of received and achieved growth will have the same effect. Research into the factors which move workplaces between different phases may therefore offer considerable advantages over research that treats all movements in membership as being around a common density, i.e. the national average. The relative importance of achieved and received growth is likely to differ according to the phases studied.

In phase 1, achieved growth is probably the main source of the initial unionization, through full-time officers' or activists' direct recruitment of the non-unionized, or, in combination with received growth, through the union signing single-union-type agreements with the employer prior to workers being hired. This phase, if the result of direct recruitment, is also likely to be the most fluid, with fairly rapid movements back into non-unionism should the initial recruitment fail to produce sufficient members to claim at least representational rights.

Phase 2 and movement into the critical phase 3, or vice versa, is likely to be determined by a combination of achieved and received growth factors. In the circumstances of the 1980s and early 1990s it is difficult to see how unions in phase 2 could force recognition for the purposes of collective bargaining on a recalcitrant employer, although it may be easier to organize resistance to its withdrawal. The power balance of the 1980s and early 1990s has moved against unions, and in the absence of a neutral or sympathetic employer or management it is unlikely that a union with a density of less than 50 per cent could achieve recognition and break through into phase 3. The danger for the union is that failure to achieve such a breakthrough may leave it with representational rights, but these may not be sufficient to retain the support of existing members. The union could therefore find itself moving rapidly back into phase 1 and through it into non-unionism. On the other hand, a union in phase 3 may well be able to mobilize opposition to the withdrawal of bargaining rights. It could well be the case that the low incidence of the withdrawal of bargaining rights in the case of manual workers is at least partially accounted for by the latent power which managers perceive unions as retaining in reserve. Thus, the maintenance of high levels of density found in some workplaces by the Workplace Industrial Relations Survey 1990 (Millward *et al.* 1992: 60–70) may well be the result of strong union organization and prove a major factor in maintaining overall density at its present level.

Movement between phases 3 and 4 and the enforcement of 100 per cent unionization on the 'free riders' has probably been made more difficult by external factors and particularly the Conservative Government's actions in outlawing the closed shop. At least some of the achieved growth of the 1970s was the result of union pressure for and management acquiescence in such agreements. However, some unions have managed to maintain 100 per cent membership in some workplaces despite these changes. Why this is possible, and why other unions have failed to stop a movement of members out of other high density workplaces into non-unionism, is also an area for further research.

The framework for analysis suggested above therefore starts with recruitment in the workplace and perceives union growth and decline as the product of a series of interrelated phases. It is a dynamic rather than a static scheme of analysis. It further assumes that each phase of development may be determined by different combinations of achieved and received growth and that, at critical points, movements of members between phases may have disproportionate effects on the next phase of growth or decline.

In conclusion, as regards union membership: many unions, including most of the leading unions in the TUC, suffered from a substantial reduction in union membership in the 1980s and 1990s for which the 'good years' of the 1970s had left them ill-prepared. At the same time, aggregate union density also fell significantly. There has been limited success in explaining the causes of this overall decline in density. A number of studies have shown that the environment, including, *inter alia*, unemployment, compositional changes in employment, and the Conservative Governments' legislation, adversely affected trade union growth. However, attempts to quantify the extent to which each of these developments reduced union density have produced conflicting results.

It is probable that a combination of the above external factors encouraged employers or managers hostile to unionization to resist attempts at recruitment of their non-unionized workplaces, and to seek lower levels of membership amongst those already unionized. Unions, weakened by the developments of the 1980s, appeared largely incapable of making inroads into the traditionally hard to unionize areas of employment, such as private services. Moreover, unions also seemed to find it difficult after 1984 to prevent significant outflows of members (and reductions in density) in workplaces in those sectors previously seen as strongholds of unionization. Nevertheless, there is evidence that even unions losing overall membership continued to recruit new members at reasonably high levels during this period. How this inflow and outflow of members was actually affected by the adverse external factors of the 1980s and 1990s is unclear and requires further research on the process and dynamics of union growth and decline. However, the resulting loss of members, and the uncertainty as to how, if at all, it could be reversed, had a most marked effect on union behaviour. Besides adopting new schemes of direct recruitment they sought to mitigate the loss of members and associated problems, including growing financial difficulties, by other means. For some unions one of these means was to seek mergers.

UNION MERGERS[4]

Trade union mergers were given a significant boost by the Trade Unions (Amalgamation etc.) Act 1964. This eased the previously restrictive balloting process required for amalgamations and introduced merger by transfer of engagements, whereby only the minor union in a merger was required to ballot its members and secure a simple majority of those voting for the merger to be agreed. The major or acquiring union in a transfer is not required to ballot its members. In an amalgamation all unions involved have to ballot their members. As shown in Table 3.6, between 1967 and 1989 there were 331 mergers (this includes all unions involved in amalgamations but only transferring unions in transfers of engagements). Also, as shown in Figure 3.2 there was, in respect of TUC-affiliated unions, a sharp upward movement in the proportion of unions merging from 1979 onwards. As we will show later in this chapter, union mergers, but particularly amalgamations, had a significant effect on the internal organization (or government) of unions.

The post-1979 merger movement as identified in Figure 3.2 at present under way, shows no sign of abating. In a survey of TUC affiliates conducted in 1990 and 1991, 60 per cent (42) of the unions surveyed did not reject merging within the next five years and 23 unions indicated that they were intending to search actively for merger partners in this period. Hence,

TABLE 3.6. Union transfers of engagements and amalgamations by years, 1967–89

Year	No. of transferring unions	No. of transferring members	No. of amalgamating unions (no. of unions after amalgamation)	No. of amalgamating members	Total members
1967	6	8,307	9 (4)	1,198,872	1,207,179
1968	6	18,051	4 (2)	437,223	455,274
1969	10	43,052	2 (1)	12,019	55,071
1970	13	90,295	9 (3)	1,392,383	1,485,678
1971	9	129,322	8 (3)	82,040	211,362
1972	11	92,056	5 (3)	41,078	133,134
1973	9	28,371	7 (2)	127,191	155,562
1974	7	26,382	—	—	26,382
1975	16	35,321	5 (2)	202,702	238,043
1976	13	58,803	2 (1)	58,000	116,803
1977	10	16,975	2 (1)	4,290	21,265
1978	9	14,354	2 (1)	79,881	94,235
1979	13	17,101	—	—	17,101
1980	12	22,701	3 (1)	90,534	113,235
1981	4	8,617	—	—	8,617
1982	8	122,082	10 (4)	1,333,125	1,455,207
1983	8	63,320	2 (1)	2,000	65,320
1984	16	101,018	6 (2)	41,284	142,302
1985	10	41,824	3 (1)	31,702	73,526
1986	32	50,530	—	—	50,530
1987	4	7,077	2 (1)	118,123	125,200
1988	9	19,800	4 (2)	653,500	673,300
1989	9	3,700	2 (1)	877,000	880,700
Total	244	1,019,059	87(36)	6,782,947	7,802,006

Total unions involved (244 + 87) = 331

Per cent of total transferring or amalgamating 1967–89:

| 74% | 13% | 26% | 87% |

Note: The figure for the total number of unions and union members used in the calculation of percentages were taken from *EG* (5.89 and 5.90) and from Marsh (1988).

the slight upturn in merger activity shown in Figure 3.2 for 1990 is likely to continue its upward movement into the mid-1990s and beyond.

Quantitative research into mergers stresses the importance of exogenous factors in shaping the merger movement and seeks to correlate aggregate mergers with economic factors such as the business cycle, wages, retail prices, and also, in some cases, political factors (Waddington 1988). There

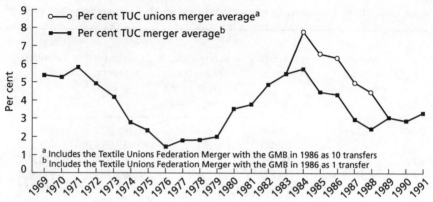

FIG. 3.2. TUC merger activity: 5-year moving averages 1969–91

are a number of problems inherent in using this approach. One key difficulty is that a merger is, in many cases, the end-product of extended negotiations, in some cases covering several years. Although the date on which mergers are legally finalized is a matter of recorded fact, the starting point of the negotiations is, in major mergers, frequently a question of dispute requiring research in its own right. Hence, to seek to correlate mergers (end dates) with the economic and political developments that may have triggered the merger search some years before is unlikely to shed much light on what actually determined individual mergers or, in aggregate, the merger movement. Further, external factors which may trigger the merger search are mediated through the union leadership and may change in importance during the merger process. They are, therefore, indirect and complex in their effect and vary from merger to merger in their importance according to the weight given them by the negotiators.

External factors tend to exert most influence on mergers at the start of the merger process. In particular they can trigger a merger search when they combine to produce a decrease in a union's membership (or growth expectations) and/or adversely change the composition of a union's membership. In these circumstances the major merging union may seek a merger as a means of restoring, partially or fully, its membership loss and/ or as a means of extending its interests into a more promising job territory. The minor union's search for a merger may also be initiated following a loss of members, particularly if the loss threatens the minor union's survival. Nevertheless, membership loss alone is not necessarily the determining factor in merger search. Unions vary widely in terms of their merger intentions and actions when faced by significant membership loss. In the survey of TUC unions referred to above, 28 (40 per cent) of respondents expressed no future (five-year) interest in mergers. These were mainly small unions. Their average size was 12,927 (median 3,770), and 21 of them had lost members since 1978 and 15 had lost over 30 per cent of their membership in this period. In contrast, 42 (60 per cent) of the unions did not reject mergers over the next five years and 23 of these indicated an intention to search actively for mergers in this period. The 23 actively searching unions included almost all the large and medium-sized unions in the TUC and accounted for 83 per cent of the TUC's total membership. These unions had, on average, suffered only an 11 per cent loss of members over the period.

The interrelationship between membership loss, financial performance, and merger intentions is therefore quite complex and varies between unions (Little 1991). As Table 3.7 shows, there is no overall positive correlation between intention to merge and membership loss, reduction in investment income, declining subscription income, or change in total income.

Thus, the external factors most likely indirectly to trigger a merger search were not sufficient in themselves to cause a merger. Indeed, unions affected by widely different changes in membership and financial well-being may react in a similar fashion to questions concerning their merger intentions. For example, three unions with over 20 per cent membership growth rates in the TUC between 1979 and 1989—the British Actors Equity Association (BAEA; 60 per cent), the National Association of Probation Officers (NAPO; 30 per cent), and the Fire Brigades Unions (FBU; 21 per cent)—perhaps not surprisingly expressed no future interest in mergers, but so did 9 small unions each experiencing a reduction of over

TABLE 3.7. Merger intentions, membership and finance: percentage average changes 1979–89 in membership, investment and subscription income

	No future interest in mergers	Actively interested in mergers	Not rejecting mergers	All trade unions
Membership	−23	−11	−22	−19
Investment income[a]	32	49	99[b]	58
Subscription income	8	27	49	25
Total income	11	30	78	18

[a] All prices used were adjusted to 1989 values.
[b] This calculation omits the TSSA, which showed an increase of 4200 per cent and in consequence distorted the group's mean. If included it raised the group's increase to 327 per cent.

40 per cent in members. Similarly, unions intending to search actively for mergers included two unions with a loss of over 40 per cent in members, i.e. the AEU and the Iron and Steel Trades Confederation (ISTC), and two unions with an increase of over 20 per cent, the NCU and the Banking Insurance and Finance Union (BIFU). There were also marked variations in the financial status of unions amongst those both intending and not intending to merge. Hence, while some merging unions may be driven to search for a merger by external factors which adversely and indirectly affect their size and financial position, not all unions respond to the same factors in the same way. It is therefore how union leaders interpret these developments and their reasons for pursuing mergers which need to be explored.

In examining why unions merge, it is important to distinguish between the major and minor merging unions and between transfers of engagements and amalgamations. The leader of the minor union negotiating a transfer of engagements is normally involved in surrendering autonomy in exchange for some gain such as security. In contrast, the major union's leaders in a transfer of engagements are primarily seeking to enhance in some way the standing of the larger union and they will probably not change significantly their present system of organization and power structure in order to accommodate the incoming minor union. However, in an amalgamation, the two parties are likely to see themselves as having similar status or as equals—otherwise why not merge by transfer of engagements? In merger by amalgamation both parties may be required to make significant changes in their rule books and organizations in order to agree the formation of a new union. In the following discussion, the major merging unions' reasons for merging will be examined before turning to examine the motives of the minor merging unions (amalgamations will be taken as involving only major unions).

Between 1978–89 a total of 98 unions were merged by transfer of engagements with TUC-affiliated unions. As regards amalgamations, nine TUC affiliates joined with eight other unions. The transferring unions had on average 8,328 members and there were 64,327 members, on average, in the smaller of the amalgamating unions. Most of the major merging unions sought mergers primarily to increase membership and/or change their job territory. A majority of the major unions considered their mergers to be primarily consolidatory[5] inasmuch as the merger built on an existing presence of some strength in an industry or amongst a particular occupational group. Of the 27 major merging unions examined, 14 fell into this category, i.e. were consolidatory. Three of the remaining major unions had been involved in defensive mergers, attempting to safeguard a position previously weakened by loss of members or increased recruitment competition from some other union. Two other major merger unions tended to adopt a predomininantly aggressive or expansionist approach to mergers. For these unions mergers were a vehicle for increasing the membership and expanding the territorial base. At certain points some of the primarily consolidatory unions also entered into expansionist mergers. The remaining eight unions did not seem to fit any of the above categories. They appeared not to have a merger policy. They were generally opportunistic or unplanned in their merger activities. Hence, the majority of the major merger unions did not use mergers to expand outside their existing industrial territories but to improve their situation within existing industrial boundaries by recruiting the same or new occupational groups. Where they involved new occupational groups these tended to be the recruitment of craftsmen into predominantly white-collar/technician unions and the addition of white-collar workers to predominantly blue-collar unions.

The above comment on the consolidatory nature of most major unions' merger activities needs to be balanced, however, by reference to the actions of those unions which pursued a more expansionist merger policy. In particular, the Association of Scientific Technical and Managerial Staffs (ASTMS) and the Technical, Administrative and Supervisory Section (TASS) (prior to their amalgamation and the formation of the MSF) and the GMB (formerly the GMWU) were more expansionist than other unions in their approach to mergers. Also, the TGWU, although not showing the same vigorous pursuit of mergers as it displayed in the 1970s, was still keen to exploit any opportunities which arose for expansion by merger. Between them the ASTMS, TASS, the GMB, and the TGWU accounted for 46 mergers in this period. The ASTMS, GMB, and TGWU covered a relatively wide area of job territory at the start of this period, although the ASTMS was mainly confined to white-collar recruitment. Thus their merger searches, even if they remained within existing industrial territories, still had a wider industrial scope than that enjoyed by more 'closed' unions. Further, the GMB and TASS deliberately used a number of mergers to take them into new occupations and industries. TASS (a draughtsmen's and technicians' union), for example, merged with a series of four small blue-collar engineering unions and in 1986 with the Tobacco Workers Union. The GMWU's break with its past, rather passive, approach to mergers occurred in 1982 when it finally amalgamated, at its second attempt, with the craft-based Boilermakers, and in 1988 it again broke new ground when the GLC Staff Association joined it by transfer of engagements. The GMWU's amalgamation with the Association of Professional, Executive, Clerical and Computer Staff (APEX) in 1989 to form the GMB was also intended to expand radically the union's rather minor white-collar membership. Thus, the most active merger unions expanded the scope of their industrial and occupational territory significantly whilst other major unions followed more conservative, consolidatory, and defensive mergers.

Apart from territorial gains the major merging unions also sought other advantages from mergers. Seventy-seven transfers of engagements and 14 amalgamations were examined from the perspective of the major merging union in an attempt to identify non-territorial advantages. Three key areas of possible advantage were identified, as shown in Table 3.8. An open-ended question was also posed seeking information about 'other advantages', but respondents referred to mainly territorial-type gains in answering this question.

As can be seen from Table 3.8, only the question concerning an increase in bargaining power received over 50 per cent positive responses. However, in subsequent interviews this positive response was frequently qualified, and only in a minority of cases was a merger mentioned specifically as having a direct and positive effect on bargaining power. For example, the TGWU noted that its merger with the Northern Textile Allied Workers Union in 1984 gave it a presence in national negotiations previously denied it. Also, the NGA argued forcibly that its merger with SLADE considerably enhanced its bargaining power. There were also a number of general comments about improved co-ordination of bargaining following a merger. Nevertheless, mention was frequently made in interviews of the difficulties in achieving an increase in bargaining power when the minor or acquired union was experiencing a decline in the demand for its members' services, and in many cases sought a merger because of a serious loss of members. Hence, claims for an increase in bargaining power in the difficult economic circumstances of the 1980s need to be treated cautiously.

The increase in political power took two main forms. Some unions saw the merger creating a stronger political alliance of like minds, for example, the TASS–Tobacco Workers Union merger. Secondly, amalgamations between relatively large unions were thought to increase the new union's political influence in the wider labour movement. The GMWU's merger with APEX to form the GMB and the AEU's merger with the EETPU to form the AEEU came into this category. In respect of financial gains, the major unions overall referred more to the financial cost of mergers

TABLE 3.8. Non-territorial advantages of mergers

	Yes		No	
Increase in bargaining power	48	(77%)	13	(21%)
Increase in political influence	21	(35%)	39	(65%)
Financial savings[a]	23	(37%)	40	(63%)

[a] Some respondents qualified a yes answer with reference to achieving savings in the longer term.

than to the savings. It would therefore appear to be the exception rather than the general rule that mergers lead to immediate financial gains.

One of the key influences on large amalgamations was the drive to reduce inter-union competition for members and inter-union disputes *vis-à-vis* a common employer. The UNISON, GPMU and MSF amalgamations respectively involving NALGO, NUPE, and COHSE (1993), SOGAT and the NGA (1991), and the ASTMS and TASS (1988) were influenced by such considerations. Technological change in the print industry created regular and fierce demarcation disputes between SOGAT and the NGA and resulted in intense competition for members. The merger was seen as one way of helping solve this problem. The ASTMS–TASS merger was also influenced by attempts to end the two unions' damaging competition for members. NALGO, NUPE, and COHSE started merger talks after a number of disputes between NALGO and NUPE in particular, and complaints by NALGO that NUPE was poaching its members. For example, at the 1988 NALGO conference a motion supporting the merger referred to such 'inter-union disputes . . . threatening effective trade unionism as a whole' (NALGO 1988: motion 116).

Lastly, some major unions also sought or used mergers as a means of reorganizing their own internal system of government. Mergers, and in particular large amalgamations, provide an opportunity for, and could be used to legitimize, a radical review of a union's system of internal government. A number of union leaders with 'problems' of internal organization—for example, too high a proportion of funds under the control of local organizations, or powerful regional- and/or district-level officials—may see mergers as a way of resolving these difficulties via the rule changes required to accommodate the merging unions' different internal structures and processes of decision-making. Moreover, in order to make the major unions more attractive to minor merging unions faced with a number of potential partners, the major union may adjust its own organization to provide the incomer with more autonomy and in this process also 'correct' some perceived governmental shortcomings. The GMB in particular, when pursuing mergers, took the opportunity to adjust its system of government for other purposes.

To conclude: in the 1980s and continuing into the 1990s there was an increase in merger activity. This ran parallel with and was influenced by the loss of members discussed previously. However, not all unions losing members and suffering the consequent financial insecurity merged. Some small unions preferred to remain independent, even though adversely affected by external developments. These unions would appear to prefer a slow death to merging with a larger organization. Major merging unions tended to seek mergers to consolidate their position in existing job territories. However, a small number of more expansionist unions had a disproportionate effect on the union map. They used mergers to break new ground and in some cases to demonstrate their effectiveness as future potential merger partners. Further, the mega-mergers between the AEU and the EETPU in 1992, and between NALGO, NUPE, and COHSE in 1993, added further impetus to the merger movement in the 1990s. They will intensify pressure on other large unions to merge in order to protect their relative influence within the wider labour movement. Thus with little sign of a recovery in union density, and with the potential minor merging unions having little if any chance of penetrating new job territories, the merger movement will continue as the major merging unions search for new partners in the late 1990s.

UNION STRUCTURE

Union structure, following convention, is taken as being the 'morphology or external structure . . . the coverage by each union of industries and occupations' (Clegg 1979: 165). There have been various attempts to classify union structure. The intention of the classifications has been to help 'separate the elements in a situation that would otherwise appear confused and chaotic' (Turner 1962: 24). The terms 'craft' (occupation), 'industrial', and 'general' were initially used to distinguish between unions which recruited, respectively, a particular group of craftsmen or several related crafts, those which recruited (or attempted to recruit) all workers within a particular industry, and those which would recruit any and all workers. These ideal types were subsequently amended, or dropped and replaced by such concepts as open and closed unions, sectoral unions, public and private sector unions, white collar unions, conglomerate unions, and enterprise unions.[6] Undy *et al.* (1981) attempted to produce a more dynamic model of union structure in terms of the degree to which unions became more or less occupationally and industrially diverse over the period 1960–75. In sum, it was found that virtually all the major unions in the TUC became more industrially and/or occupationally diverse over this period. In terms of other classifications they became more 'open' and moved towards general unionism.

The degree of union diversity was increased by a small number of highly significant unions which expanded beyond their 1970s industrial boundaries by merger. Also, the Government's privatization policies took public sector unions into the private sector. Hence, the 1970s trend towards more occupationally and industrially diverse unions gathered pace in the 1980s and 1990s. However, the kind of mergers agreed did not generally offer the major unions much scope for penetrating low or non-unionized territories. An exception to this was BIFU, which was successful in attracting into mergers a number of Staff Associations which offered considerable scope for direct recruitment of non-unionists in the growing employment field, in the mid-1980s, of banking, finance, and insurance.

In the 1980s and early 1990s union structure therefore became more and not less occupationally and industrially diverse. The previous consensus around industrial unionism was dead. Each major merging union, in what was frequently a highly competitive search for minor merger partners, therefore sought a merger for its own purpose. Some of the major union leaders saw scope for intervention by a higher authority—perhaps the TUC—in someone else's merger negotiations, but they did not wish to surrender their own sovereignty. Also, the presence of expansionist merger unions meant that a large proportion of the minor merging unions had more than one merger option and they too would not have welcomed being pressed, by some third party, into mergers on less favourable terms than could be negotiated freely. Thus, although external factors both reduced union membership and made the recruitment of replacement members more difficult, it was the manner in which union leaders responded to these and other external and internal pressures that determined union morphology. Some small unions faced with loss of members and financial difficulties chose to do very little; others sought refuge in larger organizations. Some major unions sought to expand occupationally within existing industrial boundaries; others sought to break into new industrial territory. In a small but influential number of larger mergers, political alliances seemed more important than territorial gain, and in some mergers the opportunity they offered for increased solidarity, *vis à vis* the main employer, was critical in determining the choice of merger partner. Union leaders, although constrained by financial pressures and in some cases by their internal decision-making machinery, therefore exercised considerable discretion in choosing their merger partner. In the absence of a widely accepted notion of what was an ideal structure, the result was that many unions chose partners for internal reasons and in consequence the external map became more and not less diverse. Nevertheless, a new kind of industrial or trade group structure did emerge from this process. This was because the major unions involved encouraged and facilitated those changes in job territory with greater internal differentiation between different groups of members.

UNION GOVERNMENT

In using the term 'union government', we mean unions' internal decision-making. This may be described in various ways and is an important aspect of both democratic and administrative rationalities. But for the purpose of this discussion, and prior to examining the effects of the balloting legislation on union government, it will be considered according to the analytical taxonomy developed by Undy *et al.* (1981: 37–60) for the analysis of changes in unions' internal decision-making. First, we will consider the vertical bifurcation of union government into bargaining and non-bargaining decision-making channels and processes. Second, the degree to which decision-making is centralized or decentralized within these channels will be discussed. Third, the degree to which decisions at the different levels are concentrated or diffused will be examined. Reference will also be made in this latter discussion to the informal processes and bodies of decision-making.

First, the merger movement of the 1980s and early 1990s caused a number of previously predominantly single-channel unions to adopt a bifurcated system of government, with responsibility for some bargaining decisions and industrial or trade-specific issues being allocated to a new separate channel, or channels, of decision-making. This development was most notable in the case of the GMB, and to a lesser extent in TASS prior to its merger with the ASTMS. The AEU also made a more tentative move in this direction before its merger with the EETPU.

The GMB in particular further extended and formalized the movement it tentatively first made towards vertical bifurcation in 1969 when it formed advisory national industrial committees. Following its merger with the Boilermakers in 1982 and more importantly its merger with APEX and the Greater London Staff Association in 1989, the union initiated a major reorganization of its internal structure. As the union commented in its special merger report, *Shaping up for the Next Century*, it decided 'not to try to merely bolt together the two existing Unions [i.e. the GMWU and APEX] and their various ruling bodies and institutions but to set out to create a new integrated Union' (GMB 1988: 4). The solution was to form a number of sections or trade groups combining the members of all the merged unions according to their occupation or trade. It also served to make the GMB itself more 'merger-friendly' by providing greater potential autonomy for incoming unions than would have been provided under its previous form of government. Other large unions involved in mergers also tended to adopt a similar sectional or trade group system as a means of accommodating the incoming union. Hence, although mergers led to greater diversity of membership within the individual union, the new larger unions became more highly differentiated internally in the vertical plane in order to meet and service more effectively the needs of their enlarged membership's different occupational and industrial interests. There was therefore a movement towards what may be termed a 'Transport & Generalization' of larger unions as they copied to varying degrees the TGWU's long-standing system of vertical bifurcation.

Second, the degree of centralization/decentralization in the single or dual channels of decision-making varied between unions in the 1970s and continued to do so in the 1980s and 1990s. As regards the bargaining channel: in the 1970s a number of large unions, for example the TGWU and NUPE, encouraged decentralization, whereas some, such as UCATT, preferred to retain centralized bargaining. In the 1980s and 1990s, employers tended in the main to devolve pay bargaining away from national or industry-wide negotiations, the major exceptions being general printing and some parts of the public sector.[7] Some unions, such as those in British Rail, opposed such changes and had some success in delaying or changing management's proposals. However, in the private sector in general and in some parts of the public sector, unions were faced with little choice but to accept management decisions to decentralize pay bargaining. At the same time, unions faced with major financial problems were not in a position to provide more full-time officer support to service the growing number of local negotiations. Indeed, a number of unions were cutting back on the number of local officials and merging district offices in order to save money. The AEU, for example, introduced a package of cuts in 1990, including a reduction in the number of full-time officials and a re-organization of its branch structure in an effort to reduce its deficit. Some unions, for example the NCU and NUR, attempted to 'shadow' bargaining devolution by reshaping their own internal bargaining machinery (Steele 1990: 62).

Overall, since the early 1970s there has therefore been a trend within unions towards further decentralization of the level of pay bargaining. This was primarily a response to employer initiatives to lower the level at which pay was determined and union inability to sustain higher-level negotiations against the employers' wishes. However, as will be shown in the later chapter on balloting in industrial disputes, the degree of control exercised by the leadership over the process of decision-making on industrial action has itself been centralized. Thus, the level of pay bargaining has been devolved, while the national leadership's control over the use of sanctions in support of bargaining has been centralized.

Decision-making in non-bargaining channels has tended to become more centralized. In the 1980s centralization of non-bargaining issues occurred in the AEU, GMB, and the Civil and Public Services Association (CPSA), and within the TGWU in the early 1990s. The AEU's executive promoted rule changes in the 1980s which gave it greater powers over the reorgan-ization of the union's branch and district boundaries and the movement of full-time officials and the determination of their duties. The executive also used the referendum to bypass intermediary bodies and pose questions directly to the membership on the controversial question of accepting government funds for ballots. Further, the executive sponsored a rule change which limited the rights of incumbent officials to contest other posts should their own post also be up for re-election. In sponsoring some of these changes the dominant 'Group'[8] within the executive also appeared to seek political advantage in elections affected by their boundary changes and by the restrictions placed on certain incumbent officials.

The GMB and CPSA both started the 1980s more centralized than the traditionally and relatively highly devolved AEU. The GMB's reliance on a strong regional system of government has its origins in the creation of the GMWU in 1923 and it was still identifiably the same union in 1980. In the early 1990s the full-time regional secretaries continued to play a pre-eminent role in the union's decision-making processes, but there were signs of movement towards more central direction of the union's policy and strategy. The merger process produced a trade group type structure with the result that independent sources of influence developed at the national level outside the regional secretaries' control. Further, the executive, and therefore in practice the general secretary, began to play key roles in the appointments of the regional secretaries in the late 1980s. While the regional secretaries continue to exercise considerable influence, they are now in a weaker position—at least numerically—on the executive. Finally, the election of an influential General Secretary (John Edmonds) with strong notions of where he wished to take the union itself served to centralize decision-making.

For the CPSA the major centralizing tendency in its non-bargaining activities has been associated with declining reliance on local branch organization and a movement towards regionalization. In 1989 a survey of its area co-ordinating committees found that one-third had not held a meeting in the previous eighteen months. Also, reduced time off for lay representatives under the National Facilities Agreement and an increased turnover amongst its branch officers suggested that the union's local system of organization was in difficulties. The preferred solution adopted in the late 1980s was to appoint regional officials. However, this policy was frozen in 1991 because of financial difficulties.

The TGWU in 1992 'undertook a programme of substantial internal re-organization'.[9] This followed a major review by external consultants and the executive led by Bill Morris, the General Secretary. One of the key areas of concern was the relationship between the regions and the head office. Tensions between regional (or district) organization and the centre are common to many unions. In the TGWU this was intensified by the union's financial problems. The union had a significant deficit from 1989–92, including an operating deficit of £12 million in 1991. The General Secretary election in 1991, between Morris and Wright, was also seen by many as a head office versus regions contest. Some supporters of regional organization believed that the head office spent the 'regions' profits' extravagantly while others, more supportive of the centre (or Transport House), contended that the regions behaved like eleven separate unions and did not adhere to national policy. The debate continued in 1992 and 1993 with a series of consultative meetings at all levels of the union around the strategy document 'One Union T&G'. An important part of the proposal is greater head office control of the union's total finance, its regions, and their expenditure.

The reasons for centralizing decision-making in the non-bargaining channel varied between unions. However, it is very clear that administrative concerns were very influential. The need to cut costs in the face of declining subscription income caused a number of unions to review their systems of government and question their efficacy. Drawing power back to the centre was seen as a means of exercising greater control over expenditure. It was often associated with attempts to reduce the money held at local and branch level and transfer all, or part, of this money to the head office. Further, economies were also made in expenditure incurred by the lower levels of the organization by reducing the frequency of meetings of intermediary bodies. Also, the pursuit of mergers in a competitive environment resulted in a higher degree of centralized control in the non-bargaining channel; in order to accommodate the interests of the incoming union and thus counter the competing union's offer, the national leadership of the major unions needed greater discretion to adjust their own organization. Not surprisingly, in some unions this resulted in adjustments in the newly merged union which enhanced the power of head office over other levels of organization and raised questions about the union's democratic rationality.

Third, in terms of the concentration or diffusion of decision-making there is little evidence that power became more concentrated in the hands of full-time officials, or the bureaucracy, in the bargaining channel, with the important exception of the influence of balloting legislation. Indeed, the decentralization of bargaining levels initiated by employers, and unions' general inability to fund increased numbers of full-time officials to service the increase in bargaining units, point to a greater diffusion of power in the bargaining channel. This is also borne out by other studies of shop stewards' independence of full-time officials in the 1980s (Fosh and Cohen 1990).

In the non-bargaining channel the question of whether or not there was a general concentration or diffusion of power at the national level, as decision-making became more centralized, depends on the relationship between formal and informal processes of decision-making and in particular the role of factions and parties. There appeared to be no generalized movement in this dimension of union government in the 1980s and early 1990s. However, changes associated with mergers, and, as we will show in Chapter 5, the imposition of postal ballots for elections, did serve to reduce the influence of the formal checks and balances provided by intermediary bodies. As a consequence the balance of power at the national level between conference, executive, and leading full-time officials broadly moved in favour of the executive and General Secretary.

The informal processes underwent significant changes in some unions, for example in the TGWU, and to a lesser extent in the MSF, as factionalism developed greater influence within both unions. The AEU,

NCU, and CPSA continued, much as before, to be influenced in their policy and rule-making at the national level by party or factional considerations. The AEU's diffused but stable political system continued to be dominated by the moderate 'Group'. The NCU and CPSA remained relatively unstable political organizations at the national level in the 1980s—if anything they became more diffused and volatile in this period. Both unions experienced political shifts in control of the executive and changes in the political composition of senior national full-time officials. The GMB and EETPU, by comparison, were politically stable and power remained relatively concentrated at the national level. EETPU resembled a one party—moderate—system of government. The GMB had no nationally organized party or faction, and the established Labour loyalist leadership still continued to dominate the decision-making processes despite the radical change in government structure associated with its aggressive merger policy. (The relationship between factional organization and balloting will be more fully discussed in Chapter 5.)

Union government in the 1980s and early 1990s therefore saw a movement towards more common forms of decision-making across unions with greater vertical bifurcation, primarily due to mergers; greater centralization of power in the non-bargaining channel, primarily due to financial problems; and more decentralized bargaining activity, primarily due to the actions of employers, leaving aside the impact of the balloting legislation on industrial action. At the national level there was also, in the major unions studied, either a continuation of, or a growth in, factional organization, except for the GMB and EETPU. However, the formal checks and balances on the powers of national leaders were weakened in some unions as the conference became less influential and power gravitated towards the executive and the General Secretary. It may be suggested that centralization and greater concentration of power in view of the turbulent environment and the associated difficulties facing the unions studied was an appropriate response given the need to protect the institutional framework of the union. It was, however, also associated with continuing or growing party or factional organization in some unions. In terms of democratic and administrative rationalities there were therefore some conflicting movements. Generally the drive for greater efficiency in government elevated the importance of administrative concerns, but the growth of factionalism and the continued use of existing checks and balances to diffuse power helped strengthen unions' democratic tendencies. In Chapter 7 we will examine how these particular governmental developments interacted with the balloting legislation to change union government and union democracy.

OBJECTIVES AND MEANS

Unions' political rationality includes objectives and means. These have been defined and classified in various ways.[10] For the purpose of this discussion we distinguish between 'business' and 'reformist' unionism as a means of broadly categorizing overall union objectives (Dabscheck and Niland 1981: 98–9). Business unionism refers to unions whose objective is improving their own members' limited sectional interest within the existing social system. In practice the union is therefore a bargaining agent seeking economic improvement for its members within the workplace. This leaves the union largely, if not solely, relying on collective bargaining as a means of achieving its goals. In contrast, reformist unionism, while also conscious of its members' immediate economic needs and committed to collective bargaining on their behalf, also seeks to act in the wider interests of its members and others within society. In the UK this may involve an association with the Labour Party and the TUC.

The unions studied combined elements of both kinds of unionism. They did not consistently choose to occupy one or other of the extreme positions, fully business or fully reformist. Nevertheless, in some respects the ideological stance of the unions' national leadership varied significantly, although they tended to adopt more pragmatic and opportunist positions on employment issues when it was to their advantage. Hence, in order to distinguish between unions we refine the use of 'business' and 'reformist' by introducing the notion of union character (Blackburn *et al.* 1968). 'Character' will be used to show movement, first, by reference to a union's preference for becoming more or less employment- or society-focused and, secondly, by reference to a union's preference for the use of moderate or militant strategy and tactics in pursuit of its employment objectives. As we will show, a union which adopts a moderate political position does not necessarily adopt the same stance consistently in its employment activities. Also, it should be noted that these political differences were almost always contained within a generally socialist or social democratic mould. Thus, the main characteristic was some form of association with the Labour Party; all the unions which were affiliated to the Labour Party at the start of the period reaffirmed their affiliation in the imposed ballots.

The political and industrial character of the EETPU was the most ostensibly moderate of all the unions studied. The EETPU is frequently referred to as the leading exponent of union 'new realism', which is in turn equated with business rather than reformist unionism. It involves movement towards employment-centred activities and the adoption of a moderate job regulation strategy and tactics. The emphasis is on co-operating with the employer and not assuming an adversarial posture. It reached its apotheosis in the EETPU's single-union strike-free deals. In these deals the EETPU offered employers, mainly on greenfield sites, a degree of functional flexibility and a disputes procedure incorporating pendulum arbitration. In return the EETPU wanted sole recognition, harmonization of terms and conditions, and some form of consultative machinery. By 1989 the EETPU claimed to have forty such agreements. Further, the EETPU was dominated nationally by moderates, or right-wing Labour supporters, and therefore represented the most politically conservative of the trade unions. This stance was also closely associated with a strong commitment to protecting its own sectional interest rather than those of the wider Labour movement. The union's expulsion from the TUC in 1988 for failing to accept a decision of the TUC's disputes committee reflected this commitment and further isolated the EETPU from the mainstream union organization. Nevertheless, it remained politically reformist through its continued affiliation to the Labour Party and, following its merger with the AEU in 1992, it rejoined the TUC.

The EETPU was not exceptional in signing single-union deals that excluded other unions from recruiting on greenfield sites. All the other large general unions in the study—the AEU, GMB, and TGWU—sought single-union deals and competed with the EETPU in union 'beauty contests'. The AEU, in particular, had considerable success signing major deals with the Japanese vehicle builders Nissan in 1985 and Toyota in 1991 (*FT* 23.4.85 and 1.11.91). The AEU also sought a single-union strike-free deal with Ford in Dundee in 1987, bringing itself into conflict with other major unions, leading to a complaint to the TUC's disputes committee (TUC 1988: 48–50). The craft-conscious AEU also negotiated 'Task Flexibility Agreements' removing long-standing demarcation lines between different craftsmen in its willingness to co-operate with management in job regulation in the 1980s. Also, in common with the EETPU, it was led by politically moderate leaders throughout this period, but it did not assume a similarly combative stance in relation to the TUC.

The GMB, a similarly politically aligned although more centrist union, also supported single-union deals on greenfield sites as the best option for both employer and union. The GMB developed its own model agreement with provision for training for employees, a consultative committee, flexibility, and the right to go to arbitration in disputes. In 1989 the GMB claimed to have thirty-six such agreements. In 'Shaping up for the Next Century' the GMB argued for a new approach stressing the need to co-operate with employers—a theme fitting its new slogan, 'Working together'. Moreover, by the mid-1990s the GMB was a leading exponent of 'industrial partnership'. Its General Secretary, John Edmonds, joined the President of the AEU, Bill Jordan, in signing the Involvement and Participation Association's brochure 'Towards Industrial Partnership: A New Approach to Relationships at Work' (IPA 1992). This stressed the advantages of social partnership between management and employee representatives and joint commitment to the success of the enterprise.

The TGWU stood politically more towards the reformist end of unionism. It did not reject single-union deals but consistently very strongly opposed no-strike deals. At the national level, new realism was therefore consciously rejected. As neither of the factions in the TGWU were as closely aligned with the right of the Labour movement as those in the EETPU or AEU, there was little internal political conflict over this policy. However, in such a large and geographically dispersed union, some regional secretaries and local officials did pursue job regulation practices more akin to those adopted by the AEU and GMB.

Neither the CPSA nor the NCU were consistent in their political objectives over this period. In both unions the political differences between the factions were quite marked. This was particularly so in the case of the CPSA, where the moderates and the left both held more extreme positions than their counterparts in other unions. Thus, as the controlling group changed in each union, so did their industrial and political policies and strategies. For example, within the CPSA there was a tendency to adopt a more adversarial stance in the field of job regulation under the Broad Left and to seek negotiated compromises under the moderates. The Broad Left in the CPSA also pressed for the establishment of a political fund and affiliation to the Labour Party—a policy eventually overwhelmingly accepted by the membership in a ballot in 1987 (73 per cent for and 27 per cent against) even though the Treasury's refusal to deduct such political fund contributions prevented the actual creation of the fund.

Other policy shifts initiated by unions which may be thought to reflect a movement in objectives and methods towards business unionism included the introduction or expansion of services directed towards the individual member rather than the collective membership. Virtually all the unions studied, regardless of their political leanings, moved to strengthen their services to the individual. The package provided by the AEU included assistance with mortgage arrangements, home contents insurance, motor insurance, and life assurance. This was generally a low-cost image-building exercise which made use of the newly computerized membership list to negotiate discounts with a number of financial institutions. In introducing these services, blue-collar unions were following a lead given earlier by white-collar unions, and in particular, unions with a professional or staff association origin. However, there was universal agreement within the unions' national leadership that these were supplementary to, and not replacements for, collective bargaining.

The strategy and tactics used to implement job regulation policies throws further light on the character of the unions involved and in doing so questions the degree to which the above developments indicate a 'new realism' and the adoption and practice of business unionism. First, while the combination of single-union and strike-free deals is a relatively new innovation, the practice of unions negotiating favourable terms with employers on greenfield sites is not. For example, the GMWU's northern regional secretary in the 1960s and 1970s actively pursued closed-shop agreements with firms considering moving into his region, prior to their actually employing people in his region (Undy *et al.* 1981: 136). In making such approaches, one of the advantages sometimes offered by the GMWU would be the exclusion of the TGWU. It is therefore the strike-free part of the agreement which is new, not the use of such agreements to exclude competitor unions. Second, the number of single-union strike-free deals agreed in the period studied was miniscule compared to the number of conventional agreements in existence. Even the EETPU's forty such agreements in 1989 only covered a very minor part of that union's membership. Also, similar deals signed by the AEU and GMB covered only a small fraction of their membership. The agreements were therefore more symbolic than representative of the unions' general form of collective agreements. However, in signing such agreements the unions exposed themselves to counter-claims from other employers, particularly those in the same industrial sector, for no less favourable agreements. For instance, unions in Rover came under considerable pressure and eventually agreed to sign a 'new deal' agreement which was clearly influenced by agreements made with Japanese vehicle builders (IRS 1992: 12–15). It did not, however, include a strike-free clause as such.

Lastly, although unions signing strike-free deals have rarely resorted to militant industrial action[11] under such agreements, they have been militant in other circumstances. Unions governed by parties or factions on the right of the labour movement have tended to be more sympathetic towards some aspects of business unionism but have not necessarily chosen to be more moderate than other unions in the field of job regulation when conducting bargaining under more conventional agreements. Indeed, the militant behaviour of the AEU in leading[12] the Confederation of Shipbuilding and Engineering Unions' (CSEU) campaign and selective strikes for the shorter working week in 1989–90 serves as a clear demonstration of a politically moderate union's willingness to undertake major industrial conflict. The determination of the AEU's national and moderate 'Group' leadership and not least the campaigning of Bill Jordan, who was approaching re-election for the Presidency, was critical for the relatively successful outcome. By September 1990, 1,034 agreements covering approximately 400,000 workers had been signed (providing for a 37-hour week) 'without accepting the workforce and temporal flexibility clauses which the EEF insisted upon during the 1983–87 negotiations' (McKinlay and McNulty 1992: 211).

Also, the arch-proponent of new realism in greenfield sites, the EETPU, did not reject the use of more militant methods in more traditional plants. In a series of pay claims in electricity supply in the 1980s and 1990s the EETPU, as the leading negotiator, pursued a policy of tough negotiations, joining other unions in calling a series of strike ballots (*FT* 19.4.90). Moreover, in the Ford pay claim of 1989–90 the EETPU instigated an official and indefinite strike against the introduction of flexible working practices and conditional allowances for skilled workers.[13] The strike was called and sustained for three weeks despite all the other unions supporting the proposed agreement, and resulted in 4,000 workers being laid off in the UK and Belgium. During this strike TGWU members crossed official picket lines for the first time in Halewood's long history of industrial disputes.

It can be concluded, therefore, that even in the case of the craft-conservative and traditionally politically moderate EETPU and AEU there was no movement to abandon reformism and embrace business unionism. The EETPU's expulsion from the TUC was temporary. It also owed much to the General Secretary's—Eric Hammond's—provocative approach to the pursuit of sectional industrial interests at the expense of more left-inclined unions (Lloyd 1990: 598–633). However, after amalgamating with the AEU in 1992 it rejoined the TUC, and it remained in the Labour Party throughout the period. Moreover, it also pursued an aggressive and militant job regulation strategy when it suited the leadership and had the support of members, as at Ford. Similarly, the AEU used single-union strike-free-type agreements to win recognition on greenfield sites. But it also used considerable skill in leading one of the few successful militant job regulation campaigns of the late 1980s and early 1990s. The more left-inclined TGWU, although protesting at strike-free agreements, itself signed single-union deals with Japanese companies, particularly in Wales.

Thus, while unions sought to project a new image thought to be attractive to non-unionized employees and employers alike, this did not automatically lead to a new approach towards conventional job regulation if the circumstances were thought to warrant a more traditional response. Unions adjusted their approaches to suit the particular contexts in which they operated. They generally recognized that greenfield sites required a different approach if they were to be unionized in the climate of the 1980s. New realism in the form of no-strike deals met the needs of such employers and helped the unions gain recognition in a particular segment of their membership territory. Subsequently, by the mid-1990s unions adopted a more co-operative strategy and some moved beyond this to promote industrial partnership. This was prompted, at least in part, by the leadership's recognition of their more limited power base.

SUMMARY AND CONCLUSIONS

The causes of the non-ballot-related changes were complex and inter-related, but the dramatic fall in membership and density was clearly a key factor driving a number of other changes, particularly when it was associated with a financial deficit. Changes in union government frequently originated in such developments. However, the causes of the fall in membership and density were themselves complex and are not satisfactorily explained by existing research. While quantitative and deductive studies have provided some evidence of the general impact of external factors on changes in union density, they have failed to explain satisfactorily the interaction between these factors and the dynamic process of membership gain and loss, and why it is that unions have not recruited more effectively in both existing territories and the new expanding areas of employment. As a consequence the present schemes of analysis offer little guide to how union behaviour has itself influenced this crucial change.

In circumstances of falling membership and union failure to penetrate new areas of employment, mergers were seen by some leaders as offering a more certain and possibly cheaper way of increasing the major union's membership and saving the minor unions from extinction. They may, however, have also diverted attention and energy away from a more determined attempt at the retention of existing members and the recruitment of the non-unionized. The mergers that followed were, in the absence of any widely accepted form of external union structure, largely determined by the internal concerns of the merging unions. Moreover, the major unions involved in amalgamations had a particularly important impact on union structure. They not only took large groups of members into new organizations but also caused other large unions to be sensitive to their own relatively diminished standing. In this way the large or mega-mergers of the 1990s look set to become the catalyst for future major mergers in the late 1990s.

Changes in union government, as they affected non-bargaining decisions, probably owed more to mergers and financial difficulties than any other factors. The major merging unions accommodated the incoming minor unions by becoming more vertically bifurcated around trades or industrial sectors. This in turn tended to diminish the influence of intermediate bodies, such as regional or other geographically based systems of decision-making. Also, in making cuts in expenditure and seeking to maximize income there was a tendency to draw decisions back to, and concentrate them at, the centre. Contrary to these developments, employers were primarily responsible for bargaining becoming more decentralized.

The role of the union leader (the inner ring in Figure 1.1) in exercising choice in determining the new forms of government was also important for reshaping union government. However, in some unions, such as the centralizing TGWU, the exercise of this discretion became more constrained as factional activity limited the discretion conventionally exercised by the national full-time officials and the General Secretary. Similarly, in the factionalized and volatile CPSA, and to a lesser extent in the NCU, no faction secured a dominant position for more than a few years: in these unions the centre's decision-making powers did not strengthen. In contrast, the non-factionalized GMB, the one-party EETPU, and the two-party but Group-dominated AEU, experienced relatively consistent leadership. In these unions the process of adjusting internal decision-making in response to the new climate also tended to produce changes which enhanced the national leadership's powers relative to other bodies within their unions.

The unions' commitment to some combination of reformist and business unionism remained largely intact throughout the period. Support for the Labour Party was solid. There were, however, some important variations between unions in their pursuit of business goals. In particular, unions on the centre-right of the political spectrum showed themselves more willing to accommodate the interests of employers on greenfield sites. Nevertheless, even the most craft-conservative and politically moderate and stable unions did not radically change their character; if a conventional bargaining approach and militant tactics were required by the circumstances they were used. Unions thus tended to adopt a contingent approach to strategy and tactics, provided it came within the limits of what was ideologically sound, or at least acceptable when the questions arose. However, towards the end of the period, as unions came to realize that the powers enjoyed in the 1970s were unlikely to be restored, unions began to develop a more strategic approach to their relations with employers. Notions of social and industrial partnership were explored and, in some areas, integrated with other changes to produce a new proactive strategy for regenerating the unions.

To conclude: in the unexpectedly hostile environment of the period studied, unions were initially inclined to adopt damage-limitation policies and strategies. Each union tended to defend its own interests and to give priority to institutional survival. Unions did not generally undertake a radical review or create a new movement-wide consensus around the issue of what unions were—or should be—for. Neither did they agree on a commonly desirable union structure. The general movement towards a more centralized system of government and greater vertical bifurcation was the result of a number of unconnected individual actions, although some leaders did use the opportunity these presented to draw decisions and financial control back to the centre. For much of the period, unions and their leaders therefore concentrated on dealing with internal problems as they arose, on the basis of purposeful ad hocery. Given the relatively rapid change in their fortunes and the external environment, this may have been the best they could hope for in the short term. Towards the end of the period, however, more considered and overtly strategic approaches were being developed. A number of unions initiated radical reviews of their organizational structure and in some unions this coincided with the development of new policies towards employers, including the promotion of industrial partnership.

NOTES

1. See *British Journal of Industrial Relations*, vol. 28, no. 2 (1990) for three articles which analyse changes in union density: Freeman and Pelletier; Disney; and Bailey and Kelly. Also see Waddington (1992). In this article Waddington calculates union density by reference to the labour force, excluding employers, the self-employed, members of the armed forces, *and* the *registered unemployed*. The result of this calculation is to raise the union density figures as compared to those quoted on p. 35, e.g. on p. 35 we quote figures of 41 per cent for union density in 1987 whereas Waddington produces a figure of 46.3 per cent for the same year.
2. The GMWU (forerunner of the GMB) was categorized as 'restrictive-passive' in its orientation to membership recruitment by Undy *et al.* (1981: 64–6) because in comparison with other large general unions it did not pursue membership growth as a priority in the 1960s and 1970s.
3. The initial idea concerning the process of recruitment was triggered by Disney's reference (1990: 171) to different factors affecting different stages of union membership, quoting a mimeo by F. Green of the University of Leicester. This mimeo has not been seen by the authors.
4. The material used in this section is taken largely from research conducted by Roger Undy and Lord McCarthy for the TUC. The research was primarily conducted between 1989 and 1994 using postal questions and interviews of TUC affiliates, and covered 90 per cent of the TUC's affiliated unions and 98 per cent of the TUC's total membership in 1989.
5. See Undy *et al.* (1981: 167–219) for a discussion of these terms.
6. See Salamon (1987: 166–7) for a discussion of these terms.
7. See Purcell (1991) for a discussion of changes in employers' bargaining levels in the 1980s.
8. In the AEU the 'Group' was the politically moderate party or faction which had dominated the government of the AEU since the introduction in 1972 of postal ballots for the election of all full-time officers.
9. TGWU (1993), a TGWU strategy paper used to initiate debate on further reforms at the TGWU's 35th Biennial Delegate Conference in 1993.
10. Dabscheck and Niland (1981). Chapter 4 of their book discusses the various classifications of unions according to their behaviour and how they seek to achieve their goals. We did not include reference to socialist revolutionary

unionism (Darlington (1994)) as it had little relevance to the behaviour of the unions studied.

11. *LRD*, vol. 78, no. 11 (10.89) identified five companies with 'no-strike' deals which had also experienced industrial action (p. 9).

12. For a brief discussion of the AEU's role in leading this dispute, see McKinlay and McNulty (1992).

13. See the *Financial Times* on the following dates for reports of this dispute: 30.1.90; 6.2.90; 7.2.90; 14.2.90; 28.2.90; 6.3.90; 7.3.90; and 8.3.90.

4

CONSERVATIVE POLICY AND LEGISLATION

INTRODUCTION

This chapter examines the Conservatives' balloting legislation and associated policies, and through this analysis it reveals the Conservatives' position on the critical issue of union autonomy. A number of themes and sources of Conservative ideology and strategy are developed, together with a consideration of the constraints that the Conservatives faced in terms of obtaining compliance from unions and employers, maintaining electoral appeal, and the internal management of the Conservative Party. The main discussion of the legislation itself is structured chronologically so as to demonstrate fully the incremental and cumulative nature of the Conservatives' statutory interventions in union decision-making. We also note that it was basically enabling legislation which relied on employers and disaffected members (and later members of the public) for its enforcement and thus, as indicated in the top arc of Figure 1.1, allowed the Government to remain at arm's length from its application.

In detail the chapter, first, establishes the degree of union autonomy prior to the Conservatives' election in 1979. Second, the underlying Conservative ideology and strategy for union reform is analysed. Third, the Conservatives' initial attempt to encourage more use of ballots by voluntary means is considered. Fourth, the legislation introducing mandatory elections and ballots for key national positions and, fifth, mandatory ballots for the calling of industrial action is described and analysed. The main themes regarding the legislation are developed in the discussion of mandatory ballots for elections, whereas the section on industrial action ballots emphasizes the interaction of industrial disputes, employers' responses to the legislation, and government ideology and strategy. In the sixth part we briefly consider the Code of Practice for Trade Union Ballots on Industrial Action, before drawing the various strands together in a summary and conclusion.

It should also be noted that the sections on mandatory ballots for elections and industrial action contain two tables (Tables 4.2 and 4.3) summarizing the balloting provisions of the relevant Acts, together with a note on the new Trade Union and Labour Relations (Consolidation) Act (TULR(C)A) 1992 numbering; for the reader's ease of reference, and in order to show the cumulative effect of the Conservatives' incrementalist approach as it applied to virtually all aspects of the balloting legislation, these two tables are organized thematically by reference to the different aspects of the balloting process.[1] In Table 4.2 chronological changes in the election balloting process are catalogued by reference to ENFORCEMENT and ENFORCEMENT ASSISTANCE, POSTS COVERED, PERIOD OF OFFICE, CANDIDATES, CAMPAIGNING, VOTERS/REGISTER OF NAMES AND ADDRESSES, BALLOTING METHOD, VOTING PAPER, COUNTING THE VOTE, SUPERVISION, and INFORMING MEMBERS. In Table 4.3 changes in the industrial action balloting process are similarly recorded by reference to ENFORCEMENT and ENFORCEMENT ASSISTANCE, TIMING, VOTERS, CAMPAIGNING, BALLOTING METHODS, VOTING PAPER, COUNTING THE VOTE, and INFORMING MEMBERS AND EMPLOYERS. The same sub-headings (in small type) are adopted in the text so that the reader can easily select from the tables which aspect of the balloting legislation is being discussed. A further table (Table 4.4) covers the recommendations of the Draft Code of Practice on Industrial Action Ballots and Notice to Employers 1994.

UNION AUTONOMY BEFORE 1979

Before the Conservatives came to office in 1979, unions were regarded as voluntary associations and, as such, were largely responsible for their internal affairs, including the organization of union elections and the calling and ending of industrial action: the main source of authority in union affairs was the provisions of the rule book. According to Kahn-Freund (1983: 274), 'In this country, it has, on the whole, been common ground that in the dilemma between imposing standards of democracy and protecting union autonomy, the law must come down on the side of autonomy.' The Trade Union Act (TUA) 1871 was the first major piece of legislation concerned with union government and it adopted a stance of non-intervention in union affairs, regarding union autonomy as a desirable principle (Elias and Ewing 1987: 6 ff.; Miller 1986: 276). When the position of the Certification Officer (CO) was created by the Employment Protection Act (EPA) 1975, he/she was given an independent statutory authority over certain internal union matters; however, in line with the traditional non-interventionist stance, the CO was not given the power to order unions to amend their rule books or to tell them how to conduct their affairs. The approach of TUA 1871 is consistent with International Labour Organization (ILO) Convention 87, Article 3, which gives unions 'the right to draw up their constitutions and rules, to elect their representatives in full freedom, to organise their administration and activities and to formulate their programmes'.

The common law also recognized the importance of union autonomy:

courts have treated the rule book as the contract of membership and the constitution of the union.[2] Thus membership participation, disciplinary action, and expulsion from (and in certain dubious cases admission to) unions together with the legality of calls for industrial action depended upon the court's strict construction of the union's rule book (Lewis 1986: 11–12; Miller 1986: 296–8). In theory, this approach should have allowed unions a wide discretion in setting rules and should have kept the courts out of union affairs. However, practice has been different and the courts, in applying the principles of contractual law to the relations between unions and their members, have interfered by implying terms and striking out rules contrary to public policy (Elias *et al.* 1980: 309; Miller 1986: 276). Additionally, the courts have applied the principles of public law to unions, mainly through the application of the rules of natural justice to the union's disciplining of its members (ibid.).

The common-law remedy available to a union member for a breach of union rules is an application to the High Court for a declaration of the breach and for an injunction restraining the union from, or ordering it to perform, certain actions. If the union disobeys an injunction, it can be held in contempt of court. Contempt of court in labour cases is usually punished by a fine but, where the fine goes unpaid, the court can order sequestration of the union's assets and the appointment of receivers, who then pay the outstanding fines and costs (Dickens and Cockburn 1986: 545–52). Union members also have recourse to administrative law through an appeal to the CO to ensure that they are treated in accordance with their unions' rule book (Urwin and Murray 1983: 24).

Before 1979, there was only one brief period (when the Industrial Relations Act (IRA) 1971 was in force) when there was a significant degree of state control over union internal affairs: between 1971 and 1974 a union was obliged to register as a 'trade union' if it wished to continue to enjoy legal protection, and the Registrar of Trade Unions and Employers' Associations was empowered to inspect the rule books of a registered union to ascertain whether it met a number of standards. These included union rule-book specification of the manner of appointment and removal of officials and workplace representatives, and of the bodies or officials who can instruct members to take industrial action, together with union rule-book provision of rights for members to participate in elections and meetings, to vote in secret, and not to be forced to take part in 'unfair' industrial action or a strike other than that described as an industrial dispute. Additionally, the Secretary for State was given the power to apply to NIRC, in a dispute which threatened the national interest, for an order requiring a strike ballot to be held where he considered there were doubts about whether the workers concerned supported the action (Elias and Ewing 1987: 153).

The question of what constitutes union democracy and how this ideal is best obtained was widely discussed in the UK in the 1980s (for example, Undy and Martin 1984: ch. 5; Mackie 1984, 1987; Kidner 1984; Miller 1986; Urwin and Murray 1983; and Elias and Ewing 1987). This debate is examined later in the book (Chapter 7) and we shall comment here only that the Conservative model of union democracy was and remains very limited, focusing on unions' internal affairs, and neglecting their wider role in the achievement of democracy in society. In addition, the Conservatives were afflicted with 'tunnel vision' in that they applied their model of democracy only to unions and not to the other actors in the industrial relations system such as employers or, indeed, political parties and Parliament (Mackie 1984).

CONSERVATIVE IDEOLOGY AND STRATEGY FOR UNION 'REFORM'

Beginning in 1980, the Conservative Government embarked on a massive programme of legislative 'reform' of the unions' legal framework. Major Acts so far comprise the Employment Act (EA) 1980, the Employment Act (EA) 1982, the Trade Union Act (TUA) 1984, the Employment Act (EA) 1988, the Employment Act (EA) 1990, and the Trade Union Reform and Employment Rights Act (TURERA) 1993. Two major Codes of Practice have been issued, including the Code of Practice on Trade Union Ballots on Industrial Action (first issued in 1990). The introduction of balloting requirements for union decision-making for elections and the calling of industrial action was a critically important part of the increase in state intervention in unions' internal affairs which was, in turn, part of the Conservatives' wider 'reform' of the unions' legal framework.

The Conservatives sought through their legal 'reforms' to remove the 'distortions' of the labour market caused both by statutory protection for workers and by unions' collective bargaining activities, for which they saw the weakening of union power as crucial (Wedderburn 1992: 168 ff.). The Conservatives also emphasized the importance of individual freedom in their labour market policy. These two aims pose two important contradictions. First, if the individual is free, then he/she is free to come together with fellow workers to form unions which can obstruct the free operation of the labour market. Second, the Conservatives' massive legislative programme since 1979 seems as much focused on regulating unions' internal affairs as on restricting unions' activities in the labour market. We attempt to explain these two contradictions below. In introducing so much legislation, particularly for the administration of unions' internal affairs, the Conservatives have extensively re-regulated the labour market (Wedderburn 1989: 18).

The debate over the influences shaping the Conservatives' legislative programme of union reform has focused on the different opinions held by, on the one hand, those that maintain that the Conservatives closely followed a consistent set of principles and, on the other hand, those that believe they were not influenced by 'lofty realms of ideology'. There are several versions of the former, but Wedderburn's (1989) has been the most influential: the government was driven by the theories of the New Right and in its approach to solving the 'union problem' was strongly influenced by Hayek.[3] The second position has most strongly been argued by Auerbach (1990), who maintains that the government was motivated by a complex patchwork of influences and events (including the New Right). However, this debate has been conducted on too simple a level. In discussing the 'wellsprings' of the Conservative reform of union legal frameworks, we need to distinguish clearly between ideology and strategy. On the one hand, we need to discuss whether the Conservatives pursued a particular ideology or combination of ideologies, or reacted in an *ad hoc* fashion to events as they occurred. On the other hand, we need to discuss whether they followed a planned step-by-step policy or opportunistically inserted desired changes. A better understanding of the Conservatives' legislative programme and of the contradictions posed at the beginning of this section is obtained if we view the Conservatives' ideology and strategy as shifting over time. At times the Conservatives were implementing Hayek's principles and, at other times, they were responding to other influences; at times they had a coherent plan of the reforms they wished to implement and at others they were reacting to events as they occurred.

Conservative ideology

Conservative policy during the 1980s and 1990s can be best understood if we view it as related to two deep-seated strands of political ideology, both with a long history within the party: economic liberalism and authoritarian social-political policy (Willetts 1992). The first strand looks to market mechanisms to determine effective and efficient production and distribution, while the second strand draws on traditional Tory moral absolutism to outline what individuals should do. In terms of union reform, the Conservatives' twin strands were embodied in a dual-track policy of restricting (liberal economic policy) and regulating (authoritarian social-political policy) union activities. The writings of Hayek (1980) and Hanson and Mather (1988) exemplify the first restrictive approach, which came into prominence after 1981. The aim of this approach was the removal of unions' 'special privileges' and their exposure to common law. However, we agree with Ewing (1990) that the Conservatives' 'reforms' were not wholly driven by New Right theories, as the UK in 1995 is still a long way from the paradigm: unions have not been stripped of all their 'special privileges'.

In the Conservatives' regulatory approach (which resurfaced in Conservative thinking in 1983) the emphasis was on the need to seek a more equitable balance between the rights of employers and managers, on the one hand, and employees and their unions, on the other; it was not necessary to outlaw unions. The Conservatives were able to square the imposition of regulation on union activities with their insistence on individual freedom through their particular interpretation of individual freedom, which was one of negative freedom: that is *freedom from* rather than *freedom to* (Berlin 1969). Thus union members must freely make decisions about union policy and activities, but the decision-making procedures through which they reach these decisions must accord with legally binding prescriptions. An alternative view of the Conservatives' regulatory approach is that their considerable extension of government intervention in union internal affairs was not based, or not based solely, on a concern to introduce democracy for members' sake, but was used as a means of restricting unions' efficiency, particularly in industrial action (Wedderburn 1985: 44): a case of 'regulation going where restriction fears to tread'.

Throughout the 1980s and 1990s, Conservative ideology on the 'union problem' contained, in both its restrictive and its regulatory versions, an emphasis on legal solutions: as in IRA 1971, Donovan-style voluntary solutions were eschewed. When legislation did not bring about the desired 'reforms', the Conservatives' reaction was to legislate again, to 'add another layer of cement' to the earlier legislation. Further, the Conservatives lacked consistency in their assessment of possible legislative provisions: ideas rejected in one Green Paper as unacceptable and unworkable reappeared in another as feasible and effective. However, one common thread throughout their legislation in this period was that the Government consistently pursued an arm's-length policy for enforcing the legislative requirements, in strong contrast to the approach of IRA 1971: enforcement was always placed in the hands of others—employers, members, and finally, customers.

In other respects, however, the legal solutions implemented by the Conservative Government were not novel. There was a strong tendency both to recycle legislation or proposed legislation from earlier decades and to borrow legislation from other countries. Balloting for industrial action was not by any means a new idea in British labour legislation: there were attempts to introduce mandatory industrial action ballots in the 1920s, 1950s, 1969 (*In Place of Strife*), and in the 1970s.[4] In terms of the regulation of unions' internal affairs, there was discussion of legally prescribed electoral procedures in the Conservative Political Centre's submission to the Donovan Commission in 1966, (*Trade Unions for Tomorrow*) (CPC 1966), and the provision of state funds for the reimbursement of the expenses of union election ballots was first recommended in the Conservatives' *The Right Approach* (CCO 1976). Additionally, the Conservatives were impressed by the range of common-law contractual obligations and remedies the courts recognized or granted to union members seeking to restrain their union and its officers from alleged breaches of union rule books, particularly those that arose out of the 1984–5 miners' dispute. They opportunistically built statutory provisions on this case law, expanding it and removing ambiguities (Fosh *et al*. 1993a).

A major source of influence from abroad appears to be the legislation of the USA. However, while there is a close resemblance between the provisions of the American Landum–Griffin Act 1959 for free and democratic union elections and the Conservatives' prescriptions for union elections in the 1980s and 1990s, the Conservatives' strictures on balloting for industrial action do not have an American parallel: the workers' collective bargaining agent, whose approval is generally necessary for the protection of strike activity, is not regulated by the American State as to the means of strike approval. Moreover, despite the resemblance between union election requirements in the two countries, the American State does not set out such tight prescriptions detailing how unions should conduct their affairs as is the case in the UK, nor are the American courts invited to interfere in internal union government (Fosh *et al*. 1993a). Also important to include in this discussion is the Conservatives' use as a legislative model of the practices of 'approved' British unions, particularly the politically moderate EETPU and the AUEW(E).

Some sources that have not been utilized by the Conservatives in their search for legal solutions include the European Union (EU) and the ILO. Further, the Conservatives did not fully consider research findings on union organization and behaviour: indeed, there is a very noticeable lack of substantiation in Conservative Green Papers, with frequent bland references to the expression of 'public concern', together with an ingrained perception of widespread union 'abuses'.

Conservative strategy

The Conservatives began with a coherent 'step-by-step' introduction of reforms which degenerated after 1984 into a haphazard insertion of fragments of a neo-Hayekian anti-union ideology in response to various industrial disputes and initiatives from interested parties. Margaret Thatcher began her programme of implementing union 'reform' by considering carefully the constraints imposed by the necessity to obtain union and employer compliance, maintain electoral appeal, and manage the Conservative Party; she was anxious not to repeat the failure of IRA 1971. She, and her successor John Major, grew considerably less careful of these constraints in the later 1980s and the 1990s, although union compliance was not a serious problem after 1983 given the decrease in union power associated with the hostile environment as discussed in Chapter 3. As regards employers, rather than Government ministers working closely with them to devise reforms to make the practice of British industrial relations more 'acceptable', the predominant pattern appeared to be that the Conservatives were prepared to take up suggestions for specific pieces of legislation, but they were not prepared to take generally much notice of more wide-ranging proposals. As regards electoral appeal, there was a close relationship between the publication of Green Papers and the Conservative Government seeking re-election. However, shifts in public opinion when they did not agree with the Government's views were ignored.

Finally, any consideration of restraints on the Conservatives' desire to reform industrial relations must include the negotiations, accommodations, and political infighting involved in party and pressure group management.[5] This infighting reflected the split in the Conservative Party discussed above between those to the left of the party, who favoured a step-by-step, consultative, more voluntary approach, and those on the right, who favoured a more ideologically inspired assault on unions' legal position. Further, several Secretaries of State appeared determined to make their individual mark on Conservative union policy.[6] Outside the party, policy 'think tanks' and industrial pressure groups (such as Aims of Industry, the Freedom Association, the Institute of Economic Affairs, Policy Research Associates, the Centre for Policy Studies, the Adam Smith Institute, the Engineering Employers' Federation, and the Institute of Personnel Management) also had an effect on the content of legislative proposals. This infighting also helps to explain the shifts in Conservative thinking on industrial relations reform, as different individuals and groups became influential.

A VOLUNTARY APPROACH TO ENCOURAGE UNION BALLOTS

The Conservatives had actively considered legislation on union ballots in the 1970s as part of their overall policy to increase individual rights and reduce the imbalance of power in industry, although the emphasis placed on election as against strike ballots varied, as did the preference for a mandatory or voluntary policy (see Undy and Martin 1984: ch. 1). In 1979 the Conservatives included the provision of funds for secret ballots to encourage wider participation in unions as one of three immediate changes proposed to restore this balance by encouraging responsible and representative union leadership.[7]

The Conservatives' 1979 election manifesto formed the basis of EA

1980. Margaret Thatcher had appointed Jim Prior as Secretary of State for Employment and she pragmatically backed him rather than the more hawkish Geoffrey Howe, given the problems of obtaining employer and union compliance for reform. Jim Prior's views on industrial relations were, to a significant extent, a legacy of the consensus and corporatist 1970s: he believed that the law had only a limited role in industrial relations and that unions should be consulted over proposed reforms. The Conservatives at this point accepted that unions had an important role to play in economic growth, but felt they should be less involved in formulating economic policy than they had been in the 1970s: unions should not be regarded as any different from other private voluntary organizations.

Margaret Thatcher pressed ahead with proposals for union reform in her first few months. On 9 July 1979, the government produced a working paper, *Support from Public Funds for Union Ballots*, which argued that more extensive use of secret ballots within unions would produce wider membership participation and freedom for members to express opinions without fear of future reprisal: a view that they felt was supported by the public and by unionists themselves (ibid. 18). The working paper argued that unions should decide when ballots were appropriate: the role of the Government would be to remove major financial constraints that prevented unions from holding secret ballots on important issues. Balloting matters covered by the proposed scheme included elections for full-time union officers and members of the executive committee or other governing body and the calling or ending of strikes. Unions would be able to claim refunds for reasonable postal costs in conducting a secret ballot on any of these matters. The CO was to administer the scheme: expenditure incurred was to be reasonable and secrecy must be properly secured. To qualify, ballots had to be held according to union rules. Two questions were raised by the working paper for further discussion: first, whether the Secretary of State should have powers to extend the scheme by Order in Council; and, second, whether workplace ballots should also be reimbursed (although concern was expressed over the difficulties of ensuring the secrecy of workplace ballots).

The Employment Bill was introduced in December 1979 and its proposals for union ballots (Clause 1) closely followed the proposals in the working paper, except that the provision was to be for industrial action ballots rather than just strike ballots (at the initiative of the EEF), and refunds for elections for full-time union officers were limited to those officers who, on election, would be union employees—thus excluding conveners and shop stewards.[8] The Secretary of State was to be given the power to extend the scheme by his/her own powers, answering the first of the two questions raised by the working paper. On the second question, whether workplace ballots should also qualify for subsidy, the relevant clause in the Employment Bill was unclear, referring merely to 'ballots'. At the Committee Stage of the Bill, the Government stated that its intention was to apply the scheme initially to postal ballots with power to apply it to non-postal ballots later: postal ballots incurred the greatest expense and, additionally, the Government wished to begin this innovatory scheme in a modest and limited way (ibid. 29).[9]

The Employment Act 1980

The balloting provisions of EA 1980, which received Royal Assent in August, were largely in line with those of the Bill and are laid out in Table 4.1. The Government's emphasis on voluntary reform by unions was retained: unions were still free to decide whether to apply for Government FUNDING and when to ballot. The Act empowered the Secretary of State by regulations to make a scheme providing for payments by the CO towards expenditure incurred by independent unions in respect of ballots held for certain purposes, including the calling/ending of industrial action, carrying out an election provided for by union rules, and electing a worker who was a union member to be a representative of other members employed by his/her employer. To qualify for repayment, ballots had to be secret and to conform with certain conditions laid down in the regulations. The regulations drawn up by the Secretary for State differed importantly from the requirements in EA 1980 in that the Scheme was restricted 'initially' to postal ballots and the election ballots specified were for Principal Executive Committee (PEC) members and for the positions of president, chairman, secretary, or treasurer or to any elected position held as an employee of the union, thus excluding shop stewards (Funds for Trade Union Ballots Regulations 1980 SI 1980 No. 1252). The 1980 regulations also added a number of other conditions for refunds by the CO not specified in EA 1980: these were voting in secrecy, voting by means of marking a ballot paper, entitlement to vote in industrial action being synonymous with those likely to be called upon to take action, voting without interference or restraint, cancellation of a ballot on the first day only and for a material change affecting the issue only, fair counting of votes, 'as far as reasonably practicable' a fair opportunity of voting for those entitled to vote, holding of the ballot not in contravention of union rules, and any union rule requirements as to conduct of the ballot being complied with. Most of these conditions were enacted in subsequent legislation with the exception of the last two.

The regulations for the refund of balloting expenses were altered a number of times in the succeeding years, mainly to take account of changes in legislation.[10] In 1982, the scheme was extended to include ballots referring employers' proposals affecting contractual terms and conditions

TABLE 4.1. Election and industrial action provisions of the Employment Act 1980, together with TULR(C)A 1992 numbering

ENFORCEMENT	S.1(1) & (2) Voluntary: the Secretary of State may by regulation make a scheme providing for payments by the CO towards expenditure incurred by independent unions in respect of ballots if the purposes of any of them are *inter alia* (a) to obtain a decision or ascertain the views of union members as to the calling or ending of a strike or other industrial action; (b) carrying out an election provided for by union rules; (c) electing a worker who is a union member to be a representative of other members also employed by his employer; and other purposes as the Secretary for State may by order specify.[1] (S.115 TULR(C)A 1992).
BALLOTING METHODS	S.1(5) The ballot must be so conducted as to secure, 'as far as reasonably practicable', that those voting may do so in secret (S.115(4) TULR(C)A 1992).
FUNDING/USE OF EMPLOYER'S PREMISES	S.2 Where an independent union proposes that a relevant ballot be held and requests an employer to permit his premises to be used for the purpose of giving workers employed by him who are union members a convenient opportunity of voting, the employer shall, 'so far as reasonably practicable' comply with the request.[2] (4) A union may present a complaint (within three months) to an IT that it has made a request in accordance with s.1(1) and that it was reasonably practicable for the employer to comply with it, but that he has failed to do so. Where a tribunal considers a union's complaint well-founded, the IT shall make a declaration to that effect and may make an award of compensation to be paid by the employer to the union which should be of such amount as the IT considers just and equitable in all the circumstances having regard to the employer's default in failing to comply with the request and to any expenses incurred by the union in consequence of the failure. (S.116 TULR(C)A 1992)

[1] The circumstances and conditions of the ballot refund scheme are determined by statutory instrument; these regulations have been updated as further legislation on union ballots has been passed. The regulations are contained in *The Funds for Trade Union Ballots 1984* (SI 1984 No. 1654) as amended by *The Funds for Trade Union Ballots (Amendment) Regulations 1988* (SI 1988 No. 1123), *The Funds for Trade Union Ballots (Amendment No. 2) Regulations 1988* (SI 1988 No. 2116), *The Funds for Trade Union Ballots (Amendment) Regulations 1990* (SI 1990 No. 2379), and *The Funds for Trade Union Regulations (Revocation) Regulations 1993* (SI 1993 No. 233). These regulations are summarized in a more accessible form in *Guidance for Trade*

Table 4.1. (*Continued*)

Unions Applying for Costs of a Secret Postal Ballot (Certification Office for Trade Unions and Employers' Associations 1994). Regulation 5 lists the ballot purposes for which the CO can make refunds of expenses: the ballot question must fall within one or more of a number of purposes, which include: (a) obtaining a decision or ascertaining the views of union members as to the calling or ending of a strike or other industrial action; (b) carrying out an election which includes (i) one required by s.46 TULR(C)A 1992 (duty to hold elections for certain positions); (ii) one provided for by union rules to the PEC; (iii) one provided for by union rules to the positions of union president, chairman, secretary, or treasurer or to any position which the person elected will hold as a union employee; and (c) obtaining a decision or ascertaining the views of union members as to the acceptance or rejection of an employer's proposal which relates in whole or in part to remuneration (whether in money or money's worth), hours of work, level of performance, holidays, or pensions (for this purpose only semi-postal ballots can qualify for a refund).

Regulation 8 lays down that an independent union claiming to have incurred expenditure on a ballot to which the scheme applies may apply to the CO within six months for reimbursement. Allowable costs are (reasonable) stationery and printing expenditure and postal costs (second-class post or a cheaper postal means except where the CO considers the use of a more expensive postal means reasonable in the circumstances, for example where it is particularly important to obtain the result quickly); this includes any literature enclosed with the voting papers which explains the subject to be voted on (including election addresses) or the voting procedure. Other costs are not allowable, for example expenses of collating and inserting ballot papers into envelopes, nomination costs, or transport costs. There is no right of appeal against the CO's decision.

Regulation 10 states that the CO shall not make any payments if, on consideration of any matter that has come to his notice, he is of the opinion that any of the conditions mentioned in regulation 11 (which are applicable to all ballots) or mentioned in regulation 12 (which are applicable to specific questions asked in ballots, for example the framing of the question in industrial action ballots), or any assurance he requests from the union relating to these conditions is not given. Regulations 11 and 12 together with 13 largely repeat the requirements in TULR(C)A 1992, as amended by TURERA 1993. The total amount of the payments made by the CO for ballot expenditure will be reduced (a) by a quarter, if the date of the ballot falls after 31 March 1993 but before April 1994; (b) by a half, if the date of the ballot falls after 31 March 1994 but before 1 April 1995; and (c) by three-quarters, if the date of the ballot falls after 31 March 1995. The 1984 Regulations shall be revoked on 1 April 1996.

[2] S.2(2) A ballot is relevant if (a) the purpose is one which satisfies s.1 EA 1980 and (b) the proposals for the conduct of the ballot are such as to secure, 'as far as reasonably practicable', that those voting may do so in secret. S.1(1) shall not apply where, at the time the request is made, (a) the union is not recognized by the employer to any extent for the purpose of collective bargaining, or (b) the number of workers employed by the employer, added to the number employed by any associated employer, does not exceed 20. (Where the union wished to hold the ballot outside working hours, the *IRLIB* were of the opinion that the employer would be required to keep his/her premises open to enable the ballot to take place; *IRLIB* 231 September 1980: 20).

back to members (The Funds for Trade Union Ballots Order 1982 SI 1982 No. 953). In the same year refinements were made to the definitions of reference-back ballots and 'post', and in reference-back ballots, entitlement to vote was restricted to those who were both union members and affected by the employer's offer (The Funds for Trade Union Ballots (Amendment) Regulations 1982 SI 1982 No. 1108).

EA 1980 also provided an aid for unions in terms of the USE OF EMPLOYER'S PREMISES for balloting purposes. Employers were obliged, so far as reasonably practical, to permit recognized unions to use their premises to hold secret ballots if the ballot in question was for one of those purposes specified by the Act.[11] The inclusion of this section reflected a significant body of opinion (including that of Lord Robens and the CBI) that wished to encourage workplace ballots on the grounds of their speed and lower costs; workplace ballots were additionally seen as an effective means of reducing the heightened pressures generated by mass meetings (see Undy and Martin 1984: 35–7). This attitude changed later in the 1980s.

As part of his consultative approach to the reform of unions' legal framework, Jim Prior met the TUC on a number of occasions to discuss the Government's proposals for picketing, the closed shop, and ballot refunds. However, these consultations had no significant influence on the contents of EA 1980. The TUC roundly condemned the Government's targeting of picketing and the closed shop in its first attempt to reform unions' legal framework, though its response to the Conservatives' legislation was muted compared to its response to the IRA in 1971 (and its response became more muted still in the mid-1980s and beyond): protest was confined to a demonstration and Parliamentary lobby on 9 March 1980 and a 'Day of Action' on 14 May. The TUC's position on the introduction of funds for ballots was more complex.[12] The AUEW(E) and the EETPU used postal ballots extensively and, out of concern for the expense involved, seriously considered applying for balloting refunds. The special TUC one-day conference on the Employment Bill held in January 1980 adopted a tough position: it decided to 'strongly advise' affiliated unions not to apply for balloting refunds. Its objection to the scheme was twofold; first, it objected to the CO being given control over the conduct and content of ballots in return for public funding (this represented the 'thin end of a very substantial wedge') and, second, it did not wish to compromise its opposition to other Conservative 'reforms' by accepting reimbursement for balloting costs. However, the March 1980 General Council reached a compromise position, as the TUC was concerned not to adopt a policy which might lead to the expulsion of the prominent AUEW(E) and EETPU.[13] The TUC adopted a tougher policy in 1982: the General Council recommended that affiliated unions 'shall observe Congress Policy and not seek or accept public funds for union ballots', and the TUC's Conference of Executives of Affiliated Unions, held in April

1982 at Wembley, approved the recommendation prohibiting unions from
applying for reimbursement under EA 1980 (Wilson 1986: 25–7).

All affiliated unions adhered to the TUC's policy and none applied for
the refund of balloting expenses under EA 1980.[14] Until the mandatory
balloting provisions of the TUA 1984 came into force, the pursuit of this
policy did not involve many unions in substantial losses, since few unions
used postal ballots (see Undy and Martin 1984: ch. 2). As we shall see
below, the TUC changed its policy towards compliance with the new
Conservative union laws in 1986 and dropped its boycott of the ballot
refund scheme. The response among non-TUC unions (principally staff
associations and professional bodies) to the provision of ballot refunds was
more positive, but even among these unions only a small minority applied
for refunds. Initially, applicants found it difficult to claim refunds though
the position improved afterwards.[15] Figure 4.1 shows the rate of the take-
up of Government funds from 1980 to 1994 for TUC and non-TUC unions.

Most employers' and managers' organizations were in favour of Jim
Prior's softly-softly, consultation and consensus approach to the 'reform' of
the unions' legal framework, although there was a significant faction which
proposed more speedy reform through a string of step-by-step Bills,
particularly the right-wing Institute of Directors (IOD) and the Centre for
Policy Studies (CPS) (Auerbach 1990: 62–4). The balloting refund
provisions were generally welcomed, though there were disagreements
over details. The Confederation of British Industry (CBI) had mixed
feelings: while desiring a weakening of the power of unions *vis-à-vis*

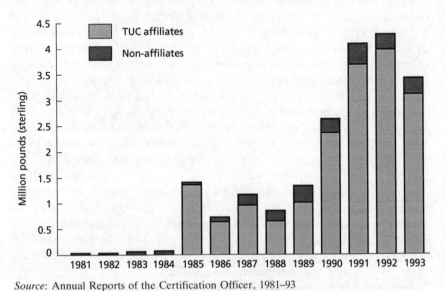

Source: Annual Reports of the Certification Officer, 1981–93

Fig. 4.1. Ballot costs refunded by Certification Officer, 1981–93

employers, they distrusted further devolution of decision-making to the rank-and-file. The IOD felt that the legislation did not go far enough: the Director, Walter Goldsmith, wished to see mandatory ballots being 'triggered' whenever a defined percentage of eligible union members requested them.[16] Public opinion, with experience of the 'winter of discontent' so recent, was behind the Conservatives' planned reform of unions' legal framework.[17]

THE INTRODUCTION OF MANDATORY ELECTIONS AND BALLOTS FOR KEY NATIONAL POSTS

In turning to examine the changes imposed on union elections and ballots we set each piece of legislation in context by, first, analysing the appropriate parts of the associated Green Paper. This establishes the Government's approach to each of the incremental changes made in elections and ballots. Second, we note the responses of the main interested parties, i.e. unions, employers, and the public at large to the Government's proposals prior to the legislation. This shows how, over time, their respective opposition to and support for the legislation developed and changed. Thus, as each of the major pieces of legislation affecting elections is examined in chronological order, its origins and purposes will have been clearly identified prior to describing the relevant parts of each Act. As regards EA 1990 we note its introduction, but as it was largely concerned with industrial action and not elections we consider this in more depth later in this chapter.

The failings of the approach adopted in EA 1980 of persuading unions to ballot their memberships more frequently were widely reported and were recognized in the Government's Green Papers *Trade Union Immunities* (DE 1981) and *Democracy in Trade Unions* (DE 1983). Nor did the provision of public funds for union ballots make the unions more amenable, as the Government had hoped, to the restrictions introduced by EA 1980 on picketing and the closed shop. Indeed, the balloting provisions provided the TUC with a focal point of opposition to the new legislation: they were the one part of EA 1980 that required active union participation. Employers' views at this time towards the reform of the unions' legal framework were mixed: while some remained cautious, the CBI shifted significantly from 'an attitude of considerable scepticism, if not hostility . . . towards robust and concerned support' (Auerbach 1990: 73).

The Conservatives continued with their incrementalist approach to the reform of industrial relations, but there was a significant shift in ideology when Norman Tebbit, who was more of a 'mirror' to Margaret Thatcher, took over from Jim Prior as Secretary of State for Employment in September 1981. Jim Prior had been cautious as to the damaging effect of legislation on industrial relations and had been reluctant to introduce any more following EA 1980. Norman Tebbit was less inhibited in his approach to legislation and believed that further legislation to 'reform' unions was politically desirable, industrially beneficial, and practically possible (Undy and Martin 1984: 41; Auerbach 1990: 74). Jim Prior was persuaded to prepare *Trade Union Immunities*, which was published in 1981 and was a rather inconclusive document, while Norman Tebbit published the more decisive *Democracy in Trade Unions* two years later. With Margaret Thatcher's Government growing in confidence, the problem of union compliance receding, and public support continuing strong, 'the sub-terranean impulses of hard-right Conservatism' acquired greater political importance (Young 1989: 115).

Norman Tebbit's EA 1982, which followed *Trade Union Immunities*, had as its central concerns a Hayek-like repeal of some of the unions' immunities and the redefinition of a trade dispute. There was some discussion of compulsory strike ballots but union election ballots received only a brief mention. In the event, there were no balloting provisions in EA 1982.

After 1982, the Conservatives continued to pursue their policy on restricting unions' activities and influence, although they stopped short of fully embracing Hayek's proposals. While the impact of the balloting provisions of EA 1980 had had little impact on unions' use of secret ballots for decision-making, the unions' refusal to adopt such ballots led to the revival of the Conservatives' interest in mandatory balloting. Norman Tebbit warned unions soon after becoming Secretary of State that if union leaders did not introduce greater controls for union democracy, he would have to legislate on the subject (Auerbach 1990: 93–4). The Conservatives' introduction of mandatory ballots drew upon traditional Conserva-tive interest in regulation, leading them to lay down detailed statutory specifications for union elections and industrial action ballots. Tebbit considered the question of union democracy eminently suitable for tackling in a single enactment (ibid. 114).

It is worth considering the Government's analysis and approach to union democracy in *Democracy in Trade Unions* (published in January 1983): while some concepts are consistent with later Green Papers, other are not. It is particularly interesting that some elements, discarded as unsuitable and unfeasible here, are adopted with enthusiasm later, when the Conservatives became less concerned with unions' ability to function efficiently and with unions' historical diversity, and became more intent on aiding aggrieved individual union members.

In its introduction, *Democracy in Trade Unions* lays out the Govern-ment's justification for legislation. Thus union leaders were seen to be out of touch with their members (neither representative of nor directly responsible to them), turn-out in union elections remained low (throwing doubt on the credibility of those elected), union rule books remained confused, self-contradictory, and obscure, and public confidence was eroded by allegations of forgery, ballot-rigging, and other corrupt practices. In particular, the government cited the increase in turn-out for the AUEW(E) on changing from voting at branches to postal balloting, attributing this to the union's adoption of a 'more democratic' voting procedure. Unions had failed to reform themselves voluntarily; 'the opportunity to extend members' rights at small cost to themselves has been thrown away' (DE 1983a: 1). Although voluntary reform was still the desired aim, the time had come for legislation to provide the impetus to move this process forward. Since the law had granted unions immunities and privileges, it was necessary to consider legislating to protect the rights of individual union members and ensure leaders' accountability; this was especially the case for 'closed shops'.[18] Moreover, unions' power to damage the economic and commercial interests of others made it essential for their internal affairs to be conducted in a manner that commanded public confidence. Hence, considerable attention was paid to the question of union elections.

The Government, which made little attempt to substantiate its claims, argued that most union elections did not meet four essential requirements: voting in secrecy; reasonable opportunity to vote; fair counting of votes; and representativeness and accountability of leaders to members. Nevertheless, at this stage, no firm proposals or a particular approach to legislation were suggested but instead the Government called for a wide-ranging debate on the statutory regulation of unions' internal affairs, focusing on a number of points. Its own preferences were as follows. First, the Government stressed that the fully postal ballot was a more democratic system than voting by show of hands, voting by the ballot box, and semi-postal ballot.[19] However, it argued that while such ballots should be possible for elections at most union levels, given accurate records of union members' names and addresses, such a requirement would place an undue burden on unions at this time. Thus a considerable step forward would be the introduction of semi-postal ballots, the return being to an independent scrutineer. Second, the Government rejected indirect in favour of direct elections on the ground that indirect elections often produced unrepresentative leadership. Third the Government suggested that elections should be held every five years for the holder of the pre-eminent position in the union, usually the General Secretary but sometimes the President, since such figures tended to be of considerable authority in the union. Another suggested approach was that General Secretaries should be subject to election and re-election only where they had a vote or casting vote on the governing body (the same principle would apply to other persons with voting rights who were co-opted on to the governing body, such as the President). However, the Government rejected the notion that all the national full-time officers in a union (including in some unions the General Secretary) should submit themselves to a confirmatory ballot of the union as a whole, as this was inconsistent with the nature of the job where a union required expertise in the office-holder rather than popular support.

In examining other electoral arrangements the Government concluded, because of wide differences in existing practices, that it was undesirable and impracticable to lay down detailed requirements for other electoral arrangements, such as the right to vote, constituencies, qualifications of candidates, election addresses, and voting systems: these were best left to voluntary determination by the membership through the rule book. However, the Government questioned whether block voting should be allowed to remain, since this could lead to an unrepresentative outcome, particularly where there was either an exceptionally small turn-out or the election was closely contested. The method was felt to be particularly unsatisfactory where a representative was subsequently allowed discretion on how to cast the block vote. The Government believed that the reform of union elections should begin at the top with the governing body, which would provide an impetus for voluntary reform for lower union levels: it considered it impracticable to specify balloting arrangements for local-level elections.

While the Government set out a number of legislative approaches for enforcing its proposals for informed discussion, it appeared to favour directly establishing the way in which elections should be held and providing a remedy for union members themselves if elections were not in compliance, feeling that giving the compliance initiative to union members themselves (a minimum number of dissatisfied members might be required) rather than a regulatory body would foster internal pressure for voluntary reform.[20]

Despite its lack of substantiation, the discussion in *Democracy in Trade Unions* of reforms of unions' internal affairs was more open, less opinionated, and less openly anti-union than that in subsequent Green Papers. For example, as an alternative and more self-regulatory approach to the suggestions for the reform of unions' electoral arrangements, the Government raised the possibility that union members should be allowed to decide democratically whether they preferred other arrangements for governing body elections. It suggested that where a majority of the total membership voted in a secret ballot expressing support for the union's election rules, and periodically confirmed that support, the specific statutory requirements would not apply.

In responding to *Democracy in Trade Unions* the TUC did not organize any days of action and confined itself to denouncing the Government's legislative policy. Nevertheless, it was totally opposed to the Green Paper's suggestions and refused to make any formal response to the Department of Employment (McIlroy 1991: 85). Instead, it published *Hands up for Democracy* in 1983, which was a general condemnation of Margaret Thatcher's policy towards unions. This document argued that unions run their affairs in a variety of ways, as laid down by their members. Just as there are many different unions so there are many different forms of union democracy, but 'every man and every woman who belongs to a trade union in Britain has a voice and a vote in their union affairs' (TUC 1983: 11): each union member was encouraged to take part in his/her union in a variety of ways and union officers, whether elected or appointed, served the union movement and were accountable to their members 'every day of the week'. In comparison the Conservative Party itself, banks, and companies were far less democratic.

The employers' attitudes towards legislative reform for industrial relations became more enthusiastic than in 1980. Some proposals in *Democracy in Trade Unions* drew mild rebukes from employers' and managers' organizations, but the Green Paper still enjoyed broad support (*FT* 1.10.83). However, most employer interest centred, as would be expected, on the Government's proposals for mandatory strike ballots. The IOD and Aims of Industry were exceptions, both responding to the mandatory election proposals with the criticism that they allowed too many loopholes and room for possible 'abuse' by unions. In the following January, Aims of Industry published a pamphlet titled *Trade Union Bill is Ballot Rigger's Charter* (Daly 1984), which was a vociferous attack on the Green Paper's proposal for union elections. Daly, the Deputy Director of Aims of Industry, urged the Government to include in the legislative proposals a computerized central membership register and fully postal ballots with an independent body handling the dispatch, receipt, and counting of the voting papers. Public opinion was still firmly behind the Government's policy on trade unions, as witnessed by the opinion polls.[21]

Hence, in the run-up to the 1983 election, the Conservatives sought political advantage by promising to bring democracy to the unions and they made it one of their top priorities in industrial relations reform.[22] They saw it as attracting union members' votes as well as emphasizing the benefits of their 'reforms' to the economy and community at large and thus gaining the support of the wider electorate. The subsequent resounding Conservative victory in June 1983 was followed by the White Paper *Proposals for Legislation on Democracy in Trade Unions* in July 1983.[23] The Trade Union Bill was published in October 1983.

The Trade Union Act 1984

TUA 1984 followed the lines of the Trade Union Bill and was piloted through Parliament by Tom King, who was appointed Secretary of State in

October 1983. Table 4.2 gives the final form of Part I, the Conservatives' first attempt to regulate the means by which unions selected their leaders. In contrast to later legislation, TUA 1984 was a more carefully planned and coherent piece of legislation.

The Government largely constructed TUA 1984 out of the alternatives presented in *Democracy in Trade Unions*. The Government chose not to involve itself directly in the ENFORCEMENT of the Act's provisions. The requirement, imposed on unions to elect PEC voting members (POSTS COVERED) every five years (PERIOD OF OFFICE) in secret ballots conducted according to certain regulations, was enforced by individual member action and, until a member took such action, there was no concrete obligation to hold elections (Kidner 1984).[24] Furthermore, the validity of the PEC's decisions was not affected if TUA 1984 was not complied with (even following a member's complaint of the lack of proper elections), nor were any union rules rendered void or unenforceable if they conflicted with the statute. Indeed, there was no obligation to change union rule books to conform to the Act's requirements: TUA 1984 simply overrode union rule books. Thus TUA 1984 established a statutory scheme which existed side-by-side with the common-law regime based on the rule book: the remedies for the two systems were kept quite separate. The only ones which applied for breach of TUA 1984 were those established by the Act; this meant that there could be no action for injunctions or damages for any union infringement of TUA 1984 and no orders for judicial review (Kidner 1984: 207). The system of remedies chosen was 'a strange combination of traditional jurisdictions' (ibid. 207) and provided two routes for the aggrieved member: (i) application to the Certification Officer, a path that the Government felt had the advantages of informality, flexibility, and lack of cost (*IRLIB* 267, 23.10.84: 4), or (ii) to the High Court, which had legal force with the ultimate sanction of contempt of court.[25]

The requirement in TUA 1984 for elections for voting members of the union's PEC, defined as that body exercising executive functions, included those voting members of the PEC who were members by virtue of their union position, such as president or general secretary, and included those holding a casting vote. The Act allowed for exemptions, most importantly for those PEC members near retirement and for newly formed unions, and in cases of union mergers.

TUA 1984 also showed its pragmatism and flexibility in terms of its choice of BALLOTING METHODS; although there was a presumption in favour of postal ballots, workplace ballots were allowed[26] where the individual members' interests were equally protected in terms of secrecy, no direct costs, freedom from interference, and so forth.[27] Note that, whereas every union member was entitled to vote, TUA 1984 only charged the union with the duty of providing such a person with a ballot paper as far as was reasonably practicable.[28] Initially, in *Proposals for Legislation on*

TABLE 4.2. Election provisions of EA 1980, TUA 1984, EA 1988, EA 1990 and TURERA 1993, together with new TULR(C)A 1992 numbering

ENFORCEMENT[1] and ENFORCEMENT ASSISTANCE

TUA 1984

S.5(1) & (2) Any union member who claims that a union has failed to comply with any provisions of Part 1 may apply (within a year of the date of the union's announcement of the result) to the CO or to the High Court for a declaration to that effect (a) if he was a union member at the date the election was held and is a member when he makes the application; and (b) in any other case, he is a union member at the time the application is made.[2]

(3) (4) & (5) On an application the CO/court may make the asked-for declaration specifying the provisions with which the union has failed to comply. (5) & (6) Where the court makes such a declaration, it shall also make an enforcement order, unless it considers it inappropriate, requiring the union, within a certain period, (a) to hold an election as may be specified in the order; (b) to take such other steps to remedy the declared failure as may be so specified; (c) to abstain from such acts as may be so specified in order to secure that the same or similar failure does not arise on the union's part.[3]

(11) Any union member shall be entitled to enforce obedience to the court's order.

S.6(1) Where the CO makes a declaration and is satisfied that the union has taken steps (or agreed to take steps) to remedy the declared failure/prevent a same or similar failure, he shall in making the declaration specify those steps. (2) The CO shall given written reasons for his decision whether or not to make a declaration and any such reasons may be accompanied by written observations on any matter arising from the proceedings. (3) An application to the CO shall not prevent a subsequent application to the court in the same matter. (4) The court shall have due regard to any declaration, reasons or observations made by the CO. (5) On an application, the CO shall make any enquiries he thinks fit, giving the applicant and union an opportunity to be heard where he considers it appropriate. (7) The CO shall ensure, 'as far as is reasonably practicable' that every application made to him is determined within six months.

S.1(5) nothing in Part 1 shall affect the validity of anything done by the PEC.

TABLE 4.2. (*Continued*)

EA 1988	

S.22 The CO may regulate the procedure to be followed (a) on any application made to him; or (b) where his approval is sought with respect to any matter, and he may make such provision as he considers appropriate for restricting the circumstances in which the identity of any applicant/complainant is disclosed to another person.

S.2 Where a member has pursued a grievance with his union for at least six months, the court cannot dismiss or adjourn proceedings on the ground that further procedures for resolving the grievance were available under the union's rules (although the court could extend the six-month period where the internal proceedings had been prolonged by the unreasonable conduct of the complainant). The grievance had to be one which (i) the union's rules required or allowed to be submitted for determination or conciliation: and (ii) came within the jurisdiction of the court.

ENFORCEMENT ASSISTANCE

S.19(1) The Secretary of State shall appoint an officer to be known as CROTUM whose function (s.20) is to provide assistance to union members/persons who are actual or prospective parties to proceedings concerning certain union activities including s.5 TUA 1984, as extended by s.12 EA 1988, and s.1 EA 1988 (industrial action ballots).[4] (3) Assistance given by the Commissioner may include making arrangements for him to bear the legal costs of advice/assistance and representation for the applicant.[5] (4) The Commissioner may have regard in determining whether, and to what extent, to grant an application, in particular to (a) whether the case raises a question of principle; (b) whether it is unreasonable, having regard to the complexity of the case, to expect the applicant to deal with the case unaided; and (c) whether, in the opinion of the Commissioner, the case involves a matter of substantial public interest. (5) Where (a) an application for assistance is arising out of an application for a court order under s.5 TUA; and (b) the CO has already made a declaration under that section; and (c) it appears to the Commissioner that the applicant would (if assisted) have a reasonable prospect of securing the making of a court order, the Commissioner shall grant the application.[6]

EA 1990

ENFORCEMENT ASSISTANCE

S.10(1) extends CROTUM's powers as laid down in s.20 EA 1988 to cover proceedings, or prospective proceedings, in the High Court (or an appeal therefrom) which arise out of an alleged breach or threatened breach of union rules relating to any of the following matters. (2) Those matters include: (a) the appointment or election of a person to, or the removal of a person from, any office; (b) union disciplinary proceedings (including expulsion); (c) the authorizing or endorsing of industrial action; (d) the balloting of members. (5) The Commissioner shall not grant an application for assistance unless it appears to him (a) that the breach of rules affects, or may affect, union members other than the applicant, or (b) that similar breaches of the rules have been or may be committed in relation to other union members.

S.11 Where an applicant wishes, the words 'assisted by the Commissioner for the Rights of Trade Union Members' may be added after his name in the title of the proceedings. The addition of these words shall not make the Commissioner a party to the proceedings.

Enforcement: ss.54–6.
Enforcement assistance: ss.109–12, ss.266–71.

TULR(C)A 1992

TUA 1984

S.1(1)(a) Every union shall have the duty (notwithstanding anything in its rules) to secure that every voting member of the PEC is elected in an election which satisfies s.2.[7]
S.1(2) S.1 also applies to voting members of the PEC[8] by virtue of holding some other union position.
S.1(3) Any term or condition of a union employee shall be disregarded if it would otherwise prevent the union from complying with Part 1.

TABLE 4.2. (*Continued*)

EA 1988	S.12(1) In ss.(1) to (3) of s.1 TUA 1984 the word 'voting', wherever it occurs, shall be omitted and after ss.(6) shall be inserted three new subsections: (6A)—A person is a member of the union's PEC if he is a voting member of that PEC or (a) that person is, under the rules of the union, a member, other than a voting member, of that committee (whether by virtue of his holding any union position or otherwise); or (b) that person may, under the rules or practices of the union, attend and speak at some or all of the meetings of that committee otherwise than for the purpose of providing the PEC with factual information or with technical or professional advice; (6B) Notwithstanding anything in rules or practices of any union, the persons who hold the positions of (a) president and (b) general secretary (if the union's rules do not otherwise provide for them to be PEC members) is deemed to be a PEC member; and (6C) Where any president or general secretary (or equivalent) (a) is neither a voting member of the PEC nor a union employee; (b) holds that position under union rules for a period less than 13 months; and (c) has held neither that position nor any other position in the 12 months before he took up that position, he does not require an election according to s.1 TUA 1984.[9]
TULR(C)A 1992	Ss.46–7, s.57, s.58, s.59, s.53.
PERIOD OF OFFICE	
TUA 1984	S.1(1)(b) No person may remain a voting member of the PEC for more than five years without being re-elected.[10]
TULR(C)A 1992	S.46(1)(b).
CANDIDATES	
TUA 1984	S.2(9) No union member shall be unreasonably excluded from standing as a candidate. S.2(10) No candidate shall be required, whether directly or indirectly, to be a member of a political party.

S.2(11) A union member shall not be taken to have been unreasonably excluded from standing as a candidate if he has been excluded on the ground that he belongs to a class all the members of which are excluded by the rules of the union.[11]

TULR(C)A 1992

S.47(1).

TUA 1988

S.13(1) adds to the requirements of Part 1 TUA 1984 the requirements in (2) that a union must (a) provide every election candidate with an opportunity of preparing an election address in his own words and of submitting it to the union to be distributed to those entitled to vote; (b) 'so far as reasonably practicable', distribute copies of the election addresses with the voting paper by post to each of the voters at his proper address; (c) do so without cost to the candidates; (d) not allow any modification of any election address except at the request of the candidate or where the modification is necessarily incidental to the method adopted for producing that copy; (e) produce copies of each election address in the same way and, 'as far as reasonably practicable' secure that no facility or information as would enable a candidate to benefit from (i) the method of producing copies; or (ii) the modifications necessarily incidental to the method are provided to any candidate without being provided equally to all the others; and (f) 'so far as reasonably practicable' secure that the same facilities and restrictions with respect to the preparation, submission, length or modification of an election address and with respect to the incorporation of a photograph or of any other matter not in words are provided or applied equally to each candidate. (3) A union may provide that election addresses submitted to it for distribution (a) must not exceed such length, not being less than one hundred words, as may be determined by the union; and (b) may incorporate only such photographs and other matter not in words as the union may determine. (4) The deadline for submission of election addresses to the union shall be no earlier than the deadline for a person to become a candidate. (5) Only the candidate shall be subject to any civil or criminal liability in respect of any publication of a candidate's election address.

S.48.

TULR(C)A 1992

TABLE 4.2. *(Continued)*

TUA 1984	S.2(1) Entitlement to vote must be accorded equally to all union members other than those belonging to one or other of certain classes of members, all of which are excluded by union rules from voting.[12] S.2(3) As long as it is in accordance with union rules and no member is denied an opportunity to vote in all elections, the union may reserve PEC seats for election by members who fall within (a) any trade or occupation; (b) any geographical area; (c) any class treated by union rules as a separate union section; or (d) any combination of (a), (b), and (c).[13] S.2(13) A union may choose whether or not to accord overseas members entitlement to vote and nothing in s.2 shall apply in relation to any overseas member or in relation to an overseas member's vote.
EA 1988	S.4(1) It shall be the duty of every union (a) to compile by 26 July 1984 and thereafter maintain a register of the names and proper addresses of its members; and (b) to secure, 'so far as is reasonably practicable', that the register entries are accurate and kept up to date. (2) The register may be kept by means of a computer. (3) Union branches may keep this register in place of the union centrally. Sch.3(5)(3) The union has the duty (a) free of charge and at any reasonable time, to allow a member, who gives reasonable notice, to ascertain from the register whether there is an entry relating to him; and (b) if requested to by a member, to supply him, 'as soon as reasonably practicable' and free of charge or on the payment of a reasonable fee, with a copy of his entry.
TULR(C)A 1992	S.50, s.60, s.24.
TURERA 1993	S.6(1) to (3) inserts after s.24 TULR(C)A 1992 a duty of confidentiality in relation to the register of members' names and addresses on the scrutineer and any independent persons not to disclose any name or address except in permitted circumstances and to take all reasonable steps to secure that there is no disclosure of any name and address by any other person except in permitted circumstances. (4) Disclosure is permitted (a) where the member consents; (b) where it is requested by the CO as part of his function; (c) where it is requested by the scrutineer or independent person as part of his function; (d) where it is required for a criminal investigation.[14]

S.2(6) Every person entitled to vote must (a) be allowed to vote without interference from, or constraint imposed by, the union or any of its members, officials or employees; and (b) 'so far as reasonably practicable' be enabled to do so without incurring any direct cost to himself.

S.2(7) 'So far as is reasonably practicable', every person who is entitled to vote must (a) have sent to him, at his proper address[15] and by post,[16] a voting paper which either lists the election candidates or is accompanied by a separate list of the candidates; and (b) be given a convenient opportunity to vote by post.[17]

S.2(8)(a) The ballot shall be conducted so as to secure that 'so far as is reasonably practicable', those voting do so in secret.

S.3(1) If the union can meet all of the conditions required in s.2, it can opt for a workplace ballot and for s.2(7)(a) & (b) may be substituted s.3(1)(a) have made available to him (i) immediately before, immediately after, or during his working hours; and (ii) at his place of work or at a place which is more convenient for him; or be supplied with a voting paper which either lists the election candidates or is accompanied by a separate list of the candidates; and (b) be given (i) a convenient opportunity to vote by post (but no other opportunity to vote); (ii) an opportunity to vote immediately before, immediately after, or during, his working hours and at his place of work or at a place which is more convenient for him (but no other opportunity); or (iii) as alternatives, both of those opportunities (but no other opportunity).[18]

S.14(2) declares that s.3 TUA 1984 (which allows for non-postal ballots in PEC elections) shall cease to have effect.

S.51(3) & (4)(a), s.51(4).

S.2(5) The method of voting must be by the marking of a voting paper by the person voting.
See s.2(7) and s.3(1) for requirement for the list of candidates to be given.

TABLE 4.2. (*Continued*)

EA 1988	Sch.3(5) Each voting paper (a) must clearly specify the address to which, and the date by which the voting paper is to be returned; (b) must be given one of a series of consecutive whole numbers every one of which is used in giving a different number to each voting paper.
EA 1990	S.5(4) EA 1990 inserts in s.2(5) TUA 1984 (voting paper requirements) the requirement for the union to state on the voting paper the name of the independent scrutineer.
TULR(C)A 1992	S.51(1), s.51(2).
COUNTING THE VOTE	
TUA 1984	S.2(8)(b) The result of the election shall be determined solely by counting the number of votes cast directly for each candidate by those voting (but the system of single transferable voting is allowed). S.2(8)(c) The votes must be fairly and accurately counted (though any inaccuracy in counting is disregarded if it is accidental and on a scale which could not affect the result of the election).
TULR(C)A 1992	S.51(6) & (7), s.51(5)(b).
SUPERVISION	
EA 1988	S.15(1) A union (a) must before the election is held, appoint a qualified independent person ('the scrutineer');[19] (b) must ensure that nothing in his terms of appointment can reasonably call his independence in relation to the union into question; (c) must ensure that he duly carries out his functions without any interference that could reasonably call his independence in relation to the union into question; and (d) must comply with all reasonable requests made by the scrutineer in connection with the carrying out of his functions. (3) A person is a qualified independent scrutineer if (a) he satisfies such conditions as may be specified by an order made by the Secretary of State; and (b) the union has no grounds for believing either that he will carry out any functions conferred on him otherwise than competently or that his independence in relation to the union or the election can reasonably be called into question. (4) The scrutineer is required (a) to supervise the production and distribution of all the voting papers and to be the person to whom those voting papers are returned by those voting; (b) to take such steps as appear to him to be appropriate for the purpose of enabling him to make his report; (c) 'as soon as reasonably practicable' after the last date for return of voting papers

to make that report to the union; and (d) to retain custody of all returned voting papers (i) for a year; and (ii) or longer where an application is made to the CO or the High Court. (5) The scrutineer's report shall state (a) the number of voting papers distributed; (b) the number of voting papers returned: (c) the number of valid votes cast for each candidate (e) whether the scrutineer was satisfied in certain matters specified in (6); and (f) if he is not satisfied in any matter, his reasons. (6) The matters are (a) that there are no reasonable grounds for believing that there was any contravention of requirements imposed on the election; (b) that the arrangements for the production, storage, distribution, return or other handling of the voting papers and the arrangements for the counting of the votes, included all such security arrangements as were 'reasonably practicable' to minimize the risk of unfairness or malpractice; and (c) that the scrutineer had been able to carry out his functions without interference.

S.49(1)–(4), (6) & (7), s.52(1) & (2).

TULR(C)A 1992

TURERA 1993

Additions to scrutineer's role

S.1(1)(a) & (c) inserts in TULR(C)A 1992 s.49 a requirement for the scrutineer to inspect the union's register (or a copy of it) of members' names and addresses whenever it appears to him to be appropriate to do so and, in particular, (3A)(a) when the scrutineer is requested to do so during the appropriate period[20] by a union member/candidate who suspects the register is not, or at the relevant date[21] was not, accurate and up to date, and (b) the scrutineer does not consider the member's suspicion is ill-founded. S.1(1)(b) inserts the requirement for the scrutineer after the election to retain a copy of the register in his custody as well as the voting papers. Also inserted is (3C) which incorporates a duty of confidentiality into the scrutineer's appointment. S.1(1)(d) inserts (5A) giving the union a duty (a) to supply the scrutineer 'as soon as reasonably practicable' after the relevant date a copy of the register of members names and addresses at that date, and (b) comply with any request by the scrutineer to inspect the register and (5B) where the register is kept on a computer, the union's duty is either to supply a legible printed copy or (if the scrutineer prefers) to supply a copy of the computer data and allow him use of the computer to read the data at any time in the period in which he is required to retain custody of the copy. S.1(2) inserts in s.52 TULR(C)A 1993 a new (2A) which requires the scrutineer's report also to state (a) whether the scrutineer (i) has inspected the register of the union members' names and addresses or (ii) has examined a supplied copy of the register; (b) if he

TABLE 4.2. (*Continued*)

has, whether in the case of each inspection/examination he was acting on a union member's request or on his own initiative; (c) whether he declined to act on any such request, and (d) whether any inspection/examination of the register has revealed any matter which he considers should be drawn to the union's attention in order to assist it in securing that the register is accurate and up to date, but shall not state the name of any member/candidate who has requested such an inspection/examination.

New requirement for an independent person

S.2 inserts s.51A in TULR(C)A 1992 (1) The union shall ensure that (a) the storage and distribution of the voting papers and (b) the counting of the votes are undertaken by one or more independent person appointed by the union. (2) A person is independent in relation to an election if he (a) is the scrutineer or (b) is another person whom the union has no grounds for believing either that he will carry out his election functions otherwise than competently or that his independence in relation to the union or election might reasonably be called into question. (3) The independent person is required to carry out his functions so as to minimize the risk of any contravention of any statutory requirements or the occurrence of any unfairness or malpractice. (4) The independent person has a duty of confidentiality towards the register. (5) Where the independent person is not the scrutineer, he is required to send the voting papers back to the scrutineer as soon as reasonably practicable after the counting has been completed. (6) The union (a) shall ensure that nothing in the terms of such an appointment is such as to call into question the independence of this person; (b) shall ensure that this person duly carries out his functions and that there is no interference with his carrying out of his functions which would make it reasonable for any person to call into question his independence; and (c) shall comply with all reasonable requests made by the independent person for the purposes of, or in connection with, the carrying out of his functions. (2)(a) The independent person's (or persons') names shall be included in the scrutineer's report or if no independent person was appointed, that fact. S.2(2)(c) inserts (2B) after (2A) (see above with respect to new requirements for scrutineer's report) the requirement that where one or more independent persons are appointed, the scrutineer's report must state (a) whether he is satisfied with the performance of the independent person/s, and (b) if he is not satisfied with the performance of the person/s, particulars of his reasons for not being so satisfied.

EA 1988

S.15(7) The union must not publish the result of the election until it has received the scrutineer's report; and the union must (a) within three months of receiving the report (i) send a copy of the report to every member of the union to whom it is 'reasonably practicable' to send such a copy; or (ii) take all such steps for notifying the content of the report to union members (whether by publishing or otherwise) as is the practice of the union to take when matters of general interest to all its members need to be brought to their attention; (b) ensure that any copy sent or notification given for the purposes of (a) is accompanied by a statement that the union will, on request, supply any union member with a copy of the report, either free of charge or on payment of a specified, reasonable fee; and (c) so supply any union member who requests the copy and pays this fee (if any).

EA 1990

S.5(5) EA 1990 inserts in s.15(2) EA 1988 (independent scrutiny of election ballots) the requirement that the union (bb) must before the scrutineer begins to carry out his functions, either (i) send a notice stating the name of the scrutineer to every union member to whom it is reasonably practicable to send such a notice, or (ii) take all such other steps for notifying members of the scrutineer's name as is the union's practice to take when matters of general interest to all its members need to be brought to their attention.

TULR(C)A 1992

S.49(5), s.52(3), s.52(4) & (5).

---

[1] S.7 TUA 1984 exempts the following bodies: (i) federated unions with no individual members; (ii) unions with individual members who are 'special members' satisfying the conditions that (a) all are merchant seamen; (b) a majority of them are normally resident outside the UK; (iii) new unions within a year of the first appointments or elections to the PEC; (iv) where one union has transferred its engagements to another union for the period of one year beginning with the date of the transfer with respect to PEC members of either union. S.2(14) A ballot is not required to be held in an uncontested election. After 1 October 1985 all PEC elections had to comply with the new requirements; however, according to s.9(3) existing elected PEC members/post holders by virtue of which they are voting PEC members could remain in post after 1 October 1985 until they would normally be due for re-election, but only for a maximum of five years since they were last elected.

[2] S.5(10) No other remedy is available. S.6(3) The making of an application to the CO shall not prevent the applicant, or any other person, from making a subsequent application to the court in respect of the same matter.

TABLE 4.2. (*Continued*)

[3] S.5(8) Where the enforcement order requires a fresh election, the court shall, unless inappropriate, require it to be a *postal* ballot.

[4] S.19(2) The Commissioner shall give his reasons if he decides not to grant an applicant assistance.

[5] The Commissioner shall not, however, provide assistance with the making of an application to the CO.

[6] Supplemental provisions for the Commissioner's role are provided by s.21. Note that in (3) the Commissioner is required to indemnify the applicant from the liability to pay costs/expenses to any other person arising out of any court judgement/order in relation to which he provided assistance.

[7] S.1(7) A person is a voting member of the PEC if he is entitled in his own right to attend committee meetings and vote on matters on which votes are taken by the committee (whether or not he is entitled to attend all such meetings or to vote on all such matters or in all circumstances, i.e. any chair's casting vote is included). S.1(3) provides for a transition period. Where a person was a voting PEC member immediately before an election and is not elected a PEC member at that election, the union shall allow him to continue as a member for a period up to six months as may reasonably be required to give effect to the result of the election.

[8] S.1(5) The PEC means the principal committee of the union exercising executive functions, by whatever name it is known.

[9] An important exemption was provided for those PEC members who were elected but not elected according to s.2 TUA 1984. S.12(3) provides that where a person to whom the provisions of s.1 TUA 1984 are extended by s.12(1) EA 1988 was elected to the PEC (or is a PEC member by virtue of holding a union position) at an election held within the last five years, that person was not required to be re-elected according to s.2 TUA 1984 for a period of five years beginning from the date of his election, but this exemption (4) did not apply to those persons elected by PEC members only. S.12(2) provides an exemption for union amalgamations and transfers of engagement: elected members could continue to rely on the one-year period of grace provided by TUA 1984, if this was more favourable, or they could rely on the transitional retirement clause (see below). Additionally, special register bodies were also exempt from s.12(1). These bodies were established under IRA 1971 to take account of professional bodies that conducted collective bargaining but were not principally trade unions. TULRA 1974 abolished the need to register in order to be in receipt of the register's benefits but the list was not scrapped, only closed to new applicants.

[10] S.8 TUA 1984 exempts voting PEC members near retirement from the requirement for such a member to be re-elected every five years. To be exempt the voting PEC member must (a) have been elected at an election which satisfies the requirements of s.2; (b) be a full-time employee who has been elected a PEC member or elected to another position by virtue of which he is a PEC member; (c) will reach retirement age within five years; (d) be entitled under the union's rules to continue as the holder of the position until retirement age without standing for re-election; (e) have been a full-time employee of the union for a period (which need not be continuous) of at least ten years; and (f) not have a period between his election and his retirement age of more than five years. This was amended by s.12(5) EA 1988, where any person (a) holds a full-time position as a union employee in respect of which the s.1 TUA 1984 would be extended to him by s.12(1) EA 1988; (b) is entitled under union rules to hold that position, without any renewal of his contract of employment, until retirement age; (c) will reach retirement age within two years; and (d) has been a full-time union employee for a period (which need not be continuous) of at least ten years, then that person shall be exempt from the extension of s.1 TUA 1984 if he continues to hold that position until retirement age.

[11] S.2(12) TUA 1984 For the purposes of s.2(11), any rule which provides for a class to be determined by reference to those members which the union chooses to exclude from so standing shall be disregarded.

[12] S.2(2) TUA 1984 These classes are (a) unemployed members; (b) members in arrears; (c) apprentice, trainee, student, or new union members.

[13] There were no restrictions in TUA 1984 on the size of the groups in proportion to the number of representatives on the PEC (*IRLIB* 267 23.10.84: 3).

[14] New s.24A(6) TULR(C)A 1992. The remedy for breach of the confidentiality requirement for the register of members' names and addresses is by way of an application to the CO or to the High Court (s.25 & 26 TULR(C)A 1992).

[15] S.9(1) TUA 1984 A member's 'proper address' means his home address or any other address which he has requested the union in writing to treat as his postal address.

[16] S.9(1) TUA 1984 'Post' means a postal service which is provided by the Post Office or under a licence granted under s.68 of the British Telecommunications Act 1981, or does not infringe the exclusive privilege conferred on the Post Office by s.66(1) of this Act.

[17] This might involve conducting the ballot over a period of time so that all those entitled to vote, including those on holiday, had an opportunity to vote (*IRLIB* 267 23.10.84: 3).

[18] If the ballot is held at the workplace, arrangements have to be made so that voters do not lose money through taking time off to vote or incur any travelling costs if they worked at different sites or would have been absent that day (*IRLIB* 267 23.10.84: 3).

[19] To satisfy the ballot supervision requirement of s.15 EA 1988, unions can appoint either a specified body or an individual. Acceptable scrutineer has been defined by SI as solicitors with a practising certificate and chartered accountants: three bodies are specifically named: Security Balloting Services, the Electoral Reform Society, and the Industrial Society.

[20] S.1(1)(c) TURERA 1993 The appropriate period (defined in the new (3B)) begins with the first day on which a person may become an election candidate and ends on the day before the day on which the scrutineer makes his report to the union.

[21] S.1(1)(e) TURERA 1993 The 'relevant date' means (a) where the union has election rules determining who is entitled to vote on a particular date that date, and (b) otherwise the date, or last date, on which voting papers are distributed in the election (new ss.(8) in s.49 TULR(C)A 1992).

Democracy in Trade Unions, the Government had proposed that any secret vote that involved the marking of a ballot paper would suffice, thus outlawing show of hands and block voting only (Urwin and Murray 1983: 25). However, this proposal was defeated in the House of Lords by an alliance of Tory, Alliance, and cross-bench peers who favoured a compulsory postal ballot on the ground that it was less susceptible to malpractice (Kidner 1984: 201). The presumption in favour of postal balloting in the Act represented a Government compromise (*FT* 10.7.84). Urwin and Murray (1983: 25) suggest that the Government did not pursue the legislative enforcement of postal ballots at this stage, as they accepted that workplace ballots produced higher turn-outs. TUA 1984 laid down various election conditions that had to be satisfied for secrecy, freedom from interference and constraint,[29] no direct cost to the voter,[30] and fairness and accuracy in vote-counting[31] (COUNTING THE VOTE).

Concerning CANDIDATES, TUA 1984 gave all union members the right not to be unreasonably excluded from standing.[32] However, this provision, unlike others in TUA 1984, could be overridden by union rules that excluded a member if he/she belonged to a 'class' of whom all are excluded from standing by the rule book. Thus, TUA 1984 exercised no control over which classes the union excluded but only over unreasonable discrimination against an individual: the exclusion of a particular class did not have to be reasonable (Kidner 1984: 205–7).[33] TUA 1984 also states that no candidate should be required to be a member of a political party: this was aimed at the common union rule that certain officials had to be Labour Party members or must attend the Labour Party Conference. However, under the class-exclusion provision above, a union could still exclude a person from office for being a member of a political party. Thus union rules excluding Communist Party members, as in the EETPU rule book, were legitimate.

As regards VOTERS, although all members had to be given equal entitlement to vote at PEC elections, the union could, if it wished, exclude classes of members, such as unemployed members, if this was specified in the union's rules. There was also no obligation on the union to provide a vote to members resident outside Great Britain. The union was also allowed to organize balloting constituencies so that representatives to the union's PEC were elected only by members in the relevant geographical area, occupational group, or trade: thus unions could still ensure that their PECs were representative of their various sections.[34] The requirement in TUA 1984 for the union to compile and maintain an up-to-date register of members' names and addresses for balloting purposes was a consequence of the considerable disquiet about the state of unions' lists of members (Kidner 1984: 201).[35] There were no requirements controlling the SUPERVISION of, or CAMPAIGNING in, elections. Although electoral supervision increasingly became a Conservative concern, campaigning did not: only a few provisions for campaigning were introduced in later legislation. In contrast to the USA, the right to nominate never became a Conservative concern (see Fosh *et al*. 1993a: 21–2).

There was a legislative lull between the passage of TUA 1984, which fulfilled the commitments of the Conservatives' 1983 election manifesto, and the publication of the next Green Paper in 1987.[36] During this period the TUC both dropped its boycott of Government ballot refunds and decided to restart talks with the Conservative Government.[37] This change in policy was at least partially influenced by the AUEW(E)'s and the EETPU's renewed interest in applying for Government ballot refunds. They in turn were concerned with the Government's announcement that no claims for back payment of ballot expenses would be met unless they were lodged before February 1985 (March 1992: 72). The AUEW(E) held a ballot and secured an overwhelming majority in favour of accepting Government funds and the EETPU applied for funds at the same time. The TUC General Council voted to discipline the AUEW(E), but at the 1985 TUC Annual Conference a compromise was reached whereby the AUEW(E) and the EETPU agreed to reballot their members on the issue, making it clear that TUC policy was opposed to refund applications. In both unions' ballots their members strongly supported acceptance of Government funds. Subsequently, a special TUC Conference of Principal Officers in February 1986 voted to drop the boycott (ibid.). After this the General Council agreed that future decisions should be left to the discretion of individual affiliates, although the TUC would inform unions that it still had grave doubts about the long-term impact on union independence of acceptance of these funds (McIlroy 1991: 103). See Figure 4.1 for the steep increase in union applications for balloting expenses refunds after 1984.

In general, unions now accepted the need to conform to the new legislation. Unions' protests were muted by the difficulty they found in opposing legislation introduced in a piecemeal fashion, the placement of the means of enforcement in the hands, not of the Government, but of employers and individual union members, and their reduced economic power. In brief, they were reluctant to wage a long and costly battle against a determined protagonist when their funds would be at risk and, as noted in the previous chapter, the consequences of taking on the Government had been demonstrated by the miners' dispute in 1984–5. Employers were still largely in favour of legislation for union 'reform' although public approval had declined from the level of 1979 and 1980 (GMB 1991).

The next Green Paper, *Trade Unions and Their Members* (published in February 1987), reviewed the Conservatives' legislation on industrial relations since 1980 and concluded that these changes had had profound and wide-ranging effects. In the case of PEC elections, it argued that the impact of the legal changes was being felt progressively as elections fell due; by 'making it easier for members to take part in secret ballots, and breaking the hold of minorities of union activists, the election requirements may have had the most profound effect of all on the way trade unions conduct their affairs and represent their members' interests' (DE 1987: 1–2). But more was required to be done in order that the rights given to union members should be 'fully developed'.[38] Hence, *Trade Unions and Their Members* proposed extending union democracy in three ways. First, it proposed that all PEC elections be conducted by the fully postal method, since many unions had retained workplace ballots after TUA 1984. Although the Government acknowledged that there was some evidence that workplace balloting yielded higher levels of participation, concern was expressed at the number of occasions where irregularities took place: reference was made to the TGWU General Secretary election in 1984 and the CPSA elections for General Secretary and Treasurer in 1986 in support of this argument. Additionally, the Government felt members' voting in workplace ballots was susceptible to subtle forms of pressure not present in postal ballots; indeed 'there is a real question whether such ballots can ever be totally free from suspicion' (ibid. 25). Compulsory postal balloting would increase election security and, further, the unions' lack of proper records of their members' names and addresses was no longer a problem following the requirement in TUA 1984 for unions to compile a register of these. Second, there were proposals for the independent supervision of ballots. The Government argued that, even under a system of postal ballots, it was still possible without independent supervision for serious malpractice to occur.[39] The Government was uncertain what form this independent supervision should take. After exploring a number of alternatives it opted for defining the criteria that an independent supervisor should meet in terms of independence and competence, thus, it hoped, avoiding a cumbersome or controversial approval system. However, it remained uncertain whether supervisors should be independent of the union whose election they were overseeing, or whether the supervisor should be independent of employers and unions generally, undesirably ruling out accountants, management consultants, and so forth. Third, the paper considered the extension of election provisions for the PEC. The Government suggested that requirements for election of PEC members in TUA 1984 provided a loophole for important elected national officials to avoid seeking re-election. It quoted the NUM's removal of the General Secretary's and President's votes, which led to their not being required to stand for re-election every five years. It believed that 'in many unions it is very difficult to argue that the non-voting General Secretary is a less powerful figure in the policy-making of the union than a voting member of the executive' (ibid. 27). Thus, it proposed that the election requirements should include all general secretaries, presidents, and executive members whether elected or appointed.

A further important aspect of *Trade Unions and Their Members,* pertinent to our interest in election and industrial action ballots, was its suggestions for offering union members assistance in enforcing their rights: the CO's powers were not comprehensive, the courts were not being used and, most seriously, several unions announced that they would not change their rules to comply with Part I of TUA 1984 (ibid. 28 ff.). The Government thus proposed to strengthen in two ways the ability of members to pursue complaints. First the CO was to be given the power (in addition to the power to specify any steps taken or agreed to be taken by the union as required under TUA 1984) to specify any steps considered appropriate for the union to take in order to remedy a declared failure accompanied by a specified time-scale. Second, where the original complainant (or other eligible union member) believed that the remedial action had not been taken within the specified time-scale, he/she would be able to seek advice from a new authority, the Commissioner for Trade Union Affairs. The Commissioner would be under a statutory duty to assist union members (if satisfied that the union had not taken the appropriate remedial action) to bring enforcement proceedings in the High Court and he/she would underwrite the complainant's legal costs. Alternatively, the Commissioner could act in his/her own name, or jointly with the complainant. In a matter of substantial public interest the Commissioner might have the power to support or take High Court action on behalf of a complainant without prior proceedings before the CO.

A further suggestion to improve union members' ability to enforce their rights was to clarify the legal position of members wishing to pursue their common-law right in court when their union rule books denied them such access, either directly or through requiring would-be complainants to complete a labyrinthine internal complaints procedure. The Government wished to assure members that they would not be deprived of the right of reasonable access to the courts in case of breach of their common law or statutory rights.

The response to *Trade Unions and Their Members* tended to be critical, though the employers' criticisms were mainly directed towards the industrial action provisions (see below). The main focus of the TUC's objection (TUC 1987) was the imbalance between the weak and ineffectual protection of the individual employees *vis-à-vis* their employer as compared to the new wide-ranging rights of the individual members *vis-à-vis* their union. In terms of the proposed changes to union elections, it pointed to the distinct lack of evidence that malpractice was anything other than a rare and isolated occurrence and that *Democracy in Trade Unions* had already commented that some unions' needs were better served by appointing General Secretaries. Further, the TUC felt that alterations to the CO's role were premature, given the limited experience in enforcing TUA 1984, and dubbed the Commissioner as the 'trade union harassment officer', whose role would be to inflict a more damaging and legalistic method of processing individual members' grievances than the present routes through union rules and the CO: the public expense involved seemed unlikely to justify the limited call for this new service. Indeed, the TUC believed the Government's underlying motives were 'malevolent' (TUC 1987: 1) and appeared to be the weakening of unions through making their internal affairs more complex and undermining union cohesion: unions should decide on their own rules and constitutions.

Turning to the employers' response, the CBI and the EEF supported the introduction of postal ballots, independent supervision, and the requirement to elect non-voting PEC members in union elections (*IDS Brief* 349, 5.87: 17, *Personnel Management* 6.87: 7). However, the IPM and the Industrial Society opposed the introduction of more union legislation, arguing that unions were putting their houses in order and should be given more time to reform themselves. All employers' organizations roundly condemned the creation of the Commissioner: the need for such a figure was unproven, the principle of enhancing democratic procedures might be prejudiced by the introduction of an external agency, and such a Commissioner would be disruptive of improving management–union relations, reinforcing adversarial attitudes. Public condemnation of unions had considerably decreased by this time.[40]

The Conservatives' election campaign leading to their election victory in June 1987 again emphasized their 'success' in reforming industrial relations and the need to provide further protection for individual members' rights *vis-à-vis* their union.[41] They saw this 'move forward' as vote-winning and they were convinced that the political rewards outweighed the opposition of most employers to their proposals in *Trade Unions and Their Members* (Mackie 1987: 155).

The Employment Act 1988

The Bill was published in October 1987 by the new Secretary of State Norman Fowler and, with substantial additions, it received Royal Assent in May 1988. The provisions of EA 1988 are laid out in Table 4.2. The overall impact of EA 1988 was to make the legal regulation of union elections much more tightly specified: furthermore EA 1988 was 'badly drafted, unnecessarily complex and obscure' (McKendrick 1988: 160).

The Government continued to remain at arm's length from the enforcement of its new regulations; as in TUA 1984, ENFORCEMENT was through union members' initiating action over union failures to abide by the new provisions. Individual enforcement was made easier with the introduction of a limit of six months for unions' internal procedures and, significantly, the courts were now allowed to grant interlocutory relief where members pursued their rights, including those relating to PEC elections and membership registers (while the former was suggested in *Trade Unions and Their Members*, the latter was not). As suggested in *Trade Unions and Their Members*, a means of ENFORCEMENT ASSISTANCE was introduced with the creation of the office of the Commissioner for the Rights of Trade Union Members (CROTUM); however, only minor additions were made to the CO's powers.

As expected in terms of POSTS COVERED, mandatory elections were now required for all PEC members. EA 1988 itself defined PEC membership widely, including as 'members' not those so defined according to the union's rule book, but those attending meetings other than for the purpose of providing any technical or professional advice.[42] Exemption was provided for short-term presidents and, in a controversial manner, for those nearing retirement. The retirement restriction appeared to be drafted specifically to catch in the election net two union leaders, both of whom would have been exempt under TUA 1984 but were not to be so under EA 1988; hence the sobriquet 'the Scargill and Todd clause'.[43] Exemption was also provided for newly formed unions and for union mergers: elected PEC members could continue to hold their positions for their full five-year term. This exemption was introduced at a late stage in the passage of the Act when the Government accepted the argument that voters in merging unions needed more than the one-year period provided by TUA 1984 to get to know the candidates for PEC elections and make reasoned choices. This lack of time for voters to familiarize themselves with candidates might lead to a reluctance for unions of similar kinds of workers to merge, whereas the Government wished to encourage such mergers (*IRLIB* 357, 19.7 88: 4–5).

Again as expected, the only permissible BALLOTING METHOD now allowed under EA 1988 was fully postal. During the passage of EA in 1987, it was argued, on the basis of Loveday's research (Loveday 1987), that the repeal of the exemption for workplace ballots was being introduced because unions had not, as the Government had hoped, voluntarily adopted postal balloting in union elections. The Conservatives countered the argument that workplace ballots were preferable as they generated higher turn-outs with the assertion that high levels of participation were not the most important factor in ensuring democracy in elections; more important was the fact that postal ballots were less susceptible to electoral malpractice.[44]

Finally, as expected, EA 1988 required unions to appoint independent scrutineers for the SUPERVISION of union elections. The regulations for the scrutineer's terms of appointment, qualifications, definition and performance of duties, the requisite union co-operation, the preparation and contents of reports, the timing of the latter's publication, and the information to be supplied to members, were all very detailed, as can be seen in Table 4.2.[45]

EA 1988 also contained regulations for two new concerns, not preshadowed in *Trade Unions and Their Members*. It introduced the right for a VOTER to inspect his/her entry on the union electoral register and the right for candidates to prepare election addresses for distribution by the union; these very detailed regulations for election addresses represent the only instance of legislation for election CAMPAIGNING.

In summary, the discussions in *Trade Unions and Their Members* and the provisions of EA 1988 demonstrated, even more clearly than those of TUA 1984, the Conservatives' return to their traditional concern with regulation. EA 1988 also concluded the major part of the legislation on union election ballots. However, instead of planned and systematic introduction of new regulations for union decision-making, the Conservatives' legislation at this time became a series of rushed opportunistic responses to events or specific pressures, conditioned by an anti-union ideology; in particular, the common-law cases brought by NUM members against their union provided the Conservatives with ideas for statutory provisions.[46] The Conservatives thus lost the sense of a coherent programme of 'reform', which characterized the 1980, 1982, and 1984 Acts, and the legislation became a 'tangled skein' (Fosh *et al.* 1993a: 28). Further, despite different Secretaries of State for Employment declaring that the necessity for further union legislation had ended, the stream of legislation continued. Even the change of leadership in 1990 from Margaret Thatcher to John Major did not appear to have any significant impact on the Conservative desire to legislate for change in unions' legal framework. Considerable effort was also expended on 'tidying-up' previous legislation and adding more and more requirements to plug loopholes that unions had 'exploited' or hypothetically might 'exploit'; the ultimate 'tidying up' being the passing of the Trade Union and Labour Relations (Consolidation) Act in 1992. The British legislation on balloting for union elections was now extremely detailed (more detailed than the Landrum–Griffin Act 1959 in the USA). This earned the UK the ILO's opprobrium.[47] Further, although union resistance was now extremely limited, employers were markedly lukewarm about further legislation and the electorate felt that union law 'reforms' had gone far enough.[48]

The Employment Act 1990

After the 'summer of discontent' in 1989, Conservative interest shifted decisively to industrial action ballots, and EA 1990 and TURERA 1993 reflected this interest, as did the issue of a code of practice for the conduct of industrial action ballots. The events of this summer and the reactions of the Government are considered in the section on industrial action ballots below. We note here, in terms of the development of our legislative themes, that the missing sense of coherence became more marked and the attempts to add 'more and more layers of cement', as unforeseen or perceived problems arose, continued.

Following the publication of two Green Papers in 1989, EA 1990 was presented by Michael Howard (appointed Secretary of State in January 1990) as the culmination of the process of ten years of reform. This Act was intended 'to limit the abuses of industrial power' and 'guarantee the democratic rights of trade union members' (Carty 1991: 3). There were two minor additions to the union election requirements: the union now had to INFORM MEMBERS of the independent scrutineer's identity and add his/ her name to the VOTING PAPER (see Table 4.2). The Government's aim was to ensure that a union member could, if he/she desired, challenge the scrutineer's competence or qualifications at the beginning of the election process. Additionally, as suggested in the Green Paper *Removing Barriers to Employment*, CROTUM's powers were increased: in particular the power to grant material assistance now covered union members' complaints over the improper observance of union rule books, that is common-law matters. A factor here may have been embarrassment on account of how little CROTUM had had to do so far.[49]

Despite the marked lack of general interest in further legislation, another Green Paper, *Industrial Relations in the 1990s*, was published in 1991. In it the Conservative Government congratulated itself on the transformation of industrial relations in the UK since 1979, in which 'without doubt' the reforms of union law and the curbing of union 'abuses' had played an essential part (DE 1991: 6). The Government now believed that it was necessary to consolidate and build on what had been achieved in the past twelve years. There were no innovative suggestions; instead the Government proposed more and more detailed regulations for the conduct of union elections. It focused particularly on the 'widely reported' instances of election ballot irregularities in the TGWU and more recent allegations that UCATT's register of members included the names of hundreds of duplicate and fictitious 'ghost' members. The Government believed that union members were entitled to be protected from 'such abuses of their democratic rights' and that union elections should be as fair and democratic as they could possibly be made (ibid. 18). It therefore proposed, first, that the right of members to inspect unions' registers should be extended to the right to inspect the union's register as a whole, thus enabling them to spot the inclusion of non-existent or duplicate names and addresses. Such a right of inspection might also be given to candidates in national elections and to the scrutineer in order to facilitate any investigation should the scrutineer receive a complaint. In addition, unions would be required to state in their annual reports the number of names appearing in their registers without a corresponding address in order to indicate to what extent unions were failing to comply with the respective statutory requirements, thus enabling a member to make a complaint to the CO or the courts. Second, the scrutineer should be required to record in his/her report the number of voting papers issued and returned down to the level of the smallest practicable administrative unit in the ballot. This, in the Government's opinion, would reveal discrepancies, for example, of turn-out per unit, and would be useful to the scrutineer or individual member who believed that malpractice had occurred but had no evidence on which to base a complaint. Third, further protection was required for candidates. The Government referred to the TGWU General Secretary election in 1990, where candidates reportedly had restrictions placed on them, effectively preventing them from addressing meetings in certain regions. It proposed that unions be put under a duty not to discriminate between candidates in an executive election in respect of campaigning facilities provided.

In responding to this Green Paper the employers' main concern was with strike ballots and the rights for consumers of public services. They made no detailed comments on further regulation of union elections. Indeed their position on further union legislation was described as 'at best equivocal and in a number of cases clearly unenthusiastic' (*IRLIB* 438, 6.12.91: 13); for example the IPM said there was no union member pressure for the changes and they could damage industrial relations (*Personnel Management Plus* 11.91: 3). The TUC again criticized the empirical base of the Government's accusations and rejected their contention that there continued to be systematic abuse in union elections, but it conceded that the relatively minor point of identifying duplicate names could be made the responsibility of the scrutineer (*IRLIB* 438, 6.12.91: 14). Nevertheless, the Government considered it had widespread employer support for almost all its proposals, including the 'tightening up' of union elections (*IRLIB* 441, 1.92: 16). However, for the electorate the reform of union law and decline of union power had gone far enough.[50]

The Conservative election manifesto published in March 1992 contained proposals for further reform of industrial action ballots, but there were no specific proposals for union elections. After the Conservatives won the general election, though with a substantially reduced majority, Gillian Shepherd was appointed Secretary of State for Employment and TULR(C)A received Royal Assent in July 1992. It introduced no new legislation; its purpose was to bring together existing industrial relations legislation in a more rational scheme.[51]

The Trade Union Reform and Employment Rights Act 1993

The Trade Union Reform and Employment Rights Bill was introduced in November 1992; this was substantially amended and the Act was even wider in scope, though significantly the Bill's proposal to provide for equality of campaigning assistance between executive election candidates was dropped (*IRLIB* 463, 12.92: 3). David Hunt became Secretary of State in May 1993 and the process of regulating union activities more and more tightly, and adding safeguard after safeguard against union 'abuses', continued.

The most important addition to the regulation of union elections in TURERA 1993 was in terms of SUPERVISION. TURERA 1993 added to the role of the scrutineer a duty to inspect the register of voters' names and addresses, whenever it appeared appropriate and particularly when requested to do so by a union member or candidate, and to include his/her findings concerning the register's accuracy in his report.[52] TURERA 1993 also introduced a second element of supervision for union elections, one not discussed in *Industrial Relations in the 1990s*. This was the appointment of an independent person (or persons) by the union to undertake the storage and distribution of the voting papers and the counting of the votes. The scrutineer had to report on the independent person's or persons' performance. Additionally, a minor addition was made as regards VOTERS; TURERA 1993 added a duty of confidentiality on any scrutineer or independent person/s with respect to members' names and addresses.

Finally, TURERA 1993 withdrew two important statutory supports for union ballots: it repealed Government FUNDING and unions' right to USE OF EMPLOYER'S PREMISES.[53] Neither of these two repeals was discussed in *Industrial Relations in the 1990s*. As regards Government funding it was to be phased out over a three-year period, reducing to 75 per cent of each qualifying claim in 1993–4, 50 per cent in 1994–5, and 25 per cent in 1995–6, before ceasing to operate completely from 1 April 1996.[54] The Government attempted to justify the withdrawal on the grounds that fewer than 50 per cent of employees had their pay determined, directly or indirectly, by collective bargaining. This decision did not surprise those cynical union leaders who had predicted in the early 1980s that, once the unions had become dependent on balloting refunds, the Government would abolish them. The repeal of the unions' right to use employers' premises for ballots followed from the Conservatives' commitment to postal balloting for both PEC election and industrial action ballots, although it also took in other kinds of ballots as well.[55]

THE INTRODUCTION OF MANDATORY BALLOTS FOR INDUSTRIAL ACTION

We now consider the Conservatives' legislation for industrial action ballots between 1980 and 1993. The structure of this section is similar to that used for examining elections: it examines the origin and purpose of the relevant

Acts by reference to the associated Green Papers; it next considers the main parties' responses to these papers, and then analyses the Acts themselves. In many ways the legislation on union elections led the way on regulating unions' other activities, for the Conservative Government appeared to find the regulation of union decision-making on industrial action more complex to tackle initially, perhaps because union rule books were usually silent on strike-call procedures. However, as we will show, after the imposition of the TURERA 1993 regulations, the two kinds of ballots were more in line.

In the Green Paper *Trade Union Immunities* (January 1981), the Government argued that secret ballots for industrial action had not been widely adopted despite the attempt of EA 1980 to promote them voluntarily and that union leaders still sought to call strikes against their members' wishes (DE 1981: 61). Compulsory ballots, such as those proposed by the Donovan Commission or those experienced in the USA and Canada and in the UK under IRA 1971, were rejected as impracticable and as likely to go in favour of strike action, to restrict union leaders' freedom of action, and to raise problems over the framing of the ballot question. *Trade Union Immunities* suggested that ballots before industrial action could be promoted either by giving a certain number or proportion of union members the right to 'trigger' such ballots (internal compulsion of this kind was considered more acceptable to the union movement than external compulsion) or by continuing to support ballots on a voluntary basis by the provision of public funds.

The Government called for views 'on the practicalities and balance of advantage of making secret ballots compulsory and on what further steps might be taken to encourage their voluntary use' (ibid. 66). However, it showed its own preferences by arguing that a voluntary approach went 'with the grain' of responsible leadership. It would avoid Government interference in unions' internal affairs and the overriding of their democratically determined constitutions and rules. Further, triggered ballots raised practical problems, for example determining the trigger threshold to be achieved, whether there would be immunity for unions whilst the ballot was conducted, making arrangements in a multi-union situation, and, particularly, whether to apply compulsory ballot provisions to unofficial action.

Following *Trade Union Immunities*, the debates in 1981 and 1982 centred on other industrial relations 'reforms', such as the reduction of union immunities, and no legislation on strike ballots was included in EA 1982. However, Norman Tebbit was particularly concerned to promote union democracy in order to protect members against the alleged irresponsibility of their leaders in calling industrial action. After the unions' failure, in his view, to reform themselves voluntarily, he strongly believed that the legal imposition on unions of industrial action ballots was desirable but he was less convinced of its practicality. Accordingly, he asked in a further Green Paper, *Democracy in Trade Unions*, published in 1983, for views on its 'analysis of compulsory strike ballots and on the possibilities for encouraging the use of ballots by both trade unions and employers' (DE 1983a: 20).

In *Democracy in Trade Unions*, the Government clearly showed that its concern for democracy was also a mechanism to reduce industrial action. It adopted an individualistic approach to ballots before strikes, with the clear assumption that the rank-and-file were more responsible and less militant than their leaders and were likely to vote against imminent industrial action. The emphasis was on the cost to the employee of his/her participating in industrial action and the cost to the economy, with little discussion of other factors which might influence a member (such as increased rewards) or any intrinsic value in the balloting process.[56] The Government argued vigorously, but with little empirical support, that 'the methods trade unions use to consult their members are often totally inadequate. Few things have done more to lower public regard for trade unions than the spectacle of strike decisions being taken by a show of hands at stage-managed mass meetings to which outsiders may be admitted and where dissenters may be intimidated' (ibid. 17).

Democracy in Trade Unions concluded that the argument of principle for legislation for strike ballots was simple and unanswerable. The question therefore remained of how unions could best be required to hold such ballots. The Government rejected universal 'automatic' strike ballots on the ground that these could not be enforced for small-scale unofficial actions. However, it felt that if such a requirement was confined to official strikes, it might encourage unofficial action. Again, if the requirement was confined to strikes, it felt that it might encourage industrial action short of a strike, equally damaging to the economy and inconvenient for the public, and it would be even more impractical to apply a balloting requirement to 'action short of a strike' than to unofficial action. Moreover, the Government recognized that if strike ballots were imposed by the state in a dispute in specific defined circumstances (as in the USA or in the UK in the 1971–4 period) they could become a test of solidarity and of support for the union leadership and policies, and prolong rather than end disputes. On the other hand, it considered that a ballot triggered by the members could not so easily be turned into a test of union solidarity or be so easily represented as external interference, and would provide union members with an opportunity to challenge and test a union executive's call to industrial action. A considerable number of practical problems were raised, including *inter alia*: What proportion of the membership would be required to trigger the ballot? Who would be entitled to vote? And what would be the sanctions for a union refusing to hold a ballot? Consideration was also given to ballots triggered by an employer, with the sanction being loss of immunity.

One further possibility was that the Government make funds available for employers to hold strike ballots where unions had refused to ballot their members.

In responding to *Democracy in Trade Unions*, the EEF, the CBI, the IOD, and the IPM all made similar comments (Auerbach 1990: 130–2). There was very limited interest in union democracy *per se* and all expressed caution on the introduction of mandatory industrial action ballots, viewing them as relevant only for large-scale strikes, particularly ones involving the public utilities (CBI). The most hard-line was the IOD, which felt that unions could exploit a loophole in the proposals by giving collective notice of employment termination to an employer on behalf of their striking members, so obviating the need for a ballot as no breach of contract had occurred (*FT* 1.10.83).[57] Finally, in those cases where a strike ballot was seen as desirable, the preferred mechanism was member-triggered ballots, with enforcement by aggrieved members through the courts (EEF), by members' appeal for breaches of a code of practice to the CO (who would have powers to impose penalties on unions) (IPM), or by loss of immunity (IOD). The electorate strongly supported the proposed curbs on industrial action.[58]

The TUC, in *Hands Up for Democracy* (1983), its general condemnation of the Conservatives' legislative programme, vehemently denied that unions were 'strike-happy' and irresponsible (TUC 1983: 33), pointing out that striking was an exceptional habit in British industry and that employers could provoke strikes. Further, it maintained that the Government was deluded if it believed that union leaders could drag an unwilling membership into unpopular strikes: unions could no more force a strike on unwilling members than a Government could force people to go to work who had a deep-felt sense of grievance. Also, while many unions held strike ballots, they would not willingly tolerate them being imposed. Finally, compulsory strike ballots could be counter-productive, prolonging a dispute and making it less easy to resolve, and the use of such laws in industrial relations did not settle conflict but instead caused it.

The Trade Union Act 1994

Proposals for industrial action ballots were included in the Conservatives' general election manifesto (May 1983), the White Paper *Proposals for Legislation on Democracy in Trade Unions* (July 1983), and the Trade Union Bill (November 1983).[59]

As can be seen in Table 4.3, TUA 1984 made union immunity in industrial action dependent on the holding of a secret ballot in which the majority of those voting voted in favour of the action.[60] Specifications were laid down in sections 10 and 11 as to TIMING, VOTERS, BALLOTING METHODS,

TABLE 4.3. Industrial action balloting provisions of TUA 1984, EA 1988, EA 1990, and TURERA 1993, together with new TULR(C)A 1992 numbering

ENFORCEMENT and ENFORCEMENT ASSISTANCE

TUA 1984	Ss.10(1), (2), & (3) remove union immunity conferred by s.13 TULRA 1974 from any act if the union has either (a) induced a person to break or interfere with the performance of his contract of employment or (b) induced a person to break or interfere with the performance of a commercial contract by inducing a breach or interference with another person's employment contract action where the union has not held a ballot in respect of the strike or other industrial action in the course of which the breach or interference occurred. A majority of those voting in the ballot have answered 'yes' to the appropriate question.[1]
EA 1988	S.1(1) A union member who claims that the union has, without the support of a ballot, authorized or endorsed any industrial action in which members of the union (including that member) are likely to be, or have been, induced by the union to take part or to continue to take part, may apply to the court for a court order.
	S.1(2) Where it is satisfied as to (1), the court shall make such an order requiring the union to take steps (including the withdrawal of any relevant authorization and endorsement) for ensuring that there is no, or no further, inducement of the union members to take part in that action and that no such member engages in any conduct after the making of the order as a result of the prior inducement.
	S.1(3) A member is treated as being induced by the union to take part or continue to take part in any industrial action if he/she has been subjected to an inducement (whether or not this would be ineffective because of the member's willingness to be influenced by it or for any other reason) and the inducement is an act for which the union was responsible under s.15(2) EA 1982 i.e. authorized or endorsed by a 'responsible person'.[2]
	S.1(5) Any industrial action is without the support of a ballot unless a ballot has been held which satisfies a list of conditions. These conditions are the same as those in ss.10 & 11 of TUA 1984 in respect of inducement to breach or interfere with a contract of employment.[3]
	S.1(8) A union is not required to hold separate ballots for the purposes of satisfying s.1 EA 1988 and s.10 TUA 1984.

TABLE 4.3. (*Continued*)

S.19 CROTUM can give assistance to union members in enforcement proceedings including those under s.1 EA 1988 (see Table 4.2).

S.23 The court shall have power, on an application under s.1 EA 1988 and s.5 TUA 1984 (remedy for failure to comply with Part I of that Act), to grant any such interlocutory relief as it considers appropriate.

EA 1990	
TULR(C)A 1992	Ss.10 & 11 CROTUM's powers are extended (see Table 4.2).
	S.226 (enforcement).
	S.62 (interlocutory relief).
	Ss.109–11, ss.266–71, (enforcement assistance).
TURERA 1993	S.22(1) Where an individual claims that (a) any trade union or other person has done, or is likely to do, an unlawful act to induce any person to take part, or to continue to take part, in industrial action, and (b) an effect, or a likely effect, of the industrial action is or will be to (i) prevent or delay the supply of goods or services or (ii) reduce the quality of goods and services supplied to him, he may apply to the High Court for an order. (2) An act to induce any person to take part, or continue to take part, in industrial action is unlawful (a) if it is actionable in tort by one or more persons, or (b) if it could form the basis of an application under TULR(C)A s.62 (union member's right to a ballot before industrial action). (3) In determining whether an individual may make an application, it is immaterial whether or not the individual is entitled to be supplied with the goods or services in question. (4) If the court finds that the claim is well-founded, it shall make such order as it considers appropriate requiring the inducer to take steps to ensure (a) that no further act is done by him to induce any persons to take part, or continue to take part, in the industrial action, and (b) that no person engages in conduct after the making of the order on account of prior inducement.[4]

ENFORCEMENT ASSISTANCE

S.22 inserts s.235B in TULR(C)A 1992. S.235(B) Provision for an individual to apply for assistance to a Commissioner for Protection Against Unlawful Industrial Action, where the action of which he complains is organized by a union. In granting assistance, the Commissioner may have regard as to whether it is unreasonable, given the complexity of the case, to expect the applicant to deal with it unaided, and whether in his opinion, the case involves a matter of substantial public interest or concern.[5]

TIMING

TUA 1984

S.10(3)(c) The first authorization or endorsement of any relevant act must take place after the date of the ballot but before the expiry of a four-week period beginning with the date of the ballot.

TULR(C)A 1992

S.234.

VOTERS

TUA 1984

S.11(1) Entitlement to vote must be accorded equally to all members who it is reasonable at the time of the ballot for the union to believe will be called on in the strike/other industrial action to act, or continue to act, in breach of, or to interfere with the performance of, their contracts of employment; and to no others.

S.11(2) The ballot will not be valid when a person, who was a union member at the time of the ballot, was denied entitlement to vote and is induced by the union in the course of the action to break his contract of employment or interfere with its performance.

S.11(9) A union with overseas members may choose whether or not to accord any of those members entitlement to vote (it will not have to satisfy s.11(1) to (7) in relation to votes cast by such members).

EA 1990

S.5(1) amends ss.10 and 11 TUA 1984 and s.1 EA 1988 so that references to a contract of employment include 'any contract under which one person personally does work or performs services for another'.[6] S.5(2) amends s.11 TUA 1984: a union member, who throughout the voting period is in Northern Ireland, shall not be treated as an overseas member (a) where workplace ballots are held and the member's place of work is in Great Britain or (b) where a general ballot is held and relates to a strike or other industrial action involving members both in Great Britain and in Northern Ireland.

TULR(C)A 1992

S.227 (entitlement to vote).
S.235 (coverage of contract of employment).
S.232 (overseas members).

TABLE 4.3. (*Continued*)

CAMPAIGNING	
EA 1990	See s.7(3)(a) under BALLOTING METHODS.
TULR(C)A 1992	S.233(2)(a).
BALLOTING METHODS	
TUA 1984	S.11(6) 'So far as is reasonably practicable', every person entitled to vote must (a) have made available to him immediately before, immediately after, or during his/her working hours and at his place of work, or at a place which is more convenient for him, or be supplied with, a voting paper; and (b) be given (i) a convenient opportunity to vote by post[7] (but no other opportunity to vote); (ii) an opportunity to vote immediately before, immediately after, or during, his working hours and at his place of work or at a place more convenient for him (but no other opportunity); or (iii) as alternatives, both of these opportunities (but no other opportunity).
	S.11(5) Every person who is entitled to vote must be allowed to do so without interference from, or constraint imposed by, the union or any of its members, officials, or employees, and 'so far as is reasonably practicable' be enabled to do so without incurring any direct cost to himself.
	S.11(7)(a) The ballot shall be conducted so as to secure 'so far as is reasonably practicable' that those voting do so in secret.
EA 1990	S.7(2) & (3) Industrial action shall not be regarded as having the support of a ballot unless it is called by a specified person and (a) there has been no call by the union to take part/continue to take part in industrial action to which the ballot relates (or any union authorization/endorsement of industrial action) before the date of the ballot; (b) there must be a call for industrial action by a specified person before the ballot ceases to be effective.[8]
TULR(C)A 1992	S.230(2) & (3) (workplace/postal).
	S.230(1) (no interference/constraint).
	S.230(4)(a) (in secret).
	S.233 (call by specified person, no call before ballot, call before ballot ceases to be effective).

TURERA 1993

S. 17 substitutes for ss. 230(2) & (3) TULR(C)A 1992 a new ss.(2): 'so far as is reasonably practicable', every person who is entitled to vote in the ballot must (a) have a voting paper sent to him at his home address or any other address which he has requested the union in writing to treat as his postal address; and (b) be given an opportunity to vote by post.'[9]

TUA 1984

S.11(4) The method of voting must be by means of marking a voting paper.

S.11(4) The voting paper must contain at least one of the following questions: (a) a question (however framed) which requires the voter to say, by answering 'yes' or 'no', whether he is prepared to take part, or continue to take part, in a strike involving him in a breach of his contract of employment; (b) a question (however framed) which requires the voter to say, by answering 'yes' or 'no', whether he is prepared to take part, or continue to take part, in industrial action falling short of a strike but involving him in a breach of his contract of employment.

EA 1988

Sch.3 para.5(8) substitutes for s.11(4)(a) & (b) TUA 1984 the following: (a) a question (however framed) which requires the person answering it to say, by answering 'yes' or 'no', whether he is prepared to take part in/continue to take part in a strike; (b) a question (however framed) which requires the person answering it to say, by answering 'yes' or 'no', whether he is prepared to take part in/continue to take part in action short of a strike.

Sch.3 para.5(8) inserts into s.11(3), at the end, the requirement that the following statement must (without being qualified or commented upon by anything else on the voting paper) appear on every voting paper: 'If you take part in a strike or other industrial action, you may be in breach of your contract of employment'.

EA 1990

S.7(1) inserts a new ss.(4A) into s.11 TUA 1984 after ss.(4). The voting paper must specify who, in the event of a vote in favour of industrial action, is authorized to call upon members to take part/continue to take part in the industrial action.[10]

TULR(C)A 1992

S.229(1) (by marking of voting paper).
S.229(2) (framing of questions).
S.229(3) (name of person authorized to call for action).
S.229(4) ('health warning').

TABLE 4.3. (*Continued*)

TURERA 1993	S.20(2) inserts a new ss.229(1A) in TULR(C)A 1992. Each voting paper must (a) state the name of the independent scrutineer, (b) clearly specify the address to which, and the date by which, it is to be returned, (c) be given one of a series of consecutive whole numbers every one of which is used in giving a different number in that series to each voting paper; and (d) be marked with its number.

COUNTING THE VOTE

TUA 1984	S.11(7)(b) The ballot shall be conducted so as to secure that the votes are fairly and accurately counted (any inaccuracy in counting being disregarded if it is accidental and on a scale which could not affect the ballot result).
EA 1988	S.17 inserts after ss(1) of s.11 TUA 1984 new ss.(1A) & (1B) which add a new requirement for a properly conducted secret ballot on industrial action.[11] Where votes are given to members at different places of work,[12] they may be aggregated if it is reasonable for the union to believe (and it does believe) that those whose votes are to be aggregated form a group consisting of (i) all its members, (ii) all its members employed by one or more employers, or (iii) members who share a 'common distinguishing factor'.[13] In other cases, where votes are given to union members with different places of work, their votes must be counted separately, producing particular results for each such place of work.
TULR(C)A 1992	S.228 (balloting constituencies). S.230(4)(b) (fair and accurate counting).

SUPERVISION

TURERA 1993	S.20(1) inserts s.226B in TULR(C)A 1992. (1) Before the ballot, the union shall appoint a qualified person ('the scrutineer') whose terms of appointment shall require him to carry out the functions of (a) taking such steps as appear to him to be appropriate for the purpose of enabling him to make a report to the union on the ballot; and (b) making his report 'as soon as reasonably practicable' after the ballot but in any case within four weeks. (2) Any person is a 'qualified person' if (a) he satisfies

such conditions as may be specified by order of the Secretary for State or is himself so specified; and (b) the union has no grounds for believing that either he will carry out his functions otherwise than competently or that his independence in relation to the union, or in relation to the ballot, might reasonably be called into question. (3) The trade union shall ensure that the scrutineer duly carries out his functions and that there is no interference with the carrying out of his functions from the union or any of its members, officials, or employees.[14] (4) The union shall comply with all reasonable requests made by the scrutineer.

S.20(3) inserts s.231B in TULR(C)A 1992. (1) The scrutineer's report shall state whether the scrutineer is satisfied (a) that there are no reasonable grounds for believing that there was any contravention of statutory ballot requirements, (b) that the arrangements made for the production, storage, distribution, return, or other handling of the voting papers, and the arrangements for the counting of the votes, included all such security arrangements as were reasonably practicable for the purposes of minimizing the risk that any unfairness or malpractice might occur, and (c) that he has been able to carry out the functions conferred on him under s.226(1) without any interference from the trade union or any of its members, officials, or employees; if he is not satisfied as to any of those matters, his report must give his reasons. (2) If at any time within six months from the date of the ballot (a) any person entitled to vote in the ballot, or (b) the employer of any such person requests a copy of the scrutineer's report, the trade union must, as soon as practicable, provide him with one either free of charge or for a reasonable fee.[15]

TUA 1984   11(8) As soon as reasonably practicable after the holding of the ballot, the union shall take such steps as are reasonably necessary to ensure that all persons entitled to vote in the ballot are informed of the number of votes cast in the ballot, individuals voting 'yes', individuals voting 'no', and spoiled voting papers.

TULR(C)A 1992   S.231.

TABLE 4.3. (*Continued*)

| TURERA 1993 | S.18 inserts s.226A in TULR 1992: the union must take such steps 'as are reasonably necessary' to ensure that not later than the seventh day before the opening day of the ballot, the notice specified in ss.(2), and (b) not later than the third day before the opening of the ballot, the sample voting paper specified in ss.(3), is received by every person who it is reasonable for the union to believe will be the employer of persons entitled to vote in the ballot. (2) The notice in (a) is a notice in writing (a) stating that the union intends to hold the ballot, (b) specifying the date on which the union reasonably believes will be the opening day of the ballot, and (c) describing (so the employer/s can readily ascertain them) the employees who it is reasonable for the union to believe (at the time) will be entitled to vote in the ballot. (3) The sample voting paper referred to in (b) is (a) a sample of the form of voting paper which is to be sent to the employees who it is reasonable for the trade union to believe (at the time) will be entitled to vote in the ballot, or (b) where they are not all to be sent the same form of voting paper, a sample of each form of voting paper. |
| | S.19 inserts s.231A into TULR(C)A 1992. 'As soon as reasonably practicable' after the ballot, the union shall take steps as are reasonably necessary to ensure that every relevant employer is informed of the ballot results (the same information is required as is given to members in s.231 TULR(C)A 1992). |

[1] TUA 1984 Considerable uncertainty exists over the exact definition of 'interference' with an employment contract, see Hutton (1984: 216). The damages obtainable by employers were, however, limited by s.16 EA 1982, where a sliding scale was set up with the highest amount being £250,000 for a union with 100,000 or more members. Unofficial action is unaffected and *threats* to break or interfere with a contract are not included. According to s.10(5), an act is authorized or endorsed by a union if it is authorized or endorsed by a responsible person; according to s.15 EA 1982 such responsible persons are: (a) the PEC; (b) any other person empowered by the rules to authorize or endorse the acts in question; (c) the President or the General Secretary; (d) any other employed official; or (e) any union committee to whom an employed official regularly reports. Additionally note that the union's ballot must satisfy s.11 of TUA 1984: these requirements are summarized in this table under our subheadings.

[2] A 'responsible person' is defined by s.15 EA 1982; see note 1.

[3] EA 1988 schedule 3 amends s.11 TUA so that references to inducements to breach of a contract of employment are replaced by references to 'inducements to take part, or continue to take part, in the strike or other industrial action'.

[4] S.22(5) TURERA 1993 The court may grant such interlocutory relief as it considers appropriate. An act of inducement shall be taken to be done by the union if it is authorized or endorsed by the union according to the provisions of s.20(2) to (4) TULR(C)A 1992 (previously according to s.15 EA 1982 as amended by s.6 EA 1990).

[5] TURERA 1993 Where the person is receiving assistance from the Commissioner, there shall, if he/she so wishes, be added after his name in the title of the proceedings the words 'assisted by the Commissioner for Protection Against Unlawful Industrial Action'.

[6] This is actually achieved by EA 1990 sch. 2 paras. 2 & 3, which change references to breaches or interference with contracts in s.10 TUA 1984 and s.1 EA 1988 to acts done by a union to induce a person to take part in industrial action, and industrial action requiring the support of a ballot (Simpson 1991: 430). The redrafting deletes all references to a contract of employment, so s.5(1) only applies to the 'health warning', thus the reference to 'you may be in breach of your contract of employment' now includes those free-lance and self-employed workers.

[7] TUA 1984 s.11(11) 'Post' means a postal service which is provided by the Post Office or under a licence granted under s.68 of the British Telecommunications Act 1981, or does not infringe the exclusive privilege conferred on the Post Office by s.66(1) of this Act.

[8] EA 1990 s.7(4) A call shall be taken as made by a union if it was authorized or endorsed by the union according to s.15 EA 1982 (as amended by s.6 EA 1990).

[9] TURERA 1993 Provisions for merchant seamen are set out in a new (2A) and (2B) for s.230 TULR(C)A 1992.

[10] According to the new s.11(4A) TUA 1984 the person so specified need not be authorized under the rules of the union but must be within s.15 EA 1982 (as amended by s.6 EA 1990).

[11] EA 1988 This account of s.17 is based upon the Department of Employment Guide (DE 1988: 4).

[12] EA 1988 s.17(3) 'Place of work' is defined as the premises occupied by an employer at which a member works or with which he has the closest connection.

[13] EA 1988 A 'factor' is one which relates to a member's terms and conditions of employment or occupational description but which is not consequent upon his place of work alone. It is 'common' if it is shared with one or more of the other members in the group and 'distinguishing' if it is not shared with any member employed by the same employer who is not entitled to vote.

[14] TURERA 1993 s.20(4) inserts s.226(C) in TULR(C)A 1992 and provides an exemption from the requirement to appoint a scrutineer or obtain a scrutineer's report if (a) the number of members entitled to vote in the ballot, or (b) where separate ballots are held the aggregate of the number of members entitled to vote in each of them, is 50 or less.

[15] TURERA 1993 Small ballot exemption applies; see note 14.

BALLOT PAPER, COUNTING THE VOTE, and INFORMING MEMBERS; however, no requirements were introduced for CAMPAIGNING or SUPERVISION. TUA 1984 was criticized for creating a 'legal minefield' for unionists by a Government more intent on diminishing the union movement than democratizing it (Hutton 1984: 220). Section 10 was particularly criticized as being convoluted and complicated, creating ample scope for judicial interpretation leading to even greater restriction on union ability to take industrial action. The Act's provisions emphasized the Government's individual approach to industrial action: the high unemployment and intense industrial conflict of the mid-1980s would, the Conservatives hoped, predispose union members to vote against industrial action (Auerbach 1990: 154).

Despite the reservations in *Democracy in Trade Unions* over the use of sanctions involving the loss of union immunity, the Government argued (as in *Proposals for Legislation on Democracy in Trade Unions*) that loss of immunity was the best means of ENFORCEMENT, as it extended members' democratic rights at the same time as it reduced the likelihood of irresponsible industrial action.[61] The Government also stated that it was responding to the increasingly hard-line approach being taken by employers since the election (Hutton 1984: 214; Auerbach 1990: 134). Membership-triggered ballots were thus rejected.

The Government, through its choice of loss of immunity as the means of enforcement for industrial action ballots, again demonstrated its intention not to become directly involved in. enforcing ballots. In contrast to IRA 1971, there were no ballots imposed by the Secretary of State and no necessity for a controversial Registrar of Trade Unions, a special court, the rewriting of union rule books, or the introduction of complex new procedures. Instead, the necessary stipulations were built into the legislation itself, and the civil courts, through their interpretations of such phrases as 'as far as reasonably practicable', would decide whether or not minor breaches could be overlooked. The employer could rely on the threat of legal action from the start of the negotiations without having to take any provocative first step (Auerbach 1990: 143). Indeed, the Government argued that a union had a choice of action: to hold a ballot or to face the possibility of legal action (ibid. 138–41).

The requirement in TUA 1984 that a majority of those voting needed to opt for industrial action in order to give immunity was a change from the Government's position in *Proposals for Legislation on Democracy in Trade Unions*. In this White Paper the retention of immunity was not to be dependent on the actual result of the ballot; the Government's position then was that no union would persist with a strike call if it did not obtain majority support in a ballot (para.9). Events in the miners' dispute of 1984–5 prompted the Government to introduce an amendment in the House of Lords that required a majority vote in favour.[62] Despite the continuing concern by employers over the disruptive effects of unofficial action, workers taking such action continued at this stage to enjoy immunity, whether or not there had been a ballot. Indeed, a number of employers expressed concern that the provisions in TUA 1984 could lead to an increase in unofficial action (Auerbach 1990: 142). Hutton (1984: 219) believes that Government strategy here was focused on separating those taking unofficial action from their union (thus rendering them vulnerable to dismissal) and on heading off attention-grabbing, large set-piece confrontations with key groups of workers in the public sector over the Government's economic and social policies.

TUA 1984 was drafted so as to encourage members to vote against industrial action. This strategy is particulary apparent in the Act's strictures on TIMING and the contents of the BALLOT PAPER. The Government adhered to the suggestion in *Democracy in Trade Unions* of a four-week period within which to call for action, despite criticism that this was too short a period: the Opposition had asked for a sixteen-week period (Auerbach 1990: 144). The Government's response was that the union should not be able to obtain a 'blank cheque' to call industrial action at the start of the negotiations, an approval for action which would form a 'backdrop to the entire negotiation' (ibid. 144).[63] The requirement for a successful ballot to precede union authorization or endorsement was a means of ensuring that the union could not call members out first and then ballot them afterwards when it became apparent that the employer really intended to take legal action (ibid. 142–3). A union therefore could not call the employer's bluff without running the risk of litigation, thereby increasing the strength of an employer's threat to take legal action if a ballot was not held.

The requirement that the ballot paper include questions asking whether the voter was prepared to take part in a strike or other industrial action that would involve him/her in a breach of contract was criticized by the Opposition as 'intimidation' (Auerbach 1990: 150). Hutton (1984: 224) notes that few union members were then aware that striking involved a breach of their employment contracts, making the 'Government health warning' appear frightening for them. Apart from having to obtain a 'yes' or 'no' answer, the union was able to phrase the question how it pleased and the words 'breach of contract' did not need to appear on the ballot paper, though the union had to make clear that the action would constitute such a breach.

In terms of ENTITLEMENT TO VOTE, a ballot could be invalidated if a member entitled to vote was denied that entitlement. However, John Gummer (Minister for Employment) distinguished at the House of Commons Committee stage between the entitlement to vote, which was an absolute right, and the opportunity to vote: the opportunity to vote had to be given 'so far as is reasonably practicable'. Therefore, if a member through some accident did not get the opportunity to vote, then, as long as his/her entitlement was not denied, the reasonable-practicability rule applied and the ballot could not be invalidated on that ground. There had to be a positive denial of the member's right to vote. So if a member entitled to vote was missed out on the list of voters and, when this was pointed out to the union, he/she was allowed to vote, the ballot would be valid. However, if, after the ballot had been held, a member complained of not having been given the entitlement to vote, it could be argued that the ballot was invalid since the mistake could not now be rectified (*IRLIB* 267, 23.10.84: 6). In this respect, Lord Donaldson in *British Railways Board* v. *NUR* [1989] IRLR 349 (CA) showed an understanding of the practical problems faced by unions in organizing ballots for large groups of workers.[64]

Other points with respect to entitlement to vote concern additional strikers and union members with an interest in the strike. The requirement to ballot only all those it is reasonable for the union at the time of the ballot to believe will be called upon to take industrial action, and no others, affects the union should it wish to call upon more members to take part in the same industrial action. The original ballot is no longer valid, as members whom the union now wished to induce to break their contracts had been 'denied entitlement' to vote in that ballot. Therefore it was not sufficient for the union merely to ballot the new groups of members whom it wishes to bring out on strike; it must ballot all the members, including those who were already taking industrial action and had voted to do so in the original ballot (*IRLIB* 267, 23.10.84: 5–6). In restricting entitlement to vote to those called upon to take industrial action, the Government took a very individualistic approach, ignoring the concerns of the EEF that a constituency wider than those taking the most direct action may have an interest in the intended industrial action: this is particularly the case in a selective strike (Auerbach 1990: 150).

In terms of BALLOTING METHOD, unlike the provisions for union elections, there was no presumption in favour of postal ballots. Voting could take place at either the workplace or by post, or by means of some combination, but show-of-hands voting was now excluded. When the ballot had been concluded, the union was required only to INFORM those entitled to vote of the bare facts of the ballot results. This posed a practical problem for employers; not only did they have no right to be informed of the ballot's results, but also they had no direct means of discovering breaches of s.11 (Hutton 1984: 220–1).

TUA 1984, as we will show in Chapter 6, had an impact on unions' use of ballots. A significant number of employers were prepared to use its provisions and the courts also demonstrated their willingness to issue injunctions where unions failed to hold industrial action ballots.[65] However, some large employers were not so willing and the Government was worried by the unions' ability both to utilize ballots tactically and produce votes in favour of industrial action. Moreover, the string of individual actions against the national and area unions in the 1984–5 miners' dispute had a big impact on Conservative opinion, convincing it to reverse its earlier opinion that it should not legislate for membership-triggered ballots on the grounds that such provisions were unlikely to be used. The miners' dispute suggested that empowering union members to control and restrain industrial action was a practical possibility and a useful device for circumventing employers' reluctance. The impending general election gave the Government the impetus to produce another Green Paper, despite Lord Young's lack of enthusiasm.

In the Green Paper *Trade Unions and Their Members*, the Government continued to presume that there was a dichotomy within unions of militant pro-strike leaders and moderate anti-strike members, but it detected a change in members who 'have on a number of occasions refused to be precipitated into industrial action contrary to their best interests and to their own better judgement'; it further asserted that there was 'now a firm and widespread expectation amongst members that they will be consulted by a secret ballot', 'they are less willing to tolerate unjust treatment by their union or be intimidated by threats made by union leaders' (DE 1987: 1).

The Government sought comments on the introduction of a union duty to its members invariably and automatically not to authorize or endorse industrial action involving breaches of contracts of employment without first conducting a secret ballot of those due to take part in the action and obtaining majority support for its authorization or endorsement. The duty would be enforceable by any individual member due to take part in the industrial action through an application to the High Court, which could be given the power to restrain the union from authorizing or endorsing industrial action before a ballot was held. The conditions governing the conduct of the ballot concerning method of voting, framing of question(s), and other matters would be in accordance with the requirements in TUA 1984. The member could be assisted in any action against the union by the new Commissioner.

The introduction of this right for members was very much in line with the Government's strong non-interventionist rhetoric, although it was clearly aimed at increasing legal challenges to unlawful industrial action. The Government's greater interest in reducing industrial action than in extending members' rights is indicated by the proposal in *Trade Unions and Their Members* that members' rights be limited to restraining their union from authorizing or endorsing unballoted industrial action. It did not recommend a corresponding right for union members to insist that a ballot be held: the decision on whether or not to ballot would remain with the union on the grounds that limiting the proposed right would 'minimize the chances of court action interfering with the resolution of a particular dispute' (ibid. 4).

Trade Unions and Their Members also proposed a right for all union members (whether or not they worked in a closed shop) not to be expelled or otherwise disciplined for refusing or failing to take industrial action. This relates to our interest in industrial action balloting, since the Government rejected the restriction of the union member's protection against a call for industrial action to circumstances where there were reasonable grounds for believing that the industrial action was unlawful (ibid. 7). This meant that the Government wished the right for members to go to work despite a strike call to apply even where the union had conducted a lawful secret ballot and had obtained a majority in favour of industrial action. The Government's argument laid stress on its individual view of employment relations: the union member should be free to decide whether to break his/her contract of employment, whatever the circumstances and regardless of whether the inducement was with or without immunity. The Government saw the individual's right to go to work despite a strike call as an 'essential freedom' that was often challenged by those who took 'a hard line of the traditional philosophy of the trade union movement based on the concept of collective strength through solidarity' (ibid. 4).

In responding to *Trade Unions and their Members* employers were lukewarm regarding the industrial action ballot proposals. While the CBI and EEF were in favour of the Government's attempts to establish the principle of pre-strike ballots, they were opposed to the introduction of the right to go to work despite a legally prescribed strike call; even more strongly opposed was the IPM; the Association of Conservative Trade Unionists and the Freedom Association joined in the condemnation as well (*IDS Brief* 349, 5.87: 17; *Personnel Management* 6.87: 7; Auerbach 1990: 166; McIlroy 1991: 139). These organizations felt that allowing members to refuse with impunity to be bound by the majority decision in an industrial action ballot would make unions less inclined to conduct ballots constructively, would undermine the authority of union officials, and reduce the stability and predictability brought to collective bargaining by TUA 1984. However, as in 1983, public opinion was firmly behind further legislation to curb industrial action.[66]

The TUC's acerbic reaction to *Trade Unions and Their Members* included strong opposition to the Government's proposals to allow members to obtain High Court injunctions in order to restrain their union from authorizing industrial action not supported by a properly held ballot (TUC 1987). It condemned this proposal as too rigid, as bypassing union rules, and as not justified by the low level of complaints from members. The TUC described the introduction of a right to go to work despite a strike call as 'contradictory and anti-democratic' (ibid. 5).

The Employment Act 1988

The Conservatives' general election manifesto (May 1987) proposed legislation empowering individuals to prevent their unions calling them out on strike without a secret ballot and preventing unions disciplining members who refused to participate. The Employment Bill (October 1987) included these proposals, but also added significant measures on other aspects of the related balloting process.

The measures in EA 1988 relating to industrial action ballots are shown in Table 4.3. In terms of ENFORCEMENT, section 1 introduced the right for a union member legally to restrain his/her union from unlawfully calling industrial action. However, the form in which it was implemented was different from that proposed in *Trade Unions and Their Members*; the member's right to demand a ballot was not linked to industrial action which broke or interfered with the performance of his/her contract of employment, but was extended to all forms of industrial action. The Government justified this extension by saying that the union member's job was potentially at risk whatever the nature of the industrial action and that the member's right to demand a ballot should not depend on the 'archaic legal technicalities' involved in proving the commission of one of the torts in respect of which the immunities had been withdrawn (Lord Trefgarne and Lord Campbell of Alloway, quoted in McKendrick 1988: 142). However, employers' cause of action remained one dependent upon the commission of a tort for which no immunity was provided: sections 10 and 11 of TUA 1984 referred to loss of union immunity for inducement to breach or to interference with the performance of a contract of employment where a lawful ballot had not been held. EA 1988 made it clear that a single ballot would satisfy both Acts. This extension meant that a union was now obliged to ballot in order to retain immunity from member action before undertaking actions that might not be in breach of the member's contract of employment (for example, a ban on voluntary overtime). Remarkably, ineffective inducement is deemed to be inducement for the purposes of this section.

Two aspects of EA 1988 offered members ASSISTANCE FOR ENFORCE-MENT of their rights. As we saw in the section on union elections, the office of CROTUM was created and the Commissioner had power to assist members in taking action against their union in connection with industrial action ballots and unfair discipline. Further, the courts were given power to grant interlocutory relief in members' applications under both EA 1988 and TUA 1984 (this had not been discussed in *Trade Unions and Their Members*). According to *IRLIB* 356 (5.7.88: 4) the purpose of section 23 was probably to get round the problem of a court order relating to a member's case being made long after the time when it was likely to be of any benefit to him/her. Thus, the provision for interlocutory relief could lead to an injunction being made at an early stage in the proceedings, before all the evidence and arguments were put. The combination of this assistance offered and the right of enforcement being given to an individual member was, according to Auerbach (1990: 167), undoubtedly designed to maximize the chances of this provision being used.

In terms of the wording of the VOTING PAPER and method of COUNTING THE VOTE, the Government introduced two new measures not mentioned in *Trade Unions and Their Members*. The Government's motivation appeared to be to reinforce the provisions in TUA 1984, which had been drafted to encourage members' supposed inclination to vote against industrial action involving their imminent participation, by eliminating union 'abuses' taking the form of making adverse comments on the Government's 'health warning' on the ballot paper and of manipulating balloting constituencies (ibid. 170–1). Additionally, section 18 of EA 1988 empowered the Secretary of State to issue Codes of Practice on ballots, a suggestion put forward by the EEF (*IRLIB* 356, 5.7.88: 5).[67] The resulting Code of Practice on Industrial Action Ballots (1989) made a number of recommendations for union practice aimed at preventing unions' using ballots as a tactical weapon and encouraging members to vote no (see below). As regards the ballot paper, the Conservatives added 'another layer of cement' by requiring unions to separate the question/s on taking part in industrial action and the 'health warning', and to use a prescribed statement for the latter, which could not be qualified or commented upon elsewhere on the balloting paper.[68] As regards counting the vote, the Government introduced a very controversial and complex regulation for determining union balloting constituencies—the infamous section 17, described by McCarthy (Wedderburn 1989: 29) as the 'gibberish' clause.[69] Section 17 attempted closely to define union balloting constituencies. The new general principle was that a separate ballot must be held for each workplace and immunity would only be enjoyed where a majority of the workplace members had voted to take industrial action (McKendrick 1988: 146). Ballot results could be aggregated across workplaces in three exceptional cases: ballots involving all union members, all members working for an employer, or members sharing a 'common distinguishing factor' (see Table 4.3).

The legal changes contained within section 17 were added when the Bill was drafted, in response particularly to concerns raised in the IPM's report *A Guide to Workplace Balloting* over unions' creating artificial constituencies in order to maximize the possibility of positive votes. However, the IPM's argument was based on only two examples, which themselves did not provide clear evidence of abuse. The clause was considerably modified during its passage through Parliament with help from the Opposition in the House of Commons and Lord Wedderburn in the House of Lords: the original drafting of this clause in the Bill (clause 16) was extremely convoluted, horrifying the IPM, *inter alios,* who concluded that 'it would be more helpful from an employer's point of view if clause 16 was omitted' (Auerbach 1990: 175–8).

The suggestion in *Trade Unions and Their Members* that protection from union discipline be introduced for union members declining to take industrial action, regardless of its lawfulness or the existence of a majority ballot in its favour, was incorporated in section 3 of EA 1988 and was very broadly drafted, both in terms of activities covered and union sanctions.[70]

After the passage of EA 1988, the next two Green Papers appeared in 1989 and both focused on the conduct of industrial action. The Conservative Government was convinced by events that took place in 1989 that further legislation was needed for industrial action ballots. Its reaction to the 1989 'summer of discontent' graphically illustrates the increasing tendency to react to events or specific pressures. However, neither employers nor the electorate were enthusiastic any longer over further reforms for the conduct of industrial action, but the Government ignored their views.[71]

The 'summer of discontent' in 1989 was an upsurge of industrial militancy which, combined with effective use of the legal process to delay or frustrate official union support, led to a significant amount of unofficial industrial action (ibid. 1990: 191). There was a rash of such action, particularly in the public sector, including British Rail and the Post Office and further disputes in the mining industry, plus industrial action in the docks following the Government's announcement of the abolition of the Dock Labour scheme, at the VSEL ship-building yard in Barrow, on construction sites (steel erectors), on North Sea oil platforms (construction maintenance workers), and at Ford and Jaguar. The most notable unofficial action was by London Underground workers, who engaged in widespread and effective unofficial action, while their unions underwent the required complex and lengthy balloting processes and fought to establish a lawful dispute. Auerbach (1990: 192) succinctly comments that 'the Government's crude monotype of militant leaders dragooning unwilling members out on strike looked more implausible than ever.' The problems that unions were so clearly seen to face in taking industrial action particularly contributed to the climate of public opinion that the Government's reform of unions' legal framework had gone far enough.

Throughout the 'summer of discontent' the Government made repeated threats that new laws would be introduced on unofficial action and strikes in essential services. In the event, it felt that banning strikes in essential services would produce insuperable practical and political problems; however, it felt that legislation for unofficial action was possible.

The first of the Green Papers published in 1989, *Removing Barriers to Employment*, had as its main concerns the outlawing of the pre-entry closed shop and prohibition of secondary industrial action. However, proposals were also included to extend the requirement to ballot on industrial action to members who worked under contracts other than those of employment and to give such members the right to restrain their union from calling on them to take industrial action without a ballot. The reason given for this extension was that many union members, such as free-lance and self-employed workers, did not work under contracts of employment, but under 'contracts for services'. As it was possible for a trade dispute to involve such workers, the Government saw no reason to deprive them of the rights accorded to members working under employment contracts (*IRLIB*, 438, 25.4.89).[72] Additionally, it proposed enhanced powers for CROTUM that could improve members' ability to bring complaints against their union for unlawful industrial action *inter alia*.

A second Green Paper, entitled *Unofficial Action and the Law*, was published later, in October 1989. The Government asserted that unofficial industrial action, particularly through its unpredictability and disruptive nature, was costing jobs and undermining the UK's economic performance and international competitiveness.[73] The Conservatives' concern to limit unofficial action also had implications for union campaigning. For, as things stood, unofficial action taken without a secret ballot could retain statutory immunity and the Conservatives had become frustrated by their discovery that unofficial action prior to the holding and outcome of a ballot could undermine much of what the new balloting requirements had been intended to achieve in terms of enhanced adherence to bargaining procedures and the defusing of the potency of industrial action (Auerbach 1990: 193). *Unofficial Action and the Law* proposed that union responsibility be extended (irrespective of the union's rule book) to make a union potentially liable for the inducement of industrial action by any official of the union (whether employed by the union or not) or any union committee to which any such official reported, unless the union repudiated the inducement in writing, individually, to all the members concerned. Alternatively, it would be open to the union to accept liability for the industrial action, in which case it would need to hold a proper secret ballot of the relevant members. If the subsequent ballot showed a majority for the industrial action, the union would be immune from legal proceedings if it proceeded to authorize or endorse that action.

Unofficial Action and the Law provoked a mixed response from employers and unions: most stressed the legal and practical problems involved.[74] The attention drawn by the TUC to the paradoxical union behaviour required in seeking to turn unofficial into official action is of particular relevance to our interest in balloting legislation. Thus, the union seeking to assume lawful and 'official' responsibility for 'unofficial' action must condemn and repudiate the action, while simultaneously organizing a ballot with the intention of supporting it (DE 1989b: 15). With respect to the more minor addition to the balloting requirements of *Removing Barriers to Employment*, the CBI, the BIM, and the IOD expressed support for the extension of balloting requirements to union members working under 'contracts for services', while the TUC called this an 'unprecedented and unwarranted interference in union affairs' (*IRLIB* 381, 25.7.89: 15).

The Employment Act 1990

The Employment Bill 1989 and the following Act largely followed the suggestions of the two 1989 Green Papers, despite the serious criticism of employers and unions and the electorate's lack of interest. These provisions are summarized in Table 4.3. The legislation on industrial action ballots contained in these four Acts was now extremely complex and the case for consolidation was pressing (see Simpson 1991: 432, 438).

The Government enacted its proposals on curbing unofficial action despite the heavy burden of repudiation imposed on unions and the dangers for union credibility (see comments by Carty 1991: 13–14 and Simpson 1991: 429).[75] In terms of VOTERS, EA 1990 extended the balloting requirements to union members working under contracts of services (as had been proposed) and to members in Northern Ireland in certain circumstances (which had not been previously discussed). The other measures below were added when the Bill was published or during its passage through Parliament, largely reflecting the Government's reactions to specific industrial disputes.[76]

With reference to TIMING, EA 1990 introduced the possibility of extending the four-week period in which industrial action had to be taken following an affirmative ballot in cases where a union had been restrained from calling for industrial action by a court order. This was introduced as a result of a problem that arose out of the 1989 docks dispute, where the union concerned, the TGWU, spent considerable time defending its actions in the courts. Litigation against the union did not finish until the four-week time limit had expired. Hence, although the union won its case, it lost its immunity and had no option but to desist from industrial action or reballot its members. This led to attempts by Lord Campbell of Alloway to push through a Bill that would extend the time limit in such circumstances. His attempts were unsuccessful, but the Government was persuaded that some provision should be made and an amendment along the lines of Lord Campbell's Bill was included (*IRLIB* 415, 21.12.90: 8–9). Both the *IRLIB* (ibid. 9) and Carty (1991: 11–12) felt that this provision was likely to draw the courts into the 'heart of a dispute', since the courts were required to make hypothetical and speculative judgments in deciding whether to or not extend the four-week rule; this would lead to considerable controversy in relations between employers and unions (see Table 4.3).

Section 7 of EA 1990 added more balloting requirements for the BALLOT PAPER, CAMPAIGNING, AND BALLOTING METHODS. The ballot paper had now to specify who was authorized to call for industrial action in the event of a successful ballot. If action was called for by an unauthorized person, the union would lose the protection of the ballot, unless it repudiated the action of this official. The Government introduced this measure in order to prevent unauthorized officials from misusing the protection of a majority yes vote to call premature industrial action when their union did not wish them to have the authority to do this. It justified it by reference to the dispute at Ford in 1989 where, following an affirmative ballot, the national officers of the union had not decided what their next step would be when the Ford shop stewards 'jumped the gun' by calling for industrial action, claiming the protection of the ballot (Carty 1991: 16; Simpson 1991: 430).[77] Further, there must be no call for industrial action before the ballot. Both the *IRLIB* (415, 21.12.1990: 8) and Carty (1991: 17) comment that the term 'call' is new to industrial relations and open to interpretation by the courts. The Government insisted that there was a difference between a call and a recommendation to vote yes, but Carty (ibid.) asks whether, in practice, a court in interlocutory proceedings would interpret an urging of the membership to vote yes as a call: a result subversive to the operation of strike ballots.[78]

In 1991 a further Green Paper, *Industrial Relations in the 1990s*, in line with previous Green Papers, emphasized the harm posed to the economy and the community by industrial action, pointed out the 'success' of the Conservatives' legal reforms (in employers' bringing proceedings against unions, in preventing industrial action, and in ensuring unions' greater commitment to consulting their members) and then went on to discuss the need for further legislation to protect the community from public sector strikes. The Government argued that strike ballots should be conducted to the same standards as union elections, given the extent to which members were directly affected by them, that businesses and jobs in the UK needed the same safeguards as those enjoyed by their counterparts in other countries, and that a distinctive feature of industrial action in the public services was its frequent deliberate targeting of the community in order to put pressure on the employer through public hardship. The employer already had a remedy in law but the members of the public had no remedy for their deprivation of their rights as citizens: if the employer is unwilling to act, or to act quickly enough, the citizen 'may be defenceless' (DE 1991: 15). If this citizen's right were introduced, unions would not be likely to escape proceedings for unlawful industrial action because the employer concerned refused to act.

In their new proposals for statutory industrial action provisions the Conservatives repeated many of the recommendations of the voluntary balloting code, which in turn echoed statutory provisions brought in for union election ballots. *Industrial Relations in the 1990s* proposed the following additional requirements to provide more secure industrial action ballots: first, industrial action ballots should be conducted by the fully postal method in every case where more than fifty union members were entitled to vote; it was for further consideration whether 'semi-postal' balloting should be required where fifty or fewer union members were entitled to vote. Second, there should be appropriate arrangements for independent scrutiny in industrial action ballots and a scrutineer's report available within four weeks of the voting to members and to the employer. Where the vote was not fully postal and it was not reasonably practicable to appoint an eligible scrutineer, the ballot could be scrutinized by one or more individuals/officials not directly involved in the dispute. Third, the employer should have the right to information about a ballot if his/her workers are entitled to vote. The union should be required to provide the employer with notice of its intent to hold the ballot, with details of which workers would be entitled to vote, and of the voting procedure to be adopted. It should also supply the employer with a sample copy of the voting paper/s and the details of the ballot result as required to be given to the union members, together with a copy of the independent scrutineer's report. Additionally, customers of public services within the scope of the Citizens' Charter should have the right to bring proceedings to prevent or restrain the organization of unlawful industrial action where their service was, or would be, seriously affected by any such unlawfully organized industrial action and where the unlawful industrial action had not been restrained by proceedings brought by an employer or union member. This new right would be available to anyone who was, or was likely to be, affected by the unlawful industrial action such that no part of the service was available or that it was available only at a reduced level. Where a member of the public brought proceedings and the court was satisfied that the industrial action was (or would be) organized unlawfully, the court would grant an order preventing or restraining the unlawful act.

Although there was a lack of enthusiasm for further legislation *per se*, there was virtually unanimous support from employers' organizations for the proposals in *Industrial Relations in the 1990s* for the extension of the legal requirements for industrial action ballots. The CBI, EEF, BIM, and IPM all supported the introduction of independent scrutiny for such ballots and employers' right to information and notice (*IRLIB* 438, 6.12.91). The organizations did differ though on the requirement for fully postal ballots: the EEF and the IPM felt, in contrast to the other two, that properly conducted workplace ballots were normally more effective than postal ballots because of the greater turn-out in the former (ibid: 13). The TUC criticized all the industrial action proposals, believing that the Government's purpose was to increase the difficulty of taking lawful industrial action, and it pointed to the greater time required for organizing postal as against workplace ballots. The extension of a right to restrain industrial action to customers of public services, if proceedings have not been initiated by the employer or union member, was condemned by the IPM, BIM, and TUC as not being conducive to the interests of the speedy settlement of disputes. Only the EEF saw the intervention of citizens in industrial disputes as beneficial (ibid.).[79]

The Conservatives' 1992 election manifesto again expressed their satisfaction with their 'transformation' of industrial relations and their wish to continue to legislate to enhance further the right of employers, employees, and customers not to have their lives and businesses disrupted by wildcat strikes (CCO 1992: 20)

Trade Union Reform and Employment Rights Act 1993

Following the Conservatives' fourth consecutive election victory, the measures on industrial action ballots contained in the 1993 Bill broadly followed the suggestions put forward in *Industrial Relations in the 1990s*. Thus, changes were introduced into current industrial action ballot requirements for the BALLOTING METHOD and the contents of the BALLOT PAPER, and new requirements were introduced for SUPERVISION and INFORMING EMPLOYERS.[80] However, there was a widening of the customer's right to bring proceedings in the case of unlawful industrial action. The amendments to TULR(C)A 1992 are shown in Table 4.3. The requirements for a fully postal ballot and independent scrutiny for industrial action ballots are likely significantly to increase unions' expenses: this is particularly significant given the phasing out of the ballot refund scheme (see above). An exemption for small ballots was introduced but this applied only to the supervision requirement, although in *Industrial Relations in the 1990s* the small ballots exemption was proposed for the postal requirement.

Turning particularly to the question of ENFORCEMENT there was a very significant difference in terms of the customer's right of action between the Conservatives' proposals in *Industrial Relations in the 1990s* and TURERA 1993. The proposed right, linked and confined to the Citizen's Charter, was replaced by an enacted right covering all sectors of the economy and all enterprises. The citizen now had the right to take action when his/her supply of goods or services was affected, or likely to be affected, by unlawful industrial action, irrespective of whether or not the individual was entitled to be supplied with the goods or services in question. This specifically included industrial action undertaken without the support of a properly conducted ballot. If the court found the citizen's claim well-founded, it should require the inducer of the industrial action to desist. The prospect of interlocutory injunctions being sought, where the citizen need only show that there is 'a serious question to be tried' and the decision rests 'on the balance of convenience', particularly worried the CBI (Morris 1993: 203). The Government justified this extension of the proposed citizen's right by the warm welcome it had received—though it did not specify from whom, by the prevention of the right's loss on the privatization of a public service, and by the avoidance of the problems of separating the public and private sphere (ibid. 196). It also appears that the Conservatives were concerned, despite a statement to the contrary in the Green Paper, that employers were not sufficiently ardent in pursuing their legal remedies (ibid. 196 fn. 16). The Conservatives refused to bow to pressure from employers' organizations to narrow the application of the right. The new right was accompanied by the establishment of a Commissioner for Protection Against Unlawful Industrial Action.[81]

TURERA 1993 thus introduces a new person into industrial disputes, whose rights are considerably greater than those of employers (though an employer can take action as a citizen). Indeed, the citizen's right to take action in an unlawful industrial dispute circumvents entirely the constraints upon the right to bring proceedings contained in the economic torts (ibid. 195). For example, the citizen has no need to demonstrate that he/she has suffered any actual material loss, damage, or even inconvenience as a result of the disruption of the supply of goods and services, nor any need to prove intent, provided that the requisite intent to constitute the tort exists in relation to another such as the primary employer. The presence of a citizen with these extensive rights to act against industrial action that was unlawful because it was not supported by ballot may seriously circumscribe an employer's freedom of action in deciding whether, or when, to take such action against the union as he/she is permitted to do: the threat of legal action as a bargaining counter for the employer is accordingly reduced (ibid. 207–8). The introduction of this citizen's right can be seen as another example of the Conservatives' re-regulation of the labour market through the reduction of employers' autonomy to manage industrial disputes as they think best. Moreover, TURERA is very uneven-handed in that it provides a citizen's right of action only when services are disrupted by unlawful industrial action, but not by a lock-out, however peremptory the employer's behaviour. Again, the introduction of this right allows the Government to distance itself behind the individual's actions (ibid. 208–10).

In summary, therefore, the imposition of mandatory postal ballots for the calling of industrial action followed a similar process to that employed in the legislation affecting union elections. It started with a very limited and voluntary means of encouraging ballots. Unions' general refusal to take advantage of this initial encouragement was used to legitimize more direct regulation. Hence, the Government incrementally expanded its legislation into a rigid statutory template which covered virtually all aspects of the process of calling industrial action and eventually drew unofficial action within its boundaries. Its enabling legislation empowered employers, disaffected union members, and the aggrieved citizen: these became its enforcement agents as the Government itself remained at arm's length from its actual application. Criticisms (informed or otherwise) remained largely ignored as the Government at regular intervals, but particularly prior to general elections, found and exposed new union 'misdemeanours' which required remedial legislation.

THE CODE OF PRACTICE ON INDUSTRIAL ACTION BALLOTS AND NOTICE TO EMPLOYERS

As we saw above, provision was made by section 18 of EA 1988 for the Secretary of State to issue Codes of Practice to promote desirable practices in elections and industrial action ballots. The introduction of a Code for industrial action ballots was not part of the Conservatives' planned reform of industrial relations when they came into office in 1979: it was not discussed in any Green Paper nor was there any debate on the extent of union abuse of the balloting laws. The adoption of this Code can be interpreted as the addition of 'another layer of cement' to reinforce the attempt in TUA 1984 to make it more difficult for unions to take collective action. Auerbach (1990: 179–80) describes the thrust of the Code, even though the published version watered down some of the most controversial draft recommendations, as an attempt both to defuse 'the potency of the ballot as a positive weapon in the hands of the union' through its recommendations such as that which downgraded the significance of a majority vote, and also to coerce unions by delivering as much evidence as possible into the hands of employers and others with the statutory right to restrain union action by injunction (see also Hendy et al. 1989: 81–2).

The inclusion of provisions in EA 1988 amending and expanding the power of the Secretary of State for Employment under section 3 of EA 1980 to include Codes to promote desirable practices in elections and ballots appears to have been the result of suggestions by employers, particularly the EEF, who were concerned over the unions' successful adoption of various strategies and tactics in order to organize industrial action, despite the strictures imposed by TUA 1984 (Auerbach 1990: 178–9). The Government itself was concerned, as we saw in the previous section, over the unions' successful adaption to industrial action ballots and it seized the opportunity both to discourage unions from holding industrial action ballots and to attempt to rectify defects in earlier legislation. The Draft Code incorporated most of the EEF's suggestions and supplemented these with provisions designed to combat numerous other possible forms of perceived union abuse in industrial action ballots.

A draft version of a Code of Practice on Trade Union Ballots on

Industrial Action was issued by the Department of Employment in November 1988 and, following revisions, the first Code came into force in April 1990. This was revised again in May 1991 (1st Revision) to take account of subsequent legislation. A further Draft Revision was issued in October 1994 following TURERA 1993; the Code was renamed the Code of Practice on Industrial Action Ballots and Notice to Employers. This Revision is expected to be completed by July 1995.

Most employers' organizations were unenthusiastic over the Draft Code and the TUC and ACAS were hostile. Even those organizations that welcomed the introduction of the Code were critical of its form and its detailed contents (*IRLIB* 372, 7.3.89: 14–15). Importantly, a number of commentators saw the Code as counter-productive (ibid. 14–15). Despite its most controversial recommendations being dropped, the first Code (and later revised versions) was still criticized on a number of grounds (see Auerbach 1990: 179–80; Hendy *et al.* 1989: 81–2, and Carty 1991: 17). Most importantly, its purpose 'to provide practical guidance to promote the improvement of industrial relations and desirable practices in relation to the conduct of union industrial action ballots' (para.1) and to 'assist unions and their members who are directly involved in such ballots, employers and their customers and suppliers, and members of the public, who may be affected by industrial action organised by a union' (para.2) was questioned. The Code's recommendations stressed occasions when a union should avoid holding a ballot; further, they are addressed to unions exclusively.[82] Thus the Code included a section on 'Whether an industrial action ballot would be appropriate', where unions were urged first to complete any agreed procedures, either formal or informal, that might lead to the resolution of the dispute without the need for industrial action or, where no such procedures were available or had been exhausted, to consider other ways of resolving the dispute, such as seeking advice from ACAS (para. 8). Further, in an attempt by the Government to discourage 'tactical balloting', the Code recommended that a union should hold an industrial action ballot only if it is contemplating authorizing or endorsing lawful industrial action (para.9). It also pointed out that even if a majority voted for action the union was under no statutory obligation to authorize or endorse industrial action (para.53), and unions were urged to consider all options as means of resolving the dispute (para.58) and to take 'relevant considerations' into account including, *inter alia*, the willingness of the employer/s to enter into further negotiations or discussions, the possibility of using ACAS, and the size of the majority and the voting turn-out (para.59).

Further, Simpson (1990: 29) criticizes the effect of the Code on 'both the function of codes of practice and the role of ballots in the law on industrial conflict'. He was concerned that the Code might constitute a form of 'back-door' legislation and that its recommendations that unions *should* undertake various tasks, when there is no statutory obligation on them to do so, adds to the uncertain legal status of the Code. He believes that the lack of consensus on industrial action practices which lies behind the Code and the detailed nature of its prescriptions will inevitably lead to its implementation through the use of labour injunctions: this, he argues, is an abuse of the proper functions of Codes of Practice.

Other general criticisms of the first Code and the new 1994 Draft Code concerned its length, excessive detail, and overly prescriptive manner, all resulting in complexity, confusion, and dysfunction: even the EEF called for greater brevity and simplicity. For example, the 1988 Draft Code ran to 103 paragraphs and four appendices (much longer than the EEF's suggested code), the 1st Revision version still consisted of 56 paragraphs and one annex, and the 1994 Draft runs to 68 paragraphs and one annex. Moreover, both Simpson (1990) and Carty (1991: 17) felt that, despite its length and detail, the Code did not help to make uncertain and complex areas of the law any clearer; for example, the Code missed the opportunity of unravelling section 17 of EA 1988 on balloting constituencies (see also *IRLIB* 387, 24.10.89: 5). ACAS found instructions regarding the ballot count unnecessarily detailed and too prescriptive, and expressed the view that Codes of Practice were likely to be more effective if they allowed reasonable latitude as to how principles of good practice could be met (ibid. 8).

The recommendations of the 1994 Draft Code of Practice on Industrial Action Ballots for preparing for an industrial action ballot, holding an industrial action ballot, and following an industrial action ballot are summarized in Table 4.4.[83] The emphasis on postal ballots and on making arrangements for independent scrutiny in the 1st Revision of the Code were removed from the 1994 Draft (both aspects being provided for in TURERA 1993). The emphasis in the 1994 Draft appears to be on providing information to help employers to minimize the disruptive effects of industrial action. Thus, the union is enjoined to check that the employer receives and understands his/her written notices from the union and to consider carefully what information the employer might need to identify potential voters and strikers, including perhaps supplying their names and workplace locations (see paras. 20, 21, 22, 64, 65, and 66). Significantly, the 1st Revision's recommendation (in para.34) that the union should consider communicating by special notices or meetings with its members in connection with a ballot was dropped from the 1994 Draft Code; this may be because the inclusion of this recommendation in the 1st Revision was criticized for implying that the union should impart information about the dispute and ballot details separately from the balloting process, although there was no statutory prohibition on such information accompanying the voting paper (*IRLIB* 387, 24.10.89: 6). Or possibly it was part of the Conservatives' continuing drive to individualize members'

TABLE 4.4. Code of Practice on Industrial Action Ballots and Notice to Employers (Draft) (1994)[1]

ENFORCEMENT	Codes of practice provide guidance as to good practice. Failure to abide by a provision does not render anyone liable to any legal proceedings but the code will be admissible in evidence and any provision which appears to be relevant will be taken into account in determining any question arising in these proceedings (s.3(8) EA 1980).
TIMING	Para.34 The period between sending out voting papers and the date by which completed voting papers should be returned should allow at least: (a) seven days if voting papers are distributed and returned by first class post; (b) 14 days if second class post is used for either the distribution or return of voting papers.
	Para.62 The union should consider delaying any call for industrial action following a ballot until it has obtained the scrutineer's report.
VOTERS	No recommendations.
CAMPAIGNING	No recommendations.
BALLOTING METHODS	Para.11 Where more than one union decides to ballot members working for the same employer in the same dispute, the arrangements for the different ballots should be co-ordinated so that, as far as practicable, they are held and the results announced simultaneously.
	Para.41 Arrangements should be such as to ensure that no mistakes are made which might invalidate the ballot through a failure to satisfy the statutory requirements. If in doubt about the nature of such arrangements in any particular case, the union should seek the advice of the independent scrutineer and be guided by that advice. If there is no independent scrutineer or if the union decides it cannot follow the scrutineer's advice, it should in any case consider (a) printing the voting papers on a security background to prevent duplication; (b) whether the arrangements for printing the voting papers, and for their distribution to those entitled to vote, offer all concerned sufficient assurance of security.
	Para.46 The union should ensure that all of its members, officials, and other employees who might—even inadvertently—interfere with or constrain those entitled to vote are aware of the potential consequences if their behaviour was regarded as having either of these effects.

TABLE 4.4. (*Continued*)

Para.47 The union should make adequate arrangements so that those entitled to vote are supplied with pre-paid reply envelopes with the voting paper so that they do not have to incur any postal costs themselves in order to vote.

Para.48 The union should make arrangements so that each of its members properly entitled to vote is supplied with a voting paper. Special arrangements may be needed to get voting papers to members who are on holiday, sickness, or maternity leave during the time when the balloting will take place so that, as far as practicable, they receive voting papers and have a convenient opportunity to vote.

Para.49 The union should establish an appropriate checking system so that (a) no-one properly entitled to vote is accidently disenfranchised; and (b) no uncompleted voting paper comes into the hands of anyone not properly entitled to vote who might use it to cast a vote to which he is not entitled. If the union is in doubt about what is required by way of such checking, advice should be sought from the independent scrutineer.

Para.50 For all ballots, any list of those entitled to vote should be compiled, and the voting papers themselves handled, so as to preserve the anonymity of the voter so far as this is consistent with the proper conduct of the ballot.

Para.51 The union should take sufficient steps to ensure that a voter's anonymity is preserved when a voting paper is returned. This means, for example, that: (a) envelopes in which voting papers are to be posted should have no distinguishing marks from which the identity of the voter can be established; (b) the procedures for counting papers should not prejudice the statutory requirement for secret voting.

BALLOT PAPER

Para.37 The relevant question/s should be simply expressed and appear on the voting paper separately from any other question that might also appear. Voters should not be misled or confused by the framing of the required question/s.[2]

Para.38 The union should ensure that neither the required question/s, nor anything else which appears on the voting paper, is presented in such a way which might encourage a voter to answer one way rather than another as a result of that presentation.

Para.40 The union should include on the voting papers information to protect the security of the balloting process.[3]

Paras. 26 & 31 The relevant union individual/s or body who would authorize or endorse the relevant industrial action should have responsibility for establishing the proper 'balloting constituency' for the ballot and decide if votes are to be aggregated across different workplaces.[4] Para.30 gives examples of aggregation across different workplaces to explain 'balloting constituencies': examples are (a) all of a union's members employed in a particular occupation by the same employer or number of employers; or (b) all of a union's members who share a particular term or condition of employment because their terms and conditions are determined by the same established collective bargaining arrangements.

Para.54:The union should consider, and apply, the following procedures:[5]

(a) destruction of unused or unissued voting papers as soon as possible after voting and voting paper-checking has taken place;

(b) rejection of late voting papers;

(c) settlement of arrangements well in advance of the ballot;

(d) proper briefing of those doing the count;

(e) ensuring no votes are counted at any location until after the official close;

(f) storage of voting papers in a locked and secure room until counting;

(g) making a neutral individual responsible for adjudicating on 'spoiled' voting papers and ensuring all such voting papers are referred to him/her;

(h) regularly removing any envelopes from the counting area after opening;

(i) locking and securing the counting room when counting staff are not present;

(j) ensuring counting staff were not disturbed or distracted by any person with a particular interest in the result during the count;

(k) storage of voting papers once counted in a secure place for at least six months after the ballot. The union should also consider putting the counting exercise as a whole into the hands of the independent scrutineer.

Para.16 The scrutineer's appointment should be made before steps are taken to satisfy any of the other requirements of the law. If such steps are completed before the scrutineer's appointment, it may be more difficult for the scrutineer to satisfy himself as to whether what was done conformed to the legal requirement.

TABLE 4.4. (*Continued*)

	Para.17 Where it would be helpful as a means of ensuring adequate standards for the conduct of the ballot, it is open to a union to entrust the scrutineer to carry out additional tasks on the union's behalf, such as supervising the production and distribution of voting papers, being the person to whom the voting papers are returned by those voting in the ballot, and retaining custody of all returned voting papers for a set period after the ballot.
	Para.18 While the scrutiny requirement applies to ballots only where more than 50 members are entitled to vote, even where fewer members are involved a union should make adequate arrangements for scrutiny of the ballot.
	Members—preparing for an industrial action ballot[6]
	Para.43 A union should give relevant information to its members entitled to vote, including:
	(a) background to the ballot and the issues to which the dispute relates;
	(b) nature and timing of the industrial action which the union may be prepared to authorize or endorse depending on the ballot result;
	(c) any considerations in respect of turn-out or size of majority that will be relevant to the decision on whether to authorize or endorse industrial action after the ballot;
	(d) potential consequences for workers of taking industrial action.[7]
INFORMING MEMBERS AND EMPLOYERS	Para.44 The union should take steps to ensure that any information it supplies to members in connection with the ballot is accurate and does not mislead voters in the process of forming their opinions about which way to vote. The union should consider (a) preparing a standard statement for inclusion with information issued in connection with the ballot about the possible effects on individual workers of taking industrial action (such as the employees' loss of their rights to take a case of unfair dismissal to an IT if they are dismissed whilst taking industrial action); and (b) making arrangements which will enable it to review, to ensure its factual accuracy, any information which its members, officials, or employees propose to issue in connection with a ballot or ballot voting papers.

Members—following an industrial action ballot

Para. 67 A union should inform all its members of its decision to induce industrial action, and its reasons for doing so, before inducing them to take or continue that action.

Employers—preparing for an industrial action ballot

Para. 20 In order to help ensure that the requirement to supply the employer with written notice of the ballot is met, a union may wish to send it out so as to allow itself sufficient time to check with the employer that the notice has been received and that the opening day of the ballot is at least seven days after the date when the notice was received. The union may also find it helpful to check that the employer believes the notice to describe, sufficiently clearly, the employees entitled to vote.[8]

Para. 24 To help ensure that the requirement to supply the employer with a sample/s voting paper is met, a union may wish to send it/them out so as to allow itself sufficient time to check with the employer that it/them has/have been received, and that the opening day of the ballot is at least three days after the date when the voting paper(s) was/were received.

---

[1] Note that there is no statutory obligation on a union to ballot, or otherwise consult, its members before it decides to call off industrial action; however, if a union decides to seek to ballot its members' views about continuing with industrial action, it should apply the same standards as in this Code (para. 68).

[2] Union members should not be led to believe, for example, that they are being asked to agree to an opinion about the union's view of the merits of the dispute/potential dispute. Nor should a voter be asked if he is prepared to 'support' industrial action as part of the question which asks him if he is prepared to take part in/continue with it.

[3] The Code gives examples of voting papers on pp. 12 & 13.

[4] The union was enjoined to review the statutory requirements when deciding how to aggregate votes.

[5] This is a brief summary of detailed recommendations.

[6] The Code also suggests in order to help the union ensure that a ballot's result can be notified as required, that the union should consider for example (a) designating a 'Returning Officer' (centralized count) or 'Returning Officers' (different location counts) to whom the results will be notified in the required form prior to their announcement; (b) organizing the counting of votes in the form required by statute; (c) utilizing its own journals, local communication news-sheets, company or union notice-boards to publicize the ballot result; and (d) checking with relevant employers that the ballot results notified to them have arrived and are understood.

TABLE 4.4. (*Continued*)

[7] The union's view of the issues and background may differ markedly from that of the employer(s) concerned in the dispute; however, there is no recommendation that employers should be given the chance to put their side to the union members. The 1988 Draft Code's suggestion that employers should be given this chance was dropped (*IRLIB* 387 24.10.89: 6).

[8] Paras. 21 and 22 offer more recommendations for unions to assist them in helping employers to identify those entitled to vote. The union has a duty under TURERA 1993 to provide a written notice which enables an employer to ascertain which of his employees will be entitled to vote. These two paragraphs offer the union advice on the amount of detail the employer might need: factors the union may need to take into account are the employer's own level of information about his work-force, his work-force's size and turnover, the variety of work undertaken and number of work locations; even the names and workplace locations of employees possibly entitled to vote may be needed. Past experience helps in demonstrating the employer's needs.

Para.27 adds that if entitlement to vote is actually given to employees other than those covered by the employer's notice—or that entitlement is given to significantly fewer employees than in the notice—the union should do its best to pass on the relevant information to the employer/s concerned as soon as possible.

decision-making in the taking of industrial action. We note also that the 1994 Draft Code's recommendations reduced even further the unions' ability to take industrial action swiftly[84] and continued the Conservatives' prescriptive and detailed approach to the legal regulation of union activities.

CONCLUSION: THE BALLOTING LAWS IN 1995 AND THEIR FUTURE DEVELOPMENTS

Since 1983 the Conservatives have radically reversed the traditional British approach towards union autonomy. In 1995 the body of legal regulations for the conduct of union elections and calling of industrial action possesses an extraordinary density and complexity, and unions and employers frequently require legal advice for previously simple decisions, such as when it is lawful to call a strike. In the early period the focus was on legislating for union elections, later the emphasis switched to industrial action, and by 1995 the weight of regulation affecting elections and industrial action ballots is relatively even. Some aspects of the balloting process for elections and industrial action are now very heavily regulated, particulary supervision, while others are more lightly regulated, such as campaigning. Some aspects, such as the nomination of candidates, have not been regulated at all. The chosen means of enforcement are complex and the Government has resolutely looked to other parties in the industrial relations process to enforce the legislative provisions—including customers, even if they are not entitled to the goods or services of whose disrupted supply they are complaining. As a consequence of this, the Conservatives have felt the need to provide a significant level of assistance for litigants. While the Government has kept at arm's length from the enforcement of its regulations, its covert encouragement of dissident members, maverick employers, and, perhaps soon, anti-union customers, has been significant in the enforcement process.

The ideological content of the Conservatives' regulations revolves around the attempt to introduce a limited version of Hayek's non-union vision, with the emphasis on individual decision-making by members at the expense of collectivism and solidarity. Accordingly, the regulations, introduced in the name of 'democracy', bear on unions alone: companies, banks, the political parties, and others have not had these standards of 'democracy' imposed on them. This is because of what unions 'are': Wedderburn (1989: 25–6) argues that the Conservatives did not apply their demands for 'democracy' to golf clubs because golf clubs do not represent an obstacle to the competitive market or a threat to individuals and private property. 'The unionized group of workers receives special treatment because of what it *is*' (ibid. 26).

The Conservatives' predilection for the legal reform of industrial relations continues and if they remain in power, it is to be seen if more and more layers of cement will be poured over the legislation to cover its cracks as unions continue to adapt to their legal restraints and strive to survive as effective organizations in a difficult economic environment. For the Conservatives, the possibilities of discovering union 'abuses' seem endless. During the signal workers' dispute in the summer of 1994, Michael Portillo revived, yet again, Conservative plans for outlawing strikes in essential services, which he felt would complete 'the unfinished business of trade union reform' (*The Independent* 30.8.94): ironically, such a ban would set aside the Conservatives' elaborate construct of hurdles for the taking of lawful industrial action and place unwelcome pressure on the Government to re-establish arbitration procedures. Additionally, at the end of this four-month dispute, Michael Portillo asked Employment Department officials to examine the possibility of enforcing refresher ballots for ascertaining whether support for industrial action is maintained (*Independent* 29.9.94). Yet later, in March 1995, the same Secretary of State, in common with a number of his predecessors, stated that there would be no further legislation for union reform (*FT*, 2.3.95) as industrial relations were now 'very good'.

The Labour Party has not published any recent proposals on their intentions, should they return to power, regarding retaining, reforming, or abolishing the balloting regulations. In the area of industrial relations more Labour Party attention has been focused on union recognition, a minimum wage, right to union representation at work, and the enhancement of individual rights. *People at Work: New Rights, New Responsibilities*, the report of the TUC-Labour Party Liaison Committee 1986, contains the fullest exposition of their views. The Labour Party's principle is that membership involvement and participation in union decisions must be assisted, and its aim is to provide a framework of measures to underpin the participative rights of union members to replace the present rigid Conservative measures. General principles would be laid down by statute for inclusion in union rule books, giving union members rights to secret ballots as the method of election for union executives and for taking decisions relating to strikes. However, the right of enforcement would belong only to union members and not to employers, their suppliers, or their customers. A new independent tribunal would be established, in consultation with the TUC, which would have the duty of hearing union members' complaints that the statutory principles have been breached. This tribunal would adopt a conciliatory and flexible approach, but would ultimately be empowered to require a union to take steps to remedy the complaint. In common with other tribunals, appeal to the ordinary courts would only be permitted on a point of law.

In the next two chapters we examine the effect of the above incremental and enabling balloting legislation on, respectively, union elections and the calling of industrial action.

NOTES

1. To save space, the tables refer to 'he' alone; however, the text refers to 'he/she' whenever appropriate.
2. Control of the powers of union officials through the contract of membership is supplemented by fiduciary constraints, although the application of these fiduciary principles to unions is uncertain (Elias and Ewing 1987: 96–7). NUM officials were held to be in breach of their fiduciary duties in the 1984–5 miners' dispute in their application of union funds (Miller 1986: 296).
3. Wedderburn would not agree with the interpretation of his views as saying that Hayek 'wrote' the Conservatives' programme of union reform. Instead, Wedderburn's main point (1989) is that the character of labour legislation can be better understood and its future course better predicted by reference to Hayek's framework than to any other. Similar views to Wedderburn's, though argued in less detail, are those of Muckenberger and Deakin (1989), McCarthy (1987), and Fredman (1992). Other writers in this area with different versions of the ideological influences on the Conservative government are Crouch (1986) and Hendy (1991).
4. For a fuller discussion see Fosh *et al.* (1993a) and the interesting paper 'Balloting before Industrial Action' TURU (1989).
5. See for example the autobiographies of Jim Prior (1986) and Norman Tebbit (1988).
6. The Secretaries of State for Employment since 1979 were appointed on the following dates:

Jim Prior	3 May 1979
Norman Tebbit	14 September 1981
Tom King	16 October 1983
Lord Young	2 September 1985
Norman Fowler	13 June 1987
Michael Howard	13 January 1990
Gillian Shepherd	12 April 1992
David Hunt	27 May 1993
Michael Portillo	20 July 1994

7. See the Conservatives' 1979 election manifesto (CCO 1979).
8. For a detailed discussion of the passage of the EA 1980, see Undy and Martin (1984: 25–35).
9. In the debate over Clause 1 in the House of Commons, attention was focused by the steel strike (which began in January 1980) on the desirability of voluntary strike ballots, particulary by ISTC's decision to call out private sector steel workers without a ballot. Right-wing members of the House of Commons expressed disquiet over the lack of a right for union members to be consulted before strike decisions were taken by their leaders: this rebellion was

unsuccessful but served notice that Jim Prior's gradualist approach to union reform might not be sustained. A prescient worry expressed by Labour MPs was that if the provision of funds for postal ballots did not produce the increase in balloting the Conservatives expected, then the government would be tempted to make ballots compulsory.

10. See Table 4.1, n. 1 for the regulations for the refund of balloting expenses in 1995.
11. Note that the employer was not obligated to offer time off to vote or attend meetings to discuss issues related to the ballot.
12. For a detailed discussion of union response to the balloting refund proposals, see Undy and Martin (1984: chs. 1 and 4) and McIlroy (1991: ch. 2).
13. The General Council recommended that affiliated unions 'should not' make use of Clause 1 of the 1980 Act but did not specify what penalties would be imposed on unions failing to comply. The AUEW(E) and the EETPU continued, along with Equity, seriously to consider applying for Government funding. However, the AUEW(E)'s national committee meeting in May 1981 voted against applying for funding and the EETPU decided not to expose itself to the wrath of the TUC.
14. Equity applied to the CO in 1982 for balloting refunds but later withdrew its application in line with TUC policy (Undy and Martin 1984: 174–5).
15. For a detailed account of the response and experiences of non-TUC unions, see Undy and Martin (1984: 176–83).
16. For a fuller discussion of the positions of the CBI and the IOD, see Undy and Martin (1984: ch. 1).
17. In September 1979, 77% of a Gallop poll replied 'too powerful' when asked 'Do you think trade unions are becoming too powerful, are not powerful enough, or the balance is about right?' (GMB 1991: 17).
18. The Conservatives' argument for the necessity for legislation to protect the rights and freedom of union members rings oddly on two counts: first, the Government omits from its reasoning the probability that pressure for a personal secret ballot is an unlikely response from members of a voluntary association where a degree of communality of interest is assumed; and second, the Government itself had introduced measures limiting the practice of the closed shop (Mackie 1984: 89; see also Elias 1990). Although in the later 1980s and 1990s the Conservatives successively legislated both against the closed shop and for workers to join a union of their choice, they continued to argue for the necessity to protect union members from the abuse of their rights by their leaders.
19. In semi-postal ballots ballot papers are issued by workplace representatives and returned through the post.
20. The alternatives presented were prescribing standard provisions (which might directly require changes in unions' rules and electoral arrangements), requiring unions to secure approval of their election rules and arrangements from some public authority, and laying down the principles to be followed in the conduct of all union elections in the form of a statutory right for members. The Government also suggested alternative court sanctions to the present penalties for contempt of court for a significant breach of a court order. These were the removal of named union officials from their 'executive status'; the freezing of

union assets; the deposit of union funds in court; and the loss of union privileges (immunities or removal from the CO's list and consequent loss of tax relief).

21. According to Gallup, in each of the years between 1979 and 1984, a clear majority of members of the public answered approvingly the question 'Do you approve or disapprove of the government's plans to reform trade union law?'; the majority declined, though, from +35% in 1979 to +13% in 1984 (GMB 1991: 11). MORI also showed that a majority agreed with the statement that 'Most trade unions are controlled by a few extremists and militants': the majority ranging from +50% in 1980 to +40% in 1984 (18). Marsh (1992: 57) reports a Gallup finding in 1983 that 88 per cent of members of the public approved of union leaders being elected by secret ballots.

22. The Conservatives' election manifesto proposed that, as some union leaders were still abusing their power, the Conservatives would, on their return to office, legislate to give union members the right to hold ballots for union governing bodies.

23. *Proposals for Legislation on Democracy in Trade Unions* proposed that union governing bodies be directly elected by secret ballots (postal or workplace) in which all members had 'an equal and unrestricted opportunity to vote' (Undy and Martin 1984: 40).

24. Wedderburn (1985) is of the opinion that TUA 1984 applies to some branch executives where the branch falls within the legal definition of a 'trade union' (s.28 TULRA 1974). In *Re: National Union of Mineworkers (Yorkshire Area)* 17.3.94 and 14.4.1994 (D/3-4/94), the CO examined the federal structure of the NUM and decided that the general secretary and executive of the Yorkshire Area had not been elected in accordance with the statutory provisions. At the time of the complaint the union was already in the process of transferring engagements from the constituent areas to the national union and this decision accelerated that process.

25. The CO is usually the first port of call for members who want to take action against their unions for failing to comply with the legislation covering union elections and his judgments have generally been more punitive than those of the courts. For example in *Re: Society of Graphical and Allied Trades 1982* 5.10.90 (D/3/90) and *Re: National Union of Mineworkers (Yorkshire Area)* 17.3.94 and 14.4.94 (D/3-4/94), the CO ruled that retired members and unemployed members have a right to complain about a union's electoral procedures (*IRLIB* 414 7.12.90). He justified his decision on the ground that the legislation does not define what is meant by the term member. However, it is questionable whether the courts would have judged these individuals to be members of their respective unions. In both cases, the members concerned had a separate status under their union's rules and were specifically precluded from entitlement to stand or vote in the election of union officers.

26. The choice for the union was not, in fact, between workplace and postal ballots, but between 'pure' postal ballots, workplace ballots, and 'hybrid' ballots. *Branch* ballots away from the workplace were now unlawful.

27. In terms of the requirement in TUA 1984 for freedom from interference in voting, the CO has limited his intervention to the wording of the statute, in contrast to his more punitive approach to other election requirements. For

example, in *Re: Film Artistes Association* 11.4.86 (D/2/86), the CO decided that telephone campaigning by a candidate in the union's NEC elections could not amount to interference or constraint within the terms of s.2(6)(a) TUA 1984. Similar decisions have been reached in complaints concerning the contents of a union's election ballot paper; in *Re: Paul and National and Local Government Officers' Association* 30.9.1986 (D/14/86), *Re: Union of Shop, Distributive and Allied Workers* 17.8.89 (D/3/89), and *Re: Union of Shop Distributive and Allied Workers* 13.1.94 (D/1-2/94), the CO declared that the practice of including a list of nominating branches on the union's election ballot paper did not contravene this requirement (now s.51(3)(a) TULR(C)A 1992). In the last of these cases, there was some evidence that the incumbent post holder had been given greater help by the union establishment in gaining nominations and had also benefited from the endorsement of the union's EC. However, the CO observed that s.51(3)(a) referred to freedom from interference in the *process of voting*; the matters about which the member complained were not part of this process (para.1.21).

28. For a discussion of the difference between entitlement to vote and supplying a member with a voting paper, see the discussion of the industrial action ballot requirements of TUA 1984 below. Early declarations by the CO took a particularly punitive line when determining whether unions had done all that was reasonably practicable to ensure that union members were afforded an opportunity to vote, and that, 'as far as reasonably practicable', the voter was able to vote without incurring any direct cost to him/herself. For example in *Re: General Municipal and Allied Trades Union* 14.10.88 (D/3/88), a member complained that at least 370 members were unable to vote in the elections for the PEC because they did not receive ballot papers—though the outcome of the election was unaffected by this omission (*IRLIB* 377, 23.5.89). The GMBATU had introduced a new and elaborate system for the 1987 elections but printing problems had delayed the distribution of voting papers. The chief scrutineer for the Ayrshire general branch refused to co-operate in distributing the voting papers to his area officials on the basis that the voting period had already begun. The regional officials quickly took over the chief scrutineer's duty and delivered the voting papers to all but two of the area officials responsible for ensuring eligible members had the opportunity to vote—in these two areas the area scrutineers refused to accept the papers. The regional officials took no further action, having concluded there was insufficient time to deliver voting papers to all those affected and that a selective approach was unacceptable. The GMBATU argued it had done all that was reasonably practicable to provide members with an opportunity to vote by the provision of an election system that would have been adequate if it had not been for the deliberate refusal of two officials to perform their duties. The CO held that the regional officials should have taken steps to distribute voting papers to some of the affected members and that their attempt to be even-handed was misplaced as 'the right to an opportunity to vote belongs to each member individually' (ibid. 10). He declared that the union had failed to do all that was reasonably practicable to ensure that members were supplied with a voting paper and an opportunity to vote. More recent decisions by the CO have been less draconian and have adopted the courts' interpretation of 'so far as reasonably

practicable'. Thus in *Re: Confederation of Health Service Employees* 17.8.90 (D/2/90) the CO refused to make a declaration that the union's postal ballot arrangements fell short of the statutory requirements on the ground that their register of members' names and addresses was not accurate and up to date (*IRLIB* 411, 19.10.90). Three members and a number of others complained that they had not received ballot papers. The CO concluded that the union's efforts to compile and maintain a comprehensive register of members' names and addresses were very impressive—particularly given the union's high membership turnover and the fact that employers (over whom it had no control) had not generally co-operated. TUA 1984 required only that the union ensure 'so far as is reasonably practicable' that members received voting papers but not to guarantee delivery of a voting paper to every member entitled to vote. In the CO's opinion the irregularities could be dismissed as being *de minimis* within the scope of the observations of Lord Donaldson in *British Railways Board* v. *National Union of Railwaymen* [1989] concerning a strike ballot (see below). See also *Re: National Union of Civil and Public Service Employees* 1.5.91 (D/1/91).

29. Note that the ballot is *not* invalidated if the voter is constrained from exercising his/her right to vote by an employer or third party (*IRLIB* 267, 23.10.84: 3; Kidner 1984: 203).

30. Note that in *Re: Paul* v. *National and Local Government Officers' Association* 30.9.86 (D/15/86), the CO upheld the applicant's complaint that the union's requirement for members who wished to vote postally to pay the costs of return postage was an infringement of the requirement in TUA 1984 to provide an opportunity to vote without incurring any direct cost. He dismissed NALGO's argument that an alternative opportunity for the member to vote without cost existed at the workplace.

31. Note that in *R.* v. *Certification Officer for Trade Unions ex parte Electrical Power Engineers' Association* [1990] IRLR 398, the Court of Appeal restored the CO's decision (quashed by the High Court) that the result of the ballot for the union's NEC had not been determined solely by counting the number of votes cast for each candidate and therefore the ballot did not qualify for a refund (*IRLIB* 394, 6.2.90). According to the union's rule book, one candidate was held to be unsuccessful, although he had received more votes than three elected candidates, on the ground that the quota for candidates from his division had already been filled. The court rejected the union's argument *inter alia* that further words should be implied to require that the election was determined in accordance with the reasonable rules of the union.

32. Note that in *Re: Paul* v. *National and Local Government Officers' Association* 30.10.86 (D/9/86), the CO decided that a member will be treated as 'unreasonably excluded' from candidature under s.2(9) TUA 1984 if the nomination procedure, although not actually closed, effectively precludes 'any real possibility that the ordinary member will put himself forward' (para.11). The union's nomination procedure for Junior President was such that it effectively precluded applications by ordinary members.

33. This contrasts with the USA, where the courts exercise considerable control under the Landrum–Griffin Act 1959 over the exclusion of classes (Kidner 1984: 206).

34. A place might be reserved for a woman on the PEC but all members of the union must be allowed to vote, unless there is a separately organized women's section with officers of its own (Kidner 1984: 198).
35. Note that the employer was put under no obligation to make a check-off list of members available to the union. Note that *Re: Association of University Teachers* 7.7.93 (D/3/93) the CO decided that there was no express requirement for a union to hold the members' names and addresses in one place.
36. The new Secretary of State Lord Young, in contrast to Norman Tebbit and Tom King, had little enthusiasm for legislation on union reform.
37. A striking illustration of the new mood was the defeat of the NGA's motion at the 1984 TUC's Annual Conference committing the TUC to automatic support for unions in conflict with the new laws (Marsh 1992: 72).
38. Influential here was a report by the centre-right Policy Research Associates (Loveday 1987) on the extent to which the 22 largest unions had adopted postal ballots for union elections. The report concluded that the time had come for the Government to close the 'ballot rigger's favourite loophole' (7) and make secret postal ballots mandatory for the election of union leaders.
39. The Government did acknowledge that there was as yet 'no evidence to suggest that gross malpractice is at all commonplace' (DE 1987: 25).
40. Thus in a MORI poll (1987) only 36% now answered 'too powerful' in response to the question 'Do you think trade unions are becoming too powerful, are not powerful enough, or the balance is about right?' (GMB 1991: 17).
41. *The Next Moves Forward* (CCO 1987) stated that the Conservatives would introduce legislation to ensure that all union governing bodies were elected by secret ballot at least once every five years, to make independent supervision for postal ballots compulsory, and to establish a new Commissioner to help individual union members enforce their fundamental rights (24).
42. Note that in *Re: Society of Graphical and Allied Trades 1982* 5.10.90 (D/3/90), the CO upheld a complaint that three non-voting members of the NEC (the President and two general officers) remained committee members for more than five years after their election without re-election. The union maintained that the three officers were not members of the NEC. However, the CO declared that the post of President was specifically mentioned in s.1 TUA 1984, as extended by s.12(1) EA 1988, as requiring election and, according to the union's own rules, the two general officers were NEC members.
43. TUA 1984 permitted both postal and workplace ballots and s.8 provided protection for those members elected by either means whose five-year term expired shortly before they were due to retire: they could remain members of the PEC without re-election until they retired provided that (i) they had been elected in accordance with the provisions of TUA 1984 at most 10 years before retirement; (ii) they were full-time union employees and had been full-time union employees for at least 5 years; (iii) they were entitled under their union rules to continue as holder of their position until retirement age. S.14(2) EA 1988 allowed only postal ballots for PEC elections after 26 July 1988. Para.5(5) of Schedule 3 of EA 1988 amends s.8 of TUA 1984: where a PEC member was elected by a workplace ballot before 26 July 1988 this member could not rely on s.8 TUA 1984 unless he/she was a voting PEC member. Since Ron Todd and

Arthur Scargill were both non-voting PEC members who had been elected by workplace ballots before 26 July 1988, they therefore had to stand for re-election before retirement.

44. It is interesting to note, in view of TURERA 1993's requirement for industrial action ballots to be postal, that the Conservatives rejected postal strike ballots in the House of Lords debate during the passage of EA 1988, on the grounds that such a proposal was 'impractical' (McKendrick 1988: 158).

45. Note that in *Re: Civil and Public Servants Association* 27.5.94 (D/5/94), the CO declared that the union had failed to satisfy s.52 TULR(C)A 1992 (scrutineer's report) in the 1993 ballot to elect PEC members. Although the union had announced the result of the ballot at its Annual Conference and had communicated the details to branch secretaries, the full details of the scrutineer's report were not made available to members and the statement advising members that a copy of the report would be provided on request was omitted.

46. See the list of examples of events and political pressures influencing Conservative legislation in Fosh *et al.* (1993: 28). The Government did react to events and pressures before 1988; for example, the provisions of EA 1980 owe much to the 1980 steel strike. However, we argue that this tendency became considerably more marked in the drafting of EA 1988, EA 1990, and TURERA 1993.

47. The ILO Committee of Experts (1989) reviewed British legislation of the 1980s to see if the overall effects were compatible with Convention 87, particularly with Article 3: its conclusion with respect to union election and industrial action ballots was that the requirements imposed by the British Government were not incompatible with Convention 87. However, the Committee did express its concern at the volume and complexity of UK legislative change since 1980. It made the point that, while most of the measures are not incompatible with the requirements of the Convention, there was a point at which the cumulative effect of legislative changes, which are in themselves consistent with the principles of freedom of association, may yet by virtue of their complexity and extent constitute an incursion upon the rights guaranteed by the Convention.

48. In a MORI survey commissioned by NALGO in August 1990, in response to the question 'In the past 10 years a range of new laws has been introduced to restrict trade union organization and action. On balance, do you think this legislation has gone too far, or not far enough?' 33% replied 'too far' and only 24% 'not far enough' (GMB 1991: 11–12). The response to an NOP survey in July 1991 produced a considerable majority disagreeing that there was any need for more union legislation. Moreover, the NALGO survey also found that 73% of the electorate felt that unions should determine their rules and constitutions through their own democratic procedures. The electorate's changing perception of unions is illustrated by the fact that the proportion in the MORI survey agreeing that unions are controlled by a few extremists and militants dropped to 50% in August 1990 (compare with n.21).

49. During her first few months of office, CROTUM (Gill Rowlands) had been forced to turn away applications for assistance from union members with

grievances concerning rule-book matters. For CROTUM's limited accomplishment during her first year of office, see her first Annual Report, in which she called for this increase in her powers (*IRLIB* 386, 10.10.89).

50. In July 1991, NOP asked the poll question 'In the past twelve years, the Government has introduced 7 pieces of legislation limiting the rights of trade unions and their members. Do you feel there is a need for any more legislation?'. While this question is to some extent loaded, yet it is significant that only 18% who replied agreed that there was (GMB 1991: 11). See also the results of a MORI survey commissioned by NALGO in August 1990 (ibid. 11–12).

51. There were a number of calls for consolidation from employers in their responses to *Industrial Relations in the 1990s*. See also McKendrick (1988: 160–1).

52. The suggestion in *Industrial Relations in the 1990s* that union members be allowed to inspect the register was not taken up.

53. S.7 TURERA 1993 repealed ss.115 and 116 TULR(C)A 1992.

54. SI 1993 No. 233 *Trade Unions: The Funds for Trade Union Ballots Regulations (Revocation) Regulations 1993*.

55. Note that the legislation does not *prevent* an employer from providing facilities for ballots.

56. If the Government were interested in the intrinsic values of balloting *per se*, that is in increasing a member's control over decisions affecting his/her interests, one would have expected *Democracy in Trade Unions* to have included proposals for ballots to accept employers' offers and call off industrial action; see Auerbach (1990: 128, 154, 161) and Mackie (1984: 87). Norman Tebbit excluded such ballots from consideration on the ground that unions enjoy legal immunity for breach of contract, but there is no breach of contract once the strike is over (Auerbach 1990: 135).

57. However, see *Boxfoldia* below (n. 65).

58. According to a Gallup poll, 83% of the public approved the Governemnt's proposal for secret ballots before strikes (March 1992: 57).

59. In *Proposals for Legislation on Democracy in Trade Unions*, the Government proposed the sanction of union loss of immunity, as did the Trade Union Bill, though amendments during the debates widened its scope considerably.

60. A number of cases in the late 1980s and early 1990s demonstrated that union organizers needed to be careful that the ballot provided 'authority' for the industrial action in question (Simpson 1993: 289–90). In *London Underground Limited* v. *National Union of Railwaymen* [1989] *IRLR* 341, Simon Brown J. granted an injunction restraining the union from organizing industrial action on the grounds that a circular accompanying the ballot paper identified four issues over which the union was in dispute with LUL, of which only one of these clearly satisfied the statutory definition of a trade dispute. This decision is in marked contrast to the view of Millet J. in *Associated British Ports* v. *TGWU* [1989] *IRLR* 291, who suggested that all that was required was that the strike called was the one voted for. More recently this issue was raised in *Newham London Borough Council* v. *NALGO* [1993] ICR 189, 198, but according to Simpson (ibid. 289) the Court of Appeal unnecessarily and undesirably confused the validity of a ballot and the

requirement for industrial action to be in contemplation or furtherance of a dispute.

61. The Government rejected amendments to confine the remedy to the employer and not to give third parties a right of action: its reasoning appeared to be to maximize the effectiveness of the legislation (Auerbach 1990: 139).

62. In the miners' dispute 1984–5, some NUM Areas balloted as unions in their own right and according to their rule books. However, several of these Areas failed to show majority support and, according to Auerbach (1990: 151), the Government drew attention to these results to make a political point suggesting that a national ballot, had Arthur Scargill called one, would have been lost. Hutton (1984: 218) also notes the importance of pressure from right-wing back-benchers for this change. He also points out that a number of union rule books actually required more than a simple majority for calling strike action, for example the NUM, the GMWU, and the AUEW(E).

63. In two important cases the issue of the validity of temporary suspension of industrial action and subsequent recommencement of such action was considered. In *Monsanto PLC* v. *TGWU* [1987] ICR 269, the Court of Appeal held that a union could lawfully suspend industrial action in order to consider an improved offer from the employer and, if the offer was deemed unsatisfactory, the action could recommence without the requirement of a further ballot. This general right to suspend action, however, has limits. In *Post Office* v. *Union of Communication Workers* [1990] ICR 258, the suspension of industrial action as a tactic in a dispute and its recommencement later when the circumstances surrounding the dispute had changed was held by the Court of Appeal to require a new ballot (Simpson 1993: 293–4).

64. Lord Donaldson rejected British Rail's contention that the NUR had infringed s.11(2) and/or s.11(6)(a) since 200 members had inadvertently not had ballot papers either supplied or made available to them (Simpson 1989: 235–6). He held that there was 'a profound difference' between such inadvertence and denying a member entitlement to vote for the purposes of s.11(2). Nor did he hold that BR's evidence was strong enough to establish a failure on the NUR's part to satisfy S.11(6)(a). The Court of Appeal dismissed BR's appeal against Vinelott J.'s refusal to grant an injunction restraining the NUR from going ahead with a 24-hour strike the following day. BR also submitted that 6,000 members entitled to vote had not received a ballot paper. Here Lord Donaldson held it was clear that BR was in error, as s.11(6)(a) provides only that members have voting papers made available to them, not necessarily sent to them.

65. Notable cases where injunctions were issued ordering the union to call off industrial action were *Austin Rover Group Ltd.* v. *Amalgamated Union of Engineering Workers (TASS)* [1985] *IRLR* 162 and *Solihull Metropolitan Borough Council* v. *National Union of Teachers* [1985] *IRLR* 211. In the Solihull case, the union argued that its call to members to refuse to cover for absent colleagues and to withdraw from certain activities during lunch-time and outside normal hours did not constitute an inducement to breach of contract on the ground that these activities were not part of its members' contracts of employment. Warner J. held that, since there was a serious question to be tried as to whether or not these activities were contractual obligations, the union had

committed inducement of breach of contract in calling for industrial action without first having held a ballot. In the Rover case and in *Boxfoldia* v. *National Graphical Association (1982)* [1988] IRLR 393, the employer was successful in claiming damages. In the *Boxfoldia* case, the union wrote to the employer on behalf of its members stating that in fourteen days' time, its members would withdraw their labour from the company. The company argued that the union should have held a ballot. The union responded that its letter gave contractual notice on behalf of its members and, as the contractual notice of termination of most of the employees concerned was two weeks, there had been no inducement to breach of contract. Savile J. held that the notification letter could not be construed as signalling the end of the members' contracts of employment and, in the absence of a ballot, the union had unlawfully induced its members to breach their contracts of employment.

66. In Gallup polls conducted in 1984, public opinion was firmly on the employer's side; in particular, members of the public were critical of the 'irresponsible' methods used by the miners; this stands in stark contrast to opinions on the miners' strikes in the early 1970s (GMB 1991: 19).

67. S.18 EA 1988 built on s.3(1) EA 1980, which empowered the Secretary of State to issue Codes of Practice containing such practical guidance as he thought fit for the purpose of promoting the improvement of industrial relations (S.203 TULR(C)A 1992).

68. TUA 1984, as we saw above, required the ballot question/s (however framed) to contain the statement that the action required the voter to take part or continue to take part in industrial action involving him/her in a breach of contract. In the prescribed ballot paper statement laid down in EA 1988, this certainty had to be changed to a *possibility*, as the proposed action did not necessarily involve a breach of the employment contract. Thus the text of the warning is: 'If you take part in a strike or other industrial action, you may be in breach of your contract of employment'.

69. S.17 soon gave rise to legal action. In *University of Central England and Kingston University* v. *NALGO* [1992] IRLR 81 Latham J. refused to grant an injunction restraining strike action by NALGO members. He rejected the employers' argument that the legislation always required unions to hold separate ballots of their members for each employer. In his opinion the common factor exception clearly contemplated a ballot covering workers with different employers, as was the case with the NALGO members who were employed by the former polytechnics and whose conditions of service were negotiated by one body (Simpson 1993: 291).

70. The remedy for a union member alleging that he/she had been 'unjustifiably disciplined' was a complaint to an Industrial Tribunal (IT). S.3 EA 1988 became ss.64–7 TULR(C)A 1992.

71. The evidence on the public's opinion is mixed. GMB (1991: 12, 19–20, 25) present Gallup evidence of strong support for the 1990 ambulance workers' dispute, and to a lesser extent for railway workers, dockers, and local authority workers in the disputes in 1989, whereas on the other hand the questions commissioned by the Conservative Party in 1991 indicated that the majority of the electorate supported more legal reforms for strikes. However, those

commissioned by the Conservative Party could be fairly categorized as leading questions.

72. Note *Shipping Company Uniforms Inc.* v. *ITF* [1985] ICR 245, where threatened blacking action by self-employed pilots was held not to amount to secondary action (Auerbach 1990: 191 fn. 8).

73. *Unofficial Action and the Law* stated that unofficial strikes were a long-standing and deep-rooted feature of British industrial relations and 'not found in most other countries', where it was normal practice for disputes to be taken through established procedures (1989b: 1–2). The Government contended that much unofficial action was organized by elected lay officials (including shop stewards) not employed by the union, or by union officials not empowered by the union rules to call industrial action, and was a useful means of exerting pressure on an employer during negotiations, and that, in some cases, the union might secretly encourage the unofficial action, despite formal repudiation.

74. The EEF and CBI expressed broad support, maintaining that unofficial action was a continuing problem and that the anomaly of greater freedom from legal restriction for unofficial action should be rectified (*IRLIB* 392 10.1.90). In contrast, the Industrial Society, the IPM, the EETPU, and the TUC criticized both the level and substantiation of the arguments in *Unofficial Action and the Law* and commented adversely on the logistical problems involved in union repudiation.

75. The unofficial action provisions were contained in ss.6 and 9 EA 1990. These are now found in ss.226 and 237 TULR(C)A 1992.

76. Note that Sir John Donaldson MR in *Post Office* v. *UCW* [1990] ICR 258 raised the possibility that in a protracted dispute a ballot may not provide authority for calling on members who were not employed by the employer concerned at the time of the ballot (Carty 1991: 10; Simpson 1991: 432). Although the Opposition urged the Government to clarify the law during the passage of the Bill, the Government chose not to.

77. According to Carty (1991: 17) the scope for legal wrangling with this measure is obvious: the union must choose either to add a long list of specified persons to the voting paper, including shop stewards, and risk an errant shop steward calling for industrial action against the recommendation of the union, or to add a short list of specified persons and risk an unspecified person calling for action—perhaps during an unwise television interview. In the case of *Tanks and Drums Ltd* v. *TGWU* [1992] ICR 1, Neill LJ addressed the problem where unions wish to retain their authority to call industrial action at the top level of the union hierarchy but where in practice the General Secretary is not 'permanently at the end of a telephone'. The TGWU's ballot papers stated that the authority for calling industrial action was vested in the GEC and through its delegated powers to the General Secretary. Some two weeks after the ballot result, the General Secretary's authority was given if a meeting with management the next day was unsuccessful. Neill LJ held that the exercise of such judgement was permissible given the day-to-day realities of industrial relations (Simpson 1993: 293).

78. During debates in the passage of the Act, it was suggested that a union

recommendation for a yes vote in an industrial action ballot, or a clear indication that the union would favour an affirmative vote, might amount to a 'call' for industrial action before the ballot. This was strongly denied by the Government (*IRLIB* 415, 21.12.90: 8). Also note that in *Newham London Borough* v. *NALGO* [1993] IRLR 81 the Court of Appeal reversed the previous decision that a NALGO letter giving details of both (1) a ballot on an indefinite strike in the six-month-old dispute over redundancies and redeployment caused by expenditure cuts and (2) a campaign for a yes vote infringed this provision. Woolf LJ held that union leaders were not required to be non-partisan in their campaigning (Simpson 1993: 291).

79. In contrast, Michael Howard claimed that the responses from interested organizations (apart from the unions) demonstrated strong support for further legislation on strike ballots and the introduction of the right for customers to take action in cases of unlawful industrial disputes (*IRLIB* 441 1.92: 16).

80. There was a significant test of the measure in TURERA 1993 requiring unions to provide the employer with a description of those employees, 'so the employer can readily ascertain them', whom the union expected would be entitled to vote. In *Blackpool and Flyde College* v. *NATFHE* [1994] CA IRLR 228, an interlocutory injunction was granted because the union's notification to the employer of the members entitled to vote was not sufficiently precise.

81. This new commissioner was not mentioned in the 1991 Green Paper; CROTUM has been appointed as the Commissioner for Protection Against Unlawful Industrial Action. The absence of a means test for citizens seeking his/her assistance in taking action is surprising in view of the Government's desire to reduce expenditure. The Government justified this on the grounds that the individual was seeking a restraining order and not damages, that the individual was seeking assistance for proceedings against unions in possession of considerable financial and legal resources, and that the individual would almost certainly be acting in a 'representative capacity', since the granting of an order would benefit many other individuals (Morris 1993: 197).

82. The TUC felt the Code would 'open the way to untold legal threats against unions, while placing no obligations on employers in respect of negotiations, arbitration, or conduct during a ballot' (*IRLIB* 372, 7.3.89). The *IRLIB* (387 24.10.89: 2), commented that for employers or others (who now included customers), 'assistance' must mean assistance in identifying possible grounds for challenging the legality of ballots and of any ensuing industrial action.

83. Note that no recommendation was made by the Code over whether the union should call for a ballot to end the industrial action. Note also that the Code's recommendation that unions should give relevant information to its members entitled to vote—including the 'background' to the ballot and the issues to which the dispute relates (para.43)—ignores the legal pitfalls unions face in providing such information. Simpson (1989: 235) points out that unions are more likely to see the advantages of keeping information supplied to members to a minimum following *London Underground Ltd.* v. *National Union of Railwaymen* [1989] IRLR 341, (No.2) [1989] IRLR 343 and *Blue Circle Cement.* v. *TGWU* 1989 July 7 (unreported). On the other hand, it would

appear that a union is unlikely to be penalized for brevity; see *Associated British Ports*. v. *TGWU* [1989] IRLR 291.

84. As well as advising the union to allow 7 days for the employers to receive their notice of the union's intention to hold a ballot (para.20), the union is recommended to consider delaying any call for industrial action following a ballot until it has obtained the scrutineer's report (para.62).

5
BALLOTS, ELECTIONS, AND UNION GOVERNMENT

INTRODUCTION

This chapter analyses the impact upon union government of the Trade Union Act (TUA) 1984 and the Employment Act (EA) 1988, both of which were examined in the previous chapter. After some initial hesitation, almost all unions had by 1992 complied with the new statutory requirements by reforming their rules and/or practice. A number waited until challenged by the Certification Officer, or until they had completed their own reviews, before making the necessary changes. In some cases amalgamation provided the opportunity for a major constitutional review which included accommodating the legislation. This process of compliance occurred when unions were confronting other changes in their environment. As illustrated in Figure 1.1, the legislation interacted with these other external developments, unions' existing constitutions, and leadership's strategies for change to cause adjustments in union government. A major reason for the differentiated impact of the legislation was the complexity of union government including, as analysed in Chapter 3, the existence of a single or dual channel for bargaining and non-bargaining issues, the degree of centralization of authority, and the concentration of authority at each level of decision-making.

The manner in which unions complied with, and the consequent impact on union government of, the legislation affecting elections is explored as follows: first, we provide an overview of the reform of the rules of TUC-affiliated unions; second, we explore, in more detail, changes in the government of a number of unions (changes in both rules and practice are analysed). This leads, thirdly, to a discussion of the organizational context of these unions. In particular, we examine the role of factions in interest aggregation, articulation, and differentiation. Fourth, the overall impact of these different processes upon political outcomes, in terms of leadership and policy-making processes, is analysed. We conclude with an assessment of the model of union government and democracy which underpinned the legislation.

CHANGES IN UNION RULES AND PRACTICE: AN OVERVIEW

This section outlines the impact of TUA 1984 and EA 1988 upon the constitutions of TUC-affiliated unions. Unions' systems and structures of government, including their method of choosing their national leaders, tended, at the start of the period, to reflect their origins: different groups of workers in discrete historical periods evolved distinctive solutions for the democratic accountability of their organizations. These were influenced both by the constituent members and the contrasting political models of union goals and government dominant at that time, hence 'Trade union forms are a product of trade union origins' (Turner 1962: 232). In the absence of radical breaks in the organizational continuity of British unions, further changes largely reflected pragmatic adjustments to the exigencies of amalgamation and accommodation to sectional interests and workplace trade unionism. Thus unions had no single organizational model, although they shared some common features.

Prior to the passage of the legislation, the relevant election methods of British unions were therefore very diverse. Thus the cumulative impact of the two Acts has been to impose a standard template for choosing key national officials upon quite different national institutions and processes. We demonstrate the extent of these changes, first, by comparing our surveys of the relevant rules of all TUC-affiliated unions in 1987 and 1992 with Undy and Martin's 1980 survey (Undy and Martin 1984).[1] Second, we examine the constitutional practices of the twenty-four unions surveyed in order to detect the extent to which unions actually conformed to the legislative requirements. The results, in terms of changes in rules and practice, are presented separately for TUA 1984 and EA 1988 in order to capture the legislation's incremental impact upon union government. However, it should be noted that, even with the high degree of compliance shown by these surveys, large areas of government and administration remained outside the scope of the legislation, especially at the subordinate levels of workplace, sectional, and geographical representative structures. Thus unions retained much of their particularity at these levels.

The main effect of TUA 1984 upon union government was to require that voting members of the principal executive committee (PEC) were directly elected, and subject to re-election at least every five years, by individual-member workplace or postal ballot. The survey of TUC-affiliated union rules regarding PEC constituencies, election methods, and term of office in 1987 (Tables 5.1, 5.2, and 5.3), undertaken three years after the passage of TUA 1984, revealed a considerable change in constituency and election method, but continuity in term of office. The number and proportion of unions specifying election by intermediate bodies (conference or other committee) fell from 37 (36 per cent) to 10 (12

TABLE 5.1. Rules, TUC-affiliated unions: Principal Executive Committee (PEC), constituency

	1980 n = 102		1987 n = 84		1992 n = 69	
	no.	%	no.	%	no.	%
Election by intermediate bodies	37	36	10	12	3	4
other national committee	3	3	1	1	0	0
area committee	12	11	0	0	0	0
subordinate committee	—[1]	—	3	4	0	0
conference	22	22	6	7	3	4
Direct election by members	59[2]	58	72	86	65	94
all members	59	58	19	23	13	19
area constituencies	—[1]	—	27	32	19	28
section constituencies[3]	—[1]	—	10	12	15	22
area-section constituencies	—[1]	—	16	19	14	20
other[4]			—[1]	—	2	3
branches	—[1]	—	—[1]	—	2	3
Combination of intermediate and direct election	6	6	2	2	1	1

[1] These figures were not collected in the earlier surveys.

[2] In Table 2.17, Undy and Martin (1984: 59), two figures are given for PEC election by the whole membership: 59 unions elected all of their executive by membership vote, while 65 used a hybrid method.

[3] Includes women's seats.

[4] The direct election 'other' category in the 1992 survey comprised the Society of Radiographers (national and regional constituencies) and NATFHE (regional, national, and women's constituencies).

per cent) between 1980 and 1987. By 1987, 72 unions (86 per cent) had rules requiring individual-member ballots in direct elections, compared to 59 (58 per cent) in 1980. Of the 74 unions (including two with hybrid systems) directly electing their PEC in 1987, 43 per cent specified only a general requirement to elect by membership ballot (1980, 20 per cent), whereas 18 per cent prescribed the use of workplace ballots (1980, 0 per cent); 19 per cent postal ballots (1980, 14 per cent); and 3 per cent half-postal ballots (1980, 9 per cent). Although not a legislative requirement, 24 per cent of the 84 unions surveyed permitted election addresses in PEC elections in 1987, compared to 16 per cent in 1980.

In comparison with the election of the PEC, the rules governing the method of selection of the General Secretary and of the President or Chair (for the sake of brevity only the former title is henceforth used) showed less change between 1980 and 1987. This was largely because TUA 1984

TABLE 5.2. Rules, TUC-affiliated unions: PEC, membership direct election, method of voting

| | 1980 n = 64[1] | | 1987 n = 74 | | 1992 n = 66 | |
	no.	%	no.	%	no.	%
Postal ballot[2]	9	14	14	19	34	52
Half-postal ballot	6	9	2	3	2	3
Workplace ballot	—	—	13	18	3	5
Ballot (other, unspecified)	13	20	32	43	23	35
General meeting (vote, ballot)	5	8	5	7	1	2
Branch ballot	13	20	1	1	0	0
Branch vote	4	6	3	4	2	3
Vote (unspecified)	14	22	4	5	1	2

[1] This is the aggregate figure from Table 2.18, Undy and Martin (1984: 59), which combines election of the PEC by the whole membership and hybrid methods. It has not been possible to disaggregate the data for the 59 unions which elected the PEC only by membership vote.

[2] The postal ballot is distributed to the member's home and returned by post; in a half-postal ballot it is returned by post but distributed by some other method, for example, the branch secretary may distribute it by hand.

TABLE 5.3. Rules, TUC-affiliated unions: PEC, term of office

| | 1980 n = 102 | | 1987 n = 84 | | 1992 n = 69 | |
	no.	%	no.	%	no.	%
One year	46	45	35	42	22	32
Two years	28	27	25	30	20	29
Three years	19	19	14	17	16	23
Four years	3	3	2	2	3	4
Five years	5	5	6	7	6	9
More than five years	1	1	0	0	0	0
Other	0	0	1	1	1	1
Not specified	0	0	1	1	1	1

only required the election of any officers who possessed a vote on the PEC and half of the General Secretaries—1980, 51 (50 per cent) and 1987, 43 (51 per cent) (Table 5.4)—and the overwhelming proportion of posts of President—1980, 98 per cent and 1987, 96 per cent—were already subject to some form of election. Nevertheless, some important rule amendments were implemented. Of those unions electing General Secretaries, the role

TABLE 5.4. Rules, TUC-affiliated unions: General Secretary, method of selection

	1980 n = 103		1987 n = 84		1992 n = 69	
	no.	%	no.	%	no.	%
Direct election	51	50	43	51	57	83
Conference election	14	14	4	5	1	1
Other	2	2	0	0	0	0
Not specified[1]	4	4	0	0	3	4
Appointment[2]	32	31	37	44	8	12

[1] The category 'Not specified' in the 1992 survey included three unions—MSF, NALGO, and POA—which did not specify any method of selection at this time.

[2] The category 'Appointment' includes the case of the appointment of the General Secretary followed by an election (1980, 0; 1987, 1; 1992, 0).

TABLE 5.5. Rules, TUC-affiliated unions: General Secretary, membership direct election, method of voting

	1980 n = 51		1987 n = 43		1992 n = 57	
	no.	%	no.	%	no.	%
Postal ballot	8	16	5	11	29	51
Half-postal ballot	0	0	0	0	1	2
Workplace ballot	0	0	6	14	0	0
Branch ballot	8	16	2	5	1	2
Branch meeting	3	6	3	7	2	3
AGM	5	10	5	12	0	0
Ballot (unspecified)	12	24	21	49	23	40
Vote (unspecified)	15	29	1	2	1	2

of intermediate bodies again declined: election by conference fell from 14 (14 per cent) to 4 (5 per cent) between 1980 and 1987, and election by branch ballot and branch meeting also declined from 11 (22 per cent) to 5 (12 per cent) (Table 5.5). In unions where the General Secretary was elected by individual members, there was a marked increase in the use of ballots, without any further specification, from 12 (24 per cent) in 1980 to 21 (49 per cent) in 1987. There was also an increase in workplace ballots from 0 (0 per cent) to 6 (14 per cent), while postal ballots fell from 8 (16 per cent) to 5 (11 per cent) over the same period (Table 5.5). The proportion of unions whose rules stipulated a term of office of five years increased from 12 per cent to 30 per cent (Table 5.6), and the permissibility of election addresses (not a statutory requirement) rose from 22 per cent to 30 per cent.

Similar trends can be observed in the case of the post of President. Intermediate bodies declined in importance: election of the President by conference fell from 41 (40 per cent) to 17 unions (21 per cent), and this was not offset by the slightly increased role of the PEC from 23 per cent (23) to 26 per cent (21) (Table 5.7). Direct election by the whole membership increased from 37 (36 per cent) to 43 (52 per cent) (Table 5.7). Within this category, 16 unions (37 per cent) elected the President by ballot, method unspecified, in 1987 (no comparable figures available for 1980), workplace ballots increased from 0 (0 per cent) to 10 (23 per cent), and postal ballots from 4 (11 per cent) to 6 (14 per cent), whereas the use of half-postal ballots declined from 6 (16 per cent) to 2 (5 per cent) (Table

TABLE 5.6. Rules, TUC-affiliated unions: General Secretary, term of office

	1980 n = 69		1987 n = 47		1992 n = 58	
	no.	%	no.	%	no.	%
One year	4	6	3	6	0	0
Two years	2	3	1	2	1	2
Three years	5	7	0	0	1	2
Four years	2	3	0	0	1	2
Five years	8	12	14	30	39	67
Six years	1	1	1	2	0	0
Other	2	3	1	2	1	2
During the pleasure of the union	45	65	27	57	15	26

TABLE 5.7. Rules, TUC-affiliated unions: President, method of selection

	1980 n = 102		1987 n = 82		1992 n = 68	
	no.	%	no.	%	no.	%
Direct election	37	36	43	52	41	60
Conference election	41	40	17	21	6	9
PEC election	23	23	21	26	20	30
Other national committee	1	1	1[1]	1	1[1]	1

[1] In the case of the NCU, the posts of president and vice-president rotate annually between the Chair of the Engineering Constituency and the Chair of the Clerical Constituency.

5.8). As regards the President's term of office (Table 5.9), this showed little change between 1980 and 1987. The great majority, 72 (71 per cent) in 1980 and 57 (70 per cent) in 1987, served for two years or less. The permissibility of election addresses increased from 11 per cent to 17 per cent.

TUA 1984 also had a marked impact on unions' electoral practice and some unions adapted their practice to conform to its provisions without formally or immediately changing their rules. This is revealed by a comparison, over the period 1980–7, of the rules and practice of twenty-four major unions, embracing 75 per cent of the TUC-affiliated membership (for details, see Chapter 3). As regards the election of the PEC, there was

TABLE 5.8. Rules, TUC-affiliated unions: President, membership direct election, method of voting

	1980 n = 37		1987 n = 43		1992 n = 41	
	no.	%	no.	%	no.	%
Postal ballot	4	11	6	14	15	37
Half-postal ballot	6	16	2	5	1	2
Workplace ballot	0	0	10	23	3	7
Branch ballot	14	38	1	2	1	2
Ballot (unspecified)	—[1]	—	16	37	17	42
Branch meeting	1	3	2	5	1	2
Vote (unspecified)	6	16	1	2	0	0
AGM	6	16	5	12	1	2
Other	0	0	0	0	2	5

[1] Comparable figures not available for 1980.

TABLE 5.9. Rules, TUC-affiliated unions: election of President, term of office

	1980 n = 102		1987 n = 81		1992 n = 68	
	no.	%	no.	%	no.	%
One year	52	51	39	48	27	40
Two years	20	20	18	22	14	21
Three years	12	12	10	12	9	13
Four years	2	2	1	1	1	1
Five years	5	5	7	9	14	21
During the pleasure of the union	11	11	6	7	3	4

a reduction in the role of intermediate bodies from 7 (29 per cent) to 3 unions (13 per cent). This included a decline in election by conference from 4 (17 per cent) (1980) to 1 (4 per cent) (1987) and other national committees from 1 (4 per cent) to zero (Table 5.10). Election by other subordinate committees was constant at 2 (8 per cent) of unions, but the identity of the cases changed. The number of unions utilizing the individual-member ballot in the direct election of the PEC increased in total from 15 (63 per cent) to 21 (87 per cent) (Table 5.10); of those using

TABLE 5.10. Electoral practice, selected TUC-affiliated unions: PEC, constituency

	1980 n = 24		1987 n = 24	
	no.	%	no.	%
Election by intermediate bodies	7	29	3	13
other national committee	1	4	0	0
subordinate committee	2	8	2	8
conference	4	17	1	4
Direct election by members	15	63	21	87
all members	1	4	2	8
geographical constituencies	7	29	6	25
sectional constituencies	0	0	2	8
geog/sect constituencies	6	25	10	42
other[1]	1	4	1	4
Hybrid	2	8	0	0

[1] Other: 1980, ASTMS 2 national seats.
    1987, ASTMS 2 national seats.

TABLE 5.11. Electoral practice, selected TUC-affiliated unions: PEC, membership direct election, method of voting

	1980 n = 17		1987 n = 21	
	no.	%	no.	%
Postal ballot	3	18	6	29
Half-postal ballot	3	18	4	19
Workplace ballot	4	24	10	48
Combination of methods	1	6	1	5
Branch vote	5	29	0	0
Ballot ballot	1	6	0	0

individual-member ballots, postal ballots increased from 3 (18 per cent) to 6 (29 per cent), half-postal ballots from 3 (18 per cent) to 4 (19 per cent), and workplace ballots from 4 (24 per cent) to 10 (48 per cent) (Table 5.11). The permissibility of election addresses in PEC elections rose from 75 per cent to 88 per cent, but the term of office (Table 5.12) remained largely unchanged.

Direct election of the General Secretary by individual-member ballot increased from 13 (54 per cent) to 16 unions (67 per cent) (Table 5.13); in this category the use of workplace ballots rose from 4 (31 per cent) to 8 (50 per cent), whereas postal ballots declined from 4 (31 per cent) to 3 (19 per cent) and the branch vote system from 39 per cent (5) to 31 per cent (5) (Table 5.14). The distribution of election addresses increased from 92 per cent to 100 per cent. All 24 unions elected the post of President (Table 5.15): direct election by individual-member ballot increased from 11 (46 per cent in 1980) to 13 (54 per cent in 1987), but the conference and PEC retained a role in the election of this post. Election by conference declined from 6 (25 per cent) to 3 (13 per cent), whereas the position of the PEC was maintained at 7 unions (29 per cent) (Table 5.15). In the case of direct

TABLE 5.12. Electoral practice, selected TUC-affiliated unions: PEC, term of office

	1980 n = 24		1987 n = 24	
	no.	%	no.	%
One year	7	29	7	29
Two years	8	33	7	29
Three years	5	21	5	21
Four years	1	4	2	8
Five years	3	13	3	13

TABLE 5.13. Electoral practice, selected TUC-affiliated unions: General Secretary, method of selection

	1980 n = 24		1987 n = 24	
	no.	%	no.	%
Appointed	11	46	8	33
Elected, all members	13	54	16	67

TABLE 5.14. Electoral practice, selected TUC-affiliated unions: General Secretary, method of voting

	1980 n = 13		1987 n = 16	
	no.	%	no.	%
Postal ballot	4	31	3	19
Workplace ballot	4	31	8	50
Branch vote	5	39	5	31

TABLE 5.15. Electoral practice, selected TUC-affiliated unions: President, method of selection

	1980 n = 24		1987 n = 24	
	no.	%	no.	%
Direct election, all members	11	46	13	54
Indirect election	13	54	10	42
PEC	7	29	7	29
conference	6	25	3	13
Other	0	0	1[1]	4

[1] In the case of the NCU, the posts of President and Vice-President rotate annually between the Chair of the Engineering Constituency and the Chair of the Clerical Constituency.

election, the use of postal ballots showed little change—1980, 3 (27 per cent); 1987, 4 (31 per cent)—whereas workplace ballots increased from 4 (36 per cent) to 7 (54 per cent) (Table 5.16). The permissibility of election addresses declined from 58 per cent to 50 per cent.

In summary, the above analysis of the rules of TUC-affiliated unions and a selection of unions' constitutional practices illustrates the impact of TUA 1984 upon union government: its provisions were relatively narrow and many unions' rules were already in compliance with at least part of its requirements. However, TUA 1984 produced a significant shift towards the direct election of the PEC by individual-member ballot. This led both to a reduction in the role of intermediate bodies as electoral colleges and other forms of voting by members. In particular it almost eliminated branch ballots. Similarly, the increased use of workplace ballots in PEC and General Secretary elections was an important innovation. Moreover,

TABLE 5.16. Electoral practice, selected TUC-affiliated unions: President, method of voting

	1980 n = 11		1987 n = 13	
	no.	%	no.	%
Postal ballot	3	27	4	31
Half-postal ballot	1	9	1	8
Workplace ballot	4	36	7	54
Branch vote	1	9	0	0
Branch ballot	2	18	1	8

the introduction of election addresses was a radical departure for many unions, and one that was not required by the legislation. Any counter-trends were of short-term duration, caused by the exigencies of amalgamation.

EA 1988 imposed four further major requirements upon union government: (1) all General Secretaries and Presidents were to be elected at least every five years; (2) General Secretaries, Presidents, and PECs were to be elected by postal ballot; (3) all persons who attended PEC meetings in any capacity other than an advisory one were to be directly elected by individual members in a postal ballot at least every five years; and (4) candidates were to be permitted to issue an election address for distribution to members. With respect to the election of the PEC the overwhelming proportion of unions—65, or 94 per cent—had by 1992 changed their rules to include the direct election of the PEC (Table 5.1). In this category there was a major increase in the proportion of unions whose rules specified the use of postal ballots, from 14 (19 per cent) in 1987 to 34 (52 per cent) in 1992 (Table 5.2). All other methods showed a decline: the use of workplace ballots fell, between 1987 and 1992, from 13 (18 per cent) to 3 (5 per cent), whilst the number of unions whose rules referred only to unspecified ballots fell from 32 (43 per cent) to 23 (35 per cent) (Table 5.2). The term of office of PECs changed: by 1992 only 22 (32 per cent) specified a one-year term compared with 35 (42 per cent) in 1987 (1980, 45 per cent), while the use of a three-year term increased from 14 (17 per cent) in 1987 to 16 (23 per cent) by 1992 (1980, 19 per cent) (Table 5.3). The effect of the amalgamation movement was reflected in the rise in the proportion of unions utilizing sectional constituencies, from 12 per cent (1987) to 22 per cent (1992) (Table 5.1).

There were similar changes in the rules governing the election of General Secretaries and Presidents: by 1992, 57 unions (83 per cent) expressly specified the direct election of the General Secretary, compared with 43 (51 per cent) in 1987 (51 [50 per cent] in 1980), leaving 8 (12 per cent) with rules still requiring appointment (1987, 37 [44 per cent]), while 3 (4 per cent) chose not to stipulate any method of selection in their rules (Table 5.4). Where General Secretaries were elected, 29 unions (51 per cent) stipulated the use of a postal ballot (1987, 5 [11 per cent]; 1980, 8 [16 per cent]), while the proportion which left open the precise form of ballot fell to 40 per cent (1987, 49 per cent) (Table 5.5).[2] Only one union retained election by conference (Table 5.4). The overwhelming majority of elected General Secretaries, 39 (67 per cent), served a five-year term of office (1987, 14 [30 per cent]; 1980, 8 [12 per cent]) (Table 5.6).

Somewhat similar but less dramatic changes were also evident in the rules governing the selection for the post of President, which remained an overwhelmingly elected position (99 per cent).[3] In this category, the use of a one-year term of office fell, between 1987 and 1992, from 39 (48 per cent) to 27 unions (40 per cent) (1980, 52 [51 per cent]), whereas 14 (21 per cent) now specified a five-year electoral term (1987, 7 [9 per cent]; 1980, 5 [5 per cent]). The trend to direct election by the whole membership continued, rising from 52 per cent (43) in 1987 to 60 per cent (41) by 1992 (1980, 36 per cent [37]). Election by conference fell from 17 (21 per cent) in 1987 to 6 (9 per cent) by 1992 (1980 41 [40 per cent]). However, the importance of the PEC in electing one of their number as President increased from 26 per cent (21) to 30 per cent (20), between 1987 and 1992 (1980, 23 [23 per cent]) (Table 5.7). Where the President was elected by the whole membership, the number and proportion of unions which now specified the use of a postal ballot was 15 (37 per cent) (1987, 6 [14 per cent]; 1980, 4 [11 per cent]); however, 17 (42 per cent) still left the ballot method undetermined by rule (1987, 16 [37 per cent]) (Table 5.8).

To summarize, EA 1988 thus had a significant effect upon unions' rules and practice. It confirmed the demise of lower-level, intermediary bodies in the election of PECs and General Secretaries as unions quickly conformed to the Act's provisions, many overriding their own rules (Smith *et al.* 1993: 370). Indeed a further survey of the constitutional rules and practice of selected TUC-affiliated unions undertaken in 1993–4 revealed near-universal compliance in practice with the new template. The PECs and General Secretaries were overwhelmingly directly elected by individual-member postal ballot. However, the PEC retained a role in the election of the post of President from amongst its membership (at 25 per cent of unions—six cases) and the conference in the selection of a PEC member as President (13 per cent—three cases, no change). All unions issued candidates' election addresses and maintained central membership address lists. Thus EA 1988's and TUA 1984's combined effect was to reshape an important feature of union government. This also had a much wider impact on other aspects of union government, as the next section will show.

CHANGING ELECTORAL PRACTICE: AN ANALYSIS OF SELECTED UNIONS

The changes in union government, both rules and practice, which resulted from compliance with TUA 1984 and EA 1988, are examined in this section for the twenty-four unions surveyed and in particular the six selected for in-depth case studies. These provide a cross section of the TUC's membership (see Table 3.3). TUA 1984's and EA 1988's impact is discussed in terms of its effect on the direct election of the PEC, General Secretary, and President, the associated changes in balloting methods, and the issuing of election addresses. The following discussion also explores other important related political processes shaping union government, particularly the development and role of factions.

Seven major unions—the AEU, EETPU, FBU, SOGAT, CPSA, NUT, and NALGO—were largely unaffected by TUA 1984 as they were already in compliance with its principal provision, namely that all voting members of the PEC should be periodically elected by individual-member ballot. The AEU's rule book, reflecting the ethos of craft unionism, had always provided for the periodic direct election, by individual-member ballot held at branch meetings, of all officers and committees at every level of the union. In 1972, following factional disputes (see below), this was amended to a postal ballot. Initially, the change from branch to postal ballot produced a marked increase in the votes cast at AEU elections. Under branch ballots between 1964 and 1972 the average vote was 7 per cent, whereas voting in postal ballots between 1972 and 1980 averaged 27 per cent (Undy and Martin 1984: 68–9). However, the average turnout has since fallen to 18 per cent for the 1989 national executive council elections. This downward trend has continued.[4] In 1984, precipitated by the financial crisis confronting the union (the result of falling membership), and in defiance of TUC policy, the AEU national executive applied to the Certification Officer for funds to offset ballot costs. This was supported by two membership referenda. In 1985 the union's constitution was brought into conformity with practice when the rule banning canvassing and electoral publications was abolished. Prior to these changes the federal AUEW had been dissolved in 1984, when two of its constituents, the Foundry Workers and the Construction Engineers, were integrated into the AEU as separate sections within its rules.

The government of the principal predecessor of the EETPU, the Electrical Trades Union (ETU), had been reformed during the 1960s when a new leadership, installed by the High Court following the conviction of senior executive officers for electoral fraud, had centralized authority in a full-time officer executive elected by postal ballot (ibid. 74–6). Although members' electoral participation increased from 10 per cent to 30 per cent as a result of the introduction of postal ballots, this was not the cause of the change in political leadership. This change would have occurred under the previous individual-member branch ballot but for electoral malpractice. In 1985 the EETPU applied for state funds for ballot costs.

Two unions, the FBU and SOGAT, had long-standing systems of government in which their PECs were elected by individual-member ballot, organized at the workplace by branches. The NUT and NALGO used half-postal ballots for their PEC elections. The CPSA had introduced direct election of the executive by individual-member branch ballot in 1979 as a result of a short-term alliance between rival factions.[5] Disputes over election procedures in the CPSA, although there was no evidence of fraud, led to successive amendments to electoral procedures in order to ensure the integrity of the ballot. The rules stipulated that members should cast their votes at a branch meeting held at the workplace, but in practice the internal post was used to distribute and receive the ballot papers. Turn-out for executive elections from 1981 to 1988 varied from 31 to 45 per cent. Following controversy over the election of the General Secretary and General Treasurer in 1986,[6] amendments to the election regulations were introduced in 1988 requiring that ballot papers and election addresses be distributed to members at work in individually sealed and addressed envelopes.

The introduction of individual-member ballots by TUA 1984 for the direct election of the PEC was a major change for those unions which had previously elected their executive by conference, other national committee, or from subordinate committees. Unions which quickly abandoned the election of their executives by conference comprised the STE, IRSF, Bakers, and NCU. The latter had been formed in 1984 from the merger of the Post Office Engineering Union (POEU) and the Posts and Tele-communications Section of the CPSA (numbering some 40,000 members), which constituted two sections—the Engineering and Clerical Groups—of the new union. The CPSA already fulfilled the requirements of TUA 1984 (see above) and its system of individual-member ballots for the election of the executive committee and senior national officials was transferred to the NCU Clerical Group. In contrast, the POEU's executive was elected at the union's annual conference, where delegations cast a block vote for candidates to all executive seats according to the decision of their branch meeting. In 1985 the conference of the newly formed NCU agreed to comply with TUA 1984. In the case of NATFHE, the abolition of the election of the executive by the national council was a significant change. It disenfranchised a body elected by the union's regional councils, which met three times a year and acted as an important forum for lay activists.

Both the TGWU and GMB similarly ended the election of their executives, in part or whole, by subordinate committees. For the TGWU this entailed a relatively minor constitutional amendment, affecting their trade group representatives on the general executive council. These were previously elected by their respective national committees, but henceforth they were elected by individual-member ballot at the same time as the territorial representatives. The new procedure was more significant for the GMB.[7] The union's central executive council (CEC), inherited from the General and Municipal Workers' Union (GMWU), had consisted of lay members elected by regional councils, the General Secretary and regional secretaries (*ex-officio*), and the senior officers of the Boilermakers Section, elected by individual-member branch ballot. From 1987 the CEC was elected by individual-member ballot, the General Secretary was subject to periodic election, regional secretaries were no longer *ex officio* but eligible to stand for election as members of regional delegations, the CEC electoral period was extended from two to four years, and election addresses were authorized. A further notable innovation was the institution of a woman's reserved seat as part of each regional delegation to the CEC.[8]

Initially the EMA retained the complex electoral system by which its PEC was elected by subordinate committees, the members of which were directly elected in separate sections. This was challenged by the Certification Officer but supported by the High Court, in effect validating its complex weighting procedures. However, the decision was overturned by the Appeal Court and the EMA was compelled to elect its PEC by direct election in an individual-member postal ballot.[9].

In contrast to those unions which abandoned indirect forms of election of the PEC, TASS adopted this method in defiance of the requirements of TUA 1984. The search by TASS for merger partners, before and after it was excluded from the consolidation of the federated AUEW in 1984 to form the AEU, had been rewarded by the transfer of engagements of four craft unions.[10] These subsequently retained their own rules and a high degree of autonomy as sections within TASS. As a consequence TASS's national executive consisted of the staff section committee (the former TASS executive committee elected by branch block vote) and representatives from the craft section committees, elected according to the rules of the transferring unions. Thus TASS was at variance with TUA 1984 on two accounts: indirect election of the executive, and individual-member branch ballots.[11]

For those unions which had elected their PEC, wholly or partly, by individual-member ballot at branch meetings or the branch block-vote (cast after a show of hands by members attending a branch meeting)— ASLEF, NUR, ASTMS, UCATT, and NUPE—the introduction of individual-member ballots, at the workplace or by post, was a major departure. Four unions—the EMA, TSSA, UCATT and NATFHE— adopted postal ballots. This was less of an innovation for NATFHE as this method was already in use for the annual election of its lay President. The Bakers Union, after the increased participation recorded in the political fund referendum conducted at the workplace, replaced postal by workplace ballots for all its elections, and extended their use to regional and district officials. This is the only known case of a union which went beyond the requirement of the legislation and extended elections to other posts as part of a wider process of union reorganization (Blackwell 1990: 23–31). Thus by 1988 the large majority of unions in the survey had adopted the workplace ballot to elect their PEC.

Individual-member ballots made new administrative demands upon unions' organizational capacities and threatened long-standing political processes. But individual ballots at the workplace also offered significant political returns. They provided union leaders with the opportunity to address members within the collective context of workplace organization. As a consequence the workplace became the primary unit in many unions' electoral processes, thus complementing its role in collective bargaining and representation. Workplace union organization provided a ready-made structure for ballot administration; and, where it was absent, ballots provided an opportunity for its construction. In this process the statutory obligation imposed by TUA 1984 upon an employer to provide facilities to a recognized union for the purpose of holding a workplace ballot became an important right.[12] Lay and full-time representatives generally discharged their tasks with efficiency, as shown by the high level of participation achieved in workplace elections. Activists performed a supportive administrative role. They provided information on the candidates and encouraged members to vote in the elections. There were a relatively small number of specific allegations of maladministration. Two notable cases involved elections in the CPSA in 1986 and the TGWU in 1984. However, in both cases accusations as to extensive ballot-rigging failed to supply any conclusive evidence.

TUA 1984's requirement that all officers who possessed a vote at the PEC should be directly elected by individual-member ballot had little effect. In our survey we found only three cases where this resulted in change. First, the NUM, otherwise unaffected by the Act, as its national executive was directly elected by individual-member workplace ballot,[13] removed the casting vote of the President in 1985 in order to avoid periodic election. Second, the GMB's General Secretary retained the right to vote through the introduction of a five-year period of office and election by individual-member workplace ballot (with postal ballot option). Third, the NUS introduced periodic re-election for the posts of General Secretary and Assistant General Secretary. Both post-holders were voting members of the executive but not previously subject to periodic election (Undy and Martin 1984: 78–80). Quite separate from the TUA 1984, both the CPSA and NCU introduced election of senior officers during the 1980s. The CPSA extended the use of individual-member ballots, in 1982, to the election of senior national officers for five-year terms. The POEU's 1983 conference had agreed to introduce the election of leading national officers by conference (this had been a long-standing goal of the union's Broad

Left),[14] but following the NCU's decision to comply with TUA 1984 for the election of the executive, the individual-member ballot was also introduced for the election of the General Secretary, Deputy General Secretary, and treasurer.

The electoral requirements in EA 1988 (see p. 89) had a greater impact upon union government than those of TUA 1984. EA 1988 affected unions qualitatively, in that its provisions overturned both entrenched union rules and the recent constitutional innovations made in response to TUA 1984, and quantitatively, in that all but a few unions came within its scope. The exceptional cases were the AEU, EETPU, and NUS: all the other unions in our survey were significantly affected by EA 1988. The least intrusive of EA 1988's requirements was the right of candidates to issue election addresses. This had been prefigured in many unions, although it had not been a statutory requirement of the TUA 1984. Nevertheless, it still had some impact, even on unions issuing such addresses. For example, the EETPU's executive abandoned its power to supervise the content of candidates' election addresses, while in the AEU procedures for the election of executive committee members from the Foundry and Construction sections were brought into compliance. The NUS did not have to make any rule changes.

EA 1988's imposition of postal ballots for PEC elections particularly affected those unions that used workplace ballots. These included unions with a tradition of workplace ballots, such as the TGWU, CPSA, FBU, NUM, and SOGAT, and also those which had recently introduced this method, mainly under the influence of TUA 1984, such as IRSF, NCU, Bakers, STE, ASTMS, NUPE, and GMB. As a result the direct and formal relationship between union government and workplace organization was broken. The role of union branches and shop stewards in electoral administration was greatly reduced and the importance of central administration considerably expanded. Electoral participation declined. To take the example of the TGWU: the turn-out in elections for the executive by workplace ballot in 1987 was 34 per cent, whereas the turn-out using the postal ballot in 1991 was 15 per cent. This trend applied also to the NUT and NALGO, where the half postal vote had been long-standing, and the role of workplace union organization had been important in persuading members to vote. Thus in the case of NALGO, 27 per cent of members voted in the 1988/9 executive council election, which was the last to use the half-postal ballot, whereas using the postal ballot the participation rate in 1990/1 was 22 per cent; 1991/2, 22 per cent; and 1992/3, 17 per cent. An internal report which examined the causes of the reduced turn-out commented that members 'feel that the candidates are remote from themselves and, with the passing of the workplace ballot, they lack the personal "feel" that could be given by a recommendation from a local NALGO officer'.[15]

The removal of discretion by EA 1988 as to whether or not General Secretaries could be appointed or elected—the Act enforced periodic elections by postal ballot—disturbed the rules and embedded norms of many unions. This included those in which this post was traditionally filled by appointment, usually by the executive (mainly white-collar and public sector unions)—including NATFHE, NALGO, NUPE, NUT, IRSF, STE, EMA, TSSA, SOGAT, ASTMS, and TASS—and those unions in which the holder was elected to serve until retirement, subject to dismissal by the executive, such as TGWU, NUM, NUR, ASLEF, Bakers, and NCU (mainly blue-collar unions). Many of the required rule changes were made on the occasion of the formation of new unions in mergers or in a subsequent constitutional review (ASTMS and TASS to form MSF; NALGO and NUPE, Unison; NUR and NUS, RMT; SOGAT and NGA, GPMU). Unions which already elected their General Secretaries for fixed terms, and therefore were not obliged to make any rule amendments, were the CPSA, FBU, AEU, EEPTU, UCATT, and NUS. Unions which had used the workplace ballot for the election of the General Secretary and other senior officers (TGWU, SOGAT), and switched to postal ballots as required by EA 1988, suffered a similar fall in electoral participation to that associated with PEC elections. For example, the turn-out in the TGWU's General Secretary election of 1984 using the workplace ballot was 39 per cent, whereas in 1991 only 22 per cent of members participated in the postal ballot.

Three unions—SOGAT, NALGO, and TASS—were reluctant to conform to EA 1988's stipulation that those who actively influenced and participated in the deliberations of the PEC should be directly elected by individual-member ballot. SOGAT's failure to arrange for new elections for the positions of General President and two general officers was the subject of a successful complaint in 1990 to the Certification Officer; and a similar complaint was also upheld in 1991 with respect to two other officers.[16] The issue was finally resolved after the amalgamation of SOGAT within the GPMU, when these posts were abolished on grounds of economy (given the falling membership). NALGO's executive council was loath to abandon a form of functional representation under which it retained the right to co-opt the chairs of the seven service committees if they had not been otherwise elected. This enabled it to ensure the direct representation of all sections. Following the threat of a complaint to the Certification Officer, the chairs of service committees, if not elected, were only allowed to attend the executive to give advice; and in 1991 the rules were revised to allow the election of representatives from the service groups, if the chair had not already been otherwise directly elected. NALGO simply avoided any mention of the method of selection of the General Secretary in its 1992 rules. TASS did not conform to the requirements of EA 1988. Its rules remained initially unchanged after its amalgamation with the ASTMS in 1988 to form the MSF (where it remained a separate section), and it only complied in 1989 following the adoption of a new constitution.[17]

As regards the election of 'other persons' attending the PEC, unions generally interpreted the scope of EA 1988 as applying only to 'executive officers', normally the General Secretary and Deputy General Secretary with occasionally additional posts, as discussed above. 'Other' officers and staff who attended the PEC on a regular basis normally did so either to advise the General Secretary on specific matters, such as finance, or by express invitation of the PEC in order to provide other specialist information. In these cases, it is usual for such officers to speak only when requested by the chair. Hence periodic elections have been unnecessary for 'other persons' attending the PEC. Further, no unions in our survey amended their rules to give the vote to senior national officers now subject to periodic election.

In summary, the combined impact of TUA 1984 and EA 1988 upon electoral practice was cumulative. It also varied widely between unions according to their initial rules and practices and its effect on individual unions was hence almost entirely contingent on their existing systems of government. The degree of change made in order to comply with the legislation may therefore be categorized by reference to a continuum of the minimal, moderate, and marked changes it wrought in different unions. The first category of unions, the smallest grouping comprising the AEU and EETPU, only had to introduce minimal changes in order to comply with the legislation. This primarily involved modifications to the rules governing existing election addresses and the supervision of elections. The second category of unions, i.e. those compelled to make a relatively moderate number of adjustments, includes all those unions which made a significant but small number of changes to their methods of choosing leaders. The NUS, CPSA, TSSA, NATFHE, UCATT, NALGO, NUT, and SOGAT came within this category. Of this group the NUS, which introduced periodic elections of both the General Secretary and President after TUA 1984, and the CPSA, which introduced the postal ballot after EA 1988, made the least number of changes. The TSSA, NATFHE, and UCATT adopted postal ballots for the election of their PEC after TUA 1984. Later, following EA 1988, they introduced periodic elections for their General Secretaries by individual-member postal ballot (in TSSA and NATFHE this had been an appointed post, and in UCATT it had been elected by branch block vote for five-year terms). NALGO, NUT, and SOGAT were already in compliance with TUA 1984 but had to make two important changes to conform with EA 1988. They introduced full postal ballots for the election of the PEC and periodic election of the General Secretary, again by individual-member postal ballot.

The majority of unions in our survey, however, fell into the third, 'marked change' category. This group of unions made a considerable number of significant changes in order to comply with the demands of the legislation, i.e. both TUA 1984 and EA 1988. This included, *inter alia*, terminating the election of all or part of the PEC by other subordinate or intermediate committees (TGWU, GMB, and EMA) or by conference (STE, IRSF, Bakers, and NCU), and its replacement by direct election using individual-member workplace ballot; abolition of individual-member ballot at branch meetings, or the branch block-vote, for PEC elections (ASLEF, NUR, TASS, ASTMS, and NUPE); periodic individual-member election of General Secretary, President, or other executive officers (all the above unions, together with the NUM); postal ballots for the election of the PEC and General Secretaries and President (all the above unions). Thus, 13 of the 24 medium and large unions at the centre of our study made a number of important changes in their national elections in order to comply with the legislation. Those that did not make such marked changes were generally in compliance with much of the legislation at the start of the period and therefore made only minimal or moderate adjustments. There was also a very small number of unions that did not totally comply with the legislation, because they came under no pressure to do so.

BALLOTING CHANGES IN THEIR ORGANIZATIONAL CONTEXT

Before analysing the impact of TUA 1984's and EA 1988's electoral provisions on policy-making processes and political outcomes it is important to set the changes imposed on the unions in their organizational context. For the imposition of a statutory template did not generally act directly to affect such outcomes. They were rather one among several other factors influencing union government. In particular the impact of TUA 1984 and EA 1988 varied between unions because it was mediated through unions' formal and informal political processes. It was influenced by internal and informal political relationships including the presence or absence of political factions. This was critically important in determining the manner in which the legislation affected political outcomes. In factionalized unions the introduction of periodic direct election of PEC members, General Secretaries, and Presidents by individual-member ballot—later specified as a postal ballot—together with the right to distribute electoral addresses, tended to provide more opportunities for factional organization and campaigning. However, if factions did not exist prior to the legislation, there is no evidence that the imposed constitutional reforms called them into being. Other factors, such as changes in members' attitudes and political preferences, possibly originating in disputes over particular issues and events, and leading to a polarization of opinion, appeared to be more important than the imposed balloting changes for encouraging factionalism.

Factionalism, where it already existed, also ebbed and flowed independently of the legislation. Many political groups were transient and did not solidify into well-established factions. If they achieved their goals and the established leadership was defeated they may then have dispersed. Some degree of broad and permanent political agreement appeared to be necessary for sustaining factional organization. This was provided, until the 1980s, by the division between the Communist Party–Labour Party left and the Labour Party mainstream. However, the decline in importance of the Communist Party during the 1970s, as it shifted its focus away from industrial work and then began to disintegrate in the 1980s before its final dissolution in 1991, left a political void in many unions. As a result the Broad Left has changed in character: in some unions it has suffered a loss of focus (e.g. the AEU), in others it is narrower (e.g. the NCU). No other left-wing organization has yet filled this vacuum, although the *Morning Star* continues to play an important if small role.

The GMB and GPMU are examples of unions where factionalism has not developed despite 'marked' changes in organization following the passage of TUA 1984 and EA 1988. The GMB, as discussed in Chapter 3, also made a series of changes in union government associated with mergers and radical initiatives which restructured the union internally on the basis of industrial sections in the later 1980s.[18] In the highly regionalized GMB this shift reduced the importance of the regions, and with them, the regional secretaries. The union's centre was further strengthened in 1990 by the creation of the new post of Deputy General Secretary and the subsequent election to this position of Tom Burlison (John Edmonds' principal opponent for the post of General Secretary in 1984). The political compatibility of the leaders of the merging unions joining the GMB further encouraged a new unified leadership. The entrenched position of the established leadership, the new sectional structure, and the four-year electoral period all combined to inhibit the development of factionalism. Following the passage of TUA 1984, the GMB's rules were amended to allow regional secretaries to stand for election in regional constituencies, and they were all re-elected in the subsequent ballots of 1988 and 1992. In the elections for the CEC from 1988 to 1991 the poll in GMW Section regional constituencies averaged 40 per cent, and there was a similar turnout for the women's seats. This represented a major increase in membership participation over the previous method of the branch block vote. The 1992 elections used the postal ballot and participation fell to between 16 and 20 per cent. Election addresses were introduced, a major innovation, but the ban on canvassing was maintained. Thus the GMB's traditional commitment to the mainstream of Labour Party politics, under the continued direction of its national and regional leadership, was maintained largely unchanged despite the imposed organizational changes.

The GPMU, an industrial union, was formed in 1991 by the amalgamation of the National Graphical Association (NGA) and SOGAT, which had straddled, with some exceptions, different sides of the craft divide in printing (Gennard and Bain 1995: 222–45). The NGA exhibited the characteristic features of 'exclusive democracy' whereas SOGAT combined aspects of both 'popular bossdom' and 'exclusive democracy' (Turner 1962: 289–96). Both unions had been dominated by left caucuses, although Dean's election as SOGAT General Secretary in 1985 represented a victory for the centre. The election of Dubbins as General Secretary of the GPMU in 1991 confirmed continuing left-inclined and craft dominance within the GPMU. However, the attempt to create a formal Broad Left organization in the GPMU in 1993 met with a hostile response from the executive council, which banned its members, national officers, and regional organizers from any participation in factional groups (GPMU 1993: 304–9).

Other unions in the survey which were markedly affected by the legislation but displayed no factional differentiation were ASLEF, EMA, NUPE, and the Bakers. In the Bakers, the prolonged and sometimes bitter internal political dispute of the 1970s did not lead to the emergence of any permanent factions (Blackwell 1990: 23–31), and the new leadership secured an unchallenged ascendancy.

The TGWU and MSF both made 'marked' changes in their electoral systems following TUA 1984 and EA 1988 and they also provide contrasting cases of the development of factions. The TGWU provides the best example of a union in which the marked constitutional changes required by the legislation coincided with newly-formed factions to transform the union's political process. During Jack Jones's tenure as General Secretary (1968–79), the election to the union's constitutional committees of a new generation of lay members, schooled in the ethos of semi-autonomous workplace unionism, led to the partial displacement of the long-standing leadership role exercised at all levels of the union by professional officers (England 1981: 24–7; Undy *et al.* 1981: 48–51). This power shift was especially noticeable on the general executive council, but its political significance only became fully apparent after the retirement of Jones in 1979. For, as the union's constitutional committees assumed a major role in the formulation of policy, so the biennial elections became a focus for factional activity. The Communist Party-Labour left caucus, which had dominated the TGWU in the 1970s during Jones's leadership, fragmented during the tenure of his successor, Moss Evans. The General Secretary election which followed Evans's early retirement in 1984 precipitated the formation of the Centre and Broad Left factions supporting, respectively, the candidatures of George Wright and Ron Todd. The factions embraced full-time officers and lay members. The validity of Todd's election was disputed by Wright and a second ballot was held which confirmed the result. Many elected and appointed positions throughout the union were also contested on a factional basis, although canvassing remained banned by rule. The Centre faction won a majority of seats on the executive council for the electoral period 1986–8. These were the first to be elected by the system of universal workplace ballots. However, the Broad Left won a majority for the period 1988–90, again under workplace ballots, and it also won majorities in subsequent executive elections using the postal ballot. Given the political differentiation within the union, the periodic election of the three senior officers (General Secretary, Deputy General Secretary, and Executive Officer) further increased the potential for organizational fragmentation and conflict between the executive and the senior officials. However, the Broad Left's candidates secured victory in all these elections. It also increased its majority on the executive council in the 1993 elections.

The introduction of the postal vote therefore did not prevent the Broad Left's victory, and in the context of the TGWU's organizational system it probably helped it. The Broad Left's influence within the trade groups and the national head office provided an effective national organizational network which benefited from the switch to postal ballots. In contrast, the Centre faction was concentrated in particular regions and found it more difficult to mobilize its support nationally under postal ballots. Its tendency to rely on full-time officer support in the regions, rather than building a broad-based lay activist structure of organization, further compounded its difficulties as postal ballots served to displace and fragment the vote. It also suffered organizationally as the Broad Left benefited from the cost-cutting exercise recommended by the Klein Report, which strengthened the head office and reduced the number of regions by two (TGWU 1992b).

Neither of the MSF's constituent unions, TASS and the ASTMS, possessed a broad-based factional system at the time of merger. Each union was dominated by a caucus, the Broad Left in the case of TASS and the Labour Party centre in the case of the ASTMS (Carter 1991: 35–71). The Broad Left in TASS was highly organized and dominated by the Communist Party, later the *Morning Star*.[19] The inauguration of the new union in 1989 was followed by an interregnum in which TASS and the ASTMS retained their identity and rules in separate sections, while their dominant political groups vied for wider support and position. The new constitution, adopted in 1989, instituted the election of the General Secretary in place of both unions' appointment systems, and terminated TASS's maintenance, in defiance of the legislation, of the role of subordinate committees in the election of the executive. The complex structure of sectional groups inherited from both unions was retained. The political infighting and the election of a new General Secretary in 1991 (following the retirement of Gill) precipitated the formation of two factions—the Unity Left (organized around the *Morning Star* within

TASS) and MSF for Labour (primarily the ASTMS). The General Secretary post and a majority on the executive were won by the moderate MSF for Labour faction.

It is too early to say whether the amalgamation of NALGO, NUPE, and COHSE to form UNISON will initiate a process of factionalization. Certainly the constituent unions were very distinct: NALGO possessed a relatively decentralized structure based on branches with access to financial resources and an active local lay leadership, and national factions, whereas NUPE and COHSE were more centralized and officer-led, and without factions or caucuses. UNISON's new constitution entrenches the representation of women, low-paid grades, and occupational groups in a structure that is unique to British trade unionism. However, the emphasis on continuing NALGO's lay-dominated system of government and the ongoing debates over leadership and policy could easily extend NALGO's factionalized contests to the new union.[20]

The highly factionalized CPSA, which made only 'moderate' changes in response to TUA 1984 and EA 1988, was, nevertheless, significantly affected by the introduction of postal ballots. During the 1980s, the union's three-way factional system, high membership turnover, and annual executive elections interacted to create a volatile political organization. In these circumstances the fluctuating views and moods of a transient membership led to rapid changes in the political balance of the executive. The introduction of postal ballots damaged the Broad Left's position, overreliant as it was upon the mobilization of votes in major concentrations of members at the place of work. However, electoral participation declined over the same period. Between 1980 and 1988 the average turn-out in workplace ballots was 38 per cent, but with the introduction of postal ballots this fell to 25 per cent (1989–90).

In the AEU and EETPU, both only 'minimally' affected by the legislation, factionalism declined during the 1990s. In the AEU, the major reason was the dominant position achieved by the Group (the moderates) over the Broad Left, which was further weakened by the disintegration of the Communist Party after 1989. Thus by 1992 the Group possessed 54 seats on the national committee compared to the Broad Left's 34 (in 1980 the respective numbers had been 29 and 23). There were also fewer opportunities for factional intervention in elections, as the officer complement was reduced in size from 220 in 1984 to 136 by 1993. Two other measures further reduced the number of candidates and contests: first, the rule change introduced in 1985 requiring existing post-holders to resign from office if they wished to challenge a sitting member[21]; second, changes to the nomination procedure introduced in 1990, whereby candidates were required to gain the support of a greater number of branches. Over the same period, for unknown reasons, some local Group supporters chose not to contest seats held by members of the Broad Left.

One result of the decline in factionalized contests was a fall in electoral participation as the factions ceased to mobilize their supporters.

The merger of the EETPU and AEU to create the AEEU will also raise new questions regarding the role of the Group. For, while the AEU has a history of tolerating organized electoral conflict, the EETPU had been characterized by one-party rule. The centralized authority of the executive (there were no subordinate bodies with any degree of autonomy) gave the established leadership control over the union, and its favoured candidates were 'sponsored' through the union's magazine *Contact*, which was posted to members at their home address. Opposition leaders thereby faced considerable barriers to gaining any national platform. Following the suspension of the union from the TUC, the leadership's position was further strengthened by the defection of the Broad Left (publishers of *Flashlight*) to form a new union, the Electrical and Plumbing Industries Union. Over time, the creation of the AEEU may cause a decline in the hegemony of the EETPU's leadership and a reorganization of political divisions.

We can therefore conclude that the new rules for the election of the PEC, General Secretary, and other executive officers imposed by TUA 1984 and EA 1988 had no consistent impact upon unions' internal political processes. Some unions which we categorized as 'markedly' affected by the legislation underwent fewer internal political changes than those identified as only 'moderately' affected by TUA 1984 and EA 1988. For example, the CPSA, which made only moderate adjustments to comply with the legislation, was significantly affected in its political activities by these changes, whereas the GMB, which underwent marked changes in response to the legislation, appeared relatively untouched politically. On the other hand, in one or two cases the legislation interacted and combined with other developments in informal political organization to produce significant changes in internal political processes. This was the case in TASS and the ASTMS following the MSF merger. The effect of the legislation was therefore largely contingent on other developments and proved amenable to negotiation by leaders and factions. Thus the reform of union government initiated by the legislation had no uniform effect upon unions' political processes, in spite of the degree of standardization which it imposed. As we will now show, the associated political outcomes have proved to be similarly diverse.

IMPACT OF THE LEGISLATION UPON UNION OUTCOMES: LEADERSHIP AND POLICY-MAKING PROCESSES

Both TUA 1984 and EA 1988 were based upon the view that the democratic processes of the majority of unions were flawed in both conception and practice. It was assumed that if these 'faults' were remedied by the legislation then the power of militant and radical leaders, unrepresentative of the members, would be broken (DE 1983a: 1–2; see Chapter 4). Thus the changes in process imposed by statute were expected to produce a politically significant shift in union leadership and policy in the direction desired by the Conservatives. However, it is not possible to discern any uniform or general changes in unions' political outcomes which were directly the result of the legislation on elections, nor is it possible to attribute those changes which did occur within particular unions solely to the legislation. There was no unidirectional trajectory of change in terms of political movement towards the 'centre' (however that might be defined). Nonetheless, the legislation did interact with other contextual and organizational factors, both general and specific, to influence particular outcomes in specific unions.

The expressed intention of the Green Paper *Democracy in Trade Unions* (DE 1983a) was to marginalize activists by the adoption of individual-member ballots for the direct election of PECs, ending both the role of intermediate bodies as electoral colleges and branch ballots (except in a few cases). In the event, however, TUA 1984's promotion of workplace balloting resulted in the enfranchisement of activists in a novel way within unions' political processes. They provided an important link with members in terms of interest articulation and aggregation (on the basis of faction, section, or geographic loyalties) and thereby gained a major role in vote mobilization. Campaigns waged to 'get out' the vote stressed the importance of the union to members independently of narrower loyalties. As a result unions achieved a new presence at the workplace, in addition to their collective bargaining function, and emerged strengthened. Thus TUA 1984 had important if unintended and unquanti-fiable consequences for union government. Generally workplace ballots favoured factions and sectional groups, which were entrenched within large workplaces and where the members could be mobilized easily. However, the period of operation of workplace ballots was probably too brief for any long-term effect on local organization and elections outcomes.

The effect of postal ballots upon political outcomes has primarily varied according to the existence and nature of factional organizations. The general impact of postal ballots is to 'reduce the effectiveness of any factions based on a small number of geographically concentrated groups of activists' (Undy and Martin 1984: 114). This conclusion was influenced by the case of the AEU, where, since the introduction of the postal ballot in 1972, the moderate 'Group' has gradually consolidated its position over the left-wing faction. This also appears to be the explanation for the increased strength under postal ballots of the Moderate faction in the CPSA and the MSF for Labour faction in MSF. However, it cannot 'be assumed that the right in all other unions with factional organization would similarly benefit from a change in balloting methods, (for) the organized right and its candidates may not always be the popular choice or, if they are, have the organizational ability to signal the nature of that choice to the membership and hence to mobilize its supporters' (ibid.). In the TGWU, for example, Broad Left candidates have won all elections to senior executive posts held under postal ballots and they also dominate the executive council.

In UCATT, the use of postal ballots and a new electoral register in 1991 interacted with the growing strength of the union's Broad Left (articulating members' dissatisfaction with electoral standards and the executives' amalgamation ambitions) to produce a left majority on the executive. This coincided with a major crisis within the union involving the suspension of the sitting General Secretary and the defection of officers and members to the EETPU. A centre-left candidate, Brumwell, subsequently defeated the moderates' candidate in the General Secretary election. UCATT's political position on the Labour party centre-right and the dominant role of the General Secretary, both characteristics since its formation in 1971, were thus ended under postal ballots. Similarly in NALGO, the Broad Left, based upon an activist cadre in the large metropolitan centres, appeared to make more gains than other factions in terms of mobilizing support under postal ballots. In the IRSF, changes in the method of electing the PEC have not resulted in a permanent shift in the union's political leadership. While the immediate effect of the introduction of both workplace and postal ballots (previously the PEC was elected at branches in the IRSF) was the decline of the Broad Left, it has, on occasion, managed to rebuild a significant presence, benefiting from superior organization and cohesion, as compared to 'moderates', who are organized in Putting Members First. In the NCU, members' support for the two factions—Broad Left and Mainstream (later NCU First)—has oscillated. Members' discontent with both British Telecom's programme of restructuring and the union's leadership's responses, regardless of political affiliation, has contributed to the NCU's political instability. In the context of a one-year electoral period, the result has been political destabilization as each faction has controlled the national executive in turn: 1986, NCU First; 1987, Broad Left; 1989, NCU First; 1993 Broad Left. The present dominance of the Broad Left may again be short-lived, especially since it has 'narrowed' its appeal with the decline of the Communist Party and no longer has the support of the General Secretary.

EA 1988's introduction of periodic elections for General Secretaries and other senior national officers provided an opportunity for referenda on their performance. But the statutory rules also provided transitional arrangements for appointed officals approaching retirement age, which, given the age profile of successful candidates for General Secretary posts, has inevitably meant that a large number did not face re-election. Further, formal and informal arrangements made by individual unions have also limited the effect of EA 1988 on General Secretaries. For example, two of our surveyed unions, the STE and IRSF (plus the AUT outside the survey), require their executives to make a nomination for the post of General Secretary. As a consequence one person emerges as the 'official' candidate. In addition, EA 1988 has been at least partially neutralized in some unions by the development of a 'self-denying ordinance', whereby no other leading candidate has stood against an incumbent officer forced to submit to re-election. Examples within the survey where sitting General Secretaries have been returned unopposed are: NUPE, Sawyer; GMB, Edmonds; STE, Petch; and FBU, Cameron. However, this constraint has never been universal and clearly may weaken over time. Nevertheless, there have been some important contests during 1994: in the RMT, Knapp, General Secretary (9,471 votes) was opposed by Guy (7,174 votes) and Hime, Deputy General Secretary (8,244) was opposed by Connolly (8,129); NCU—Young, General Secretary (23,565) was opposed by Fry the President and Broad Left candidate, (13,552);[22] NUT—McAvoy, General Secretary, successfully, but only narrowly (38,881), defeated Hufford (37,329), while Hufford herself was subsequently defeated by Sinnott, a past President, in the contest for Deputy General Secretary later in the same year by 25,763 votes to 16,512; IRSF—Brooke, General Secretary (16,043) was opposed by Ellis (Broad Left, 12,074); NATFHE—Woolf, General Secretary was defeated by Akker, Deputy General Secretary of the AUT (7,349 votes to 6,855), and Woolf had previously defeated the incumbent General Secretary, Dawson, in 1989. Outside the survey, USDAW's General Secretary, Davies, was returned with a vote of 35,004 to the 22,766 cast for Savage (a national officer).

We only identified two unions in which sitting General Secretaries have been defeated: NATFHE on two occasions, 1989 (Dawson) and 1994 (Woolf), and, outside our survey, the NUJ in 1989. These defeats seem best explained by the incumbents' identification with specific difficulties besetting their particular unions. In the case of NATFHE the members identified Dawson with policy failures associated with the further education negotiations in 1989, and later, in 1994, they objected, via the ballot, to Woolf's response to the radical changes in contract sought by the College Employers' Forum. In the NUJ the key issues appeared to be the management of the union and derecognition. But these were exceptional cases, and given the institutional bias towards office-holders (Martin 1968), it is scarcely surprising that national union officials, or their nominees, have rarely been defeated in EA 1988 ballots. Thus, most unions' members appear satisfied with their established leaders despite the difficulties they experienced in achieving substantive gains in the hostile political and economic environment of the period.

Similarly the new rules for the election of PECs and senior executive officers (General Secretary, Deputy General Secretary) have not automatically led to any consistent and radical adjustments in the unions' hierarchies. Any developments were contingent on other factors. The TGWU illustrates the complexity of such changes. Under the union's rule book (formulated in 1922) the post of General Secretary was permanent, but subject to an initial ballot of the whole membership. This gave the holder a separate legitimacy from the members of the general executive council, who were elected by different sections of the membership. The latter's constitutional authority was in practice reduced by the turn-over and passivity of its members, and throughout most of the TGWU's history the General Secretary's role in policy formulation was pre-eminent (Allen 1957: 260–9). As previously argued, the authority of the General Secretary was undermined in the 1970s and visibly waned in the 1980s as the power of the executive council grew. This trend was further enhanced by increased factional organization which increased the cohesion and policy-making capacity of the executive. For example, the whole executive selected the Deputy General Secretary and Executive Officer. These positions had previously been in the 'gift' of the General Secretary, acting through the executive's finance and general purposes committee and subject in practice only to the executive's formal confirmation. In determining such decisions the executive assumed a new importance in decision-making. This helped change the political character of the union and in the process the majority on the executive secured the succession of the left's candidates to the post of General Secretary.[23] Nevertheless, the new-found power of the lay national executive was, to some degree, eroded by EA 1988's requirement for the periodic election of the General Secretary and by the union introducing periodic ballot elections for Deputy General Secretary and Executive Officer. These changes gave the holders of these posts a source of legitimacy largely independent of the executive. In the case of the latter two posts, they also gave the two newly elected officers greater independence *vis à vis* the General Secretary. Thus, in the TGWU, the changes imposed by the legislation strengthened the leading national full-time officials' authority, against the trend to greater executive influence which originated in the late 1970s.

In contrast TUA 1984 and EA 1988 had little effect on the internal power balance and political outcomes in the GMB. The reforms implemented to comply with the statutory template (identified earlier as producing a marked change in the GMB's electoral system) were incorporated in a wider process of reform changing the union's structure and ethos. This involved radical adjustments associated with mergers (see Chapter 3). While these developments entailed the abandonment of much of the distinctive conservatism and some of the structure of the former NUGMW, the union remained officer-led at all levels, and regional secretaries continued to act as the principal power brokers in determining the nomination and election of lay members to the executive. In effect, the legislation was responded to by the GMB's leadership as one part of its ongoing process of constitutional reform. The GMB therefore stands as a monument both to the failure of TUA 1984 and EA 1988 to achieve any transformation in unions' political complexion, and the vigorous autonomy of unions, which allowed their leaders to create their own agendas of political change.

In summary, therefore, changes in leadership and policy-making processes resulting from TUA 1984 and EA 1988 were contingent on the presence or absence of factions and the unions' existing formal systems of decision-making. Leadership changes varied widely across unions. Few sitting General Secretaries were defeated and more general political change was problematic. In non-factionalized unions the members faced no known political choice. Hence, even if the newly enfranchised members wished, they could not have knowingly altered the political make-up of the national leadership. Moreover, even when they had the option in factionalized unions they did not automatically vote for the moderate ticket. Where political changes were made, a number were influenced by the shift to postal ballots. However, in some cases this favoured the left and in others the centre-right faction. In other unions leaders associated with unpopular policies—regardless of political persuasion—were voted out of office. Changes in union policy-making processes also varied between unions. However, the legislation consistently diluted the role played by intermediate bodies and the postal ballot dispersed the vote to the home and reduced the influence of workplace activists. In unions which previously appointed the General Secretary or used the block branch vote for electing the national executive, this clearly created the potential for a new populist mandate. But even in unions which made marked changes in election procedures to comply with the legislation, such as the GMB, there was still considerable continuity in policy-making. Nevertheless, the legislation generally altered unions' policy-making processes by strengthening the influence of the centre and weakening that of intermediate bodies and local activists.

SUMMARY AND CONCLUSIONS: A FLAWED CONCEPT OF UNION DEMOCRACY

TUA 1984 required the PEC to be elected by individual ballot. As a consequence it abolished the election of the PEC by intermediate bodies—conference and sectional and area committees—or by branch ballots. This change stemmed from the Conservative view that unions' political processes and hence their policies were unduly influenced by the opinions of the activist minority, unrepresentative of the mass of members. However, the initial attempt to displace this cadre of opinion formers through the enfranchisement of the individual member was not achieved.

They readily found a new role in the administrative and political process of workplace ballots. Moreover, workplace ballots reinforced the collective ethos of trade unions, integrated workplace organization within the national union, and thus helped legitimize unions' national leaders and their policies.

This co-option of workplace ballots by unions was ended by the EA 1988, which required unions to use postal ballots to elect the PEC and certain other national senior officers, such as the General Secretary. EA 1988 was inspired by a view of democratic rationality which valued the individual above the collective interest. Unions were also conceived as quasi-contractual organizations in which union services were ideally assessed by members according to their individual interests.[24] However, the extent to which posting ballot papers to the home rather than the workplace elevated individualist values, and thereby subverted collective organization, must be open to doubt. Unions were not passive objects of Conservative policy. They complied with the legislation but the consequent rule changes were subsumed within unions' existing collectivist ethos and organization—their political and supporting democratic rationalities—and these were not amenable to change by legislation alone. There was, therefore, no simple and direct route from postal ballots to the reconstruction of union government. Ballots may have changed the location of the vote and increased the potential electorate, but their effect on union government was determined by a combination of context, existing decision-making systems, and leadership responses. Even unions most 'markedly' affected by the legislation did not experience the transformation in decision-making intended by the Conservatives.

The failure of TUA 1984 and EA 1988 to initiate a general transformation of trade union government, despite widespread compliance, was followed by its failure to promote the emergence of a 'moderate' leadership and associated changes in union policy. The legislators presumed that union members would display different political preferences when voting by secret individual ballot from when voting in a public forum. The latter method was considered more open to the influence of lay activists and the existing leadership. However, even the compulsory move from workplace to postal ballots did not change members' voting patterns in any consistent political direction. The imposed shift from the collective environment of the workplace to the individual vote in the home did not have the expected effect. The legislators overestimated the importance of ballots, which previously rarely had a privileged or proscribed status within union government. They were but one method—along with formally prescribed open votes, delegate meetings, and representative committees—by which collective interests were defined and support assessed. Further, the informal relationship between ballots and voting behaviour in factionalized and non-factionalized unions was not understood. Indeed, in certain circumstances the switch to postal ballots actually aided left-wing factions in some unions. If unions' democratic processes, both formal and informal, despite inadequacies, did not lead to the general, sustained, and pronounced distortion of members' views, the statutory template imposed by TUA 1984 and EA 1988 could not in itself precipitate the kind of major changes in union leadership and policy-making processes envisaged by the legislators.

Beyond its practical consequences, however, the legislation played an important symbolic role. Enshrined within its template were assumptions as to how unions should be constructed and operate. Legislation reinforced by Conservative rhetoric served to discredit union autonomy, their collective norms and practices, and claimed union democracy as the creation of government policy (DE 1991: 17). In practice, TUA 1984 and EA 1988 left an indelible if uneven mark upon the processes of union government, but where political outcomes changed, in whatever direction, these can be attributed to a combination of factors, including the wider context and internal political processes. In some cases, statutory inter-vention interacted with these factors to promote change. But in general the legislation singularly failed to initiate a transformation in the political complexion of union leadership or a reorientation of union policy in a 'moderate' direction, nor was this outcome ever likely. Thus the model of union government and its inadequacies held by the Conservative Government, and underpinning the legislation, was flawed.

NOTES

1. See the Technical Appendix for a detailed commentary on the rule-book surveys.
2. In fact the number of unions which specified only that the General Secretary be elected by ballot rose from 21 cases in 1987 (49 per cent) to 23 cases in 1992 (40 per cent), but this increase was subsumed in the wider move to elect General Secretaries prompted by EA 1988.
3. In one other union, the NCU, the posts of President and Vice-President rotated between the chair of the Engineering Section and the chair of the Clerical Section, both of which were elected members of their respective section executives.
4. In an executive election in 1992, contested by Weakley (Group) and Bevan (a left candidate not supported by the Broad Left), the turnout fell to 17 per cent.
5. During the 1970s a three-way factional contest had developed within the CPSA between the Moderates (embracing the Labour Party right to those with no party allegiance), the Labour Party left (at present organized under the label of the Broad Left '84), and the socialist left (the Broad Left). The executive committee was elected by annual conference but in 1979, as a consequence of a temporary alliance between the Moderate Group and the socialist left, the

conference resolved (in the face of executive opposition) to introduce individual-member ballots (retaining the one-year term). See Undy and Martin (1984: 97–100).

6. The first elections for the post of General Secretary and General Treasurer were won by Broad Left candidates (39 per cent turn-out for each position), but after new elections, Moderate candidates were victorious (62 per cent turn-out).

7. The GMB had been created in 1982 as a result of the merger between the National Union of General and Municipal Workers (NUGMW) and the Amalgamated Society of Boilermakers.

8. Attempts in 1989 by Edmonds to introduce individual-member ballots for the election of annual conference and regional councils, to hold the conference every two years, and to establish authoritative section conferences, met with failure.

9. See *IRLIB* (1990) 394: 10–11 for a report on *R. v. Certification Officer ex parte The Electrical Power Engineers Association* case.

10. National Union of Gold, Silver and Allied Trades; National Union of Sheetmetal Workers, Coppersmiths, and Heating and Domestic Engineers; Association of Patternmakers and Allied Craftsmen; and National Society of Metal Mechanics.

11. The Certification Officer commented that 'no evidence was produced to me on behalf of the Union of any steps taken or even contemplated since then [the passage of TUA in 1984] to resolve the difficulties . . . , and to move towards meeting the law's requirements' *Re: J. W. Whiteman and others and TASS* 3.2.87 (D/1/87).

12. One GMB officer commented that workplace ballots were an opportunity to 'run up the flag'.

13. Members of the executive were elected in regional constituencies, the autonomous unions which constituted the NUM.

14. The POEU had a history of factional political activity (the rules banning canvassing and electioneering were not enforced) but the Broad Left only effectively challenged the Labour right at annual conference, hence its support for conference election of officers.

15. Lorna Tee Consultancy, *Report to NALGO on Members' Attitudes to Voting at NEC Elections*, September 1991, Appendix 67/92—Annexure (1) General Purposes Committee 18 July 1992, NALGO. This decline is emphasized by the high rate of electoral participation in the workplace ballot held in 1991 for the post of General Secretary of the Graphic, Paper, and Media Union, formed by the merger of the National Graphical Association (NGA) and the Society of Graphical and Allied Trades (SOGAT), with a turn-out of 76 per cent in the NGA and 66 per cent in SOGAT.

16. As Gennard and Bain (1995: 240–3) show, this action by the Certification Officer (D/2/91) had unforeseen consequences for the subsequent election of the General Secretary of the newly formed GPMU. It resulted in a delay in the vesting day of the new union, as the two unions involved came to terms with the decision. This gave the NGA time to organize a more effective campaign on behalf of Dubbins (NGA), who subsequently defeated the more moderate Dean (SOGAT) in the contest for the General Secretaryship of the GPMU.

17. The MSF constitution also makes provision for women's seats on the executive.
18. By 1994 the GMB's sectional structure comprised: General; Technical Craft; APEX Partnership; Clothing and Textile; Food and Leisure; Construction, Furniture, Timber, and Allied. Proposals to establish three new sections—Public Services, Energy and Utility, and Processing and Chemicals—from the GMB Section have been shelved.
19. When TASS was a constituent of the AUEW, its Broad Left was part of the wider Progressive faction.
20. We are grateful to Mike Terry, Warwick University, for access to his research on the UNISON amalgamation.
21. The so-called 'Duffy rule', which was ostensibly introduced to save money, but which, when combined with a six-month delay in the election, had the effect of preventing Airlie, the Broad Left's preferred candidate, from competing for the post of President (subsequently won by Jordan).
22. A third candidate, Wiltshire, gained 2,278 votes.
23. The TGWU general executive council 'appointed' Morris to the post of Deputy General Secretary (he had not been on the original short-list), giving him a powerful position for a future bid for the post of General Secretary, which he subsequently won in 1991.
24. Ford (1992: 251–5) argues that this is the implicit Conservative view; see also Offe and Wiesenthal (1985: 207–9).

6

BALLOTS AND INDUSTRIAL ACTION

INTRODUCTION

We now examine the effects of the legislation imposing individual-member balloting prior to industrial action. The Trade Union Act 1984 (TUA 1984) included a legal requirement for trade unions to achieve a majority vote in favour of industrial action. As shown in Chapter 4, over the next ten years these initial measures were refined and amended no less than five times by the Employment Act 1988 (EA 1988), the Code of Practice for Trade Union Ballots on Industrial Action 1990 (CPTUBIA 1990), the Employment Act 1990 (EA 1990), the Code of Practice for Trade Union Ballots on Industrial Action 1991 (CPTUBIA 1991), and the Trade Union Reform and Employment Rights Act 1993 (TURERA 1993). As with the imposition of election ballots, the legislation interacted with the wider environment and unions' existing decision-making systems (as shown in Figure 1.1) to affect changes in union processes and outcomes. However, in the case of industrial action ballots an external party, employers (including managers), had much greater influence over the processes and outcomes of these ballots than did any external party in the case of election ballots. Employers acted both to ensure compliance with the legislation and responded to the ballot result. Further, the wider environment had a much greater and more direct effect on the outcome of these ballots than it did on the outcome of election ballots. Thus, it is necessary to disentangle a particularly complex web of interacting external and internal factors to assess the effects of the balloting legislation.

We examine four important issues which were repeatedly raised regarding the potential effect of the legislation. First, we assess trade union reactions to the statutory imposition of balloting procedures on industrial action. It was expected that unions would either alter their practices to accommodate the law or, on the other hand, resist this incursion into their internal democratic procedures. We establish the actual impact of the legislation on the processes of union decision-making by reference both to union rules and to union practice. The use of ballots for referring offers to union members is also examined. Second, we focus upon the effects of ballots on the internal organization of trade unions. In particular, the effect of the requirement to ballot on the centralization or devolution of power is considered, and the Conservative argument that 'the fundamental purpose of the statutory requirement for unions to hold strike ballots is to guarantee the democratic rights of union members, and thereby prevent the abuse of union power' (DE 1991: 12) is questioned.

Third, we investigate the effect of the above changes upon the management of the balloting process. We are concerned here with the balance of bargaining power between management and trade unions. According to two authoritative reviews, ballots could provide the means whereby unions might strengthen their negotiating positions, and secure concessions from employers (Donovan 1968: 114; ACAS 1987: 11). Employers' organizations further argued that manipulation of balloting constituencies, the timing of the votes, and the orchestration of members' voting behaviour could be used by union negotiators to boost perceptions of their power and thereby hoodwink management negotiators into making better offers (Wilkinson 1987: 34; EEF 1987). In these circumstances unions could achieve significant gains without incurring the costs of strike action. By contrast others argued that the imposition of ballots represented another strand in the convergence of state and managerial policies designed to undermine the collective power of trade unions (Wedderburn 1989; Hyman 1989: 247). Balloting, it was argued, contributed to the fragmentation and individualization of the employment relationship and left union negotiators hamstrung in a web of regulation. We examine these and other associated arguments.

Fourth, we analyse the impact of the changes on balloting and collective bargaining outcomes. Early interest in the imposition of ballots was dismissed because of fears that strike ballots were, in the words of the Donovan Commissioners, 'overwhelmingly likely to go in favour of strike action' (Donovan 1968: 114). By contrast, the Government has consistently claimed that industrial action ballots have contributed to a reduction in the incidence of strikes (DE 1988, 1989a: 10, 1989b: 1, 1991: 3–5, 11 and 1994: 53). Lastly, we summarize and draw conclusions from the above discussions.

CHANGES IN UNION RULES AND PRACTICES: AN OVERVIEW

This section considers the impact on union processes of the legal regulation of trade union balloting, as applied to collective bargaining. We distinguish between reference-back ballots and national and local industrial action ballots. Reference-back ballots are membership votes which test the acceptability of a proposed negotiated settlement between management and trade union representatives. For example, a ballot may ask members to endorse a new pay agreement, or accept a change in working conditions.

By contrast, national and local industrial action ballots, as the name implies, refer to votes in which trade union members express support for, or rejection of, proposed strike action, or action short of a strike.

Industrial action ballots, whether national or local, were subject to considerable legislative intervention throughout the period. The Employment Act 1980 (EA 1980) introduced a scheme which entitled unions to reclaim some of the costs associated with individual-member ballots, as long as the votes complied with regulations drawn up by the Certification Officer. TUA 1984 extended this regulation by stipulating that unions engaging in industrial action could only maintain their statutory immunity from action in tort if the action was supported by a majority of members in an individual workplace, semi-postal, or full postal ballot. This was amended by TURERA 1993, which, amongst other things, specified that such ballots must only be conducted by the full-postal method.

In comparison with industrial action ballots, the conduct of reference-back votes has been subject to less statutory intervention. The Employment Act 1982 (EA 1982) introduced an amendment to the regulations governing the refund of balloting costs and thereby allowed unions to reclaim the costs of reference-back ballots conducted by the full postal method. This regulation, like that governing the refund of full postal industrial action ballots, will be phased out between 1994 and 1997 as a consequence of provisions contained within TURERA 1993.

The account which follows examines how these legal changes affected union rules and practices. In making this assessment evidence is again drawn from the rule book surveys of 1980, 1987, and 1992; interviews with national officials from 24 unions in 1987–8, and 21 unions in 1993–4; and the in-depth case studies conducted over the period. The first part focuses on revisions and amendments to trade union rules and the second concentrates on changes in practice.

As regards rule changes, Undy and Martin (1984: 124–5) concluded that the conduct of collective bargaining was not traditionally regulated in detail by trade union rules. The results of our 1987 and 1992 rule book surveys confirm the enduring validity of this assessment and suggest that, with a few notable exceptions, unions have not sought to adapt to the new legislation by detailing in rule the steps which should be taken when organizing a reference-back or industrial action ballot.

The number of unions with mandatory rules covering the reference back of collective agreements declined from 6 unions (6 per cent) in 1980 to 4 (5 per cent) in 1987, and 2 (3 per cent) in 1992. The numbers with rules which provided for reference-back ballots at the discretion of the union's executive also declined from 42 (41 per cent) in 1980 to 29 (35 per cent) in 1987, and 22 (32 per cent) in 1992. The steady decline in the number of unions with rules in this area clearly demonstrates that the leaders and members of these unions had no desire to alter the *de jure* position of ballots in response to the introduction of regulations governing the refund of balloting costs in 1982. The reduction in rules in this area came about largely as a consequence of mergers and the attendant simplification of rules which often accompanied this process.

Union rules regarding the conduct of industrial action ballots tended to remain unaltered or become either silent or relatively unprescriptive (see Table 6.1). The percentage of unions which mandatorily required a membership vote before authorizing national industrial action remained reasonably constant despite the extensive legal regulation imposed over the twelve-year period. Of the 26 unions (31 per cent) which had rules requiring a ballot in 1987, 20 (29 per cent) had the same or similar provisions in 1992. Where change occurred this tended, as in the case of reference-back ballots, to be the result of merger activity rather than concerted reassessments of existing rules. Eight of the unions with mandatory balloting provisions in 1987 had amalgamated or transferred engagements by 1992; six of the new unions formed by this process did not have mandatory provisions governing the conduct of ballots.

Concerted changes were more evident where union rule books explicitly provided discretion over the organization of a national-level industrial action ballot. The significant reduction in the number of unions in this category between 1980 and 1992, from 41 (40 per cent) to 6 (9 per cent), reflected a conscious decision by many union leaderships to remove reference to balloting procedures altogether, rather than produce new rules covering this area.

A similar picture of change was evident regarding the organization of local-level industrial action. While the number of unions with rules making a vote mandatory remained relatively constant between 1980 and 1992—17 (17 per cent) in 1980 and 17 (25 per cent) in 1992—the number which made reference to discretionary procedures or other decision-making machinery decreased significantly from 42 (41 per cent) in 1980 to 0 in 1992. This change reflected a decision by many union leaders to remove all reference

TABLE 6.1. Rules, TUC-affiliated unions: vote of the membership required before authorization for national industrial action

| | 1980 | | 1987 | | 1992 | |
| | n = 102 | | n = 84 | | n = 69 | |
	no.	%	no.	%	no.	%
Mandatory	25	25	26	31	20	29
Discretionary	41	40	19	23	6	9
No or other specified procedure	36	35	39	46	43	62

to their decision-making methods in this area rather than attempt to comply in rule with legislative prescriptions.

At both the national and local levels the number of unions specifying postal or workplace ballots in rule did not change significantly over the period (see Table 6.2). However, this stability was largely illusory, as different unions adopted or relinquished rules specifying the voting method. Those unions which retained or adopted rules specifying postal balloting procedures tended to be relatively 'closed' unions which represented, or were predominately organized by, members with a strong professional ethos (Turner 1962: 233–68). Over the same period, many of the organizations with a strong craft ethos which had previously specified (or granted their executive discretion to use) the postal voting method in their rules dropped their commitment. To be specific, in 1980 the British Airline Pilots Association (BALPA), the Health Visitors Association (HVA), British Actors' Equity Association (Equity), the Amalgamated Engineering Union (Engineering Section) (AEU), and the Electrical, Electronic, Telecommunications and Plumbing Union (EETPU) all had rules regarding the use of postal ballots in national or local industrial action (Undy and Martin 1984: 123). Between 1980 and 1987, apart from BALPA they all dropped their postal balloting rules. BALPA continued and was joined in this category by the British Association of Colliery Management (BACM), the Hospital Consultants and Specialists Association (HCSA), the Prison Officers Association (POA), and the Bakers' Union. These changes were generally introduced as a consequence of pressure from

TABLE 6.2. Rules, TUC-affiliated unions: voting method used to test membership support for the proposed national industrial action

	1980 n = 66		1987 n = 45		1992 n = 26	
	no.	%	no.	%	no.	%
Full postal ballot	4	6	5	11	3	12
Half postal ballot	6	9	1	2	0	0
Workplace ballot	3	5	3	7	5	19
Ballot (method not specified)	9	14	27	60	15	58
Combined workplace and postal ballot	0	0	2	4	0	0
Vote at branch	3	5	1	2	0	0
Vote (method not unspecified)	31	47	2	4	3	12
Other	10	15	4	9	0	0

Note: Analysis of the voting methods specified in rule prior to the authorization of local-level industrial action reveals a similar distribution of procedures.

activists, rather than originating in the statutory regulations. Over the next five years the BACM, POA, and Bakers dropped their postal balloting rules and replaced them with less specific provisions.[1] In the final survey, only three unions retained a commitment to postal ballots in their rule books—BALPA, FDA, and the Hospital Consultants and Specialists Association.

Of those unions specifying the required majority in ballots before national industrial action, the percentage specifying a simple majority increased sharply (30 per cent to 61 per cent) between 1980 and 1987 and slightly thereafter (see Table 6.3).

In comparison, the number of unions specifying majorities in local industrial action ballots was consistently lower in each category. In 1980, 1987, and 1992, the number specifying a simple majority stood at 4 (4 per cent), 14 (17 per cent), and 11 (16 per cent) respectively, whilst the corresponding numbers specifying a two-thirds majority were 11 (11 per cent), 5 (6 per cent), and 4 (6 per cent).

Despite the general lack of mandatory rules requiring industrial action ballots and the number of rule books which were either silent or specified alternative procedures, decision-making power over the authorization of local industrial action was by 1992 almost entirely in the hands of unions' executive committees (see Table 6.4). In 1980, 56 unions (55 per cent) gave their executives this authority. By 1992, 60 (87 per cent) had adopted this position. Furthermore, in 1980 34 unions (33 per cent) did not specify such responsibilities in rule, but by 1992 this had fallen to only one union (1 per cent).

A similar pattern of increased centralization was revealed by rules governing the authorization of national industrial action (i.e. a dispute involving all the union's members) (see Table 6.5). In 1980, 53 unions (52 per cent) placed control over these issues in the hands of the executive committee; in a further 10 (10 per cent) power was vested in other

TABLE 6.3. Rules, TUC-affiliated unions: majority of those voting required before approval can be given to national-level industrial action

	1980 n = 23		1987 n = 28		1992 n = 20	
	no.	%	no.	%	no.	%
Simple majority	7	30	17	61	13	65
Two-thirds	13	57	6	21	6	30
Three-quarters	1	4	1	4	0	0
Other	2	9	4	14	1	5

Note: Figures exclude unions which organize votes but do not specify the required majority in rule.

TABLE 6.4. Rules, TUC-affiliated unions: body authorizing local-level industrial action

	1980 n = 102		1987 n = 84		1992 n = 69	
	no.	%	no.	%	no.	%
Executive committee	56	55	64	76	60	87
Other national committee			6	7	2	3
Conference	3	3	0	0	0	0
Union officers	1	1	1	1	0	0
Conference and/or executive	3	3	2	2	0	0
Section/area/region or district committee	5	5	6	7	3	4
Other	0	0	3	4	3	4
Not specified in rule	34	33	2	2	1	1

TABLE 6.5. Rules, TUC-affiliated unions: body authorizing national-level industrial action

	1980 n = 102		1987 n = 84		1992 n = 69	
	no.	%	no.	%	no.	%
Executive committee	53	52	72	86	64	93
Other national committee	0	0	5	6	2	3
Conference	4	4	0	0	0	0
Union officers	1	1	0	0	0	0
Special delegate conference	1	1	0	0	0	0
Conference and/or executive	4	4	3	4	1	1
Other	—	—	—	—	1	1
Not specified	39	38	4	5	1	1

intermediary bodies; the position in the remaining 39 unions (38 per cent) remained not specified or ambiguous. In 1992, 64 (93 per cent) specified the authority of the executive committee, 4 (6 per cent) relied on intermediary bodies, and only one small union still lacked an explicit rule-book provision.

Interviews with national trade union officers in 1987–8 and 1993–4 revealed that the decision to centralize power and widen the discretion of the national executive committee was prompted by pressure from four sources. First, there was increased uncertainty about the legal regulation of trade union activities. In the period before 1979 it was relatively easy for unions to keep pace with changing legal regulations through the normal cycle of quinquennial, biennial, or annual rule revisions at conference. During the 1980s and 1990s this became less practicable as the pace of change in statutory reform and judicial precedent accelerated markedly. Second, employer-led initiatives to decentralize and fragment collective bargaining arrangements increased the number of bargaining units and variety of bargaining procedures confronting union negotiators. Faced with this additional source of uncertainty, union leaders sought to maximize their control over local union representatives in order to prevent the union from being exposed to legal injunctions and fines. This pressure was exacerbated by the extension of unions' responsibilities by EA 1990. As discussed in Chapter 4, this Act made unions vicariously liable for the organization of unlawful industrial action by their officers and activists unless the union's leadership could demonstrate that they had taken steps to repudiate the action. Third, the issue of compliance or non-compliance with balloting legislation became a significant political issue within the labour movement during the 1980s. By removing all reference to balloting procedures from the union's rule book, union leaders and activists could demonstrate their hostility to government-imposed regulation whilst simultaneously obscuring whether in practice they had chosen to comply. Finally, amalgamations and transfers of engagements often provided the means by which these changes in rule were effected. The merger process required the parties planning and implementing this change to agree a set of rules for the new union. In these circumstances it was often easier to remove reference to balloting procedures rather than argue over a comprehensive set of rules for the whole union, or the detailed specification of different procedures within constituent sections.

In summary, the majority of unions did not amend their rules in order to conform with the new balloting laws. Those unions which did introduce changes to their reference-back balloting procedures normally did so as a consequence of a merger with another union. With regard to industrial action balloting procedures, as well as merger-inspired changes, the leaders of a number of unions initiated steps to delete reference to balloting procedures from their unions' rule books. Whatever the cause of the change, rules revisions produced a movement away from the detailed prescription of balloting practice and thus increased discretion. In the case of industrial action ballots, the power to exercise this discretion was formally centralized and placed in the hands of the national executive committee.

In respect of changes in balloting practice, we use evidence gleaned from the Workplace Industrial Relations Surveys (WIRS), and our own interviews with national officials in 1987–8 and 1993–4, to examine how the pattern of reference-back balloting changed between 1980 and 1994. We then examine the more contentious issue of industrial action ballots.

Throughout this analysis two issues are addressed: first, the reaction of trade unions to the statutory encouragement of postal ballots in EA 1980 and EA 1982; second, the extent to which they complied with the requirement for workplace or postal ballots in TUA 1984.

The most comprehensive survey of workplace trade union consultation techniques is provided by the WIRS surveys. Although they make no distinction between industrial action, reference-back ballots, and other procedures, they give a nationally representative indication of the level of trade union consultation with members at the workplace level. Evidence from the first WIRS (1980) revealed that unions consulted their members before the acceptance of agreements in 72 per cent of bargaining units covering manual workers, and 64 per cent of bargaining units with non-manual workers (Daniel and Millward 1983: 194). This practice became more widespread over the next ten years. By 1990, consultation was evident in 77 per cent of bargaining units covering manual workers, and 70 per cent of bargaining units covering non-manual workers (Millward *et al.* 1992: 235). The WIRS survey results in 1980, 1984, and 1990 also showed that the amount of consultation varied with the level of bargaining. Individual-member consultation was least prevalent where national multi-employer negotiations were the dominant form of bargaining, and most prevalent where greater emphasis was placed on workplace level bargaining. Worker representatives also reported that consultation over the terms of a proposed agreement was more common in larger workplaces.

As well as increasing the level of consultation during the 1980s, union negotiators also demonstrated a growing willingness to use more formalized methods for gleaning membership opinions. Information from the WIRS surveys reveals a decline in show-of-hands votes and a corresponding increase in secret workplace and postal ballots (Millward and Stevens 1986; Millward *et al.* 1992) (see Table 6.6). Voting by marking a ballot paper increased in manual unions from 19 per cent to 40 per cent and in non-manual unions from 30 per cent to 64 per cent. Thus, formal balloting more than doubled in both manual and non-manual consultative processes.

The overall impression of increased formality presented in Table 6.6 is supported by evidence of practice within specific unions. Evidence gained from our interviews with national officers from 24 unions in 1987–8 revealed that reference-back ballots were becoming more prevalent. However, diversity of practices persisted. According to our interviewees, collective agreements were normally referred back to the membership for agreement (88 per cent of unions), either via a show of hands/secret ballot (57 per cent of unions) or by reference to shop stewards and/or a delegate conference (62 per cent of unions). Many unions did both, either favouring one practice for a particular regional or industrial group, or alternatively, combining the practices so that a ballot was held after an initial delegate conference, or a straw poll of stewards had agreed to recommend the offer.

TABLE 6.6. Consultations with union members by union negotiators prior to a final pay settlement, 1984–90 (%)

	Largest manual bargaining unit		Largest non-manual bargaining unit	
	1984	1990	1984	1990
Any consultation with members	64	77	45	70
Method if consulted:				
General feeling of meeting without a vote	19	14	14	21
Show of hands at meeting	62	47	56	19
Voting slips/secret ballot at workplace or other meeting place	14	26	18	31
Postal ballot/secret postal ballot	5	14	12	33
Other answer	5	1	5	3
Base: worker representatives from recognized trade unions.				
Unweighted	894	716	946	663
Weighted	533	362	557	334

Note: Minor changes to question wording were made in two pre-coded responses in 1990. The 1984 wording 'voting slips' was changed to 'secret ballot at workplace or other meeting place'; 'postal ballot' in 1984 was altered to 'secret postal ballot'.
Source: Millward *et al*. 1992: 235.

Where ballots were held, the most common format was a workplace ballot (9 of the 12 unions used this method). We did not repeat the questions concerning the reference back of agreements in 1993–4; however, Elgar and Simpson (1993b: 9), in a survey of 846 union lay officials, full-time officers, and executive committee members, reported that more than half of the respondents (58 per cent) used workplace ballots or show-of-hand votes for the reference back of agreements. A third used postal ballots (32 per cent). Regrettably the extent of reference to delegate conferences was not reported in this survey.

Evidence of the level of industrial action balloting at the workplace level in 1990 is provided by the third WIRS survey. This shows that approximately three-quarters of worker representatives had consulted the membership before the start of industrial action (74 per cent for manual strike and non-strike action; 76 per cent for non-manual non-strike action).[2] The figure was higher in the case of strike action by non-manual trade union members (87 per cent). With regard to the method of consultation, as Table 6.7 shows, a wide variety of methods were used. Secret postal ballots were the most common means of endorsing strike action for both manual (35 per cent) and non-manual (59 per cent) groups, with secret workplace ballots (29 per cent) coming a close second for manual workers. Both groups preferred to use a show-of-hands vote at a meeting as a means of ascertaining members' views about non-strike action (see Table 6.7).

Consultation in general, and ballots in particular, were far less common when calling off strike and non-strike action. The third WIRS survey in 1990 revealed that approximately half of the manual union representatives surveyed reported membership consultation before ending strike or non-strike action. Amongst non-manual bargaining groups nearly two-thirds reported consultation before ending strike action, but only slightly over a third consulted before ending action short of a strike. The low level of responses to questions concerning the method of consultation limits the generalizations which can be made from these responses, but the figures appear to indicate that secret balloting, especially postal balloting, is much rarer in these situations (Millward *et al.* 1992: 299).

In summary, during the 1980s and early 1990s unions significantly increased and formalized membership consultation prior to the acceptance of pay offers and the authorization of industrial action. Results from the third WIRS survey in 1990, five years after the introduction of the requirement to hold workplace ballots and three years before the

TABLE 6.7. Consultation on industrial action, 1990 (%)

	Manual		Non-manual	
	Strike action	Non-strike action	Strike action	Non-strike action
Method of consultation:				
Ascertained views without a vote	2	5	—	1
General feel of meeting	5	8	6	17
Show of hands at meeting	24	72	23	39
Secret workplace ballot	29	12	22	27
Secret postal ballot	35	2	59	12
Other answer	3	—	—	—
Don't know/not answered	6	—	—	—

Base: worker representatives belonging to recognized trade unions reporting consultation with members before industrial action named in column heads began.

Unweighted	55	124	115	90
Weighted	23	38	67	29

Source: Millward *et al.* 1992: 298–9.

introduction of the postal balloting requirement, indicate that approximately two-thirds of unions representing manual workers and three-quarters
of unions representing non-manual employees used workplace or postal
ballots to consult their members before deciding whether to call industrial
action. Although there is no definitive data currently available, it also
seems probable that the level of postal balloting continued to increase after
1990, before being made mandatory by TURERA in 1993.

BALLOTS AND TRADE UNION ORGANIZATION

This section considers the effects of changes in industrial action balloting
practice on the internal organization of trade unions. In terms of Figure 1.1
this is represented by the arrows filtering through the decision-making
system from the balloting legislation.

We begin with an examination of the development of union policy in this
area before considering the effects of this policy on the distribution of
decision-making power within trade unions. The section concludes with an
analysis of the different effects of these changes on the organization of
industrial action ballots at different bargaining levels. Interviews with
national full-time officers in 1987–8 and 1993–4 showed that formal
balloting increased in the four years following the third WIRS survey in
1990. Of the 24 unions examined in 1987–8 only 6 provided for industrial
action ballots by rule, but 23 required in practice that workplace or postal
ballots be held before calling industrial action. The remaining union
changed its practice to comply with the legislation shortly after our
interview. In 1994 and following the imposition of postal ballots in
TURERA 1993, out of 21 unions the number with mandatory rules
requiring a ballot had declined to 5, but all of those interviewed reported
that their unions held (20 unions), or intended to hold (1 union), postal
ballots prior to the authorization of industrial action.[3]

In order to ensure that ballot votes complied with the legislation, unions
developed and issued their own detailed regulations to full-time officers
and lay activists. By the 1993–4 survey all 21 unions interviewed had
issued, or were in the process of issuing, formal regulations covering postal
balloting procedures. An example of the detail and precision of these
regulations is provided by the GPMU. Their balloting regulations, issued
to branch secretaries in 1993, ran to 16 pages and included: a timetable for
the organization of an industrial action ballot; advice on compiling a list of
members' addresses; outline plans for initiating industrial action; a model
ballot paper; and a series of *pro forma* letters with which to notify
employers of the intention to ballot and to inform members and employers
of the result of the ballot. In the final paragraph of these regulations,
branch secretaries are reminded that 'this procedure is *interim* and *must*

only be used after consultation with the Deputy General Secretary. Branches *must not* commence any Industrial Action Ballots without first consulting with this office' (GPMU 1993; italics in original).

Formal regulations, similar to the above, were used by all 21 unions' national officers to monitor and control the actions of other officers and local activists involved in disputes and contemplating industrial action. Thus, the most recent legal constraints on balloting prompted national officers to become more involved in workplace organization and collective bargaining. It also provided an opportunity for national officers to exert authority over local activists by demonstrating their expertise in this area of the law. Examples of such changes in previously highly decentralized unions included the AEU and TGWU. In the AEU the head office circular accompanying the balloting regulations stipulated that divisional, district, and area officers should sign and return a form to indicate that they had read, understood, and circulated the regulations to shop stewards in their area. Local union representatives within the TGWU were similarly required to gain the signatures of the independent scrutineer, local, and regional officers, as well as the General Secretary, before a ballot could even be organized. Unions with quite different traditions of control, including, amongst others, the GMB, TGWU, NCU, CPSA, EETPU, and AEU, also identified a senior national officer to take responsibility for, and exercise control over, all industrial action ballots and deal with related enquiries about the legality, or otherwise, of such action.

TURERA's introduction in 1993 of independent scrutineers produced further complications for trade unions. The twenty unions in our survey which had organized postal industrial action ballots under the provisions of the new Act all used independent supervisors to conduct the vote counts where more than fifty members were involved. Fourteen retained the services of the Electoral Reform (Ballot Services) Ltd. and six used the Unity Security Balloting Services. This represented a substantial external-ization of the related administration. As a result several unions closed their own internal balloting departments. However, according to union officials and scrutineers, this did not lead to the anticipated loss of control over the balloting process, but did improve the organization of ballots. In more than one case, scrutineers acted as consultants as well as a conduit for the exchange of information and best practice between national officers in different unions. These developments further encouraged centralization of control at the union's national office and helped concentrate power over the authorization of industrial action. For in practice, the union's liaison role was generally given to the senior national officer responsible for ensuring blanket compliance with the legislation. He, or she, therefore both policed industrial action procedures within the union and effectively secured the power of veto over any proposed industrial action by acting as gatekeeper to the independent scrutineer.

The externalization of ballot administration increased centralization and concentration of power within many of the unions in our study. It also had repercussions on the negotiating timetable and the financial cost of calling industrial action. A survey by the Labour Research Department in February 1993 revealed that most unions could organize industrial action in less than two weeks under TULR(C)A 1992 and the attendant CPTUBIA 1991. The additional notification and postal balloting requirements imposed by TURERA 1993 extended the process by some three weeks. Furthermore, the requirement to engage independent scrutineers to supervise the conduct of industrial action ballots involving more than fifty members exposed all of the unions to additional costs. For a union the size of the GMB, the costs of printing and distribution alone were estimated at 50p for each member involved in a ballot, a total of £10,000 in the first year of the 1993 Act's operation.

The adoption of increasingly formalized and centralized systems of control largely ensured compliance with the law when the union was policing the actions of its members in a well-organized company or workplace. However, monitoring and controlling industrial action which arose outside the annual pay round or occurred in smaller, less well-organized workplaces was more problematic.

In the majority of company-level bargaining units, the new balloting procedures fitted easily into established negotiating procedures (ACAS 1993: 16). Our in-depth case studies showed this was particularly evident where trade union organization was sophisticated, and the annual negotiations formally institutionalized. In these circumstances ballots were valued as an additional stage in the negotiating process; they were not seen as a 'bolt-on extra' which could be used or discarded. If the annual negotiations broke down, both sides knew that a ballot would have to be held before the dispute escalated. However, the place of ballots within the timetable of discussions surrounding localized grievances or spontaneous disputes created difficulties. Although examples exist of the adoption of balloting procedures in these areas, notably the Ford Motor Company (Hougham 1992: 229), this was not commonplace and the difficulties associated with these incidents were illustrated in two of our case studies in 1988–9.

Union members at the Jaguar Car plant in Coventry were involved in three incidents of unofficial industrial action between 1988 and 1989. The first, in October 1988, was in protest at the movement of labour by managers in breach of the agreed procedures. The second, in November, was a strike by stores staff in protest at the dismissal of a worker who allegedly assaulted a manager after refusing to account for unauthorized use of the photocopier. A third incident in May arose when a steward accused a manager of assaulting him after he had challenged the lay-off of employees in breach of an agreed procedure. In only one of these three incidents was an industrial action ballot organized, and then only after the employees had returned to work following a walk-out. The problems of organizing ballots after these 'flare-ups' were recognized by the company's industrial relations managers, who issued elaborate guidance notes to line managers at the site. A series of flow diagrams attached to these notes specified that after unconstitutional industrial action, 'informal discussions with union officials to obtain compliance with [the] appropriate stage of procedure [a ballot], should take place' (JIRD 1988).

In smaller workplaces and the growing number of enterprises which lacked sophisticated trade union organization these problems were even more pronounced. At an airport in the East Midlands, where one of the unions in our investigation had only a few members represented by one shop steward, we were told that the responsible full-time officer had only become aware of an unlawful and unconstitutional ballot over a collective grievance when he caught a ballot paper 'blowing in the wind'. In this case the local representative had organized a ballot and instigated a walk-out without contacting the relevant full-time officer. Fortunately for the union the dispute had been resolved rapidly and the full-time officer was therefore relieved to find that the employers had not contemplated taking legal action.

In summary, despite the absence of rule-book provisions all of the unions in our survey had adopted by 1994 a formal policy of conducting postal ballots before authorizing industrial action. These policies were universally accompanied by the formalization of balloting procedures, a centralization of power at the national level, and increased contact between the national officers and local activists. Furthermore, the introduction of postal balloting substantially increased the costs associated with organizing ballots, externalized much of the administration of these votes, and added to the tendency within a number of unions to concentrate decision-making power in the hands of senior national officers with competence in this field. As a consequence of these changes, first workplace balloting and later postal balloting became an accepted feature of the negotiating process in most bargaining units. Unions thus acted to ensure compliance with the statutory regulation. This was most effective in set-piece annual wage negotiations in large well-organized workplaces. However, when disputes arose within smaller workplaces, or as a consequence of spontaneous grievances, ballots were less common.

MANAGING THE BALLOTING PROCESS

The unions' national leadership's responses to the legislation were not solely determined by the legislation. The leadership had a number of choices to make in dealing with its balloting requirements. There were elements of discretion in organizing ballots which could have significant effects upon the processes and outcomes of these votes—whether workplace or postal. We identified, from our studies, five important issues commonly raised by union and management negotiators. These were: establishing the bargaining objectives; defining the balloting constituencies; co-ordinating inter-union activities and ballots; interpreting the ballot results; and determining when a ballot should be held. The way in which the negotiators chose to deal with these issues could have a profound effect upon the success or otherwise of the ballot and could influence perceptions of the union's bargaining power. If these issues were clearly thought through in advance of the ballot, and were not subject to legal challenge, there is evidence that ballots could assist the union's negotiators. By pre-planning to meet the administrative demands, and actively campaigning to gain democratic legitimacy for the proposed course of action, unions could bolster their bargaining power. Where this did not take place the organization of the ballot could expose differences of opinion between negotiators and members, as well as competing sectional interests within and between trade unions.

Full-time officers interviewed in 1987–8 and 1993–4 highlighted the role ballots played in defining and communicating bargaining objectives as well as assessing membership attitudes. The importance of this contribution to internal democratic processes should not be underestimated. A number of studies conducted before the widespread introduction of ballots noted the difficulties that this task presented to trade union negotiators (Lane and Roberts 1971: 85; Batstone *et al*. 1978: 46–62). Defining a set of objectives upon which everyone is agreed and can move forward together is a difficult task. The balloting legislation helped to concentrate attention on this issue by requiring negotiators to state their areas of agreement and disagreement in a straightforward and easily understandable manner. It also encouraged union and management negotiators to codify their respective claims and offers in a manner which produced a forced-choice vote. As one interviewee commented, 'there is no place in a ballot for questions over a range of issues' (AEU representative 1988).

In short, members must be asked to support a particular position or reject it. The results of this exercise, unlike membership meetings, can be summarized succinctly and placed before negotiators in black and white. However, this simplicity conceals dangers; ballots may address a particular well-defined issue, but the vote may be influenced by other concerns not addressed on the ballot paper. At BT in 1987, when the company chairman initially challenged the unions to ballot their members, both management and trade union negotiators were confident that the pay offer outlined in the reference-back ballot would be accepted. Lack of balloting experience, including failing to test the feelings of members and lay activists before going to a vote, left union and management unprepared for the results of the ballot. Members rejected the pay offer, and used the vote to give manifest expression to their latent dissatisfaction with the rapid pace of recent organizational changes. This initial vote also provided union members with a quantifiable indication of the feelings of their colleagues in more geographically remote parts of the company. Contrary to union and management expectations the initial ballot thus encouraged militancy, not moderation, and contributed to an even larger majority for a strike in the subsequent industrial action ballot.

Other problems related to ballots involving relatively large numbers of members concern the issue of aggregation. Regional or occupational differences may be submerged in aggregated ballot results, or exposed to a wider audience if not aggregated. In the return-to-work ballots in the BT dispute, referred to above, disaggregated results demonstrated very wide differences of opinion. Members in Northern Ireland, the West of Scotland, Merseyside, the North East, and Inner London recorded majorities for prolonged action. This produced internal tensions and highlights the dangers union representatives face if they release disaggregated results and do not maintain close links with all their constituents throughout the negotiations. It also demonstrates the problems associated with using a ballot to end a strike. As many negotiators rapidly realized, ballots should be used as a supplement to, and not a substitute for, membership meetings and other informal means of gauging and mobilizing membership opinion. When used appropriately these traditional trade union activities can help test opinion, develop commitment to the bargaining objectives, and build the solidarity needed to realize union goals prior to the formal ballot.

The importance of finding appropriate ways to define voting constituencies and co-ordinate different groups of members was clearly demonstrated by the engineering hours dispute between 1989 and 1990. During this dispute, the CSEU pursued a claim for the 35-hour week at EEF plants through a co-ordinated programme of pattern bargaining and rolling strike ballots. In this case the requirement to define balloting constituencies was turned to the unions' advantage. In the first stage of this programme, ballots were held at workplaces where a majority for action could be assured (McKinlay and McNulty 1992: 209). The negotiators hoped that by achieving votes in favour at these plants the profile of the dispute could be raised and the momentum maintained in subsequent votes. As ACAS noted in their assessment of this dispute, 'it was notable for the coherent planning of the trade unions involved and their skill in organizing the complex balloting arrangements required before industrial action involving different companies and different groups of members could be taken or contemplated' (ACAS 1991: 10).

However, the definition of balloting constituencies did not always produce advantages for the union and could give rise to legal challenges. In

Blackpool and Flyde College v. *NATFHE* [1994] *IRLR* 228 CA, Bingham MR, interpreting section 21 of TURERA 1993, granted an interlocutory injunction because the union's notification of the intention to ballot was not sufficiently precise in describing the members who would be called upon to take part in the vote. This last decision was greeted with alarm by many unions. The salami-slicing of bargaining constituencies was felt to have reached its logical conclusion, as union members would in future be required to register their intentions individually. However, all of our interviewees in 1993–4 reported, shortly after the NATFHE judgement, that they had been able to adapt their practice to describe the balloting constituency without supplying employers with the individual names of those who would be required to vote. At this stage the wider decollectivizing effects of this judgement seem to have been averted. It would appear that unions have no obligation to name names when they have cohesive collective bargaining arrangements and maintain high levels of membership amongst the *group* of workers called upon to ballot. Whether this will continue to be the case in the longer term remains to be seen.

The balloting legislation also aggravates the problems associated with co-ordinating action between members in different trade unions. TUA 1984 required that each union should ballot its members separately, and independently, before endorsing industrial action. However, as was demonstrated above, before the introduction of postal ballots by TURERA 1993 unions adopted different balloting methods. The EETPU, for example, adopted postal ballots in 1984 and maintained this general policy throughout the 1980s, although it did not introduce rule book provisions to this effect. The low level of its membership in many manufacturing workplaces meant that they did not take a lead in single-table negotiations and therefore their ballot results were frequently announced after the results of workplace ballots by other unions. Balloting also exposed other differences between the procedures of unions. The GMB, for example, originally required a two-thirds majority before calling industrial action, although most other unions require only a simple majority. At Eng Co, the EETPU ballot result was announced two weeks after those of the other unions, and 65 per cent of the GMB members voted in favour of industrial action short of a strike—the average vote in favour by members of the other four unions was 75.6 per cent. In this case the GMB and EETPU members were placed in the invidious position of either defying the overtime ban taken by other unions, or alternatively supporting the action without the benefit of a confirmatory ballot.[4]

Apart from procedural differences, ballots may expose substantive differences between unions when an offer or proposed industrial action differentially affects the members of unions party to the negotiations (Manning 1991: 2). We found this to be most pronounced when unions representing white-collar and professional employees bargained alongside blue-collar unions. In the railway, engineering, and telecommunications industries in particular, ballots by the TSSA and RMT, the MSF and AEU, as well as the STE and NCU, frequently produced different results and reduced inter-union co-ordination in any ensuing negotiations or dispute. The problems of maintaining co-ordination within and between unions were most pronounced when the issue under negotiation was redundancy or establishment closures. In these situations the lack of solidarity between workers in different workplaces and regions of the country was publicly displayed in ballots and could rarely be effectively ignored. Pit-head ballots by the NUM on a national basis in 1981 and 1984 and the campaign by the NUR against work-force reductions at BREL in 1986 provide good examples of this phenomenon. In each case significant differences in the majorities for action recorded at different workplaces effectively prevented or undermined the union's position in the ensuing industrial action.

The announcement of ballot results did not necessarily end the arguments about the intentions and solidarity of the membership, particularly if there was a low turn-out and/or only a narrow majority for taking action. Employers occasionally challenged the representativeness of the ballot by suggesting that abstentions represented votes against action. Management in effect questioned the legitimacy of the vote in favour of action. These challenges could also give rise to court action. For example, in *British Railway Board* v. *NUR* [1989] *ICR* 678 CA the employer argued, albeit unsuccessfully, that 200 union members had been denied a vote and that this invalidated the ballot. In response to this type of challenge, the GMB altered its rules. In 1991 it gave the executive power to overrule the general requirement for a two-thirds majority and in 1992 it clearly specified that action could be authorized by a two-thirds majority of those who actually voted, not those who were eligible to vote at the time.

The unions in our study also took strenuous steps to ensure that there were high turn-outs in any ballot. In 1988 this typically meant that ballot votes were taken after a workplace meeting. Where meetings could not be held or attendance was low, several unions distributed ballot papers to members' desks to encourage them to vote and raise any queries about the issues under dispute. Five years later all 19 of the union officers whose unions had been involved in industrial action under TURERA 1993 reported meetings before and/or during the postal balloting period. In the case of the STE and GPMU it was reported that employers had refused facilities for these meetings on more than one occasion. Within the Scottish Prison Officers Association (SPOA), not part of our survey, the employer even sought an injunction preventing a meeting at which a ballot would take place (*Scottish Prison Service* v. *Scottish Prison Officers Association* [1991] *IRLR* 371, CS Outer House). All of the unions which had been involved in a postal ballot also reported putting considerable effort into collecting the names and addresses of those members who would be called upon to vote. Several interviewees commented that the collection of this information encouraged direct contact between activists and members, facilitated direct discussion of the issues, and in the case of more than one union led to substantial increases in union membership. Such consultation was seen as vital in providing a true indication of the democratic wishes of the members, as the following extract from the GMB's regulations demonstrates:

the ballot, while complying with the law, may give no real indication of the overall support for the action. It remains legal for the union to assess support in other ways, e.g. consultation with lay officials; mass meetings etc. However nothing should be done which might be interpreted as interference with the right to vote freely or in secret. It is advisable for any mass meeting or other consultation to take place either before ballot papers have been dispatched, or after the last day of voting (GMB: 1993, para. 21).

The importance of these pre-meetings was further demonstrated by the contradictory results some unions achieved in reference-back and industrial action ballots. At Eng Co, according to the deputy works convenor, members were inclined to use reference-back ballots tactically, an approach which was clearly demonstrated in 1988 when members rejected the management's pay offer in a reference-back ballot but refused to endorse industrial action in the subsequent workplace ballot. This voting behaviour was explained as follows:

the workforce are sophisticated in their outlook . . . They realize that they will always be given another bite at the cherry after a reference-back ballot . . . The only time members actually gave their real position [on the pay offers in 1987 and 1988] was in the final pre-industrial action ballot (interview with deputy works convenor).

In other words, the members knew that the union would have to ballot them again before authorizing industrial action and therefore they could refuse any offer without personal loss. As a consequence of these problems the negotiators at Eng Co decided to dispense with a preliminary reference-back ballot in subsequent negotiations. The failure to judge their members' real attitudes had temporarily undermined their bargaining credibility and they did not want this to happen again. For similar reasons none of the unions in our study reported tactically encouraging members to vote for action they were not really prepared to take. However, all of the unions, including the NUM, reported that achieving a majority in an industrial action ballot could improve their bargaining power and may make some members more willing to engage in action. As an official of the construction union UCATT noted in a 1993 interview, 'Where ballots are called they help as a negotiating weapon, and may help taking the proposed action.'

When, contrary to the expectations of the members, ballots were not held, the effects could be debilitating. Indeed, it has been argued that 'The absence of a ballot [before the miners' strike]—the centre piece of the NUM constitution—was poisoning the dispute. The moral legitimacy of the strike and therefore its potentially explosive political power was crippled' (Wintour, quoted in Meredeen 1988: 219).

But even where the ballot revealed that a majority of members supported the proposed action, the threat of action had to be a credible threat. As one full-time ASTMS officer commented in 1985: '[strike ballots] are a bit like a nuclear deterrent, employers have to believe that you are prepared to do it [take strike action] or it has no credibility whatever.'

The bargaining power provided by a successful ballot may be further enhanced by the judicious timing of the ballot. At Eng Co in 1989, the unions planned their approach to the negotiations carefully and pencilled in a schedule for the negotiations and ballot before the talks formally began. This tactic was used to bring management to the negotiating table at a time convenient to the unions. As a consequence negotiations which had in previous years been delayed for six months began on time. By planning their approach in advance, the unions were able to complete the requisite stages of the procedural negotiating agreement quickly and then concentrate on organizing the ballot. At BT in 1987 by contrast, the timetable for the negotiations and subsequent ballot were largely made in response to management's challenge to test opinion. The hurried and ill-prepared ballot which followed had unforeseen consequences and caused severe problems for all involved.

The importance of assessing and influencing the attitudes of union members was not overlooked by managers. During disputes at BT in 1987 and 1990, employees were effectively asked to engage in a management-sponsored ballot when senior managers asked them to sign forms indicating that they were prepared to work normally. When workers refused they were suspended and sent home.[5] Similarly, during the railway dispute in 1994, managers commissioned MORI to undertake an attitude survey of 250 striking signal workers in an attempt to assess their attitudes and resolve. When this exercise failed other tactics were used to attack the collective resolve of the strikers. An improved local offer was made to staff in the South West division and details of this package were sent direct by post to employees' homes, bypassing the union negotiators who had earlier dismissed the offer. These practices were not widespread and frequently backfired as employees questioned the legitimacy of management taking these actions. The control of the balloting process was seen to be a union preserve which could give moral as well as legal legitimacy to industrial action. Management tests of members' opinions prior to a lock-out were not seen in the same light, as the ambulance workers' dispute amongst others demonstrated (Kerr and Sachdev 1992). As a consequence, employers were more likely to limit their campaigning to management briefings and the circulation of leaflets, rather than attempt to organize their own ballots. However, the introduction of postal balloting and the request to give seven days' notice of such a ballot, in TURERA 1993, clearly provides more time for employers to employ such tactics prior to the strike ballot itself.

In summary, within many unions ballots exposed the lack of consensus over bargaining objectives and methods, as well as contributing towards the centrifugal forces for sectionalism. However, where union negotiators were able to draw upon a strong and disciplined workplace organization, the balloting requirement could provide a focus for agreeing the bargaining objectives, resolving or concealing internal differences, and planning effective action. In these circumstances ballots provided a useful means of increasing a union's bargaining power and legitimized any resultant industrial action in the minds of union members and management.

BALLOTING AND BARGAINING OUTCOMES

It is not easy to assess how the outcomes of collective bargaining have been altered by changes in the law governing industrial action ballots. The outcomes of negotiations between union and management representatives are clearly influenced by a wide range of factors, inside and outside the enterprise (Martin 1992: 14–15). The way in which the leaders and members of trade unions, as well as the managers with which they bargain, react to these changes is only partly affected by the law. A range of other pressures are at work, including employers' business strategies and the strength of union organization, as well as wider changes in social attitudes, the economy, industry structure, and the range of available technology. In this context, the effects of union and management bargaining tactics generally, and ballots specifically, may be very small. Moreover, even where unions are able to extract concessions through the use of ballots, these gains may be short-lived as employers use other means to reassert their bargaining power after the dispute. With these caveats in mind, this section considers the following six points in turn. First, the extent to which increased legal regulation of the balloting process reduced the number of times unions organized industrial action ballots. Second, the relationship between different balloting methods and the level of membership turn-out. Third, the results recorded by trade unions in industrial action ballots. Fourth, employers' responses to the announcement of ballot results. For example, we ask if the use of industrial action ballots has made strikes more likely, or encouraged employers to make improved offers and thereby remove the need for industrial action by union members. Fifth, we consider the direct effect of increased legal regulation of industrial action ballots on employers' willingness to use the courts in order to challenge trade union actions. Finally, we assess the indirect effects of the legislation on the willingness of trade union members to take part in industrial action.

A number of commentators have suggested that the gradual introduction of increasingly complex statutory regulations governing the organization of industrial action ballots would reduce the number of times they were organized by trade unions.[6] However, a cursory examination of the overall level of industrial action balloting activity during the 1980s and 1990s does not appear to support this view. Figures collated by ACAS reveal that after a steady increase in the level of balloting following the imposition of the requirement for workplace ballots in TUA 1984, the number of votes plateaued in the early 1990s (see Table 6.8). More recent information is provided by the Electoral Reform Ballot Services (ERBS), which in the seven months following the introduction of a postal balloting requirement in September 1993 reported organizing approximately 500 ballots for 11 TUC-affiliated trade unions—representing 73 per cent of the registered membership of TUC-affiliated trade unions (ERBS 1994: 3).[7]

TABLE 6.8. Number of industrial action ballots, 1985–93

	85–6	87	88	89	90	91	92	93
Number of ballots[1]	253	280	331	359	n/a	300	269	352
Number of stoppages in progress in year[2]	—	1,016	781	701	630	369	253	211
Ratio of ballots to stoppages in progress in year	—	28	42	51	—	81	106	167
Number of workers involved in stoppages (thousands)	—	887	790	727	298	176	148	385
Number of working days lost (thousands)	—	3,546	3,702	4,128	1,903	761	528	649

[1] These figures are based upon reports compiled centrally by ACAS head office staff and upon reports from local ACAS officers about disputes with which they have been involved, disputes which they have shadowed but have not been directly involved in, and the details of ballots described in newspaper articles. As a consequence of this procedure, the recorded number of ballots may misrepresent the total number of votes, for three reasons. First, ACAS officers may not be aware of every dispute where a ballot has been organized. Second, the results of separate ballots in a multi-union situation may not be recorded individually. Finally, the reliance on local officers may lead to more than one report about the same dispute in difference parts of the country (source: interview with ACAS officer).

[2] These figures are based upon reports collected from the local office network of the Employment Service. No distinction is made between strikes and lock-outs. Political strikes, work to rules, and go-slows are excluded, as are small stoppages involving less then ten workers or lasting less than one day, except where the aggregate number of days lost exceeds 100.

Sources: ACAS internal records and Bird (1994: 200).

Although the number of ballots organized by trade unions remained relatively constant in the late 1980s and early 1990s, the proportion of disputes preceded by a ballot increased (see Table 6.8). This changing ratio reflects both the decline in overall strike activity in the early 1990s and the steps taken by senior trade union officers to ensure that union members remained within the law. Thus, while the number of recorded ballots in 1987 fell well short of the number of recorded stoppages, by 1993 the position had reversed. These figures would appear to support the previous observation that the proportion of disputes preceded by a ballot has increased in the four years since the third WIRS survey conducted in 1990. However, this is not to say that all stoppages were preceded by a ballot. Evidence from a survey of union representatives by Elgar and Simpson in 1992 revealed that 30 per cent of respondents were aware of unballoted industrial action taking place within the preceding three years (1993b: 8). Our investigations confirm this picture. In interviews following the passage of TURERA 1993 we found union officials were still required to monitor closely a number of disputes to ensure compliance with the law.

The introduction of a statutory requirement for trade unions to hold workplace industrial action ballots in 1984 was also accompanied by ministerial assertions that this procedure would increase the representativeness of these votes (DE 1983: 17, 1987: 3). Workplace ballots, it was argued, would involve more people than a block vote at conference or a show of hands at the workplace or branch. Analysis of the turn-out in workplace ballots between 1985 and 1993 supports this claim. Although it is difficult, if not impossible, to obtain accurate measures of voter turn-out in show-of-hand votes, a number of the trade union officers interviewed in 1988 estimated that turn-out in these votes averaged 20 per cent in branch-based systems and 50 per cent when conducted at the workplace. By contrast the average level of voter turn-out in secret workplace ballots was considerably higher. Within one district of the AEU an average turn-out of 81 per cent was recorded in the 17 workplace industrial action ballots held during 1987. The level of turn-out was higher still in well-organized workplaces. At Eng Co between 1987 and 1989 the plant's trade unions held three industrial action ballots; the average turn-out in these ballots of approximately 6,000 workers was 87 per cent.

The representativeness of postal ballots is a more contentious issue. In debates within the House of Lords over the TURERA Bill 1993 it was suggested that the average turn-out would decline under this new regime. It was argued that the reliance upon a disparate membership casting votes from their home addresses would produce membership participation figures comparable with the average of 30–40 per cent recorded in union election ballots. In practice these pessimistic predictions have not been wholly realized. According to the Electoral Reform Balloting Services, the participation rate in the 242 postal ballots they conducted between January and March 1994 was 73 per cent (ERBS 1994: 3). This unexpectedly high level of turn-out probably reflects both membership interest in industrial action decisions and the small size of most ballots. Ninety per cent of industrial action ballots over the period of the ERBS study involved 500 or fewer members and not surprisingly the turn-out varied according to the size of the voting constituency. In ballots of under fifty members the turn-out averaged 79 per cent and in ballots of over 1,000 members it fell to approximately 44 per cent (see Table 6.9).

Another common assumption made by the advocates of industrial action ballots was that these votes would enable a moderate membership to express their dissatisfaction with the militant action of their leaders (see Chapter 4). As a consequence it was expected that many ballot votes would produce majorities against industrial action. However, in practice the results of ballots conducted under both workplace and postal balloting systems produced consistently high majorities in favour of the union leadership's recommendations (see Table 6.10). As can be seen from Table 6.10, the lowest percentage of ballots supporting the union recommendation, and therefore almost certainly some form of industrial action, was 78 per cent in 1985–6, rising to a high of 94 per cent in 1989.

The high proportion of ballot results supporting the union negotiators' recommendation at least partly reflects the general unwillingness of union officers to hold a ballot if they were not reasonably confident about

TABLE 6.9. Membership turn-out in postal industrial action ballots by size of membership constituency, January–March 1994

	0–50	51–100	101–500	501–1,000	1,000+
Number of ballots	76	49	95	10	12
Percentage turn-out	79	73	73	66	44

Source: ERBS (1994: 3).

TABLE 6.10. Relationship between ballot result and union recommendation, 1985–93

	85–6	87	88	89	90	91	92	93
Number of ballots	253	280	331	359	n/a	300	269	352
Number in support of union recommendation	196	251	305	336	n/a	276	244	316
Percentage of votes in support of union recommendation	78	90	92	94	n/a	92	91	90

Source: ACAS internal records.

securing the desired result. The majority of union officers in our interview
surveys during 1987–8 and 1993–4 indicated that they would only
countenance the organization of a ballot where there were good chances of
success. Exceptions to this general approach were provided by the few
cases where ballots were either held at the behest of the employer, or
alternatively used to resolve otherwise intractable disagreements between
union negotiators and activists.

The high level of voter support for the union negotiators' recommendations was also influenced by a change in unions' industrial action tactics
during the 1980s and 1990s. As documented elsewhere, there is evidence
that over this period industrial action by unions was more likely to take the
form of action short of a strike or one-day strikes, rather than all-out strike
action (Edwards 1992: 377–8). Some unions also chose to use highly
selective strike action, as in the CSEU dispute for the shorter working
week, noted above. Both these developments suggest a moderation in
unions' chosen forms of industrial action. This change in the form of
industrial action was doubtless affected by a number of social and
economic factors, not least increases in unemployment and perceptions of
employment insecurity. It may also have been considered more cost-
effective by unions conscious of the cost of paying strike benefit over a
longer period. However, it also appears to have been influenced, at least in
part, by the introduction of detailed legal specification of the acceptable
wording of questions on industrial action ballot papers. TUA 1984
specified that the ballot paper should distinguish between a call for strike
action and action short of a strike; the two issues could not be dealt with by
one question. This requirement was further elaborated in CPTUBIA 1991.
As a consequence a majority of the unions covered by our interview
surveys in 1987–8 and 1993–4 included both questions on their ballot
papers. According to staff interviewed at the ERBS, implicit in this policy
was a desire on the part of many union negotiators to begin any dispute
with action short of a strike, whilst reserving the right to escalate the action
if required at a later date. It probably also helped to secure an initial
majority for a form of action which required a limited and known sacrifice
by the members involved, as compared to the all-out and indefinite strike.

The detailed specification of proposed action on the ballot paper was
further encouraged by a number of employer challenges to the wording of
union ballot papers in the late 1980s and early 1990s.[8] As a consequence of
these challenges unions were frequently forced to provide their members
with a detailed specification of the proposed action on the ballot paper. For
example, in the Thames Water dispute in November 1993, the TGWU
asked their members the following question on the ballot paper:

Are you prepared to take three separate one day strikes in a seven week period to
demonstrate your anger at the Company's recent actions and persuade the
Company to enter into further meaningful negotiations?

Similar questions were asked by the other three unions involved in this dispute—the AEU, the GMB, and UNISON. This and evidence from the Eng Co and Engineering Hours disputes, discussed earlier, indicates an increased sophistication in the degree of pre-planning of some industrial action, inspired in part by the legislation.

The effect of the announcement of the ballot result upon the resolution of a dispute is more difficult to ascertain. As previously mentioned, although the number of ballots organized by trade unions remained relatively constant throughout the late 1980s and early 1990s, the number of stoppages and working days lost declined dramatically. These changes raise a number of important questions. Did the introduction of a requirement for unions to hold industrial action ballots undermine the unions' ability to organize action, or alternatively, did it lead employers to concede settlements in response to ballot results rather than risk industrial action?

The previous section drew on the case studies to demonstrate that the requirement to ballot presented unions with a number of organizational problems which, if not resolved, could undermine union bargaining power and limit their ability to call industrial action. However, the effect of these problems on the overall pattern of industrial action is difficult to disentangle from other contextual changes. The evidence which we have suggests that in the majority of cases where unions effectively organized a ballot this was generally followed by the authorization of industrial action. In 1991 and 1992, ACAS reported that where a ballot revealed a majority for industrial action, the union involved went on to call for industrial action in two-thirds and three-fifths of cases respectively. In the majority of the remaining cases where the union gained the support of a ballot vote, it would appear that the union either gained an improved offer from the employers or alternatively withdrew the threat of action. Given the general reluctance of union negotiators to call for a ballot when the results could not be assured, and their preference for one-day strikes or action short of a strike, these figures appear to demonstrate that unions were less likely to organize a total and unlimited strike in the early 1990s than they had been a decade earlier. However, how much of this change can be attributed to the imposition of a requirement to hold a confirmatory ballot prior to calling action is less certain. The union officials interviewed in 1987–8 and 1993–4 commented that although it took their unions some time to adapt to each change in the law, and that this could result in legal action, in the longer term they did not believe that the requirement to organize a ballot had independently reduced trade union bargaining power. This is not to say that other legal restrictions upon trade unionists' rights to take industrial action during the 1980s and 1990s had not reduced the number of recorded strikes during the period. Indeed, several interviewees commented that their ability to organize effective industrial action had been limited by the legal curtailment of unions' ability to organize effective pickets, limitations on unions' internal disciplinary procedures, and the effective outlawing of unofficial and secondary action.

An examination of the use of the law by employers to challenge the legitimacy of industrial action ballots appears to support the observations of the full-time union officers in our surveys. The use of injunctions in the late 1980s has been widely documented (Evans 1985, 1987; LRD, 1985, 1987, 1988, 1989, 1991, and 1994). Evans's surveys report the grounds for 80 injunctions, of which 47 were issued due to balloting irregularities. The LRD surveys report a further 76 legal actions, of which 30 concerned ballots. Of the 47 cases analysed by Evans, 43 involved no ballot before strike action, 3 were over the wording of the ballot paper, and one related to the balloting procedures. Evans's surveys reveal that of the 36 cases in which injunctions were granted, 16 led to the withdrawal of industrial action. The LRD surveys detail 18 cases where a request for an injunction was granted, 10 where it was refused or subsequently lifted, and 3 cases where an action for damages was abandoned or settled out of court. Of the 18 disputes where a legal challenge was successful, 14 led to the organization of a fresh ballot and 3 resulted in the union terminating the action. In the remaining case union members continued with unofficial action despite the court ruling.

The injunctions reported by Evans and the LRD demonstrate that employers rarely took legal action against their unions during the 1980s and 1990s. Overall, injunctions were sought in less than 2 per cent of all disputes, and those employers prepared to take this action were heavily concentrated in a few litigious companies and industrial sectors. Of the 156 injunctions sought by senior managers on all grounds over the period between 1983 and August 1994, 104 arose from actions by employers in 5 industry groupings—newspaper publishing and distribution, 37; road, rail, and marine transport, 28; manufacturing, 16; local government, 12; and the Royal Mail, 11. Despite the low level of litigation and its heavy concentration in a few sectors, a large number of unions were affected by these actions. In all, a total of 29 separate unions were named in injunction applications and a larger number were threatened with legal actions. Hence, it is not surprising that, as we found in interviews, unions' decisions to comply universally with the balloting legislation were heavily influenced by their concern to avoid the threat of legal injunctions. In this context, the willingness of senior managers at Austin Rover to take eight of their company's trade unions to court in 1985 for failing to comply with the balloting requirements in TUA 1984 had a very significant impact upon the subsequent policy of compliance adopted by a number of TUC-affiliated trade unions.

Aside from documenting employers' applications for injunctions, surveys of their awareness of the law and preparedness to threaten legal action give an indication of the extent to which the law had permeated and coloured the relationship between management and union representatives. A survey of senior personnel managers in 144 unionized organizations by Income Data Services in 1992 revealed that 66 per cent of respondents said that the legislation had not changed their approach to the handling of industrial disputes. Of the more detailed responses, 4 per cent had used the courts to prevent industrial action, 10 per cent had threatened to take a trade union to court over industrial action, and 55 per cent had contingency plans to determine the lawfulness of threatened industrial action (IDS 1992a: 4). A survey of union negotiators in the same year revealed similar findings, with 28 per cent of respondents reporting legal challenges to industrial action (Elgar and Simpson 1993b: 5).

Consideration of the effects of the threat of legal action on the outcome of specific disputes suggests that one of the most significant effects was not the prevention of action but the delay it entailed for negotiators on both sides. In the late 1980s, strikes within the Post office, London Underground, and Associated British Ports were called off or delayed after injunctions were successfully obtained by the employers.[9] Whether these injunctions significantly affected the union's chances of victory in these cases is difficult to ascertain. In the Post Office dispute three-quarters of the staff had ignored the initial call for industrial action and the strike would probably have collapsed without the injunction. In the Underground dispute another ballot was organized which produced a reduced majority for action—4-to-1 instead of 7-to-1 in favour. Both parties then sought mediation from ACAS and reached a higher settlement. In the case of the docks dispute the delay undermined the resultant strike, although the willingness of the union's leadership and wider labour movement to back this action was questioned in several quarters while the union fought the legal challenges before authorizing industrial action.

Legal challenges by employers were more successful in preventing industrial action where members feared victimization, either because workplace organization was weak or the action was unofficial. In *University of Central England and Kingston University* v. *NALGO* [1992] *IRLR* 81, the employers argued that the union should have released the results of its industrial action ballot at each institution instead of combining the results on a nation-wide basis. Although the legal challenge was unsuccessful, staff at the affected institutions did not engage in strike action because they feared being dismissed. Other studies over the period suggest that a significant minority of employers have been more willing to exercise their common-law right to dismiss employees engaging in industrial action, particularly when this action is unofficial (Elgar and Simpson 1992). Whether these developments should be attributed to the use of balloting legislation, or the more widespread diminution of trade union power, remains a moot point.

Although the law played an important part in a minority of disputes, most employers were content not to use these new legal remedies. During our investigations it became evident that there was some underreporting by employers of balloting irregularities by trade unions. Closer analysis revealed that this practice reflected the pragmatic desire of negotiators on both sides to achieve a workable agreement and maintain a relationship based on trust. In several cases, management negotiators were clearly unaware of the complexities of the workplace balloting laws and attendant code of practice. Where they were aware, they had not attempted to monitor or challenge their trade union counterparts over the conduct of any ballot or industrial action, because this could be seen as undermining the good faith upon which the successful conclusion of their negotiations depended. One employer summed up this attitude with the remark, 'I'd rather not go looking for problems' (Eng Co Employee Relations Manager, 1989).

The wider effects of the balloting legislation upon union activities and the climate of industrial relations is even more difficult to assess. The detailed regulation of industrial action ballots may reasonably have been expected to affect members' preparedness to vote for industrial action, especially the 'Government's health warning' covering breach of contracts of employment. However, only 7 of the 24 trade unions surveyed mentioned this in 1988 and none referred to it in 1994. The 'cooling-off period' which inevitably accompanies the organization of the ballot vote was similarly seen to have little effect under workplace balloting systems although the added delays associated with postal balloting created some problems. As the AEU respondent commented, employers occasionally take advantage of this delay in order to 'move the goalposts' during a dispute. In some cases this involved the employer making an improved offer before the ballot result was announced and then claiming that the ballot was no longer relevant to the current dispute.

Apart from legal interventions, the number of cases where ballots demonstrably led to outcomes which could not have been anticipated in their absence was small. The BT dispute in 1987 provides one example of industrial action which could perhaps have been averted if management had not challenged the unions to ballot over their offer. Similarly, management negotiators at Ford in 1986 increased their final offer by 2.5 per cent and removed an important productivity string when a ballot by manual workers revealed a 2-to-1 majority in favour of industrial action. As Paul Root, Ford's Industrial Relations Director at the time, commented: 'the secret ballot put the unions in a much stronger position because they were completely free of the usual criticisms such as that of rigging the ballot' (Thomas 1986). In this case, the use of a ballot at the end of negotiations enabled the unions to make gains without the costs associated with industrial action, but the ballot was not a substitute for the latent bargaining power the unions required to make the threat of a strike credible.

In summary, the proportion of disputes preceded by an industrial action ballot in the late 1980s and early 1990s increased. Between 1985 and 1993 workplace ballots raised participation rates. The introduction of the requirement to hold postal ballots in 1993 did not affect the proportion of disputes preceded by a ballot. It did produce a marked reduction in membership participation in large disputes. In smaller disputes turn-out remained largely unaffected by the imposed switch from workplace to postal ballots.

Throughout the period of study, under both workplace and postal ballots, the results of industrial action ballots invariably went in favour of the union negotiators' recommendations. This was probably helped by both the tendency for national and local full-time officers to authorize a ballot only when they were reasonably confident about winning the vote and the inclusion of more 'moderate' forms of industrial action on the ballot paper. Under postal ballots, the national leadership's greater control over the balloting process probably also exercised a moderating influence in this latter period. Faced by considerable financial and other related problems, they had good cause to err on the side of caution when sanctioning a request for a strike ballot if the result was thought to be finely balanced. In these circumstances national officials would be more prone to take the wider view and safeguard the union's funds and position by refusing a ballot, as against the local activists' concern for the immediate issue. Further, it appeared from our interviews that many national leaders were moving to adopt and promote a more moderate or conciliatory stance in the 1990s, and this too probably influenced their cautious response to requests for industrial ballots.

Whether the more targeted approach to industrial action in both workplace and postal ballots produced less and not more industrial action is difficult to assess. Other things being equal, it could be argued, on the one hand, that the inclusion of questions proposing more selective and limited action helped secure majorities for some form of action, when in the absence of such an option the members would have rejected an all-out strike. On the other hand, if the voters had only been offered an all-out strike they may, in some ballots, have preferred this to no industrial action. Further, even if the more targeted and more moderate approach did secure more majorities for some form of industrial action—as seems likely in the climate of the period—it may not necessarily have actually produced more industrial action. It may only have served to restart negotiations and produce a more acceptable offer. Thus the inclusion of more restricted forms of action on the ballot paper probably had little if any overall effect on the incidence of strike action.

To some extent the impact of workplace balloting, but particularly postal balloting, on industrial action was contingent on its organizational context. In well-organized bargaining units involving single-union negotiations with co-operative or neutral employers the imposed balloting provisions caused few problems for the trade unions. Indeed, they may have aided union negotiations by giving a new legitimacy to their claims and thus helped secure better settlements. However, in multi-union, industry-wide bargaining units with poorly-organized work-forces, postal ballots in particular added a further obstacle to effective action. They reduced turn-out, as compared to workplace ballots, and made it more difficult for unions to co-ordinate their bargaining tactics. In these circumstances they probably reduced the union's ability to organize effective sanctions. It may therefore be concluded that the imposed systems of balloting, but particularly postal balloting, contributed at the margin to the moderating tendencies of the period. However, the impact of both workplace and postal ballots on the very marked decline in strike incidence and the number of days lost by strikes from the late 1980s to the mid-1990s was insignificant when compared to other factors.

SUMMARY AND CONCLUSIONS: THE BUREAUCRATIZATION OF DECISION-MAKING, FRAGMENTATION OF COLLECTIVE BARGAINING, AND MODERATION OF INDUSTRIAL ACTION

The imposition of industrial action ballots and statutory encouragement of reference-back ballots produced a number of important changes in internal union organization and unions' external relationships with employers. However, these changes were not determined solely by the balloting legislation. In practice the influence of the legislation was mediated and influenced by wider contextual trends and the processes of internal organizational decision-making (as shown in Figure 1.1). External pressures (as documented in Chapter 3), including increasingly antagonistic relationships with some employers and growing financial problems, sometimes closely associated with loss of members, caused union leaders to be very sensitive to the balloting legislation. However, despite the sizeable problems posed by these changes, union leaders retained considerable discretion when dealing with negotiations and disputes. The way in which they exercised this discretion had a significant effect upon the manner in which they implemented the legislation and the associated outcomes.

Trade unions sought to comply strictly with the legislation on industrial action ballots. Bargaining practice was also changed by the introduction of more reference-back ballots. However, union leaders did not generally extend formal balloting to questions concerning the termination of industrial action. In the majority of cases they preferred to deal with these questions by the more traditional means of show-of-hand votes. Further-more, union leaders were extremely reluctant to change their rules in order to accommodate the new laws. They chose instead to comply with the letter of the law in practice, by issuing detailed regulations and instructions to local-level officials regarding industrial action. The resulting changes in union processes for controlling industrial action thus led to a bureaucratiz-ation of procedures and increased centralization of power. The subsequent imposition of postal balloting strongly encouraged these tendencies. Union leaders sought in this latter period to ensure universal compliance by concentrating decision-making power in the hands of the executive and/or national full-time officers, whilst simultaneously externalizing the adminis-tration of the balloting process.

The effect of the balloting legislation on the mobilization of support for industrial action in general tended to be contingent upon the industrial context. In particular, the level at which negotiations took place, and the sophistication of workplace trade union organization, influenced the balloting processes and outcomes. When ballots were conducted at the end of annual negotiations within workplaces with one dominant trade union, high membership levels, a sophisticated pattern of local membership representation, highly institutionalized negotiating procedures, and a not overly antagonistic relationship with the employer, there is evidence that the union negotiators became adept both at ensuring high membership turn-outs and producing ballot results which supported their recommenda-tions. Indeed, the results of several disputes indicate that well-planned action supported by a ballot demonstrating the membership's commitment to action could significantly increase the bargaining power of the union's negotiators. However, in less well-organized workplaces with poorly developed negotiating procedures, or in situations where union leaders were forced to respond to spontaneous disputes and belligerent employers, the requirement to ballot created significant organizational problems. In these circumstances full-time union officers were often placed in a defensive position and forced to cancel, reorganize, or repudiate the action.

Unions also experienced some problems when organizing votes as part of the process of multi-union industry-level bargaining, especially when the ballot results revealed divisions within, or between, trade unions over the substance of negotiations. These difficulties became most pronounced with the introduction of postal balloting. In these situations the problems associated with defining agreed bargaining objectives and balloting constituencies, as well as co-ordinating the activities of several different unions, added to the difficulties of ensuring high membership turn-out and often gave rise to questions about the representativeness and meaning of ballot results.

Industrial action ballots did not of themselves therefore strengthen or undermine workplace trade union organization. Weak organization could, however, undermine the effectiveness of a ballot. The sectional and individual interests which have been an enduring feature of British trade unionism since its inception could be palpably exposed in a ballot. In this context, the well-documented fragmentation and constriction of collective bargaining, together with the exclusion of trade unions in some companies and erosion of union membership in others, did not provide an environment conducive to the extension of balloting practice. These problems were heightened by the financial pressures placed on trade unions as a consequence of the requirement to ballot by post.

Independent of the organizational context, the net effect of the changes outlined above on moderation or militancy and the overall incidence of industrial action was small in comparison with other environmental changes affecting the pattern of management–union relations during the 1980s and early 1990s. However, in the climate of the period, the following balloting characteristics probably tended to aid moderation rather than increase militancy. First, balloting provided a comparatively low-cost and credible way of demonstrating the resolve of union members without calling on them to engage in strike action. This helped produce new offers and settlements without recourse to industrial action. Second, the imposition of specified ballot questions also appears to have encouraged many union leaders to offer their members more moderate forms of industrial action, including action short of a strike and targeted programmes of one day strikes—although whether this reduced or increased industrial action is a moot point, for it might have encouraged action which would not otherwise have occurred if the alternative choices had been an all-out strike or no strike. Third, the threat, and demonstration of the damaging financial effects, of legal actions by employers made many union negotiators more cautious and risk-averse in their dealings with employers during disputes. On balance therefore, and in the hostile environment surrounding union negotiations, the balloting legislation probably made a minor contribution to increased moderation.

Thus, union leaders responded to the threats posed by the new balloting laws, the fragmentation of previously established collective bargaining arrangements, and a decline in membership levels in a generally defensive manner. Faced with the threat of legal action, an increasing number of hostile employers, and a less secure membership base, as well as wider economic and social uncertainties, they adopted more 'moderate' bargaining tactics and engaged in less strike action. They therefore centralized and bureaucratized the relevant decision-making processes to ensure compliance with the legislation and in order to avoid the legal sanctions. The imposition of industrial action ballots, and particularly postal ballots, in the context of the period hence encouraged oligarchic rather than democratic tendencies.

NOTES

1. The Bakers' Union replaced its rules governing postal ballots with a system of workplace ballots because it was felt that this would increase the turn-out and representativeness of industrial action votes.
2. The question on industrial action ballots in the third WIRS survey may have led respondents to confuse industrial action ballots with reference-back ballots over the acceptability of an offer. Despite this problem the survey data provide the most comprehensive picture of national practice currently available (Millward *et al*. 1992: 297, 312).
3. Elgar and Simpson report similar findings based upon a survey of 846 full-time union officers and officials from 15 of the 23 TUC unions with over 100,000 members in 1991–2 (1993b: 9). 71% of respondents referred to workplace ballots and 41% to postal ballots as the most common means of consulting members. Only 3% of respondents referred to show-of-hands votes at members' meetings.
4. In *British Aerospace* v. *CSEU* (1989) (unreported), Schiemann J. refused the employer's request for an injunction when he ruled that the CSEU's rules requiring a two-thirds majority in an industrial action ballot did not supersede the requirements of TUA 1984 as amended by EA 1988. Whether this same principle could be invoked in a legal challenge by members to the calling of industrial action on the basis of the contractual nature of their union's rule book remains unanswered at the present time.
5. In *Ticehurst and another* v. *British Telecommunications PLC* (1992) *IRLR* 205 CA, Ralph Gibson LJ held that when Mrs Ticehurst, a member of STE, refused to sign an undertaking to 'work normally' she was in breach of an implied contractual duty to serve her employer faithfully and therefore the employer's decision to send her home without pay was justified.
6. See, for example, DE (1983a).
7. The figures from ACAS and ERBS are not strictly comparable. ACAS records the number of ballots at the workplace level and therefore does not separately record ballots in multi-union situations. By contrast, ERBS registers the number of ballots by union and therefore would individually record the number of ballots in disputes involving several unions.
8. In *London Underground Ltd.* v. *National Union of Railwaymen* [1989] *IRLR* 341, Simon Brown J. granted an injunction restraining the union from organizing industrial action on the grounds that a circular accompanying the ballot paper identified four issues over which it was in dispute with LUL whilst only one of these clearly satisfied the statutory definition of a trade dispute (Simpson 1993: 289). This decision is in marked contrast to the view of Millet J. in *Associated British Ports* v. *TGWU* [1989] *IRLR* 291, who suggested that all that was required was that the strike called was the one voted for (Simpson 1993: 289). Similar issues were raised by *Newham London Borough Council* v. *NALGO* [1993] *ICR* 189, 198, where it was held that the taking of industrial action must relate to an issue identified on the original ballot paper. In this case the original dispute was settled and the reason for industrial action, although

related to the issue identified in the original ballot, was of a different nature. Similarly, in *Blue Circle* v. *Transport and General Workers Union* [1989] 7.7.89 (unreported), Alliot J. held that industrial action must be limited to that originally called for on the ballot paper and associated literature (Simpson 1989: 235). In this case the union had obtained support for a 24-hour strike, but had subsequently sought to increase the action without a further ballot.

9. *London Underground Ltd.* v. *National Union of Railwaymen* [1989] *IRLR* 341; (No. 2) [1989] *IRLR* 343; *Post Office* v. *Union of Communication Workers* [1990] *ICR* 258 and *Associated British Ports* v. *Transport and General Workers' Union* [1989] *IRLR* 291; [1989] *IRLR* 305 CA; [1989] *IRLR* 399 HL.

7

UNION BALLOTS, BEHAVIOUR, AND STRATEGY

INTRODUCTION

This chapter summarizes and concludes the analysis of the impact of legally prescribed ballots on union behaviour in the UK. In summarizing these changes we follow the pattern of the previous two chapters and distinguish between process and outcomes. First, we consider the causes and nature of the change in process. In this analysis we stress the importance of context and associated contingent factors. Second, we establish and assess the relative importance of the factors which mediated between the modified processes and their outcomes—the key factors examined are union decision-making systems and the hostile environment. Third, we examine the choices made by union leaders in responding to the legislation and in dealing with the non-ballot-related changes discussed in Chapter 3. In analysing these choices we present them as strategic choices, i.e. discernible patterns of behaviour (Mintzberg 1987), and explain them by reference to the leaders' political, democratic, and administrative rational-ities, as shown in the centre of Figure 1.1 (p. 5). In this manner we both qualify the emphasis placed on contingent factors when analysing changes in processes and examine the interactive effects of the balloting legislation and other developments affecting changes in trade unions previously considered in Chapter 3. We conclude with an assessment of the effect of the above changes and leaders' choices on the management of the unions in the 1980s and early 1990s.

BALLOTS AND CHANGES IN UNION PROCESSES

The legislation prescribing secret ballots—initially postal and workplace ballots, and subsequently postal ballots only—for important national elections and industrial action was ostensibly intended by the Conservatives to improve union democracy by increasing lay participation in secret votes in critically important decisions. Its underlying intention was to release the voice of the supposed moderate majority and thus reduce industrial and political militancy. It was also an important part of a much wider political and economic agenda, including related legislation, aimed at reducing union power, encouraging individualism at the expense of collectivism, deregulating the labour market and winning favour with the wider electorate. The legislation was supported by a rhetorical attack on trade unions. They were portrayed as outmoded institutions and, as such, obstacles to industrial efficiency. In Mrs Thatcher's period of office, this was accompanied by strong Government resistance to unions' industrial action in the public sector. In effect the Government led by example in defeating the NUM in 1984–5 and in doing so demonstrated to unions at large its determination to oppose industrial action. Thus, the balloting legislation was an important and integral part of a prolonged and relatively consistent attempt by successive Conservative Governments to change union behaviour in a radical manner.

The wider economic, industrial, and managerial context was generally favourable for realizing Conservative objectives, in as much as it too tended to weaken union influence. In particular, changes in the level and composition of employment militated against trade unionism. An historic-ally low level of employment and a shift of employment out of traditionally highly unionized sectors into traditionally low or non-unionized sectors contributed to a marked reduction in union membership. Competitive pressures also caused managers to search for new means of securing improvements in labour productivity. In these circumstances employers and managers in the non-unionized sectors were generally not supportive of trade unionism, while some in the unionized sectors derecognized unions. The growing use of human resource management techniques was also associated in some organizations with strategies seeking to marginalize trade unions. The result was that unions found it extremely difficult to increase union membership by recruiting in the non-union sectors, while also encountering problems in maintaining density in the shrinking unionized sectors. In this context unions were, for most of the 1980s, pushed on to the defensive and managers, compared to the 1970s, given both cause and opportunity to take the initiative in managing labour.

The above developments were critically important for the application of the balloting legislation concerning industrial action and, to a lesser extent, elections. For the balloting legislation was fundamentally enabling legisla-tion: the Government itself remained at arm's length from its application. It relied on unions' compliance, or the threat of sanctions, to impose its balloting and related provisions on unwilling unions. It was the role of employers or managers, disaffected members, and, in some areas, members of the general public to use or threaten to use the available sanctions and secure for the Government compliance with the proposed balloting templates for elections and industrial action. Thus, given the origins of the legislation and union antipathy to externally imposed regulations, the hostile environment was centrally important for gaining compliance. It provided employers and managers with the power and encouragement to use the legislation. In these circumstances it only needed a few important cases to demonstrate to the unions in general the disadvantages of non-compliance.

Trade unions over the period 1979–94 thus complied with, rather than embraced, the processes prescribed by the legislation for ballots on elections and industrial action. This required changes in virtually all processes of decision-making. However, the degree of change varied widely. Some unions already had systems of decision-making which included periodic elections of officials and executives by postal ballots, for example the AEU and EETPU. Other unions did not have periodic elections of leading national officials, but they did ballot on industrial action. This was the case in NALGO (but not always postal ballots) and BIFU. Thus, as shown above in respect of elections, different clusters of unions changed minimally, moderately, or markedly their processes to comply with the legislation. The degree of change required to comply with the legislation was therefore contingent on existing decision-making processes. One result of the legislation was therefore to reduce diversity.

Unions required to change their processes generally did the minimum necessary to comply with the legislation. Thus, they modified their processes incrementally in response to the incremental changes in the law between 1980 and 1993. Moreover, they did not extend postal balloting to other related decisions, or positions, such as the reference back of agreements and the appointments of officers other than those directly affected by the legislation. Regarding elections, there was no general move by disaffected members to enforce the changes via the legal process, even with the help of the CROTUM. However, a small number of unions slow to comply were threatened with such action and eventually almost all unions changed their electoral rules and practices to give effect to the legislation. As the union rule book normally prescribed electoral processes in some detail, unions found it necessary to change their existing rules in order to comply with the legislation and avoid complaints from disaffected members. In contrast, in respect of workplace and subsequently postal ballots for industrial action, unions did not generally comply by changing or inserting in their rules the detailed procedures required by the legislation. As many of them did not start the period with detailed rules governing the calling of industrial action, it was not necessary to amend them. By the end of the period their rules either complied in very general terms or were silent or unprescriptive regarding the processes to be employed in calling industrial action. Even union leaders who saw general advantages in strike ballots were averse to rules which satisfied the legislation and made ballots mandatory in all circumstances. Nevertheless, they changed their practices through a series of very detailed regulations in an attempt to ensure strict and blanket compliance with the legislation. The threat of effective sanctions, in the form of fines, injunctions, and ultimately sequestration, was critically important for influencing these changes. The Conservative legislation, which reduced union immunities and made unions liable, and subsequently vicariously liable, for any industrial action taken by their members and not officially repudiated by the union, was critically important for making union leaders sensitive to the costs associated with non-compliance. Hence, the primary reason for unions' religious but unbelieving compliance with the *detail* of the legislation on industrial action was fear of sanctions.

In summary, the combination of legislation and the wider hostile environment placed the unions on the defensive for much of the period. They felt compelled to comply with the legislation. In this context refusal was perceived as ultimately self-defeating and, in the case of industrial action ballots, potentially very costly. However, they tended not to incorporate the changes in rule if they could be accommodated by modifying practice. The degree of change was therefore contingent on the rules and practices of the individual unions prior to the legislation and, as a consequence, varied widely between unions. Nevertheless, the changes made were, in each union, the minimum necessary for compliance. The unions did not extend the prescribed methods to other processes of decision-making and, as we will show below, sought by other means to limit the adverse effect of the imposed changes on the related outcomes.

FROM PROCESS TO OUTCOMES: THE MEDIATING FACTORS

In this section we examine the manner in which the changes in process prescribed by the Conservatives interacted with existing decision-making systems and non-ballot related changes to affect outcomes. This complex interrelationship between process and outcomes is shown in Figure 1.1 by the arrows filtering from balloting legislation through union's decision-making systems to changes in union government and industrial action. These changes are also shown as influenced by the arrows on the curved lines emanating from non-ballot related changes in unions.

We examine the outcomes by reference primarily to the Conservatives' ostensible or more immediate objectives. These may be summarized as more moderate unions, in both the political and industrial sense, and more democratic unions. The changes in electoral processes were expected to produce leaders more attuned politically to the newly enfranchised, and presumed moderate, majority. Similarly, the introduction of postal ballots in the calling of industrial action was expected to reduce industrial militancy by allowing the same moderate majority free play in controlling the more militant union activists and leaders. Further, the intention was also to improve union democracy by the introduction of workplace and subsequently postal ballots and associated changes which would: increase membership participation and influence (at the expense of the lay activists' influence); increase accountability through periodic elections for key national posts; provide more detailed information on both candidates in elections and the extent of any proposed industrial action; introduce external scrutineers and hence eradicate malpractice in both elections and the calling of industrial action; exclude non-elected persons from the national executive; and ensure secrecy in the casting of the individual vote. We examine the relationship between changes in processes and the moderation of outcomes before examining their effects on union democracy.

The attempt to moderate union behaviour will be examined first by reference to election outcomes, followed by reference to industrial action. The Conservative approach toward the election of moderate rather than left-wing candidates was flawed on three important counts. First, their assumption that union malpractice was a significant factor in union elections was ill-founded. Hence, the eradication of malpractice had very little, if any, effect on electoral outcomes. Second, and more importantly, the assumption that members were generally faced with known political choices in competitive elections—or that the newly imposed election addresses would present members with such choices—was not correct. A significant number of unions, including some major TUC affiliates, did not offer their members such a choice prior to the imposition of ballots. Further, the imposition of postal ballots and the associated legislation did not, of itself, even when it prompted marked changes in process, encourage the factionalism needed for political choice. For example, in the GMB and NUPE, both large and influential unions which changed their electoral processes markedly to comply with the legislation, the established leadership, and particularly the dominant national full-time officials, continued to win elections in the absence of any factional opposition worthy of note. Similarly, in other non-factionalized organizations, established leaders of different political persuasions continued to win elections unopposed by any alternative organized groups. The traditional reliance and trust placed by members and activists in their established leaders combined with the supporting decision-making processes which remained unaffected by the balloting legislation to ensure that there was generally no change in political alignment and outcomes in non-factionalized unions despite frequently marked changes in their election processes.[1]

Third, and most importantly, the assessment that the legally imposed changes in process and potentially higher turn-outs would necessarily shift factionalized unions to the right was not well grounded in empirical studies. As Undy and Martin (1984: 64–74) explained, despite the AEU moving to the right in the 1970s after the introduction of postal ballots in

1972, it did not follow that similar changes elsewhere would have similar results. Changes in the method of voting, independent of an assessment of the nature of the employees organized, the issues of importance to the members at the time, the wider context, other decision-making structures and processes, and the level and nature of factional organizations, do not give confidence in achieving a consistent change in political fortunes. Further, the expectation that newly enfranchised union members who voted Conservative in general elections would naturally vote for moderate union candidates (mostly right-of-centre Labour Party supporters) once they had identified them via the new election address was mistaken. As shown in the most politically volatile of the factionalized unions, the CPSA and NCU, the failure of either faction to live up to members' expectations frequently resulted in their being voted out of office, regardless of their political persuasion. Also, the notion that lay activists associated with the left (or the right) would not, under postal ballots, continue to exercise significant influence over how ordinary members cast their votes was mistaken. Well-organized factions with extensive networks of lay supporters would, under whatever voting system, exercise some influence over the 'floating' voters. Under postal ballots, when the turn-out ranges from some 15 per cent to 30 per cent, the mobilization of a relatively small percentage of the floating membership by the activists, particularly in finely balanced contests, could still be expected to help determine the outcome of such elections. Moreover, as trade union elections to executive posts largely ceased to be considered newsworthy by the popular press in the late 1980s and early 1990s, the role of the lay activists in providing information on the merits of the rival candidates probably increased over the period. In the TGWU and UCATT the Broad Left made significant gains under the new legislation in the late 1980s and early 1990s. In the TGWU they won a majority on the executive and secured the General Secretary post, under both workplace and postal ballots. The Broad Left in UCATT made significant gains from the moderate faction after the introduction of postal ballots. In both unions the left appeared to hold the political advantage under postal ballots because they had broad-based activist support, whereas the moderate factions were more dependent on full-time officers and, in the case of the TGWU, were relatively narrowly organized in particular regions. In contrast the moderate faction in the MSF won a majority on the executive and the General Secretary's post against well-organized Broad Left opposition. However, this was probably just as much a product of the political infighting between ASTMS's and TASS's activists and officials following the 1988 merger to form the MSF as it was the result of changes in balloting method. Thus, despite compliance, both in rule and practice, with the imposed changes in electoral processes the politically moderate outcomes desired by the Conservatives were not forthcoming.

In examining the relationship between the changes in processes and industrial action the Conservatives' desired outcomes will be taken as a reduction in union power, and a reduction in strike incidence—the first may be seen as causing and the second reflecting moderation in union behaviour. The relationship between the imposed changes in process, union power, and strike incidence is more complex and hence more difficult to assess than the relationship between process and outcome in elections. For example, it is extremely difficult to disentangle the effect of changes in the balloting process from other legislation aimed at limiting union power, including restrictions on picketing, secondary action, and the union's ability to discipline members. But, most importantly, the effects of the wider environment, including unemployment, inflation, and the actions of employers, make it difficult to isolate the effects of the balloting legislation. Furthermore, within this given external context other organizational factors, such as the level of union membership, the work group's cohesiveness and leadership, and its previous experience of industrial action—in combination with the employers' bargaining strategies and tactics—continued to be of more importance in shaping union power than the enforced switch from show-of-hands votes to workplace and, finally, to postal ballots. If the union was well organized the switch to workplace ballots was probably of no consequence and the later change to postal ballots did not, of itself, prevent the union from mobilizing support for industrial action by calling meetings and testing and taking opinion by show-of-hands votes prior to postal balloting. Moreover, if the union chose it could adjust its bargaining timetable, procedure, and tactics to include either a workplace or postal ballot at the point it considered most effective for persuading the employer to improve the offer. On the other hand, if the union was poorly organized and part of a multi-union negotiating team, the added complexities associated with balloting, and particularly postal balloting, could further weaken its bargaining power. The planning and co-ordination needed to deal with the new requirements was lacking in these situations. Hence, in these latter circumstances, balloting became another obstacle to organizing industrial action.

The effects of workplace and postal ballots on bargaining power, in a given hostile environment, were therefore both contingent on the organizational context and the ability of the union. As shown in Chapter 6, when unions used ballots in well-organized bargaining units they invariably registered relatively high turn-outs in both workplace and postal ballots. Further, the participation rates in postal ballots were much higher than those achieved in elections using the same process. Moreover, a clear majority for one of the proposed courses of industrial action was achieved in almost all ballots. In these circumstances the shift in the location of the vote and its individualization did not decollectivize the union's voice. Indeed it may have given it a new legitimacy in the eyes of both members and management by removing all doubts about its validity, as compared to the much-maligned show-of-hands car-park votes. Thus, if the union was weak the balloting legislation made it weaker, but if it was well organized its effects may have been positive or relatively neutral.

The impact of the balloting legislation on strike incidence is more difficult to assess. Clearly the number of strikes and days lost through strikes fell very sharply over the period of the legislation. The fall also coincided with the growing use of workplace ballots and, at the end of the period, postal ballots. However, it is certain that factors other than the specific balloting legislation contributed most to the marked decline in both strike incidence and days lost: changes in the external environment and the employing organization did most to reduce strikes. These developments made the unions' members less prone to strike. Nevertheless, on balance, and in the circumstances of the period, the balloting legislation probably marginally contributed to increased moderation in the form and quantity of industrial action. First, ballots generally helped unions demonstrate substantial support for some form of industrial action in a clear and unambiguous manner. This mandate was then used in a significant number of cases to bring the employer back to the bargaining table with the hope of negotiating a better and more acceptable offer. To the extent that this resulted in an agreed settlement the ballot substituted for the strike. Second, in attempting to ensure they achieved a majority vote for industrial action, while complying with the detail required on the ballot paper, union leaders became more cautious in calling for all-out strikes. They moved to opt for more selective and limited action, whilst also soliciting votes for action short of a strike. Thus, action was likely to be more limited and more focused in its length and purpose than in the 1970s. However, this may have secured more frequent votes for action of some kind than proposals for all-out stoppages, which members may have been more prone to reject. Therefore, as strikes diminished other forms of action short of a strike probably increased. Third, the threat of legally imposed sanctions probably reduced the length of industrial action which was not procedurally correct. Faced by fines or injunctions union leaders moved to repudiate unofficial strikes: such strikes, devoid of official backing, could scarcely be sustained solely by local activists. Fourth, the transfer of authority for calling the ballot from local level to the national level at a time of retrenchment also made the 'marginal' ballot vote less likely to be sanctioned, as the national leadership sought to protect the union's wider credibility and financial well-being. Thus, on balance, the balloting legislation tended to reduce militancy and promote moderation. However, it was of very minor significance compared to other external and organizational factors and thus served more to articulate the members' reluctance to engage in all-out strikes than to cause such behaviour.

Turning now to issues of union democracy: the Conservatives had a simple model of union democracy in mind when promoting the balloting legislation. It was implicitly pluralist and recognized the potential in unions, as representative democracies,[2] for a divergence of goals between national leaders, lay activists, and ordinary members (Undy and Martin 1984: 186). As a result the Conservatives valued a high level of individual participation by ordinary members in key elections and decisions on industrial action. This was expected to reconcile existing goal conflict in favour of the ordinary members. These, as noted above, were seen as inherently moderate while leaders and lay activists were perceived as militant. Unions' existing decision-making systems which enabled national leaders to be chosen by lay activists were therefore seen as reinforcing the militant spiral. Such systems were perceived as unrepresentative of the wider membership's interest and hence undemocratic. It should be noted, however, that this kind of analysis runs contrary to one of the dominant themes in studies of union democracy which, following Michels's iron law of oligarchy (Michels 1962: 365), perceives the leading national officials as intrinsically moderate and acting together to protect institutional interests, and hence their own position and status, against the interests of lay activists.

The Conservatives' attempts to operationalize their concept of democracy had different effects within different unions. Those unions which elected their executives, general secretary, or president by branch (block or individual-member votes), or by conference votes at regional and/or national level, experienced a clear and unequivocal increase in membership participation when they moved to workplace ballots. For example, such major unions as ASTMS, the GMB, the NUR, and the NCU saw a very significant increase in membership participation in elections following the introduction of workplace ballots. In some cases this produced a tenfold increase from some 5 per cent to 50 per cent. Further, the imposition of periodic elections for general secretaries previously appointed, or elected until retirement, extended membership participation and, no doubt, made the general secretary more responsive to their interests, particularly when approaching re-election. However, a minority of unions already used postal ballots to elect their executives and leading national officials prior to the legislation. For example, the AEU, EETPU, and FTAT fell into this category. Such unions obviously experienced no change in participation rates following the legislation. Hence, the effect on participation rates, and therefore, union democracy as conceived by the Conservatives, was contingent on unions' existing rules and practices. Finally, following the subsequent imposed movement in 1988 from workplace ballots to postal ballots, turn-out dropped quite sharply in those unions previously using workplace ballots. For example, the TGWU had a turn-out of 39 per cent in its executive elections under the last of the workplace ballots in 1988, but this fell to 16 per cent in the 1994 executive elections under postal ballots.

Such reductions were common across unions forced by the imposition of postal ballots to cease using workplace ballots. Thus, on the basis of the Conservative's own limited model of representative democracy the introduction of postal ballots had the effect, in many unions, of reducing union democracy.

The impact of workplace ballots on participation rates in the calling of industrial action was, across a wide spectrum of unions, generally and significantly to increase participation. Although it is difficult to generalize on turn-outs under show-of-hand votes or branch ballots it is very unlikely that they approached the 80-per-cent-plus rates reached in workplace ballots. This was the figure recorded in our case studies involving the AEU and also the level achieved, prior to the legislation, in the NUM's traditional workplace ballots (Undy and Martin 1984: 134). The evidence regarding the effect of postal ballots, imposed in 1993, suggests that, as in elections, they reduced turn-out compared to workplace ballots. However, their effect was much less marked than in elections. As we have shown above, in Chapter 6, turn-out was significantly affected by the number of members balloted. In small bargaining units—fifty or fewer members—postal ballots still recorded very high turn-outs, averaging over 75 per cent. In contrast, if there were 1,000 or more members in the ballot, turn-out dropped to 44 per cent on average. This may be compared to a system which distributed ballot papers at the workplace (via the pay-packet), but used a postal return in disputes involving similar large groups of members, i.e. the electricity supply workers. This process had recorded 89 per cent and 87 per cent participation rates in 1979 (ibid. 140). Such a comparison would suggest that logistical problems reduce participation rates when posting ballot papers to the homes of large groups of members. Thus, the switch from workplace to postal ballots was again detrimental to participation rates, even if its effect was less dramatic than in elections. This was no doubt because members called on to vote in industrial action ballots felt both better informed about the choices on offer and had more at risk if they failed to influence the vote. Nevertheless, large turn-outs did not correlate with the rejection of industrial action. As shown in Table 6.10, between 1987 and 1993 90 per cent of those balloted voted consistently in support of the union recommendation for some form of industrial action.

In terms of union democracy, therefore, the imposition of postal ballots on key elections and the calling of industrial action was, on the Conservatives' own definition of democracy, only a partial success. While it no doubt improved secrecy, compared to branch and workplace ballots, and provided some additional information regarding the choices on offer— and in industrial action ballots provided a reminder that the consequences of voting yes could involve breaching their contract of employment—it also reduced participation rates and, hence, reduced democracy. However, the

Conservatives' notion of what comprised union democracy is itself limited. If this restrictive interpretation is relaxed, other developments associated with the imposition of postal ballots may also be assessed by reference to their impact on democracy. At least five different approaches or models may be used to assess the nature and degree of union representative democracy by reference to a union's constitution and behaviour (ibid. 190–210). One focuses on the level of participation and competition in elections, and is therefore similar to the Conservative notion of democracy. However, this is generally considered a rather weak measure if not associated with some of the other features of democratic government, including the existence of factions or parties. These, almost certainly unofficial groups, are seen as critically important for both offering the electorate a choice of candidates in elections and forming an opposition to the established leadership. Further, it is argued that the existence of such an opposition is helpful in ensuring that the checks and balances in the union's constitution—for example, the rights of the conference, regional committee, district committee, or other intermediary bodies to challenge and exert influence over the executive—are activated in practice. Also, there are some arguments in favour of decentralizing power over decisions, such as the calling of industrial action, in order to ensure that the centre, even if tending to oligarchy, does not have control over issues which can be more effectively determined at the district, local, or workplace level—a form of union 'subsidiarity'.

The balloting legislation did little to encourage or discourage factional organization and it had only marginal impact on existing factions. Nevertheless, if one faction had a more extensive network of lay activists, postal ballots could help give it a competitive edge by making its ability to reach more of the electorate with its propaganda and advice on how to vote more important for determining the election result. However, such advantages could be countered—or reinforced—if the faction in power at the time of postal ballots also used its control of the union journal or newspaper to give its candidates favourable exposure prior to elections. Thus the effect of the introduction of postal ballots in factionalized unions was again contingent on a range of other factors largely untouched by the legislation. By comparison with the well-organized faction's electoral activities, the enforced issuing of election addresses had little impact on voters' preferences.

The main democratic weakness in the balloting legislation was, however, associated with its impact on intermediary bodies and its consequent centralizing and bureaucratizing effects. In practice the imposition of postal ballots for elections and later for industrial action significantly reduced the role played by intermediary bodies across a wide range of unions. In the case of elections, all unions which had formerly and by rule involved region, district, branch, or trade group committees in the selection or election of their key national leaders had to remove them from this process. Further, unions which had previously seen their General Secretary as the leading professional officer chosen by and responsible to the elected lay executive or delegate conference found that he or she was no longer so directly accountable to such bodies. Hence, as the executive members and leading full-time officials became legitimized, respectively, by a vote of a section of the membership and the total membership, the role of intermediate bodies was diminished. In addition, the imposition in 1993 of postal ballots for calling industrial action reinforced the centralizing and bureaucratizing tendencies associated with elections. With very few exceptions, one of which was the highly regionalized GMB, decisions over whether or not to call a ballot and whether or not to proceed with industrial action were generally removed from intermediary bodies and drawn back to the centre of the union. In some cases these powers were given to a single member of the executive or the General Secretary. Moreover, the issuing of centrally determined formal and very detailed regulations on how to conduct such ballots reduced any discretion previously enjoyed in this respect by the local organization. Thus, the balloting legislation had the general effect of strengthening the centre at the expense of intermediary bodies. It served primarily to centralize and concentrate decision-making powers.

Thus, as regards the outcomes associated with the imposed changes in balloting processes, it can be concluded that they were not always those sought by the Conservatives. Outcomes were contingent on factors other than the type of ballot. Nevertheless, during the period of workplace ballots turn-outs in elections and industrial action ballots were generally and significantly increased. The introduction of both workplace and postal ballots in the calling of industrial action also probably helped moderate industrial action by helping achieve negotiated settlements without strikes. However, the contribution of the balloting legislation to reducing strike incidence and days lost was insignificant compared to the effect of the hostile environment, and the perceived ineffectiveness of strikes, on members' inclination to take such action. Further, the effect of the ballots on election outcomes was problematic. Both left and right won and lost elections under workplace and postal ballots. The subsequent imposition of postal ballots also reduced participation—sometimes more than halving turn-out in elections. Moreover, the use of postal ballots reduced the influence of intermediary bodies and consequently reduced the existing checks and balances on executive power. Overall, therefore, the imposition of postal ballots for industrial action and elections tended to weaken rather than strengthen representative democracy.

LEADERSHIP STRATEGIES FOR MANAGING CHANGE

At various points in the above discussions we have noted the degree to which the changes made in response to the legislation were contingent on other factors, especially the environment and unions' existing processes and structures of decision-making. In this section we focus on the importance of the choices exercised by union leaders and thus qualify our primarily structuralist contingency model of change. The relationship between the leaders and the changes made in union behaviour is shown by the central area of Figure 1.1. Leaders are presented as operating according to political, democratic, and administrative rationalities which have rather indeterminate and overlapping boundaries. In referring to leaders' decisions as strategies we follow Mintzberg (1967) and 'read' the strategies from the patterns of union behaviour. They may not, therefore, be strategies in the sense that they were consciously developed as a consistent, cohesive, and integrated set of policies. We are concerned rather with unions' realized strategies as discernable patterns of behaviour. However, by the 1990s some unions were adopting the language and approaches of corporate strategists.

In using a 'rationalities' framework we extend and amend the work of Child *et al.* (1973: 71–92), which in turn owed a debt to Weber (1978: vol. i, pp. 63–74). Political rationality refers to the ultimate purpose and primary means of trade unions. It thus embraces both unions' ideological positions and their general approach to industrial relations. Unions' different positions on such questions may be categorized according to their reformist or business orientation. For our purposes we take a union's reformist orientation to be demonstrated by its affiliation to and support for the Labour Party and its business orientation to be concerned with bargaining for improving members' terms and conditions of employment amongst other means. Political rationality thus covers means and ends. Democratic rationality refers both to unions' ideas of what constitutes democracy and the associated processes and structures of union government. Democratic processes and structures are intended to support the unions' political rationality and not dominate it. Unions seek to balance the need for members' participation and the articulation of their views with the effective pursuit of collective objectives. They therefore organize themselves internally to accommodate the different industrial relations needs of different groups. Hence, as mergers made unions more heterogeneous, they introduced trade groups or similar divisions to cater for different groups' bargaining interests, as described in Chapter 3. Administrative rationality refers to procedures designed to achieve specified objectives in the most effective manner. It was defined by Weber (ibid. vol. ii, pp. 973–4) as bureaucratic rationality, the principal features being centralization of authority, long-term planning, organizational unity, rapid decision-making, operation according to rule, and professionalization. However, unions' concerns with administrative rationality cannot be simply equated with those of profit-maximizing, or profit-satisficing, business organizations. Unions do not have such unambiguous goals. Nevertheless, in the 1980s and 1990s as unions encountered financial difficulties, many leaders became very concerned with organizational efficiency. Finally, as regards 'rationalities', it is *not* our intention in using this term to suggest that unions' decision-making is as precise or calculative as the term may be taken to indicate in normal usage. Union leaders were subject to a restricted range of options and operated in organizations which bounded and structured their rationality. Hence much of the decision-making was concerned with resolving differences between competing claims, satisfying internal pressure groups, and achieving what was politically acceptable, rather than reaching an ideal 'rational' solution. The result tended to be a negotiated rationality.

In the following discussion we will generalize on the basis of the strategies of the twenty-four unions at the centre of our study and in particular the six case-study unions (see Table 3.3), while noting significant differences between these unions. We will also combine analysis of the balloting changes with the non-ballot-related developments examined in Chapter 3. These covered external union structure or job territory (critically, membership loss and mergers), union government, and union objectives and means. These developments will now be examined by reference to the three rationalities, moving from political to democratic and, lastly, administrative rationality. In each case we will describe the threats or problems faced by the unions before examining the leaders' responses.

Unions' political rationality was directly and indirectly challenged by the Conservative legislation and other developments in the unions' environment. In particular the legislation posed two threats to core union values. First, there was the attempt to depoliticize unions' external associations and change their internal political complexion. Second was the attempt to individualize unions' industrial relations activities. The attempt to depoliticize unions was largely confined to the legislation requiring confirmatory ballots on political funds in the 1984 Act and accompanying Conservative rhetoric. It was hoped that this would end or weaken unions' formal association with the Labour Party. The balloting legislation on elections, as discussed above, aimed to change and moderate unions' internal political bias by helping the 'right' defeat the 'left'. Broadly, the underlying purpose of both pieces of legislation was to shift unions away from their traditional reformist activities towards a modified, more individualized, form of business unionism.

Both moves were unsuccessful. Unions' external political allegiances and their internal political biases remained consistent throughout the period.

Despite the legislation on political funds, the Labour Party's repeated failures to win an election, and subsequently its own attempts to dilute union influence, the unions remained committed to the Labour Party and their wider reformist aims. Following the 1984 Act on political funds the unions mounted a very successful campaign under the umbrella organization of thirty-seven unions titled the Trade Union Coordinating Committee (TUCC) to persuade members to support the retention of their political funds. By 1986 all the unions concerned had voted to retain their funds with majorities of between 59 per cent and 93 per cent (Webb 1992: 29). Moreover, Conservative antagonism towards trade unions made the return of a Labour Government an even greater priority for many union leaders. Thus, instead of withdrawing support unions tended to allocate more money and resources to their external political activities. As previously noted the GMB and TGWU contributed some £40 million to the Labour Party and, in the words of a leading GMB official, 'paid for four election defeats'! The organization 'Trade Unions for Labour' (TUFL) also allocated human resources, often full-time officials, to work for the Labour Party, particularly in the run-up to general elections. Further, towards the end of the period, following the Labour Party's failure to win the 1992 election, some unions strengthened their political activities *vis-à-vis* the European Parliament. The GMB opened an office in Brussels with the purpose of being more proactive in lobbying at the European level, and in common with several other unions established its own group of MEPs (Members of the European Parliament). The MSF in 1994 also claimed a group of some eleven MEPs. Even unions not affiliated to the Labour Party, such as NALGO, extended their political activities. They established a political fund and developed stronger European contacts via consultancy arrangements with two MEPs. NALGO, in common with other TUC affiliates, were also more active in the ETUC (European Trade Union Confederation).

Union leaders therefore used their discretion to organize campaigns and sponsor different kinds of political relationships to counter the effects of Conservative policy and legislation. The unions' commitment to the Labour Party was seen as central to this continuing regard for wider social improvements. Further, and probably more importantly, the return of the Labour Party to power was also perceived as an essential condition for restoring their political and industrial influence. In this respect, therefore, the Conservative attempt to change unions' political rationality, by reducing their attachment to democratic socialist objects as represented by the Labour Party, was counter-productive.

The continuing commitment to the Labour Party also survived Conservative attempts to change unions' internal politics. As discussed above, non-factionalized unions remained so, while amongst the factional-ized unions changes in political bias were noted in the TGWU and

UCATT—gains for the left—and in the MSF gains for the right. There was little consistent internal political change in the other factionalized unions studied. The CPSA and NCU tended, as usual, to oscillate between left and right, although the CPSA showed greater political stability under the moderates' control towards the end of the period. The left, in some unions, appeared to suffer from the collapse of the Communist Party and fragmentation of the different Trotskyist groups. Also, where the moderates had held power for a long period, as in the AEU, they too suffered from political infighting between leading members of the same faction. There were also signs, particularly in unions which suffered from severe membership loss and consequent financial difficulties, that factional disputes tended to be less frequent and less severe towards the end of the period. The need to resolve major internal problems, associated with mergers and/or financial problems, appeared to push factional differences into the background and concentrate minds on issues of common concern to all political groups. This was particularly noticeable in the TGWU and the newly merged AEEU. As we will show later, in these circumstances questions of administrative rationality came to the fore and national leaders became more concerned with resolving financial and organizational problems and less concerned with championing their faction's causes.

Unions continued to act in defence of their sectional interests, particularly pay and conditions, through collective bargaining. The 'business' interest thus continued to be the unions' *raison d'être*. They also displayed considerable continuity in pursuit of this dominant interest throughout the period. Almost all moved to introduce a new range of individual services, including credit cards and other financial services, a range of discounted retail outlets, and extended access to legal advice; but these additions were seen as supplementing their traditional collectivist activities and not the means of replacing them. Unions shielded from the worst of the hostile environment also appeared to function in their bargaining relationships much as before. For example, the FBU made few concessions to either the legislation or the climate. When Government policy on public sector pay threatened to veto an increase due under the FBU's 14-year-old guaranteed pay formula in 1993, it responded with a threatened strike ballot and finally resolved the dispute to its satisfaction: a sequence of events reminiscent of the late 1970s. NALGO, prior to forming UNISON, also appeared to function much as before in its bargaining activities.

In contrast unions more adversely affected by the combination of severe membership loss, the decentralization of bargaining, and aggressive human resource management strategies tended to revise their bargaining objectives and styles of negotiation in the late 1980s and early 1990s. This process was given further impetus by the Labour Party's failure to win the 1992 election. This reinforced the view that unions were very unlikely to see the kind of change in their political and economic context which would restore them to the position and influence they enjoyed in the 1970s. In these circumstances they took more seriously the need to develop bargaining policies and strategies aligned to the new environment. This resulted in a number of changes common to most unions, most commonly adjustments in the bargaining agenda and changes in attitudes towards bargaining with employers.

The bargaining agenda was broadened to include more non-pay issues. The TGWU and GMB jointly proposed a shift from 'pay to prospects' (T&G/GMB, 1992). This involved giving greater emphasis to training, equal opportunities, and health and safety issues. At the same time unions' bargaining style was generally moderated. According to a leading NUPE official in interview, their attitude to negotiations became 'more circumspect'. In the case of the TGWU it was described by a senior official as 'more co-operative'. More concretely, in the 1991 recession the Confederation of Shipbuilding and Engineering Unions (CSEU) suspended its militant, and relatively successful, campaign for the shorter working week. Whether or not the national leaders led or followed their members' preferences in moderating their bargaining style in this period is difficult to assess. However, as it coincided with the centralizing of decision-making in unions, itself influenced by the balloting legislation on industrial action, it may be suggested that moderation was at least encouraged by the national leaders, if not initiated by them. Further, it also ran parallel with the shift, as noted by a number of national officials in interviews, with the trend in industrial action ballots to propose strictly limited strikes, or action short of a strike, rather than open-ended strike action when negotiations failed to reach agreement. Such moderating changes may, of course, be seen as no more than unions' short-term and temporary adjustment to the difficult economic circumstances of the early 1990s. Clearly, as union power was further diminished by the recession, the adoption of a more militant bargaining style could well have been perceived as self-defeating. Such considerations no doubt helped shape union strategy. However, these changes were also consistent with longer-term developments in unions' strategies towards employers.

In protecting their sectional bargaining interests not all unions chose to respond to the circumstances of the period in exactly the same manner. Unions' national strategies differed, in some important respects, according to their leaders' political biases. This was most noticeable in two areas of bargaining activity. First, in the 1980s and 1990s, it affected approaches to employers for recognition agreements. Second, in the mid-1990s, it again surfaced in respect of the more consensual approach to industrial relations embodied in the 'social partnership' strategy developed and promoted by the TUC and several individual unions in submissions to the House of Commons Select Committee Inquiry into the Future of Trade Unions in

1993–4. First, as shown in Chapter 3, during intense inter-union competition for recognition on greenfield sites the EETPU, followed by the AEU and the GMB (all politically moderate unions), offered employers single-union no-strike deals in return for sole recognition agreements. The TGWU, a more left-inclined union, resolutely refused at the national level to sanction no-strike deals. It did, however, enter into several single-union agreements. The TGWU explained its position in 1992 in its policy statement paper 'One Union T&G' as follows: 'Some unions chose to . . . pursue employers rather than workers. The T&G chose to remain a workers' union and a progressive union.' However, this did not prevent the TGWU from co-operating with and signing strong peace clauses short of no-strike deals. For example, in common with the more moderate AEU, GMB, and MSF, the TGWU signed the Rover 'New Deal' which committed the union to supporting a wide-ranging programme of work re-design and human-resource-type initiatives, including a very strong peace clause providing for a joint reference to arbitration as the final stage of the procedure. Thus, while the TGWU's stand against no-strike deals was a significant indicator of its political bias and its practice regarding recognition on greenfield sites, in the much more important field of existing agreements it behaved in a very similar manner to other major unions recruiting in the private sector. In common with more politically moderate unions the TGWU agreed to a series of changes in different parts of the private sector, and particularly in the vehicle industry, that heralded a less militant stance on bargaining issues and a greater willingness to co-operate in moves to increase industrial efficiency.

Second, by the mid-1990s several union leaders representing the centre and moderate wing of union politics espoused a more consensual approach to relations with employers as a strategy for union regeneration. This strategy emphasized the value of creating social or industrial partnerships with co-operative employers. In articulating this new approach in 1994, Bill Jordan, President of the AEU, argued that unions, as well as management, must set aside 'the ideology of confrontation and acknowledge that all have a shared interest in the success of the enterprise' (Jordan 1994: 20). Further, he claimed that 'there is no more effective or productive tool than a genuine partnership between employers, unions and employee' (ibid. 21). This approach was also similar to that outlined to the Commons Select Committee Inquiry into the Future of Trade Unions by the AEU, GMB, and MSF. It was also reflected in the Involvement and Participation Association's document 'Towards Industrial Partnership—A New Approach to Relationships at Work', published in 1993. This paper was signed by the General Secretaries of several major unions, including the GMB, USDAW, BIFU, UCW, and NCU, and the aforementioned President of the AEU. It too emphasized the changing role of unions and argued that they would need to become facilitators of change working together with management. Again, the result of partnership was claimed to be economic success and prosperity. In a similar vein the TUC argued, in its evidence to the Select Committee, 'social partnership . . . is delivering results across the developed world'.[3] Hence, seen from the perspective of the moderate union leader the circumstances of the 1990s required unions to rethink their bargaining strategy and develop a new consensual approach of mutual benefit to employer and union.

Unions' political rationality thus survived the Conservative's legislative programme largely intact. Unions remained committed to political reformism and the Labour Party. This applied just as much to the politically moderate AEU as it did to the more left-inclined TGWU. Union national leaderships also continued to represent a similar range of political opinion to that which existed prior to the legislation. The unions' underlying character remained predominantly collectivist rather than individualist—although services to the individual members were generally improved and extended. Nevertheless, although resistant to legally imposed changes, unions' political rationality, particularly in terms of 'means', changed in several other important respects. Politically, as it became clear that there was little hope of immediate improvement in national politics, the unions moved to extend their European influence. Individually they also became more pragmatic. They recognized their power base had been eroded and was unlikely to recover in the near future. Initially they both extended their bargaining agenda and moderated their bargaining style. Subsequently they agreed with established employers to provide the kind of co-operation previously given to greenfield employers on such questions as the reorganization of work and flexible working. Under the influence of domestic pressures, and aware of European precedents, the moderate union leaders, in particular, sought to maintain and extend collective representation by arguing that it was mutually beneficial to employers and employees. This consensual strategy was promoted nationally under the heading of social and/or industrial partnership. Thus, by the end of the period unions' political rationality was under review. However, this was not a result of the balloting legislation. This only had a minor impact on this aspect of trade unionism. It was rather that union leaders at the national level started to come to terms with the new environment. Those to the right of the movement were in the vanguard of the shift towards consensual unionism. Those of the left were more reluctant to jettison their traditional bargaining position; as the TGWU expressed it: the 'Union's strategy has remained focussed on positive traditional values and activities' (TGWU 1992a: 8). Yet they too were, in the right circumstances, willing to bargain co-operatively, agree radical changes in working practices, and establish new forms of union–management relations. Thus, changes were occurring across the political spectrum. However, some were prepared to move further than others and hence we summarize the developing strategies of the politically moderate union leaders as 'consensual realism' and those of the political left as 'co-operating traditionalism'.

Democratic rationality, in terms of unions' notions of democracy and its actual operation, varied widely between unions at the start of the period. All unions normally claim to be democratic, but their means of taking decisions, in both rule and practice, do not conform to any general model. This diversity is clear in the typology outlined in Table 1.1. Thus, the imposition of workplace and then postal ballots for key national elections and for calling industrial action only prescribed changes in one part of what were different and often complex processes of decision-making. Moreover, the legislation was not imposed on static processes and structures of government. Other things did not remain equal as the unions adjusted to the new balloting requirements. Responses to legislation were linked to developments initiated by national leaders, who attempted both to sustain their preferred version of democratic rationality against that imposed by the Conservatives and to adjust internal government in response to other developments, such as the decentralization of collective bargaining and union mergers.

In terms of general changes in internal union structure the larger unions, under the influence of mergers, moved to a greater vertical internal differentiation of government. This divisionalization of the larger unions into sections or trade groups resulted in responsibilities for collective bargaining and related decisions being allocated to the appropriate sections or groups. These changes ran parallel with the employer-instigated shift to decentralized bargaining. Hence there was a controlled fragmentation of union government in the bargaining channel and a reduction in national negotiations. However, over the same period the balloting legislation affecting industrial action was, as we have shown above, perceived by union leaders as requiring greater central control of the decision to take industrial action. Unions' national leaders were thus attempting to reconcile two contrary movements in the bargaining channel. They needed to decentralize bargaining in response to employer-led changes in bargaining level, while also safeguarding the union as an institution against the legal and financial consequences of failing to comply with the balloting legislation. As a consequence they imposed on the existing and continuing system of workplace meetings, by which local officials and lay activists assessed support for industrial action, the very detailed regulations they developed centrally in response to the legislation. Hence, although local negotiations continued much as before, there was a strong centralizing movement in respect of any form of industrial action and a concentration of responsibility at the centre for ensuring compliance with the highly formalized and detailed balloting regulations. This aspect of union government was therefore bureaucratized.

Over the period, unions' democratic rationality was thus affected in several different ways by the legislation requiring industrial action ballots and the leaders' responses. Membership participation was clearly increased in a number of unions by the imposition of workplace ballots. In many cases they complemented the employers' moves to decentralize bargaining and achieved very high participation rates. Thus, although union leaders did not welcome the imposition of ballots they were not diametrically opposed to workplace ballots. Also, as Undy and Martin (1984: 129–30) showed, extensive consultation on industrial action took place in many unions prior to the legislation and therefore the imposition of workplace ballots to some extent formalized an existing process, rather than introducing an alien one. Further, workplace ballots assisted the trade unions' own devolution of bargaining responsibilities down the internal structure to trade groups and sectors following mergers. However, the imposition of postal ballots for the calling of industrial action ran counter to the above trends in union government and democracy. They generally reduced turn-out, particularly in large bargaining units, and union leaders, in seeking to protect the union from the potential sanctions, responded by centralizing and concentrating decision-making. This process of bureau-cratization, following the imposition of postal ballots, ran parallel with the national leaderships' adoption of more co-operative or consensual bargaining strategies. Bureaucratization in this context therefore gave a greater say to generally moderating forces intent on both safeguarding the union from conducting ballots they could not win and avoiding commitment to open-ended all-out strikes. Thus the period ended with a much greater degree of commonality across unions in terms of their bargaining processes and structures compared to the variety of government forms identified in 1980. However, this also produced a reduction in union democracy as assessed by reference to participation and decentralization, while it also made a small contribution to increased moderation in bargaining tactics.

Changes in the non-bargaining channel of decision-making of union government which affected unions' democratic rationality tended to owe more to union leaders' strategies than to the imposition of elections for key national posts and the associated workplace, and subsequently postal, ballots. For, in responding to membership loss, financial difficulties, and associated union mergers, national leaders in the larger unions instigated much more radical changes in union government than those associated with the legislation. This included adjustments in the structure and levels of decision-making, and, in some unions, these changes had a secondary effect on competition for union office. In particular, mergers directly affected the internal structure of unions and frequently altered the balance of power as exercised by different groups or committees. For example, in merging to form UNISON, Britain's largest union, in 1993, the three unions involved drafted 'aims and objects'—a form of mission statement—

which included reference to promoting 'a member-centred union . . . and fair representation in all the union's structures for women, members of all grades, black members, members with disabilities and lesbians and gay men'.[4] All three unions were concerned to establish at the very centre of the talks agreement over the new union's democratic rationality and government structure. At NALGO's insistence the two smaller partners accepted NALGO's traditionally lay-member-dominated structure, including an important role for its disparate groups and a high degree of branch autonomy. Thus, for NUPE and COHSE, both previously highly centralized and faction-free unions with a strong full-time official influence at the national level of policy-making, the merger produced a far more decentralized and lay-member-dominated system of government influenced by the factional divisions well established in NALGO, but foreign both to NUPE and COHSE.

UNISON's movement towards greater decentralization and more lay influence was not common to many other unions in this period. If, however, one of the parties in a merger insisted on adhering to a particular form of decentralized organization as the price of agreement the other unions had to comply or forego the merger. This was also the case for the NGA in merging with SOGAT to form the GPMU. In making its agreement with SOGAT the NGA accepted both a more federal structure and a higher degree of branch autonomy. In particular, SOGAT insisted on protecting its existing branch boundaries, and to a large extent its branches' financial autonomy, as part of the merger agreement. Thus some merging unions experienced a clash of democratic rationalities. The resulting changes in government in the above two mergers resulted in the smaller merging partners accepting a more decentralized system of government, which gave greater autonomy to bodies outside the centre's control.

Periodic reviews of union government instigated by the national leadership also affected changes in existing democratic rationalities. Partly as a result of mergers, but also related to internally sponsored reviews of union government, the TGWU, AEU, GMB, MSF, and CPSA, amongst others, chose to make (or were initiating in 1994) changes which had the effect of centralizing decision-making and reducing the role of intermediate bodies. In some cases these proposals also ran parallel with changes to encourage minority groups, or in some cases majority groups, such as women, to play a greater role in union government. In the case of the CPSA the changes reduced the role played by the branches and enhanced the influence of the regional level of organization. The union also placed more reliance on its appointed officials and less on its lay activists. Similar centralizing movements in the TGWU and GMB involved shifting some responsibilities from regional to national level and in the AEU from districts to national level. In the TGWU this followed a major review of the organization by consultants. The recommendations, originating in the 'Klein Report' in 1992, resulted in a major restructuring including the decision to cut the number of regions from eleven to eight. This was followed by a further strategic review of the TGWU in its paper 'Focus for the Future' in 1993. Broadly, it concluded that the TGWU was too diverse in its operations and in need of a stronger lead from the centre to deal with the issues and financial difficulties facing it in the 1990s. Similarly, the GMB's national leadership, looking to expand by mergers, considered its highly regionalized structure unsuited to the new growth strategy and it too sought to strengthen the centre.

In response to internal difficulties associated with a major loss of members, the AEU's national executive initiated a series of rule changes which increased the executive's power over the organization, produced a marked reduction in the number of districts and branches, and restricted their autonomy. The number of lower-level AEU officials facing elections was also noticeably reduced by the boundary changes associated with the reduction in the number of districts. For these structural changes were accompanied by an agreement that full-time officials taking on a new territory would be allowed an extension of their electoral period. This followed an earlier rule change which required a sitting full-time official to resign his/her seat if contesting an election involving another sitting official seeking re-election. This change effectively deterred many aspiring and ambitious officials, who had previously contested higher or national executive office from the safety of a secure seat, from fighting such elections. Both changes, coupled with the decline in the left's factional organization, had the effect of markedly reducing the number of elections and electoral competition. In addition, the national executive's right to use the referendum to test membership opinion on important policy issues, if opposed and defeated by lay activists at the equivalent of the AEU's national conference, was retained by the executive of the new merged AEU (formed by the amalgamation of the AEU and EETPU in 1992). In 1985 this had been used to overturn the conference's decision not to accept government money for postal ballots. Thus, although the AEU's democratic rationality was largely untouched by the balloting legislation on elections and the same faction continued in power, the national leadership instigated and executed radical changes in government. The result was that in 1994 the union was much more centralized and national-officer-led than it had been in 1980, when it was probably the most decentralized of all the large unions.

Unions' democratic rationality, although ostensibly targeted by the balloting legislation, was therefore much more radically and directly affected by the manner in which union leaders chose both to reorganize the union in the light of other developments in the environment and to respond to the legislation. Moreover, the leaders making these changes were not a new political breed of leaders produced by the enforced changes in the electoral process. They were, in the main, the union's existing leaders and factions. The resulting government changes included a marked tendency to greater vertical bifurcation, in the form of industrial sectors or trade groups. This often followed, or facilitated, a merger and it also helped unions deal more effectively with the general decentralization of bargaining initiated during the period by employers. Unions also provided more scope for interest-group representation at the national level, particularly by reserving national executive seats, or full-time officer posts, for women. These changes therefore produced a greater degree of devolution and dispersion of authority. In addition, if a merger involved a clash of democratic rationalities, as it did in the NALGO, NUPE, and COHSE merger, and the dominant union was the more decentralized of the merging partners, the likely result was that the other unions changed to adopt the more decentralized system of government. In general therefore, the unions in our study ended the period more divisionalized and, in a small number of cases, more decentralized, in their systems of government than in 1980.

The decentralizing changes considered above were, however, exceptional and in most unions overwhelmed by the opposite centralizing tendencies. In the bargaining channel this was particularly noticeable in respect of the leaders' moves to centralize and bureaucratize decision-making in response to the imposition of postal ballots for calling industrial action. This effectively denied intermediary bodies between shop floor and the national level of government any discretion in this activity. These changes were introduced concomitantly with developments in the non-bargaining channel which involved changing structures—mainly reducing the number and/or frequency of lower-level bodies and meetings—and transferring authority for a range of decisions up the remaining structure to the next, or to the national, level. These changes occurred across a range of unions and appeared independent of different government structures and previous democratic traits. For example, the relatively centralized, moderately factionalized, and left-led TGWU was joined in this trend by the highly regionalized, non-factionalized, and centrist GMB, and by the decentralized, highly factionalized and right-led AEU. By adopting such a centralizing process they reinforced the effect of the balloting legislation in reducing the influence exercised by those intermediary bodies which previously determined a range of issues and mediated between members on the shop-floor and the national level of government. Thus, individual members and national leaders gained in influence, while lay activists found their power diminished. This further weakened the effective application of the formal checks and balances on national power. The main movement in union government, with the exception of some of the smaller merging unions, was therefore greater divisionalization and centralization. In the absence of factionalism, or with factions weakening in several unions, this produced, in terms of democratic rationality, a movement towards popular autocracy, rather than greater representative democracy.

The above changes in unions' democratic rationality were primarily motivated by the leadership's concern for administrative rationality. This became the paramount concern in many unions in the hostile climate of the period, and particularly in the late 1980s and early 1990s. It was in this latter part of the period that the loss of membership made itself most strongly felt in terms of consequent financial difficulties. In these often dire financial circumstances cost-cutting emerged as the central issue to be resolved by the national executive and particularly the General Secretary, who frequently carried ultimate responsibility for policy in this area. As Willman *et al.* (1993: 203) noted, while financial issues were not normally given such importance they could come strongly to the fore in a crisis—in most unions at this time they formed the crisis. It gradually became clear to a number of union leaders, as hopes of a revival in union membership faded, that if they did not act to reduce expenditure the survival of the union could be threatened. The balloting legislation itself did little to precipitate this crisis. It may have added to such problems indirectly by being one amongst many other environmental factors that contributed to a reduction in union membership, and it also, through the threat of fines, appeared capable of compounding unions' financial problems. However, the most important interactive effect was that the difficult financial circumstances ensured that most union leaders did their utmost to avoid falling foul of the law on industrial action ballots because of the financial consequences.

Unions as diverse in their systems of government and job territories as the AEU, CPSA, GMB, MSF, NGA, NCU, NUPE, TGWU, UCATT, and, after the merger, UNISON were all affected by financial problems of differing degrees of severity. In these circumstances the MSF stated, 'Finance is the lifeblood of the unions. We must therefore have a stable financial base which generates sufficient income to meet costs' (MSF 1993: 5). This was a sentiment felt at the time by several other unions. Initial union response to such problems was to address the issue of financial control directly by a combination of means, including introducing more expertise into the management of the union's finances and investments, improving budgeting systems, and transferring greater control over income and expenditure to the centre and the union's executive officers. For example, the CPSA appointed a qualified accountant as treasurer and the TGWU appointed a finance director with commercial experience to oversee its financial reforms. Several unions also commissioned studies of their financial systems and as a consequence introduced new and more effective budgetary controls. In the case of the MSF this included a tight programme of debt repayment. Some unions also drew back to the centre money previously collected by, or allocated to, other levels of the organization. NALGO, in the formation of UNISON, for example, changed to collecting subscriptions at the centre instead of through the branches. This was expected to result, eventually, in the centre benefiting from the kind of fund-holding previously enjoyed by the comparatively wealthy branches. UCATT also cut the money allocated to branches. Many unions also raised contribution rates and in the TGWU responsibility for adjusting contributions was transferred from the conference to the national executive.

As the scale of the financial problems began to be fully appreciated most leaders initiated cost-cutting measures throughout their unions. In particular they moved to cut expenditure by reducing the number of full-time officials and staff, reducing the number of offices and other properties, cutting back on the frequency of meetings, and reducing the number of intermediary bodies. To some limited extent, and often following extended internal wrangling, mergers also eventually facilitated similar changes as the partner unions agreed to avoid duplication of officials and departments. This frequently included closing one or other of the merging unions' research and legal departments and offering full-time officers and staff voluntary redundancy. Full-time officials in the AEU were reduced from 220 in 1984 to 136 in 1993, a reduction of 38 per cent. This disproportionately affected the small number of national organizers whose posts were eliminated and the divisional level of organization, which was reduced from 26 to 13 officers by 1994. The executive itself was not reduced in size at this stage. The NCU cut its national officers by 20 per cent between 1988 and 1994 and the TGWU, under extreme financial pressure, reduced its full-time officers by 124 between March 1991 and October 1992. Over a somewhat longer period the TGWU, at a time of falling membership, changed its officer–members ratio from one officer to 3,000 members in 1990 to one to 3,800 in 1992. The MSF between 1988 and 1994 cut its regional officers from 160 to 100. Some annual conferences were made biennial, for example, the AEU's moved from annual to biennial meetings. Similarly, branch, district, regional, and trade group councils or conferences, in a wide range of unions, extended the period between meetings, thus cutting such administrative costs as delegates' fees and travel expenses.

Unions' administrative rationality in this period thus displayed many of the classic features of bureaucracy as described by Weber. It involved the centralizing of authority for financial decisions and, in some unions, the adoption of a more professional approach to managing the organization. Budgets were imposed on the lower levels of the organization and their previous discretion to spend and generate income independent of the centre's control restricted. More care was taken in planning changes and in costing the consequences of planned developments. Reductions in the number of officials and the rationalization of branches, districts, divisions, and regions further extended the centre's control over the union and helped strengthen organizational unity. At the same time the centre sought, in several unions, to use its newly enhanced power to co-ordinate and direct local resources in support of a new recruitment strategy in an attempt to stem, and if possible reverse, the loss of numbers. Given the reduction in the number of officers and the growing demand for them to service the newly decentralized bargaining activities, this was a highly desirable, but also very under-resourced, policy. Thus, the use of detailed balloting regulations for determining industrial action in order to ensure compliance was just part of a much wider bureaucratizing tendency.

There were, however, significant differences in the manner in which the unions determined changes in their administration. Unions such as the TGWU, GMB, and MSF took an overtly strategic view of their restructuring and employed the language of the corporate strategist. The managerialism displayed in these, and some of the white-collar unions, such as NALGO, reflected the lay executive's previous traditional reliance on the appointed national officials for expert advice in such matters. Moreover, the emphasis placed on administration was reflected in the weight accorded this aspect of union behaviour by the national leadership. For example, the TGWU's General Secretary considered himself acting in this regard as the union's chief executive, and his counterpart in the MSF was, in the same period, leading the union's 'top management team', composed of the union's four leading full-time officials (as described in interview). In the same period the TGWU and MSF both opted to increase their employment of professionals to run their key departments and provide internal expert services. In its strategy paper the TGWU also examined the possibility of adopting a cost-centre approach to its planned internal restructuring. This kind of administrative rationality we therefore term 'strategic modernization'.

In contrast, the approach of the two former craft unions, the AEU and NGA, to the same kind of problems we term 'purposeful rationalization'. They tended to deal with issues as they arose without developing the kind of all-embracing and integrative approach resonant of the corporate strategists. Further, they did not generally welcome the introduction of outside professionals. Indeed, following the AEU's merger with the EETPU the latter's previous reliance on such assistance was diminished. They were, therefore, more self-reliant and *ad hoc* in their administrative adjustments. Thus, although there were many common bureaucratizing elements in the different unions' approaches to the problems of the late 1980s, their approaches diverged under the influence of traditions which were established well before they encountered the financial crises of the period.

SUMMARY AND CONCLUSION: MANAGING THE UNIONS IN A HOSTILE
ENVIRONMENT

The balloting legislation was but one factor influencing union behaviour in
an almost unremittingly hostile environment. It changed decision-making
processes as unions reluctantly complied with its ever more restrictive and
detailed requirements. In the case of elections it achieved these limited
procedural objectives through extensive changes in unions' rules and
practices, whereas in respect of industrial action, although some unions
changed their rules, it was largely accommodated by changing practice. It
also served, as part of the Conservatives' overall policy on trade unions, to
set an agenda which denigrated collectivism and encouraged individualism.
Moreover, in the economic circumstances of the period and given the
associated and critically important large reduction in union membership,
the legislation helped shift the balance of power in the employer's favour
and, by doing so, pushed trade unions on to the defensive.

The outcomes achieved by the legislation were contingent on existing
systems of decision-making (both formal and informal), the wider
environment, and the choices made by union leaders in response to the
legislation. The legislation was therefore attempting to effect particular
changes in behaviour in unions with widely different processes and
structures of government, which were themselves changing in response to
other external pressures and leadership initiatives. It is therefore extremely
difficult both to generalize on the effects of the legislation across all unions
and to disentangle the effects of the legislation from those of other
developments shaping union behaviour. Nevertheless, and with the above
caveats, the general effect of the incrementally imposed legislation on
elections was, by the end of the period, to reduce membership participation,
and to weaken the checks and balances on the power of the national
leadership, by intentionally undermining the decision-making roles
previously played by intermediate bodies. The imposition of postal ballots
for the calling of strike action also reduced turn-out, but not to the same
extent as experienced in elections. Moreover, the union leadership's
response to the industrial action legislation reinforced the centralizing
tendencies associated with election ballots. The manner of their response—
the imposition of highly detailed regulations for calling industrial action—
helped further bureaucratize decision-making processes. Finally, for many
unions the dominant need in the late 1980s and early 1990s was to correct
unions' financial difficulties. As a result the national leadership gave
administrative rationality a new primacy as they increasingly bureaucratized
decision-making in the interests of greater efficiency. Thus, while the
balloting legislation helped enfranchise and individualize membership
participation at the very local level—in the home—other changes enhanced

the power of the national leadership. The result of the change was, therefore, not increased union democracy, but a shift towards popular autocracy.

The national leaders instigating the above changes represented in 1994, with a small number of notable exceptions, the same political factions, or, in non-factionalized unions, the same established political orientation, as existed in 1980. The balloting reforms did not, therefore, shift union leadership in one politically consistent direction. Nor did they change radically unions' political rationality. Unions remained committed fundamentally to the same reformist and business union objectives. Indeed, as regards reformism, several unions extended their political involvement, despite their financial difficulties. Ironically, as the Conservatives continued to tighten incrementally the restrictive union legislation, they gave the unions even more cause for supporting political reform, via the return of the Labour Party and/or a stronger European influence on Britain's social and employment policies. This political strategy was seen for a long period by union leaders as representing their best hope of a return to 'normality' in industrial relations.

In terms of business unionism and their bargaining activities, unions still retained their collectivist character. Despite the imposition of individual postal ballots, unions regularly secured support for the most collectivist of all unions' means, industrial action. There was nothing in the legislation that prevented unions continuing to call local workplace meetings for testing members' feelings, mobilizing support for industrial action, and thus winning majorities in the subsequent ballot. However, in the very difficult economic circumstances of the 1980s and 1990s, affecting both employment and the unions' own financial situation, unions were very cautious about sanctioning open-ended strike action. In this context they preferred limited and tactically effective strikes, or action short of a strike, as a means of securing acceptable offers. Thus, although union government became more divisionalized and the negotiations themselves more localized, the centre found a new role for itself in controlling the process used for determining the unions' response to the final stage of deadlocked negotiations.

Growing centralization of control, the general bureaucratization of decision-making, driven by administrative concerns, and a more sophisticated and strategic approach to organizational restructuring coincided with a review of union–management relations. Individual unions and the TUC began to espouse a more proactive approach to industrial relations. Social or industrial partnership was adopted as their theme for the 1990s. Unions sought to promote themselves to employers, employees, and the wider public as socially responsible institutions capable of adding value to industry and commerce through collective representation. Union leaders on the political left tended to stress co-operation with those employers willing to work with, rather than marginalize, the unions, whereas the centre/right were more prominent and vocal in supporting the more consensual approach. Thus, while the balloting legislation achieved little or nothing in terms of political reorientation and democratization, the leadership itself, acting under often intense financial pressure, initiated significant administrative reforms and sought, some in a strategic fashion, to reposition their unions more effectively in relation to their environment. Whether or not this will be sufficient to launch the regeneration of trade unionism remains to be seen. However, unlike the damage limitation strategy which dominated the 1980s, it reflected a more positive and proactive, rather than reactive, policy. Hence, it may herald a new phase of union development under the more effective control of a national leadership unintentionally strengthened by the balloting legislation.

NOTES

1. See Edelstein and Warner (1975: 188–205) for a discussion of why there is an absence of factionalism in many British unions and a comparatively low level of competition for sitting-officer posts.
2. For a discussion of the different approaches to the nature of union democracy in practice including discussion of the role of lay activists and members, see Fosh and Cohen (1991: 107–46). This work also examines the notion of participatory democracy, of which representative democracy is but one aspect.
3. This was the TUC's concluding reference to 'social partnership' in the final section of its written evidence (House of Commons Employment Committee Third Report [1994], The Future of Trade Unions, vol. ii: Minutes of Evidence, p. 14).
4. UNISON Rule Book (1993) B2: Union Democracy, p. 2.

8

UK—EXEMPLAR OR EXCEPTIONAL CASE?[1]

INTRODUCTION

This last chapter turns outwards from the UK to compare and contrast the present tight legal framework in the UK for the election of union officers and the calling of industrial action (which as we saw in Chapter 4 has been progressively introduced by Conservative Governments since 1980) with union legal frameworks in a selection of other EU countries. In contrast to the UK, legal frameworks for the conduct of union business over the past fifteen years have not significantly changed: with the exception of Greece other EU states remain firmly non-interventionist. We seek to explain this difference by considering the approach of the State towards union autonomy and the role it accords to unions in national decision-making, together with the constraints imposed on the state by the character and organization of the union movement and by the country's constitution. We consider whether these other EU countries are likely to move towards the present British model of severe union regulation.

For reasons of space we could not include a comparison of all EU countries and, in selecting some rather than others, we have attempted to include examples of Crouch's (1993) different classes of 'state traditions' (particulary neo-corporatist as opposed to pluralist/contestation, both of which can be associated with strong or weak labour movements) and to pay attention to Due et al.'s (1991) classification of EU industrial relations systems based on the different traditions of regulation.[2] The selected EU countries have also all experienced similar economic pressures in the 1980s and 1990s to those experienced by the UK. These economic pressures were particularly a consequence of German reunification in 1989 and the spill-over effects of the rise in German interest rates, through the Exchange Rate Mechanism, into other European economies. France and Spain, in particular, suffered from this fall-out: Spain experienced very high levels of unemployment (for example 22.4 per cent in 1993). Both France and Spain adopted monetarist-style economic policies, which included considerable reform of their labour markets. Spain is a particularly interesting example to include in this comparison as, following the death of Franco, the State has retreated from intervention in union affairs. The UK, in its most neo-corporatist period 1971–4, is also included in the comparison.

No other EU country has chosen to introduce changes in union legal frameworks as part of its response to the economic pressures of the 1980s or 1990s. Thus in Spain, for example, the only significant constraint on union activities is the forthcoming introduction of certain legal restrictions on striking, targeted at strikes in essential services—at the time of writing the legislation has yet to be passed (*EIRR* 210, 7.91; *EIRR* 214, 10.91; *EIRR* 227, 12.92; *EIRR* 235, 8.93). Instead, the thrust of the Spanish approach has been to increase labour flexibility, to improve qualifications and training, to reduce the deficit of the National Employment Institute's (INEM) unemployment benefit spending and provide individuals with greater incentives to work, and to pursue more moderate wage settlements (*EIRR* 220, 5.92; *EIRR* 242, 3.94). To take another example, in Balladur's five-year plan for employment and social reform in France the only proposal related in any way to unions' legal framework was for the simplification of the employee representation system to make it less burdensome for small- and medium-sized companies while at the same time safeguarding workers' rights (*EIRR* 242, 3.94).[3] The emphasis of the incoming RPR-UDF government in France was on job creation (by lifting employers' social security burden and by reducing 'rigidities' and 'blockages' preventing employment creation, for example the restrictions on working time), on cutting redundancies and saving the social security system from bankruptcy, on improving the position of workers both by an increase in direct pay and by developing employee participation in the management and profits of their companies, on fighting 'social exclusion' of the young and unemployed, and on training for young people (*EIRR* 232, 5.93; *EIRR* 235, 8.93). While British Conservative Governments have also been concerned to introduce different measures for job creation, union reform has been the outstanding item on their agenda for the reform of the UK's labour market, particularly when fighting general elections.

UNION GOVERNMENT: ELECTIONS FOR NATIONAL AND LOCAL LEADERS

Table 8.1 compares state intervention in union affairs through the imposition of regulations for electing union officials (both national and local) and the calling of industrial action in the selected EU countries, together with the UK in 1995 and in the 1974–9 period.

From Table 8.1 it is clear that the UK differs sharply from the other selected countries in the degree to which methods of election for national union leaders are specified by statute. The only country where the State plays a role resembling that of the British State is Greece, where Law 1264/1982 on union democracy includes special provisions concerning the government and internal decision-making procedures of unions: regulations provide for the organization, functioning, and government of unions,

TABLE 8.1. A comparison of state regulation of union elections and calling for industrial action in selected EU countries[1]

	Denmark	France	Germany	Greece	Ireland	Italy	The Netherlands	Spain	UK 1974–9	UK 1995
Selection of national union leaders	No regulation	No regulation	No regulation[2]	Moderate regulation, elections required[3]	No regulation	No regulation	No regulation	Only regulation is that union officials must be elected[4]	No regulation	Extensive regulation for elections
Selection of local union representatives	No regulation[5]	Partial regulation[6]	No regulation	Moderate regulation, elections required	No regulation	No regulation	No regulation	Only regulation is that union officials must be elected[7]	No regulation	No regulation[8]
Membership approval of proposed industrial action	No regulation[9]	No regulation	No regulation[10]	Partial regulation[11]	Moderate regulation[12]	No regulation, voluntary codes	No regulation, voluntary codes[13]	Regulation[14]	No regulation	Extensive regulation

Definitions

No regulation: absence of direct State regulation of union procedures and activities.

Extensive regulation: direct regulations with wide coverage and detailed prescriptions for union procedures and activities.

Partial regulation: direct regulations for union procedures and activities with narrow coverage.

Moderate regulation: direct regulations on union procedures and activities with coverage of some but not most aspects and prescriptions of a general rather than a detailed nature.

[1] Adapted from Table 1 in Fosh et al. (1993b). The sources for this table are the collection of articles edited by Ferner and Hyman (1992); Blanpain, R.: *International Encyclopedia of Labour Law and Industrial Relations* (Deventer, Netherlands: Kluwer, 1991); IDS/IPM, *European Management Guides: Industrial Relations* (IDS/IPM: London, 1991); and *EIRR* (1991).

TABLE 8.1 (*Continued*)

[2] There is no direct statutory regulation of the internal decision making processes of unions in Germany. However, the legal underpinnings of the collective bargaining process are provided by the Act on Collective Agreements 1949, as amended in 1969. The interpretation of the provisions of this Act by the Federal Labour Court has led to the formulation of nine criteria against which the competence of the parties to a collective agreement is assessed and, therefore, the validity of the final agreement. Of particular relevance to trade unions, is the requirement that the union should be organized in a manner such that members are able to democratically influence its activities.

[3] The Greek Act 1264/1982, on the democratization of the syndicalistic movement, includes special provisions about the governmental and internal decision-making procedures of trade unions. Among the detailed regulations governing trade unions are sections dealing with the organization, functioning and government of these bodies, the system of elections (both national and local), and the operation of proportional representation schemes.

[4] Article 7 of the Spanish Constitution provides that unions' associations, foundation, and performance are free and that their internal structure and functioning must be democratic. The only stipulation upon the unions' choice of democratic model is that, under *Ley Orgánica de Libertad Sindical 1985*, union officials be elected.

[5] While there is no statutory provision in Demark for shop-floor representation, s.8 of the General Agreement (*Hovedaftalen*) between the LO (*Landsorganisation*) and the DA (*Dansk Arbejdsgiverforening*) provides that industry agreements should make provision for shop stewards (*Tillidsrepæsentant*) to be elected and recognized; industry agreements in turn lay down detailed regulations for their elections and their specific rights and duties.

[6] In France the Act of 27 November 1968, as modified by the Act of October 1982, created the legal concepts of a union section and union delegates. Under the terms of these regulations, each 'representative union' within an enterprise may constitute a section, except where the enterprise employs certain specified categories of employees. The function of the union section is to ensure the representation of the material and moral interests of its members. The establishment of a section entitles the union to informational, organizational and facility rights, which vary according to the size of the enterprise. Each union section within an enterprise employing more than fifty employees may appoint one or more delegates, the precise number is determined by a formula linking representation to the number of employees. These delegates represent the union and are competent to conclude collective agreements, demand modifications to work rules, end strikes, etc.

[7] As mentioned above, trade unionists in Spain are guaranteed the right to freely elect their representatives. However, the principal means of workplace representation is via staff representatives (*delegados de personal*) in workplaces of less than fifty employees. In larger workplaces employees are represented through works councils (*comités de empresa*). The election of these workplace representatives is heavily regulated by the Workers' Statute of 1980.

[8] However, the balloting prescriptions of the Trade Union Act 1984 in the UK apply to some branch executive committees, where the branch falls within the legal definition of a 'trade union' (Trade Unions and Labour Relations Act 1974 s.28) (Wedderburn 1985).

[9] Note, however, that the General Agreement in Denmark provides that no stoppage of work may lawfully be initiated unless it has been approved by at least three-quarters of the votes cast by a competent assembly under the rules of the relevant organisation. Also the General Agreement prescribes the holding of reference-back ballots: 35% of workers concerned must vote against a draft settlement for it to be rejected.

10 Although there is no direct statutory regulation of pre-strike procedures, according to the German Federal Labour Court's interpretation of the right to strike, the following prerequisites must be fulfilled for a strike to be lawful. First, both parties must respect the peace obligation. Second, before a union can call a strike, there must be a secret ballot of the members involved. Third, the strike must be proportionate to the objectives pursued by the union. Finally, the strike must be a weapon of last resort. The Federal Labour Court has also ruled that not only strikes as such, but any preparation for industrial action (including balloting), is illegal where it is in violation of a prevailing peace obligation.

11 In Greece, the controls on the calling of industrial action vary according to the level at which the action is proposed. Greek law makes a distinction between three levels of trade union organization: local, district/industry groupings, and national confederations. Detailed regulations apply differently to these three levels; for example, the authorization of industrial action at the first of these levels requires prior endorsement by a ballot at a general meeting.

12 In Ireland, the Industrial Relations Act 1990 'provides that two years after the passing of the Act the rules of every trade union shall contain a provision requiring a secret ballot before organising, participating in, sanctioning or supporting a strike or other industrial action. Entitlement to vote is to be given to all members whom it is reasonable at the time of the ballot for the union concerned to believe will be called upon to engage in the action. They are to get a "fair opportunity" of voting . . . unions failing to incorporate the Act's secret ballot requirements . . . will lose their negotiating licence.' Evidence of compliance is supplied by way of forwarding to Registrar of Friendly Societies a copy of the union's rules' (Redmond 1991: 187).

13 In The Netherlands, ballots are governed by the trade unions' internal regulations. Generally, rejection of a settlement requires a two-thirds majority and a vote for strike action a three-quarters majority.

14 In Spain, the decision to strike must be reached by an express decision of the work-force, though no percentage figure is stipulated. The decision may be that of the staff representatives, the workers' delegates, the works council, or the workplace unions: in each case it must be a majority decision. Provisions of the 1977 Decree-law which specified precise percentages were declared unconstitutional.

the system of elections, and the operation of proportional representation schemes (Kritsantonis 1992: 616). In contrast to the extensive regulation of union national elections in the UK, the state in the other EU countries (and in the UK prior to 1984, except in the 1971–4 period) regards the method of election of such officials as a matter for the membership, in keeping with the spirit of ILO Convention No. 87. It should be noted, however, that in a number of these countries the state may be involved in the specification of representational rights and electoral procedures for work councils/committees, for employee participation at board level, and for various national tripartite bodies (for example in France and Germany). The activities of these institutions may overlap with those of British unions.

In terms of state specification of the methods of elections of local officials, the Conservative Government decided at an early stage of its union reform programme (as we saw in Chapter 4) that it would be impracticable to specify balloting arrangements at this union level. Most of the other countries in Table 8.1 (including the UK in the 1974–9 period) also do not regulate union local elections; however, the rationale is not impracticability but the view that this is properly a matter for the membership to decide. Greece is again more in favour of regulation and the election of local officials is covered by Law 1264/1982. In France there is partial regulation for the election of union delegates, but in devising the regulations the State was concerned not to become involved in regulating unions' internal decision-making processes (see note 6 in Table 8.1).

CALLING INDUSTRIAL ACTION: REQUIREMENT FOR STRIKE BALLOTS

Table 8.1 shows that the UK in 1995 and Greece again differ markedly from the other selected countries in the extent to which the State lays down regulations concerning the method by which unions can call for industrial action. However, Ireland joins these two countries in having State regulation for this aspect of union decision-making. However, neither the Greek nor Irish State regulates to the same extent as the British State in 1995. Thus, in Greece, the balloting requirement that applies to the first tier of local union organization does not extend above this to the regional or national union organizations, and, in Ireland, the requirement that unions should ballot their work-forces before organizing industrial action (introduced by the Industrial Relations Act 1990) is phrased in terms of principle rather than detailed prescription (see note 12 in Table 8.1). In the other EU countries in Table 8.1 (and in the UK prior to 1984), unions to varying degrees are free to organize the way in which they call industrial action and to decide whether and how they will ballot. In countries such as The Netherlands, it is usual for the union's rule book to specify voting methods and procedures; in Denmark the manner in which strike decisions are taken is regulated by the General Agreement between the *Landsorganisation* (LO) and the *Dansk Arbrejdsgiverforening* (DA).[4]

In sum, Table 8.1 shows that the UK in 1995 and Greece differ significantly from other EU countries in having a pattern of strong state intervention in union procedures, both for electing union officials and calling industrial action: the British prescriptions are, however, more stringent than those of Greece and the pattern of strong state intervention in union affairs is repeated in Britain, but not in Greece, for other aspects of unions' internal decision-making such as unions' discipline of strike-breakers (see Fosh *et al.* 1993b and 1993c). In the other EU countries in Table 8.1, the state very largely refrains from intervening in unions' internal affairs.

EXPLANATORY FACTORS IN THE DIFFERENTIAL REGULATION OF UNION DECISION-MAKING

In this section, we set the British Conservative Government's strong interventionist policy towards the conduct of union affairs in the 1980s and 1990s in its EU context and we draw on the international comparison to shed further light on why the Conservatives have been able to legislate so successfully for the introduction of regulations for union activities. None of the other selected EU countries have followed the British lead so far, despite similar economic pressures, and we consider why they did not.[5] We consider two aspects of State policy: first, the approach taken towards union autonomy and second, the role allocated to unions in national economic and social decision-making. We then go on to consider the constraints on State regulation of union affairs: the strength and organization of the labour movement and constitutional constraints. These aspects of State policy and the constraints on the State are summarized in Table 8.2.

The State's approach to union autonomy

Union democracy is a valued goal in all western societies. However, there are two distinct strategies for its realization, depending on who is seen as responsible for achieving it and what means should be utilized. The choice lies between, on the one hand, the State enacting rules to provide for union democracy and ensuring union adherence to them and, on the other, the State relying on unions themselves to establish democracy in their internal affairs (Blanc-Jouvan 1988). General social values play a part in the extent to which union autonomy is recognized by the State. Such values also play

TABLE 8.2. Explanatory factors in the differential regulation of union decision-making among selected EU countries

	Denmark	France	Germany	Greece	Ireland	Italy	The Netherlands	Spain	UK 1974–9	UK 1994
State approach to union autonomy	State has respect for union autonomy	State has respect for union autonomy	State has respect for union autonomy	Anti-labour and authoritarian intervention in union affairs	Partly respect for union autonomy, partly State has duty to regulate union decision-making	State has respect for union autonomy	State has respect for union autonomy	State has respect for union autonomy	State had respect for union autonomy	State has duty to maintain union democracy
Role of unions in national decision-making	Declining neo-corporatism	State-led attempts at neo-corporatism: bargaining/contestation	Neo-corporatism with strong branch component	Contestation	State-led attempts at neo-corporatism: bargaining/contestation	Incipient regional neo-corporatism in limited areas; elsewhere bargaining/contestation	Declining neo-corporatism	State-led attempts at neo-corporatism: bargaining/contestation	Government-led attempts at neo-corporatism on bargaining and contestation base	Dis-aggregating collective bargaining; contestation

	Strength of union movement	Organization of union movement
	Strong union movement with high density (79%), strong political ties	Highly co-ordinated union movement with craft and general base
	Low union density (9%) but considerable union impact on wage-setting and influence through strong political ties	Politically pluralist unionism, moderate centralization
	Powerful union movement, only moderate density overall (29%) but high density in strategic areas	Branch-level-co-ordinated union movement, strict industrial unionism
	Weak, repressed union movement with density of approximately 30%	Extremely party-dependent and riven by factions, with a mixture of forms including industrial, craft, occupational, company, and general
	Strong union movement with 43% density	Dominated by general unions, moderate centralization
	Union movement (density 39%) with a pivotal role through political interests in Italian socio-economic relationships	Political pluralism with three main confederations
	Weak union movement with density of 24%	Politically and religiously divided union movement
	Weak union movement with density of 15%	Political pluralism with two large national confederations
	High union density (54% in 1979), unions had significant political influence and role in public life	Craft and occupational fragmentation, central union body weak in comparison to large general unions
	Rapidly declining union density (43%), political influence and role in public life	Craft and occupational fragmentation, central union body weak in comparison to large general unions

TABLE 8.2. (*Continued*)

	Denmark	France	Germany	Greece	Ireland	Italy	The Netherlands	Spain	UK 1974–9	UK 1994
Union universalistic or sectionalist policy	Universalistic	Universalistic: strong focus on 'representative' democracy	Composite	Universalistic	Sectional	Universalistic: strong focus on 'representative' democracy	Sectional	Universalistic: strong focus on 'representative' democracy	Sectional	Sectional
Union rule-making capacity	Unions' administrative abilities respected	Unions' administrative abilities respected	Unions' administrative abilities respected	Government and media have negative view of unions' ability	Government and media have positive view of unions' ability	Unions' administrative abilities respected	Government and media have positive view of unions' ability	Unions' administrative abilities respected	Government had positive view of unions' ability, not shared by media	Unions' ability perceived as weak by government and media but this view contested by unions
Legal constraints on state intervention	Moderately strong	Strong	Strong	Strong	Strong	Strong	Strong	Strong	Weak	Weak

Sources: Crouch (1993) and the collection of articles edited by Ferner and Hyman (1992): the figures for union density are from the latter.

a part in the extent to which unions are allocated a part in national decision-making and are considered capable of devising their own rules for democratic administration: these issues are discussed below. Where unions are valued in public opinion and not lampooned by the media, union autonomy is more likely to be respected by the State, unions are more likely to be consulted in national decision-making, and there is more likely to be electorate resistance to State-imposed regulations on union activities.[6]

Table 8.2 shows that the predominant State approach among the selected EU countries towards union internal affairs is one of respect for unions' autonomy: a view that unions are private associations and therefore subject only to the same laws as other private associations, and a perception that unions have an important function as one of the checks-and-balances in a democratic society. Unions are relied upon to regulate themselves to produce responsiveness (to members' desires) and respect (for individual rights).[7] Further, legislative intervention is seen as stunting the autonomous development of unions, as inimical to the maintenance of democracy on a societal level, and as counter-productive in that it would generate ill-afforded hostility among union members (Blanc-Jouvan 1988; Wedderburn 1988). An extreme version of this view is Giugni's (1988: 43–4) notion that true democracy allows the existence of undemocratic unions, given freedom of exit.

In France, the State chooses not to intervene in the relations between unions and their members, although it has chosen to intervene powerfully in the relation between capital and labour in order to balance the power of the former (Blanc-Jouvan 1988). Unions are officially recognized by the law and this recognition means that they are subject to some legal constraints. However, these constraints are the same as are applied to any non-profit organization: the Labour Code merely states that any member can take part in the administration of the union, with minor exceptions. The law does not lay down prescriptions for union organization, for matters such as the competence and operation of the general assembly, the appointment, powers, and liability of the unions' officials, the decision-making process, the relations between unions and their members (admission, exclusion, discipline, and so forth), and the rights and duties of individuals (apart from the individual's right to withdraw from the union). The French courts have had little opportunity to intervene in union's internal affairs as such matters are rarely submitted to them. Where the courts do exceptionally intervene, they decide cases on the basis of general principles of law applicable to all private organizations, for example to ensure equality of treatment. Moreover, this non-interventionist approach has survived the advent of Balladur's right-wing RPR-UDF government in 1993 and its massive reforms of French social and employment legislation.

The State approach in Spain to union autonomy provides a clear contrast between the Fascist era and the return of democracy after the death of Franco in 1975. Under Franco, the State played an authoritarian role, both in industrial relations generally and in the determination of unions' internal affairs.[8] The *sindicatos verticales* compulsorily organized both workers and employers; autonomous workers' organizations were illegal. The *sindicatos verticales* were run first by State-appointed officials at the national, provincial, and local levels and, even after indirect elections were introduced, they were tightly controlled by the Falangists. After the death of Franco, the State attempted to construct a liberal-democratic model of industrial relations and an appropriate legal framework. It renounced its authoritarian control, although it retained a key role in devising a legal framework for autonomous decision-making and in providing assistance to the employer and worker organizations to enable them to re-establish themselves (*EIRR* 224, 9.92). Unions were seen, as in pre-Franco Spain, as free to organize their own affairs. However, the law in Spain is not entirely 'silent' on union autonomy, since the final part of Article 7 of the 1978 Spanish Constitution stipulates that unions' internal structure and functioning must be 'democratic'. This means both that the rules governing the organization of collective participation must accord with democratic principles and that the rules are adhered to.[9] However, the union is free to determine its own democratic model: the Constitution does not define rules for democratic union structures or functioning. Nor does the *Ley Orgánica de Libertad Sindical* 1985 (Law of Trade Union Freedom) stipulate an obligatory democratic model: the only obligation is that officials are elected and not appointed or nominated. Unions are free to decide what election model and rules to adopt.[10] This approach survived, as in France, the Socialist PSOE Government's move to monetarist economic policies and its considerable reform of the Spanish labour market.

The State's approach in Ireland to union autonomy is a hybrid of the French and Spanish approaches considered above and the British and Greek considered below. Irish industrial relations have been subject to a number of different influences including the neo-corporatist tradition, multinationals' non-unionism, and other EU countries' industrial relations systems as well as that of the UK (von Prondzynski 1992). While the Irish Government introduced regulations for the calling of industrial action in the Industrial Relations Act 1990 modelled on the British legislation, and introduced this for much the same reasons, it has refrained from legislating for the control of union elections, preferring to follow here the western European model of respecting union autonomy.

The above accounts of the State approach to union autonomy in France and Spain contrast sharply with that of the UK in 1995. The UK today is the most interventionist of the States under consideration here. The British approach before 1979 also contrasts with the present Conservative approach; in both the traditional *laissez-faire* British approach to the legal regulation of unions and in the neo-corporatist approach of the 1970s, the Government regarded unions as voluntary associations and largely responsible for their own internal affairs. As we saw in Chapter 4, the Conservatives in the 1980s and 1990s had a particular view of unions: first unions were privileged in legal terms and therefore their conduct should be subject to public accountability; second individual union members were in need of protection from their leaders, particularly those coerced into membership; third union power to initiate industrial action was damaging not only to the disputants but also to the general public and the economy; and fourth union leaders were unrepresentative, their survival ensured by malpractice and corruption. From this perspective the need for a competitive market logically leads to the legal regulation of union affairs: State intervention is necessary to protect the individual, society and the market from 'coercion' by collective labour organizations and their 'distortion' of the labour market (Wedderburn 1988; McCarthy 1992: 48–57). Instead of there being a perceived separation between political and organizational democracy, it is considered necessary for unions to be bound by the same principles and standards as those binding the State. Thus unions should follow the practices adopted by the State, including strong reliance on majority rule. However, the Conservative regulations and safeguards for union elections in 1995 now far exceed the requirements laid down for political elections.

The only country where the State approach towards union autonomy resembles that of the UK today is Greece, which has had a very different history of industrial relations. The Greek state, according to Kritsantonis (1992), is anti-labour, authoritarian, and pro-capitalist in attitude; its approach in a situation of political polarization and intense industrial conflict has been to enclose industrial relations in a comprehensive and complex framework, which includes the detailed regulation of unions' internal affairs. This approach to industrial relations is not a product of monetarist economic policies of the 1980s and 1990s but has been sustained in Greece from the inter-war military dictatorships, through wartime Nazi occupation, the right-wing administration which held control after the civil war of 1946–9, and the regime of the Colonels (1967–74) to the present day.

In both Greece and the UK the State has sought to take upon itself, despite the possible dangers and questions about its utility, the goal of promoting union democracy by legal means. However, it is questionable whether the imposition of regulation for unions' internal affairs is driven by a quest for 'democracy' or by a desire to weaken unions, which are seen as unwelcome political opponents or as representatives of illegitimate interests (Offe and Weisenthal 1985).

**The role accorded to unions in national
decision-making**

A government's approach to the role of unions in national economic and
social decision-making, and indeed in public life, can vary significantly
and is linked to its approach to union autonomy. A neo-corporatist State
that values unions as 'social partners', and includes them along with
employers in tripartite national decision-making, may feel it inappropriate
to dictate how one of its partners elects its representatives and makes
internal decisions, for example when to call a strike or whether to
discipline a strike-breaker. Indeed, political problems may ensue if the
State is open to accusations of manipulating the political affiliation and
militancy of the leaders of one of its partners. Further, the State may fear
the objections of a strong union movement to the legal regulation of its
affairs when it wishes to retain the unions' co-operation. Alternatively, the
State may be seeking to build up unions' weak bargaining strength in order
that they may function efficiently as social partners and accordingly feel
that creating a comprehensive legal framework for running unions' internal
affairs would be counter-productive.

It is useful in this section to adopt Crouch's (1993) typology of the
differing relationships between unions, employers, and the State: his two
variables—the 'level of organizational articulation of both labour and
capital' and the 'power of organized labour' produce a fourfold typology
consisting of neo-corporatist States with weak and strong labour movements and pluralist/contestation States with weak and strong labour
movements. Table 8.2 classifies the selected EU countries in terms of this
typology. Germany is an example of Crouch's neo-corporatism, with a
strong 'branch' (i.e. industry) component combined with a powerful union
movement. German unions are seen as important 'social partners' and,
although *Konzertierte Aktion* was disappointing and came to an official end
in 1977, German unions continue to have a powerful voice in decision-
making at industry level and at company and establishment levels (Jacobi
et al. 1992). The Netherlands is also classified as neo-corporatist by
Crouch[11] but, compared to Germany, the Dutch union movement is weak.
However, despite their weakness, Dutch unions play an essential part in
national decision-making through the machinery of the *Sociaal-Economisch
Raad*, whose advice the Government is obliged to seek on all proposals for
major social and economic legislation. There is also the bipartite Labour
Foundation, which acts as a forum for negotiation and consultation
between employers and unions; the Government looks to the Labour
Foundation for a consensus position on pay in its autumn consultation
(IDS/IPM 1991: 153–4; Visser 1992). As we have seen, the State in neither
Germany nor The Netherlands has thought it appropriate to legislate for

the regulation of unions' internal affairs; and this is so for Germany despite the high degree of juridification of its industrial relations system.

We turn now to compare the national role of unions in Crouch's pluralist bargaining and contestation types. We look here at Spain in particular and note that overall, since the death of Franco, unions have participated in and influenced national decision-making to a significant degree, even though Spain does not possess the fully developed corporatism of Germany and The Netherlands.[12] In Spain the pluralist bargaining/contestation base has been combined with an intermittent government strategy of encouraging tripartism. Thus the Spanish Socialist (PSOE) government has alternated since Franco's death between excluding employers and unions from influence and involving them to a significant extent, in particular, the PSOE's commitment to *concertation* diminished as political stability was achieved (Lucio 1992: 503–8).[13] However, in the 1990s the PSOE returned to *concertation* following the 1988 general strike, the challenge of European integration, the rapidly rising level of unemployment, and the loss of its absolute majority following the 1993 general election; in 1992 the PSOE set up the Social and Economic Council to further tripartism. The introduction of union involvement in national decision-making in Spain after the death of Franco was accompanied by a withdrawal of the repressive State intervention in union activities: the Spanish Constitution and the legal framework for industrial relations were rewritten to ensure union freedom.

The contrast with the UK under Conservative rule in the 1980s and 1990s is stark. Crouch (1993: 267–8) classifies the UK in 1990 in a contestation class of its own as 'disaggregate collective bargaining' on account, not only of the dismantling of almost all state and national institutions of neo-corporatism, but of a virtual collapse of branch-level or any other form of co-ordinated cross-company bargaining. The Conservatives on taking office in 1979 firmly rejected tripartism and systematically denied unions any role in public life—they did not see unions as appropriate bodies to consult on economic and social matters or leading trade unionists as appropriate people to whom to offer public appointments (Crouch 1986; Wedderburn 1989; Marsh 1992). As noted in Chapter 3, Conservative Acts of particular significance were the abolition of NEDC in 1992 and first the restriction, and then in 1993 abolition, of the Wages Councils. The Conservatives have also been strongly opposed to tripartism at the enterprise level, hence their rejection of the EU Works Council Directive. This approach by the State in the UK towards the role of unions in society has meant that considerations of union opposition to the detailed regulation of their internal affairs were not an important consideration in policy-making: unions were not respected 'social partners' but an opposition force to be 'brought down to size'.

Constraints imposed by the State through the strength and organization of the union movement

The State that wishes to intervene in union affairs will face union resistance; the strength of this resistance will vary according to the strength and organization of its union movement. A government may choose not to implement a desired policy of intervening in union affairs through fear of the consequence or a Government may be defeated by a powerful adverse reaction from the labour movement to the legal regulation of its affairs. The strength of a union movement depends most importantly on its density, the industrial distribution of its membership, and its alliance with powerful political parties, together with employer strength and the demand for labour. However, the union movement's strength is also closely linked to its organization. A number of options exist here: centralized or decentralized; unitary or pluralist; industrial unionism or occupational and craft fragmentation (Treu 1988: 51–3). A further important aspect of union organization is the distinction between union adoption of universalistic as opposed to sectionalist policies: that is, whether unions view their role as representing the interests of the working class in a societal context or those of its members *vis-à-vis* its members' employers. A final feature of the union movement is its capacity to provide rules for satisfactory internal democracy and the union leadership's responsiveness to its members; this is important where a state seeks justification for intervening in union affairs. Table 8.2 summarizes the features of the union movements in the selected EU countries.

The union movement in Germany is perhaps the strongest in the present EU, though its density is not strikingly high (35 per cent in 1990). However, key groups, such as blue-collar workers in the strong manufacturing industry and public sector employees, do have relatively high density and, in an historically tight labour market, have set the pace in wage agreements (Jacobi *et al.* 1992: 230–6); and the system of industrial unionism and sectoral bargaining discourages employers paying below-union rates. Further, the German union movement with its absence of ideological and status divisions, has a strong sense of unity and the unions, owing to the high level of commitment, can mobilize their members in 'disciplined, protracted, and effective strike action' (ibid. 233). The German unions do not have a strong tradition of universalism but the works councils, which represent all employees, and unions are mutually dependent: (ibid. 243) describe the works councils as 'the arm of the union in the workplace'. The final feature accounting for the strength of the German union movement is its respectability both in the eyes of employers and the Government. In particular, German unions, though they have clearly oligarchic tendencies (ibid. 234), are seen as responsible and fairly organized and administered: for example, most unions have voluntarily adopted the requirement that at least 75 per cent of the membership must vote in favour of a strike before industrial action can begin (*EIRR* 1989). The strength and organization of the German union movement suggest that it could mount an effective resistance to the imposition of legal controls on its internal affairs. This would presumably deter the State from adopting such a policy, even if it wished to. The Danish union movement is also strong, with a high degree of coordination between LO and the other two smaller union centres, FTF (Central Confederation of Salaried Employees) and AC (Central Confederation of Professional Associations), though it has a craft and general base rather than an industrial one (IDS/IPM 1991: 31–2).[14]

It is possibly more relevant to look at countries with 'weak' labour movements to assess the role of possible union resistance in the State's decision whether to intervene or not in union affairs. What, for example, would be the possible resistance to State intervention in union affairs in Spain and France, countries which are both frequently described as having weak and politically divided labour movements? In the case of France, the weakness of the politically divided, fragmented, and poorly resourced union movement faced by increasingly large and powerful employers is countered to a considerable degree through the unions' close ties with French political parties and through State sponsorship, in particular by the State granting unions legal rights to represent the interests of all employees (not only their limited number of members), by social legislation providing workers directly with benefits the union has been unable to obtain through collective bargaining, and by the State granting unions a substantial role in public bodies (Goetschy and Rozenblatt 1992). Such State sponsorship is, of course, reversible, but it has created a set of expectations concerning French unions' universalistic and public role that could lead to strong resistance to change. Linked to the French unions' universalistic approach is the lack of a debate over the unions' capacity to regulate their internal affairs in a democratic manner and to be accountable to their members. This debate has not taken place because the emphasis has been placed on the achievement of external rather than internal democracy (Blanc-Jouvan 1988). Thus the focus has been on the extent to which unions represent the will and aspirations of the working class, both members and non-members, to employers and public authorities.

The position of the unions in Spain is similar to France, though the predominance of small employers is increasing in the former. The weak, pluralistic, and rivalry-torn union movement has close ties with sponsoring political parties; there are particularly close ties between the UGT and the ruling PSOE—though Lucio (1992: 503) feels the closeness of the ties may have led to overdependence and organizational weakness. Moreover, Spanish unions maintain an important influence through the 'capture' of the system of workplace representation by the UGT and the COOO (ibid. 501). The workplace elections for works councils (*comités de empresa*) and workers' delegates (*delegados de personal*) (in which members and non-members vote) determine union 'representativeness' for participation in tripartite bodies and for reaching collective agreements. Additionally, as in France, the universalism of the Spanish union movement gives it strength: Spanish unions represent diffuse interests beyond the sphere of their members, for example participating in bodies such as INEM and INSERO. Again, the capacity of Spanish unions to regulate their internal affairs in a democratic manner is of less importance for their reputation than their ability to represent 'fairly and truly' the interests of the working class.

In the 1970s, the British union movement was strong, both in terms of membership density (54 per cent in 1979) and influence and prestige, and it faced a decentralized and ineffective employers' organization. The unions' rejection of the interventionist IRA 1971, the ensuing high rate of industrial action, and the union resistance to wage restraint were a very significant factor in the defeat of Ted Heath's Conservative Government in 1974, and the incoming Labour Government repealed IRA 1971 in 1974. Union power declined steeply in the UK in the 1980s and 1990s. As noted in Chapter 3, a variety of factors, including the marked rise in unemployment, the shift in the industrial mix, the change in the composition of the labour force, and the reduction in firm size in the UK in the 1980s and 1990s, played a significant part in the decline of union power. But while union density declined in other EU countries as well, the British unions' influence in Government decision-making and role in public life declined in a way that was not mirrored in these countries. Various features of the British union movement—not so disadvantageous in times of neutral or pro-union Governments and economic prosperity—handicapped it severely in resisting the combined assault of unfavourable economic and demographic influences, the employers' pushing back of the 'frontier of control', and the antagonism of the Conservative Governments under Margaret Thatcher and John Major.

The handicaps of British unions relate to political, organizational, and policy matters. British unions have been traditionally closely linked to the Labour Party, but the lack both of proportional representation and a tradition of coalition government, coupled with the Labour Party's failure to win a general election since 1979, has meant that the unions have had little or no access to the Government in power or influence on labour legislation. The 'new' Labour Party in 1995 under Tony Blair, which possibly has more electoral chance of success, is at present emphasizing its separateness from the unions and is unlikely to repeal all the Conservative union legislation since 1979. The resistance of the British union movement to aggressive legal reform has been hampered, not only by its political distance from the legislators, but also through its lack of cohesiveness: it is characterized by marked decentralism, a considerable craft and occupational fragmentation, and a marked orientation towards sectoral bargaining and inter-union competition. Further, there is an absence of representative authority: British unions put their efforts into recruiting and retaining union members and on pursuing policies to benefit those members. There is thus a strong British preference for union security and sectional policies.[15] A final weakness of the British unions was their failure to counteract effectively the damaging allegations, made by the Conservatives since 1979, that British unions are unable to provide rules for internal democracy and leader responsiveness. As we saw in Chapter 4, the Conservatives accused the unions of failing to reform themselves, despite being offered the opportunity to do so by EA 1980: this was held to justify the introduction of legislation to ensure union democracy and abolish union malpractice.

We have shown that union movements in France, Spain, and the UK are weak in the 1990s. However, our analysis suggests that the political and organizational links of the French and Spanish unions would enable them to mount effective resistance were their Governments to seek to introduce major reforms of their legal frameworks.

Constitutional constraints

In the countries in Table 8.2, apart from the UK, unions have substantial constitutional or otherwise enshrined freedoms to organize themselves as they wish.[16] It would be difficult for the State in these countries to adopt a policy of intervention in union affairs and introduce radical new controls for union activities. Italy and Spain are interesting examples to consider as substantial union rights were introduced in both countries after the fall of Fascism. Thus in Italy, Article 39 of the 1947 Constitution declares that 'labour organizations are free'. This has been held to imply not only that individuals have the right to organize, to join a union of their choice, to resign from a union, and not to join a union, but also that the State is prohibited from interfering in unions' internal affairs: the State may not predetermine union aims and models of organization, nor define areas of union jurisdiction. The only condition explicitly required by Article 39 of unions asking for recognition is that unions' constitutions and rules be inspired by the principle of internal democracy. When Article 39 was found to be of limited effectiveness in protecting union freedom in employer–employee relations, the *Statuto dei Lavoratori* 1970 (Statute of Workers' Rights, Act No. 300 of 30 May) was passed to confirm and specify the principle of union freedom in the workplace (Treu 1991).

In Spain, Article 28 of the 1978 Constitution gives workers freedom to form unions and the right to belong to one of their choice, and Article 7 provides that unions' and employers associations' foundation and perform-ance are free, provided that the Constitution and the law are respected and that unions' internal structure and functioning is democratic. The *Estatuto de los Trabajadores* 1980 (Workers' Statute) 1980 and the *Ley Orgánica de Libertad Sindical* 1985 draw upon the Constitution closely for their authority. The first lays down the procedures and scope of collective bargaining and formalizes workers' participation within the enterprise through workers' committees and delegates. The second develops the right of freedom of association and provides statutory support for workplace union branches (*secciones sindicales*) and union delegates, and stipulates the facilities to which they are entitled (Lucio 1992: 497–8).

The lack of constitutional protection for union freedom in the UK stands in sharp contrast to that offered in the other EU countries in Table 8.2. The UK has no written Constitution guaranteeing, *inter alia*, union freedom and British unions owe their legal existence to a relatively precarious system of immunities which protect union members and their leaders from the consequences of their actions under common law. As labour legislation passed by one Government can be repealed by the next, the sovereignty of the British Parliament places union freedom in jeopardy when an anti-union Government takes power. Further, there was a very different tradition in the UK in terms of unions' preference for legal protection. The British unions had become established before the development of universal suffrage and the founding of the Labour Party in 1913. After 1913 they preferred to continue to rely on their own strength in negotiations with employers to obtain recognition and favourable condi-tions of work, rather then pressing through Parliament for legal protection. The British unions were not opposed to all protective legislation but they were averse to legislation that had the effect, or appeared likely to have the effect, of bringing unions and their members into the courts—as one would expect given unions' experience of the judiciary (Flanders 1974). There was also a fear that intervention by the law, for example the introduction of legal support for collective bargaining, might bring in its wake less welcome legal intervention in other areas such as industrial action (Davies and Freedland 1984: 133–4). While the British unions were strong enough in 1971 to defeat Ted Heath's IRA 1971, when their strength diminished with recession and restructuring in the 1980s and 1990s they had no constitutional or legislative resources to protect themselves against the onslaught of Margaret Thatcher and John Major's anti-union Govern-ments. The unions found their immunities from the common law progressively whittled away and draconian controls imposed on their organizational freedom. As we saw above, the UK's ratification of ILO Convention 87 had not offered the unions any practical protection: the Conservative Government has ignored the judgments of the ILO's Committee of Experts.

CONCLUSION: IS THE UK AN EXEMPLAR OR AN EXCEPTIONAL CASE?

This review of the approach in selected EU countries towards union autonomy and their incorporation of unions in economic and social decision-making, together with a consideration of the constraints exercised by the strengths and organization of their labour movements and their constitutions, suggests that movement by these EU countries towards the British example of adoption of a strong regulatory framework for union organization is unlikely.[17] If the economic crisis affecting other EU States were to worsen drastically and unemployment were to rise even higher, particularly among the politically sensitive group of young people, and if union leaders in these countries did not accept the retrenchments in employment and social protection which their governments considered necessary, it is possible that their governments might be tempted to curb union resistance by the imposition of legal controls on union activities. However, a more likely outcome, given such an economic situation, is for the governments, employers, and union leaders in these countries to work together for economic recovery. Friction would be more likely to occur between union leaders and their members: the latter might resist wage constraints and reduction of entitlements, and be tempted into undertaking unlawful industrial action. Given such friction, the government in power would not logically consider the introduction of legislation designed to empower the membership and 'return unions to their members'.

From the discussion in this chapter, it appears that the factor with the most explanatory power in the analysis of why the UK in the 1980s and 1990s has diverged so sharply from the EU continental model of granting unions the autonomy given to other private organizations is Government ideology. The British Conservatives have taken to its utmost conclusion the precept that the logic of the policy of competitive market forces and individual enterprise leads not to State withdrawal but to State intervention in industrial relations to protect the individual, society, and the market from 'coercion' by collective labour organizations and their 'distortion' of the labour market: 'the "free market" requires a strong—not a weak—state intervening to protect it' (Wedderburn 1988: 130). The Governments in other EC countries have not been, and are unlikely to be, tempted to follow. Thus the UK is an *exceptional case* and not an *exemplar*.

NOTES

1. This chapter uses some of the same material as Fosh *et al.* (1993b and 1993c).

2. Thus we include examples of the Roman-Germanic system, the Anglo-Irish system (Ireland and the UK), and the Nordic system (Denmark).
3. Alterations were made to the employee representation system for *délégués du personnel* and for works councils.
4. A minor amendment needs to be made to the above argument in the case of Germany: although there is no direct statutory regulation of pre-strike procedures, the German Federal Labour Court has held that for a strike to be lawful, it must be preceded by a secret ballot of those involved (see note 10 in Table 8.1).
5. The State approach to union regulation in Greece resembles that of the recent Conservative Governments in the UK since 1980 but, in contrast to the UK, State intervention in unions' internal affairs in Greece is part of a long tradition of union repression and political conflict.
6. For a survey of adverse reporting of union activities in the UK, see Jones (1986).
7. Wedderburn (1988: 125) argues strongly that political and union democracy are not analogous.
8. Although some liberalization took place in the 1950s; see Lucio 1992: 486 ff.
9. Olea and Rodriguez-Sanudo (1987: 117) add that interpretation of Article 7 and the Trade Union Freedom Act also require more important union decisions to be made at the assembly or congress, and for there to be free expression and free deliberation.
10. This union obligation to elect officials comes from Paragraph C of *Ley Orgánica de Libertad Sindical* 1985, which refers to minimal terms to be included in union rules: particular emphasis is laid on the 'organs of representation, government and administration and their functioning, as well as systems for the election of officials, which must be in keeping with democratic principles' (Valdes Dal-Re 1988).
11. Though Crouch places The Netherlands in the category of declining neo-corporatist following the relaxation of its previously high level of corporatist relations. Crouch also classifies Denmark as declining neo-corporatist: Scheuer (1992) notes without regret the 'failure' of the 1970s attempts in Denmark to establish Scandinavian-type high-trust relations between the leaders of (social-democratic) governments, the LO, and the DA and sees the decentralization of collective bargaining in the 1980s as the rediscovery of a 'lost pattern'.
12. Even when the PSOE Government has taken action of which the unions disapproved, the unions have had the opportunity of making their feelings known (for example during the passage of the Decree-Law of 3 December 1993, which was intended to promote employment).
13. The process of *concertation* in Spain involved at various times the Government, political parties, the CEOE, and one or both of the major union confederations in tripartite or bipartite exchanges; wage control was accepted by unions in return for Government or employer concessions/reforms in areas like union law and job creation.
14. Note, however, the important influence of the close links between unemployment insurance and union membership in Denmark.
15. See Treu (1988: 52). For the notion of union 'security' see Clegg (1976) and for its critique as a tactic see Brown (1993).

16. In contrast to most of the other selected EU countries, the Danish Constitution does not enshrine any specific right to strike but s.78(1) provides for freedom of association.
17. We do not include Greece in this observation, with its historically strong State regulation of union activities.

TECHNICAL APPENDIX: NOTES ON THE RULE-BOOK SURVEYS 1980, 1987, AND 1992

In 1980 Undy and Martin (1984), and in 1987 and 1992 the present authors, surveyed the rule books of unions affiliated to the TUC. Over the period between these surveys there were significant changes in the number, government, and structure of TUC-affiliated unions. Thus, despite the conscientious efforts of those involved in the analysis, there are a number of differences between the surveys undertaken in 1980, 1987 and 1992. As a consequence, interpretation of the results of these surveys should take account of the following four factors: (1) changes in the units of analysis; (2) unions missed out from the surveys; (3) changes in the sample composition and characteristics; and (4) amendments to the construction of the coding schedule and associated conventions.

1. Changes in the units of analysis between 1980 and 1992

In the 1980 rule-book survey, constituent sections of federal unions were treated as separate entities and coded accordingly. In the 1987 and 1992 surveys the union as a whole has been treated as a single entity and national rules have been assumed to apply to all the unions' constituent sections. This convention has been adopted because far fewer unions today than in 1980 maintain separate sections with any real degree of autonomy.

2. Unions missed out from the three surveys

In 1980, 1987, and 1992 requests for union rule books were sent to the general secretaries of all unions affiliated to the TUC: 114, 87, and 73 respectively. The unions which did not reply to this request were contacted again by letter or telephone. Finally, visits were made to the Certification Officer's Records Department to gain access to the remaining missing rule books. Despite these efforts a number of unions were left out of the three surveys and those omitted were not always the same unions in each survey. The total number of rule books included in the surveys were as follows: 1980, 102; 1987, 84; and 1992, 69. Nevertheless these unions represented a significant proportion of the members of unions affiliated to the TUC (1980, 98.7%; 1987, 99.99%, and 1992, 99.99%). It is important to note that the 1992 survey omitted the Chartered Society of Physiotherapy, which did not technically affiliate to the TUC until the middle of that year's congress (i.e. September 1992). Similarly the EETPU (latterly the Electricians Section of the Amalgamated Engineering and Electrical Union (AEEU)) was included although it did not formally vote to reaffiliate until May 1993.

In the 1980 survey, the following eight unions and two constituent sections were missed out from the coding because their rule books could not be obtained.

Sections and members
AEU Construction Section, membership in 1980: 25,100
ASTMS Medical Practitioners Section, membership in 1980: 5,109

Unions
National Union of Lock and Metal Workers, membership in 1980: 6,843.
Spring Trapmakers' Society, membership in 1980: 200.
Scottish Union of Power Loom Overlookers, membership in 1980: 90.
Yorkshire Association of Power Loom Overlookers, membership in 1980: 1,130.
Healders and Twister's Trade and Friendly Society, membership in 1980: 174.
The National League of Blind and Disabled, membership in 1980: 4,250.
Film Artistes Association, membership in 1980: 2,581.
Society of Civil and Public Servants, membership in 1980: 108,697.[1]

In the 1987 survey, the following three unions were missed out from the coding because their rule books could not be obtained.

Military and Orchestral Musical Instrument Makers Trade Society, membership in 1987: 36.
Spring Trapmakers' Society, membership in 1987: 90.
Scottish Union of Power Loom Overlookers, membership in 1987: 71.

Five TUC-affiliated unions were excluded from the 1992 survey. In the case of the Chartered Society of Physiotherapy this was because the union was a recent affiliate to the TUC, joining in 1992. The Scottish Union of Power Loom Overlookers and the Military and Orchestral Musical Instrument Makers Trade Society were excluded because they had been excluded from the 1987 survey. The Society of Shuttlemakers was excluded because it had begun the procedure for disbanding the union, and the Sheffield Wool Shear Workers, with a membership of 16, were judged too small to include. It is important to note that the Yorkshire Association of Power Loom Overlookers is included in the survey although it is not formally listed as a TUC affiliate in 1992. Finally, the EETPU was included in the 1992 survey although it was not formally affiliated to the TUC when rule books were requested.

Chartered Society of Physiotherapy, membership in 1992: 24,416.
Scottish Union of Power Loom Overlookers, membership in 1992: 60.
Sheffield Wool Shear Workers' Union, membership in 1992: 16.
Society of Shuttlemakers, disbanded in January 1993, membership in 1992: 19.
Military and Orchestral Musical Instrument Makers Trade Society, membership in 1992: 44.

The rule books of the Spring Trapmakers Society and the Scottish Union of Power Loom Overlookers were excluded from both the 1980 and 1987 studies. Both of these unions no longer exist but remain registered as TUC affiliates for historical reasons.

3. Changes in the sample composition and membership characteristics

As previously stated, there were fewer unions in the 1992 survey than in the 1987 and 1980 equivalents. This change arose primarily as a result of amalgamation and transfers of engagements. Between 1980 and 1987 there was also one dissolution, one disaffiliation and one new affiliate to the TUC. Between 1987 and 1992, these figures were added to by a further dissolution, 2 disaffiliations and 2 new affiliates. See Annex 1 for a full list of the unions that have amalgamated, transferred engagements, dissolved, or disaffiliated from the TUC.

Amalgamations sometimes had an unanticipated effect upon unions' balloting policies between 1980 and 1987. For example several unions, which previously used ballots to elect their officers and lay officials, transferred engagements to TASS during the period covered by our analysis. As TASS was the dominant union by size, some of these bodies adopted its branch block vote-based procedures for the election of national officers including the General Secretary. Similarly, other unions which have attempted to grow during the 1980s through mergers have adopted federal structures. This often means that the national officials are elected either by the method previously used by the larger partner, or that some compromise solution has been reached.

Table 1 summarizes the general decline in the membership of unions affiliated to the TUC.

TABLE I. Total membership and index for unions affiliated to TUC unions (1980–92)

Year	Membership (000s)	Index (1980 = 100)
1980	12,173	100.0
1981	11,601	95.3
1982	11,006	90.4
1983	10,510	86.3
1984	10,082	82.8
1985	9,855	80.9
1986	9,586	78.7
1987	9,243	75.9
1988	8,797	72.2
1989	8,652	71.0
1990	8,417	69.1
1991	8,193	67.3
1992	7,786	63.9

The general effects of these changes on the membership size categories used in the 1980, 1987, and 1992 surveys are set out in Table 2.

TABLE 2. Rule-book survey unions classified according to membership
(1980, 1987, and 1992)

Membership category	1980 n = 102		1987 n = 84		1992 n = 69	
	No.	%	No.	%	No.	%
1–1,000	11	10.8	10	11.9	6	8.7
1,001–10,000	22	21.6	18	21.4	16	23.2
10,001–50,000	31	30.4	28	33.3	22	31.9
50,001–100,000	13	12.7	8	9.5	6	8.7
100,001–500,000	20	19.6	15	17.9	13	18.8
500,001+	5	4.9	5	6.0	6	8.7

The number of unions in each of the membership categories declined between 1980 and 1992, with the exception of those unions with over 500,001 members. This change reflects the overall decline in trade union membership and also indicates a relatively even decline across each of the membership categories. Despite these general trends there were significant variations between unions, as Table 3 overleaf demonstrates.

4. Amendments to the construction of the coding schedule and associated conventions

The major problems encountered in undertaking the rule book analyses reflected the nature of the trade union rule books themselves. These instruments of union governance evolve, and reflect both the regularity with which unions alter their contents and the patience of the drafters. It should also be noted that union policy on balloting was the subject of considerable controversy in the mid-1980s. The decision to apply or not apply for Government refunds of balloting costs became the focal point of discussion about responses/resistance to Government trade union legislation. For this reason the rules governing elections and industrial action may have been designed to obscure as much as enlighten. Unions that complied may have wanted to appear not to comply and vice versa.

There are two differences between the surveys undertaken in 1980 and 1987. First, the 1980 survey made no distinction between appointment and election as methods of selecting lay and full-time officers. As a consequence the codings dealing with the post of General Secretary were recoded in 1987 with figures drawn from the original rule books.

Second, in 1980 reference-back and industrial action ballots were divided into two categories, ballots mandatory by rule and ballots discretionary by rule. Every attempt has been made to reconcile the two sets of data by recalculating the 1980 data to fit the 1987 categories. However, it would appear that the 1980 codings may have overstated the incidence of ballots. In the 1987 and 1992 coding a slightly less optimistic convention has been adopted. For example, where a rule book makes no mention of ballots during collective bargaining but the executive reserves the right to initiate other unspecified actions in furtherance of the union's stated aims, this has not necessarily meant that the union has been categorized as holding ballots at the executive's discretion, although in reality this may be the case.

In the table below, changes in membership figures are calculated on the basis of TUC quoted figures in 1980 and 1987 plus the membership of any merger partner at the time of amalgamation/transfer of engagements minus the membership in 1987 or 1992, as appropriate. The figures do not take account of additional membership from mergers with unions who were not affiliated to the TUC. This is of little general significance, but may mean that the membership decline of some unions, such as the MSF and EETPU, is understated.

TABLE 3. Changes in the membership figures of unions affiliated to the TUC (1980–7 and 1987–92)

		1980–7	1987–92
	*Amalgamated Association of Beamers, Twisters and Drawers (Hand and Machine)**	−595	*Disaffiliated*
1.	Amalgamated Engineering Union*	−441,665	−234,937
	*Amalgamated Union of Asphalt Workers**	−1,018	*Merged with TGWU 1987*
2.	Associated Society of Locomotive Engineers and Firemen	−6,032	−2,580
	*Association of Cinematograph, Television and Allied Technicians**	+5,445	*Merged with BETA 1991*
3.	Association of First Division Civil Servants	+188	+2,127
	*Association of Professional, Executive, Clerical and Computer Staff**	−67,592	*Merged with GMB 1989*
	*Association of Scientific, Technical and Managerial Staffs**	−106,109	*Merged with TASS 1987*
4.	Association of University Teachers	+814	+1,266
5.	Bakers, Food and Allied Workers' Union	−8,233	−1,670
6.	The Banking, Insurance and Finance Union	+26,972	+3,683
7.	British Actors' Equity Association	+6,813	+9,878
8.	The British Airline Pilots Association	−712	+1,675
9.	The British Association of Colliery Management	−5,045	−5,461
10.	Broadcasting, Entertainment, Cinematography and Theatre Union*	+10,227	−24,452

TABLE 3. (*Continued*)

		1980–7	1987–92
11.	Card Setters and Machine Tenters' Society	−28	−14
12.	The Ceramic and Allied Trade Union	−12,053	−4,541
13.	The Civil and Public Servants Association	−73,370	−26,491
	*Civil Service Union**	*−15,696*	*Merged with SCPS 1987*
14.	Communications Managers' Association	−15,696	−1,708
15.	Confederation of Health Service Employees	−618	−10,319
16.	Educational Institute of Scotland	−5,564	+4,254
17.	Electrical, Electronic, Telecommunications and Plumbing Union	−83,845	+20,845
18.	Engineering and Fastner Trade Union	−2,100	−160
19.	Engineering Managers' Association	−7,618	−666
20.	Electrical and Plumbing Industries Union ■	(Affiliated in 1991)	
21.	Film Artistes Association	−298	−346
22.	The Fire Brigades Union	+14,919	+6,962
23.	Furniture, Timber and Allied Trade Union*	−39,339	−12,417
24.	GMB*	−282,781	+48,701
25.	General Union of Associations of Loom Overlookers	−1,235	−645
	*Greater London Staff Association**	*−4,849*	*Merged with GMB 1988*
26.	Graphical, Paper and Media Union* (formerly SOGAT and NGA)		−54,198
27.	The Hospital Consultants and Specialists Association	−1,382	−23
	*Health Visitors Association**	*+4,320*	*Transferred to MSF 1990*
28.	Inland Revenue Staff Federation	−9,959	+1,713
29.	Institution of Professionals, Managers and Specialists*	−25,379	+1,645
30.	The Iron and Steel Trades Confederation*	−50,234	−5,000

TABLE 3. (*Continued*)

		1980–7	1987–92
31.	Manufacturing Science and Finance* (formly TASS and ASTMS)		−27,000
32.	Musicians' Union	−3,185	−1,386
33.	National and Local Government Officers' Association*	−2,796	+9,305
34.	National Association of Colliery Overmen, Deputies and Shotfirers	−6,429	−6,967
35.	National Association of Cooperative Officials	−1,559	−176
36.	National Association of Licensed House Managers	−1,642	−4,177
37.	National Association of Probation Officers ■	(Affiliated 1984–5)	+677
38.	National Association of School Masters/Union of Women Teachers	+1,887	−2,803
39.	NATFHE—The University and College Lecturers Association	+11,556	−2,825
40.	National Communications Union	+29,920	−4,940
	*National Graphical Association**	*−10,875*	*Merged with SOGAT 1991*
41.	The National League of the Blind and Disabled	−1,424	−316
42.	National Union of Civil and Public Servants	−35,655	−5,745
43.	National Union of Domestic Appliances and General Operatives	−2,400	−700
	*National Union of Hosiery and Knitwear Workers**	*−21,511*	*Merged with NUFLAT 1991*
44.	National Union of Insurance Workers	−1,773	−689
45.	National Union of Journalists	−1,271	−2,202
46.	National Union of Knitwear, Footwear and Apparel Trades*	−21,511	−69,448
47.	National Union of Lock and Metal Workers	−1,706	−471
48.	The National Union of Maritime, Aviation and Shipping Transport Officers*	−14,938	−5,283
49.	National Union of Mineworkers	−148,241	−60,589
50.	National Union of Public Employees	−34,137	−106,468
	*National Union of Railwaymen**	*−55,000*	*Merged with NUS 1990*

TABLE 3. (*Continued*)

	1980–7	1987–92
51. National Union of Rail, Maritime, and Transport Workers (formerly NUR and NUS)		−33,795
*National Union of Seamen**	*−24,150*	*Merged with NUR 1990*
52. National Union of Scalemakers	*−940*	*−247*
*National Union of Tailor and Garment Workers**	*−43,452*	*Transferred to GMB 1991*
53. National Union of Teachers	−64,441	−19,737
*National Union of Footwear, Leather and Allied Trades**	*−27,944*	*Merged with NUHKW 1991*
54. Northern Carpet Trades' Union	−1,235	−109
Pattern Weavers' Society	*−40*	*Ceased affiliation 1989*
55. The Power Loom Carpet Weavers' and Textile Workers' Union	−2,823	−1,033
56. Prison Officers' Association	+3,388	+3,368
57. The Rosendale Union of Boot, Shoe and Slipper Operatives	−1,755	−1,790
58. Scottish Prison Officers' Association	+543	+989
59. The Society of Radiographers ■	(Affiliated in 1990)	
*Society of Civil and Public Servants**	*−19,959*	*Merged with CSU 1988*
*Society of Graphical and Allied Trades '82**	*−60,654*	*Merged with NGA 1991*
60. Society of Telecom Executives	+5,736	−3,276
*TASS**	*−570,997*	*Merged with ASTMS 1987*
*Tobacco Mechanics Association**	*−245*	*Merged with MSF 1989*
61. Transport and General Workers' Union*	−886,322	−252,525
62. Transport and Salaried Staffs Association	−26,426	−5,442
63. The Union of Communication Workers	−11,493	−5,110
64. Union of Construction, Allied Trades and Technicians	−98,292	−47,151
65. Union of Shop, Distributive and Allied Workers	−88,033	−40,635
66. Union of Textile Workers	−2,943	−1,112

TABLE 3. (*Continued*)

		1980–7	1987–92
67.	United Road Transport Union	−5,850	−2,669
	Wire Workers' Union*	−4,628	*Transferred to ISTC 1991*
68.	The Writers' Guild of Great Britain	−82	+144
69.	Yorkshire Association of Power Loom Overlookers	−548	−63

* indicates the Union was involved in merger or transfer of engagements with other TUC unions between 1980 and 1992.

■ indicates the union affiliated to the TUC after the first survey in 1980.

NOTE

1. The responses of the Society of Civil and Public Servants were hand-coded into the tables used in Undy and Martin (1984), but the codings were not included in the original data set.

ANNEX 1: CHANGES OF NAME, AMALGAMATION, TRANSFERS OF ENGAGEMENT, NEW AFFILIATIONS, DISAFFILIATIONS, AND DISSOLUTIONS

The following section describes how the composition of the sample of unions included in the survey has altered as a consequence of: (a) changes of union name, (b) amalgamation, (c) transfers of engagement, (d) new affiliations, (e) disaffiliations, and (f) dissolutions. It is important to note that the changes listed below only take account of changes within the TUC. Non-TUC-affiliates transferring their engagements to existing affiliates are therefore excluded from the lists.

a) Changes of Union Name

The Post Office Managers Staffs' Association changed its name to the Communications Managers Association in 1981.

The Greater London Council Staff Association dropped the word 'Council' from their name following the dissolution of the GLC in 1983.

The National Union of Domestic Appliance and General Metal Workers changed its name to become the National Union of Domestic Appliance and General Operatives between 1984 and 1985.

The Society of Post Office Executives became the Society of Telecom Executives in 1984–1985.

The Amalgamated Society of Wire Drawers and Kindred Workers became the Wire Workers' Union between 1985 and 1986.

The Entertainment Trade Alliance changed its name to the British Entertainment Trades Alliance in 1986.

The Screw, Nut, Bolt and Rivet Trade Union changed their name to the Engineering and Fastner Trade Union in 1989.

The Associated Society of Textile Workers and Kindred Trades changed its name to the Textile Workers Union in 1991.

b) Amalgamation

The Amalgamated Union of Engineering Workers (Technical Administrative and Supervisory Section) AUEW (TASS) merged with the Gold, Silver and Allied Trades in 1981, retaining the name AUEW (TASS).

The Society of Lithographic Artists, Designers, Engravers and Process Workers merged with the National Graphical Association in May 1982 to become the National Graphical Association '82 (NGA '82).

The National Society of Operative Printers, Graphical and Media Personnel merged with the Society of Graphical and Allied Trades to become the Society of Graphical and Allied Trades 1982 (SOGAT '82).

The Amalgamated Society of Boilermakers, Shipwrights, Blacksmiths and Structural Workers merged with the General Municipal Workers Union to form the General Municipal, Boilermakers and Allied Trades Union (GMBATU) in December 1982.

The Amalgamated Textile Workers' Union merged with the General Municipal, Boilermakers and Allied Trades Union in 1983, retaining the latter union's name.

The Amalgamated Union of Engineering Workers (Technical Administrative and Supervisory Section) AUEW (TASS) merged with the National Union of Sheet Metal Workers, Coppersmiths, Heating and Domestic Engineers in December 1983. In the following year the new union merged with the Association of Patternmakers and Allied Craftsmen.

The Association of Broadcasting and Allied Staffs merged with the National Association of Theatrical, Television and Kine Employees in 1984 to form the Entertainment Trades Alliance.

In 1985–6 AUEW (TASS) merged with the National Society of Metal Mechanics and the Tobacco Workers Union, splitting from the AEU to become TASS, an independent affiliate to the TUC.

The three sections of the Amalgamated Union of Engineering Workers—the Construction, Foundry, and Engineering sections—and the Roll Turners Trade Society merged during the period 1983–6 to become the Amalgamated Engineering Union.

The Merchant Navy and Airline Officers Association merged with the Radio and Electronic Officers in 1985–6 to form the National Union of Marine, Aviation and Shipping Transport Officers (NUMAST).

Civil Service Union and the Society of Civil and Public Servants merged to form the National Union of Civil and Public Servants in 1988.

The Association of Scientific, Technical and Managerial Staffs and TASS merged to form Manufacturing, Science and Finance in 1988.

The General, Municipal Boilermakers and Allied Trades Union merged with the Association of Professional, Executive, Clerical and Computer Staff to form GMB in March 1989.

The National Union of Railwaymen and the National Union of Seamen merged to form the National Union of Rail, Maritime and Transport Workers in September 1990.

The National Union of Hosiery and Knitwear Workers merged with the National Union of the Footwear, Leather and Allied Trades to form the National Union of Knitwear, Footwear and Apparel Trades in January 1991.

The Association of Cinematograph, Television and Allied Technicians merged with the Broadcasting Entertainment Trade Alliance to form the Broadcasting Entertainment, Cinematograph and Technicians Union in January 1991.

The Society of Graphical and Allied Trades 1982 (SOGAT) merged with the National Graphical Association 1982 to form the Graphical Paper and Media Union in September 1991.

The Amalgamated Engineering Union merged with the Electrical, Electronic, Telecommunication and Plumbing Union to form the Amalgamated Engineering and Electrical Union in May 1992.

c) Transfers of Engagement

In January 1981, the Huddersfield Healders and Twisters' Trade and Friendly Society transferred engagements to the National Union of Dyers, Bleachers and Textile Workers.

In 1982, the National Union of Dyers, Bleachers and Textile Workers transferred engagements to the Transport and General Workers Union to form the Dyers, Bleachers and Textile Workers Trade Group of the TGWU. In the same year the National Union of Agricultural and Allied Workers transferred engagements to the TGWU and formed another trade group within the union. Following a subsequent review of the structure of the TGWU, both of these trade groups were combined with the main body of the union.

The Amalgamated Society of Journeymen, Felt Hatters and Allied Workers, together with the Amalgamated Felt Hat Trimmers, Woolformers and Allied Workers Association, transferred engagements to the National Union of Tailors and Garment Workers in October 1982.

The Medical Practitioners Section of the Association of Scientific, Managerial and Technical Staffs (ASTMS) was integrated into the main body of the union following the TUC's review of sections in 1982.

The National Society of Brushmakers and General Workers transferred engagements to the Furniture, Timber and Allied Trades Union (FTAT) in 1983.

The Association of Government Supervisors and Radio Officers transferred engagements to the Institution of Professional Civil Servants in February 1984.

The National Union of Blast Furnacemen, Ore Miners, Coke Workers and Kindred Trades transferred engagements to the Iron and Steel Trades Confederation (ISTC) between 1984 and 1985.

The Sheffield Sawmakers Protection Society transferred engagements to the Transport and General Workers Union in May 1984.

The Post and Telecommunications Section of the Civil and Public Services Association transferred to the Post Office Engineering Union (POEU) to become the National Communications Union in 1985.

Amalgamated Union of Asphalt Workers transferred engagements to the Transport and General Workers' Union in December 1987.

The Greater London Staff Association transferred engagements to the General, Municipal and Boilermakers and Allied Trades Union in September 1988.

The Tobacco Mechanics Association transferred engagements to the Manufacturing Science and Finance in 1989.

The Health Visitors Association transferred engagements to the Manufacturing, Science and Finance Union in August 1990.

The National Union of Tailor and Garment Workers transferred engagements to the GMB in March 1991.

The Wire Workers Union transferred engagements to the Iron and Steel Trades Confederation in April 1991.

d) New Affiliations

Throughout the early 1980s the TUC pursued a policy of advising potential new recruits to pursue a merger with an affiliated union rather than affiliate in their own right. This policy was enforced less strictly as membership numbers continued to decline towards the end of the decade.

The National Association of Probation Officers (NAPO) was accepted into affiliation in 1984–5.

Society of Radiographers was accepted into affiliation in October 1990.

The Electrical Plumbing and Industries Union, a breakaway section of the EETPU, was accepted into affiliation in April 1991.

Chartered Society of Physiotherapy was accepted into affiliation in September 1992.

Note: the Union of Democratic Mineworkers applied for affiliation in 1989 but was refused.

e) Disaffiliations

The Associated Metal Workers Union withdrew from affiliation in 1987.

The Electrical, Electronic and Plumbing Union was suspended from TUC membership in 1988 and subsequently disaffiliated in 1989 in advance of formal expulsion.

The Pattern Weavers Society ceased affiliation in 1989.

The Amalgamated Association of Beamers, Twisters and Drawers (Hand and Machine) ceased its affiliation in 1992.

f) Dissolutions

The Cloth Pressers' Society was formally dissolved in December 1984.

The Spring Trapmakers' Society dissolved in 1988.

BIBLIOGRAPHY

ACAS (1987), *Annual Report* (London).
—— (1991), *Annual Report* (London).
—— (1993), *Annual Report* (London).
Adeney, M., and Lloyd, J. (1986), *The Miners Strike* (London: Routledge).
Auerbach, S. (1990), *Legislating for Conflict* (Oxford: Oxford University Press).
Bailey, R., and Kelly, J. (1990), 'An Index Measure of British Trade Union Density', *British Journal of Industrial Relations* 28.
Bain, G. S., and Price, R. (1993), 'Union Growth: Dimensions and Density', in Bain, G. S. (ed.), *Industrial Relations in Britain* (Oxford: Blackwell).
Bassett, P. (1987), *Strike Free* (Basingstoke: Macmillan).
Batstone, E., Boraston, I., and Frenkel, S. (1978), *The Social Organization of Strikes: Warwick Studies in Industrial Relations* (Oxford: Blackwell).
Berlin, I. (1969), *Four Essays on Liberty* (Oxford: Oxford University Press).
Bird, D. (1994), 'Labour Disputes in 1993', *Employment Gazette*, June.
Blackburn, R. M., Prandy, K., and Stewart, A. (1968), 'White-Collar Associations: Organizational Character and Employee Involvement', in Mann, M. (ed.), *Proceedings of an SSRC Conference on Social Stratification & Industrial Relations, 1968*.
Blackwell, R. (1990), 'Parties and Factions in Trade Unions', *Employee Relations* 12.
Blanc-Jouvan, X. (1988), 'France' *Bulletin of Comparative Labour Relations* 17.
Blyton, P., and Turnbull, P. (eds.) (1992), *Reassessing Human Resource Management* (London: Sage).
Brown, W. (1993), 'The Contraction of Collective Bargaining in Britain', *British Journal of Industrial Relations* 31.
Buxton, T., Chapman, P., and Temple, P. (1994), *Britain's Economic Performance* (London: Routledge).
Carter, B. (1991), 'Politics and Process in the Making of Manufacturing Science and Finance (MSF)', *Capital and Class* 45.
Carty, H. (1991), 'The Employment Act 1990: Still Fighting the Industrial Cold War', *Industrial Law Journal* 20.
Child, J., Loveridge, R., and Warner, M. (1973), 'Towards an Organizational Study of Trade Unions', *Sociology* 7.
Clegg, H. A. (1976), *Trade Unionism and Collective Bargaining: A Theory Based on Comparisons of Six Countries* (Oxford: Blackwell).
Clegg, H. A. (1979), *The Changing System of Industrial Relations in Great Britain* (Oxford: Blackwell).
Common, R., Flynn, N., and Mellon, E. (1992), *Managing Public Services* (Oxford: Butterworth Heinemann).
CCO (Conservative Central Office) (1976), *The Right Approach: A Statement of Conservative Aims* (London).
—— (1979), *Conservative Manifesto 1979* (London).
—— (1987), *The Next Moves Forward* (London).

—— (1992), *The Best Future for Britain: The Conservative Manifesto 1992* (London).

CPC (Conservative Political Centre) (1966), *Trade Unions for Tomorrow: The Memorandum of Evidence Presented to the Royal Commission on Trade Unions and Employers' Associations by the Inns of Court* (London).

Crouch, C. (1986), 'Conservative Industrial Relations Policy: Towards Labour Exclusion', in Jacobi, D. (ed.), *Economic Crisis, Trade Unions and the State* (Beckenham: Croom Helm).

—— (1993), *Industrial Relations and European State Traditions* (Oxford: Clarendon Press).

Dabscheck, B., and Niland, J. (1981), *Industrial Relations in Australia* (London: George Allen & Unwin).

Daly, J. (1984), *Trade Union Bill is Ballot Rigger's Charter* (London: Aims of Industry).

Daniel, W., and Millward, N. (1983), *Workplace Industrial Relations in Britain: The DE/PSI/ESRC Survey* (Aldershot: Gower).

Darlington, R. (1994), *The Dynamics of Workplace Unionism* (London: Mansell).

Davies, P., and Freedland, M. (1984), *Labour Law: Text and Materials* (London: Weidenfeld and Nicholson).

DE (1981), *Trade Union Immunities*, Cmnd. 8128 (London: HMSO).

—— (1983a), *Democracy in Trade Unions*, Cmnd. 8778 (London: HMSO).

—— (1983b), *Proposals for Legislation on Democracy in Trade Unions*, (London: HMSO).

—— (1987), *Trade Unions and their Members*, Cmnd. 95 (London: HMSO).

—— (1988), *Employment for the 1990s*, Cmnd. 540 (London: HMSO).

—— (1989a), *Removing Barriers to Employment: Proposals for the Further Reform of Industrial Relations and Trade Union Law*, Cmnd. 665 (London: HMSO.

—— (1989b), *Unofficial Action and the Law: Proposals to Reform the Law Affecting Unofficial Industrial Action*, Cmnd. 821 (London: HMSO).

—— (1991), *Industrial Relations in the 1990s*, Cmnd. 1602 (London: HMSO).

——(1994), *Competitiveness: Helping Business to Win*, Cmnd. 2563 (London: HMSO).

DEP (Department of Employment and Productivity) (1969), *In Place of Strife: A Policy for Industrial Relations*, Cmnd. 3888 (London: HMSO).

Dickens, L., and Cockburn, D. (1986), 'Dispute Settlement Institutions and the Courts', in Lewis, R., *Labour Law in Britain* (Oxford: Blackwell).

Disney, R. (1990), 'Explanations of the Decline in Trade Union Density In Britain: An Appraisal', *British Journal of Industrial Relations* 28.

Donovan (1968), *Royal Commission on Trade Unions and Employers' Associations 1965–1968* (London: HMSO, Cmnd. 3623).

Due, J., Madsen, J. S., and Stoby-Jensen (1991), 'The Social Dimension: Convergence or Diversification of IR in the Single European Market?', *Industrial Relations Journal* 22.

Edelstein, J. D., and Warner, M. (1975), *Comparative Union Democracy* (London: Allen & Unwin).

Edwards, P. K. (1992), 'Industrial Conflict: Themes and Issues in Recent Research', *British Journal of Industrial Relations* 30.

EEF (1987), *Response to the Green Paper* Trade Unions and their Members (London).

EIRR (1989), 'The Regulation of Industrial Conflict in Europe', EIRR Report no. 2, Dec.

Elgar, J., and Simpson, R. (1992), *The Impact of the Law on Industrial Disputes in the 1980s*, Centre for Economic Performance, Discussion Paper No. 104 (London: LSE).

—— —— (1993a), *The Impact of the Law on Industrial Disputes in the 1980s: Report of a Survey of Engineering Employers*, Centre for Economic Performance, Discussion Paper No. 150 (London: LSE).

—— —— (1993b), *The Impact of the Law on Industrial Disputes in the 1980s: Report of Negotiators in Twenty-Five Unions 1991–1992*, Centre for Economic Performance, Discussion Paper No. 171 (London: LSE).

Elias, P. (1990), 'Law and Union Democracy: The Changing Shape', in Fosh, P., and Heery, E. (eds.), *Trade Unions and their Members: Studies in Union Democracy and Organisation* (Basingstoke: Macmillan).

—— and Ewing, K. (1987), *Trade Union Democracy, Members' Rights and the Law* (London: Mansell).

—— Napier, B., and Wallington, P. (1980), *Labour Law Cases and Materials* (London: Butterworth).

England, J. (1981), 'Shop Stewards in Transport House: A Comment on the Incorporation of the Rank and File', *Industrial Relations Journal* 12.

EPI (1992), Sept. 1992 Report (London).

—— (1993), July 1993 Report (London).

ERBS (1994), *ERBS Update* (London).

Evans, S. (1985), 'Research Note: The Use of Injunctions in Industrial Disputes,' *British Journal of Industrial Relations* 23.

—— (1987), 'The Use of Injunctions in Industrial Disputes, May 1984–April 1987,' *British Journal of Industrial Relations* 25.

Ewing, K. (1990), 'Labour under the 1980s' Conservative Government', paper presented at the Cardiff Business School Conference on Employment Relations in the Enterprise Culture.

Fairbrother, P. (1983), *The Politics of Union Ballots*, Workers' Educational Association: Studies for Trade Unionists, 9.

—— (1984), *All Those in Favour: The Politics of Union Democracy* (London: Pluto).

Fatchett, D. (1987), *Trade Unions and Politics in the 1980s* (New York: Croom Helm).

Ferner, A., and Hyman, R. (eds.) (1992), *Industrial Relations in the New Europe* (Oxford: Blackwell).

Flanders, A. (1974), 'The Tradition of Voluntarism', *British Journal of Industrial Relations* 12.

Ford, M. (1992), 'Citizenship and Democracy in Industrial Relations: The Agenda for the 1990s?', *Modern Law Review* 55.

Fosh, P., and Cohen, S. (1990), 'Local Trade Unionists in Action: Patterns of Union Democracy', in Fosh, P., and Heery, E., *Trade Unions and their Members* (London: Macmillan).

—— Morris, H., Martin, R., Smith, P., and Undy, R. (1993a), 'Politics,

Pragmatism and Ideology: The "Wellsprings" of Conservative Union Legislation (1979–1992)', *Industrial Law Journal* 22.

—— —— —— —— —— (1993b), 'Union Autonomy, a Terminal Case in the UK? A Comparison with the Approach in other Western European Countries and the USA', *Employee Relations* 15.

—— —— —— —— —— (1993c), 'Union Autonomy in Context: An International Comparison', *Employee Relations* 15.

Fredman, S. (1992), 'The New Rights: Labour Law and Ideology in the Thatcher Years', *Oxford Journal of Legal Studies* 12.

Freeman, R., and Pelletier, J. (1992), 'The Impact of Industrial Relations Legislation on British Union Density', *British Journal of Industrial Relations* 28.

Gall, G. and McKay, S. (1994), 'Trade Union Derecognition in Britain', 1988–1994', *British Journal of Industrial Relations* 32.

Gennard, J., and Bain, P. (1995), *A History of the Society of Graphical and Allied Trades* (London: Routledge).

Giugni, G. (1988), 'Italy', *Bulletin of Comparative Labour Relations* 17.

GMB (1988), *Shaping up for the Next Century* (London).

—— (1991), *Poll Position: Public Attitudes to Trade Unions 1979–1991* (London).

—— (1993), *Industrial Action Guide for Officers* (London).

Goetschy, J., and Rozenblatt, P. (1992), 'France: The Industrial Relations System at a Turning Point?', in Ferner, A., and Hyman, R. (eds.), *Industrial Relations in the New Europe* (Oxford: Blackwell).

GPMU (1988), *Biennial Delegate Conference Report* (Bedford).

—— (1993), *GPMU Branch Circular* (Bedford).

Green, F. (1992), 'Recent Trends in British Trade Union Density: How Much a Compositional Effect?', *British Journal of Industrial Relations* 30.

Guigni, G. (1988), 'Italy', *Bulletin of Comparative Labour Relations* 17.

Hanson, C. G., and Mather, G. (1988), '*Striking Out Strikes: Changing Employment Relations in the British Labour Market*', Hobart Paper no. 110 (London: Institute of Economic Affairs).

Hayek, F. (1980), *Unemployment and the Unions* (London: Institute of Economic Affairs).

Hendy, J. (1989), *The Conservative Employment Laws: A National and International Assessment* (London: Institute of Employment Rights).

—— McCarthy, Lord, and Wedderburn, Lord (1989), Ballots on Industrial Action: The Draft Code of Practice (London: Institute of Employment Rights).

Hougham, J. (1992), 'Law and the Working Environment: The Ford Experience', in McCarthy, W. (ed), *Legal Interventions in Industrial Relations: Gains and Losses* (Oxford: Blackwell).

Hutton, J. (1984), 'Solving the Strike Problem: Part II of the Trade Union Act 1984', *Industrial Law Journal* 13.

Hyman, R. (1989), *The Political Economy of Industrial Relations: Theory and Practice in a Cold Climate* (London: Macmillan).

IDS (1992a), 'Management and the Law', *IDS Focus* no. 62, Mar.

—— (1992b), *IDS Focus* no. 65, Dec.

IDS/IPM (1991), *European Management Guides: Industrial Relations 1991* (London: IDS/IPM).

ILO (1989), *Report of the Committee of Experts on the Application of Conventions and Recommendations* (International Labour Conference, 76th Session), report iii, pt. 4a (Geneva).

IPA (1993), 'Towards Industrial Partnership' (London).

IRS (1992), 'Rover's New Deal', *Employment Trends* 514.

Jacobi, O., Kellner, B., and Muller-Jentsch, W. (1992), 'Germany: Codetermining the Future', in Ferner, A., and Hyman, R. (eds.), *Industrial Relations in the New Europe* (Oxford: Blackwell).

JIRD (Jaguar Industrial Relations Department) (1988), 'Procedure for the Avoidance of Disputes' (internal paper).

Jones, N. (1986), *Strikes and the Media* (Oxford: Blackwell).

Jordan, W. B. (1994), Speech to the Foundation for Manufacturing and Industry.

Kahn-Freund, O. (1983), *Labour and the Law*, Third Edn. (London: Stevens).

Kelly, J. (1989), 'British Trade Unionism 1979–1989: Change, Continuity and Contradictions', paper delivered to the Conference 'Work, Employment and Society—Decade of Change', Durham.

—— (1990), 'British Trade Unionism 1979–89: Change, Continuity and Contradictions', *Work, Employment and Society* Additional Special Issue, May.

—— and Heery, E. (1989), 'Full-Time Officers and Trade Union Recruitment', *British Journal of Industrial Relations* 27.

Kerr, A., and Sachdev, S. (1992), 'Third among Equals: An Analysis of the 1989 Ambulance Dispute,' *British Journal of Industrial Relations* 30.

Kessler, I. (1994), 'Performance Pay', in Sission, K. (ed.), *Personal Management* (Oxford: Blackwell).

Kessler, S., and Bayliss, F. (1992), *Contemporary British Industrial Relations* (Basingstoke: Macmillan).

Kidner, R. (1984), 'Trade Union Democracy: Election of Trade Union Officers', *Industrial Law Journal* 13.

Kritsantonis, N. (1992), 'Greece: From State Authoritarianism to Modernization', in Ferner, A., and Hyman, R. (eds.), *Industrial Relations in the New Europe* (Oxford: Blackwell).

Lane, T., and Roberts, K. (1971), *Strike at Pilkingtons* (London: Collins/Fontana).

Lewis, R. (1986), 'The Role of Law in Employment Relations', in *Labour Law in Britain* (Oxford: Blackwell).

Lincoln, Y. S., and Gubba, E. G. (1985), *Naturalistic Inquiry* (London: Sage).

Little, K. (1991), *Trade Union Mergers 1979–1989: The Financial Considerations*, M.Phil. thesis, University of Oxford (unpub.).

Lloyd, J. (1985), *Understanding the Miners' Strike* (London: Fabian Society).

—— (1990), *Light & Liberty: The History of the EETPU* (London: Weidenfeld and Nicholson).

Loveday, M. (1987), *Postal Ballots and the Unions* (London: Policy Research Associates).

LRD (1985), 'Rise in Legal Actions against Unions', *Labour Research*, Oct.

—— (1987), 'Bosses Resort to Tory Union Laws', *Labour Research*, Oct.

—— (1988), 'Tightening the Legal Grip around the Unions', *Labour Research*, Sept.

—— (1989), 'Judges Move Nearer Strike Ban', *Labour Research*, Oct.

—— (1991), 'Unions in a Legal Minefield', *Labour Research*, Oct.

—— (1993), 'The Tories' Union-Ballot Mania', *Labour Research*, Feb.

—— (1994), 'Employers Step Up Legal Challenges', *Labour Research*, TUC Special, Sept.

Luico, M. (1992), 'Spain: Constricting Institutions and Actors in a Context of Change', in Ferner, A., and Hyman, R. (eds.), *Industrial Relations in the New Europe* (Oxford: Blackwell).

Lukes, S. (1974) *Power* (London: Macmillan).

McCarthy, Lord (1987), in Mather, G., and McCarthy, Lord, 'The Future of Labour Law: Two Views', *Warkwick Papers in Industrial Relations* no. 14.

McCarthy, Lord (1992), 'The Rise and Fall of Collective *Laissez Faire*', in McCarthy, W. (ed.), *Legal Intervention in Industrial Relations: Gains and Losses* (Oxford: Blackwell).

McIlroy, J. (1991), *The Permanent Revolution? Conservative Law and Trade Unions* (Nottingham: Spokesman).

McKinlay, A., and McNulty, D. (1992), 'At the Cutting Edge of New Realism: The Engineers' 35 hour week Campaign', *Industrial Relations Journal* 23.

McKendrick, E. (1988), 'The Rights of Trade Union Members—Part 1 of the Employment Act 1988', *Industrial Law Journal* 17.

Mackie, K. (1984), 'Law Commentary: Three Faces of Democracy and Three Missing Persons: the Trade Union Act 1984', *Industrial Relations Journal* 15.

—— (1987), 'One More Time: How do we Democratise Organizations', *Industrial Relations Journal* 18.

Manning, A. (1991), *Pre-Strike Ballots and Wage Employment Bargaining*, Centre for Economic Performance, Discussion Paper no. 19 (London: LSE).

Marsh, A. (1988), *A Trade Union Handbook* (London: Gower).

Marsh, D. (1992), *The New Politics of British Trade Unionism* (Basingstoke: Macmillan).

Martin, R. (1968) 'Union Democracy: An Explanatory Framework', *Sociology* 2.

—— (1992), *Bargaining Power* (Oxford: Clarendon Press).

Meredeen, S. (1988), *Managing Industrial Conflict: Seven Major Disputes* (London: Hutchinson).

Michels, R. (1962), *Political Parties* (Glencoe, Ill.: Free Press).

Miller, K. (1986), 'Trade Union Government and Democracy', in Lewis, R., *Labour Law in Britain* (Oxford: Blackwell).

Millward, N. (1994), *The New Industrial Relations* (London: Policy Studies Institute).

—— and Stevens, M. (1986), *British Workplace Industrial Relations 1980–1984* (Aldershot: Gower).

—— —— Smart, D., and Hawes, W. (1992), *Workplace Industrial Relations in Transition: The ED/ESRC/PSI/ACAS Surveys* (Aldershot: Dartmouth).

Mintzberg, H. (1987), 'Crafting Strategy', *Harvard Business Review* 65.

Morris, G. (1993), 'Industrial Action: Public and Private Interests', *Industrial Law Journal* 22.

MSF (1993), 'MSF into the 21st Century' (London).

Muckenberger, Z., and Deakin, S. (1989), 'From Deregulation to a European Floor of Rights: Labour Law, Flexibilisation and the European Single Market', *Zeitschrift fur Auslandisches und Internationales Arbeits und Sozialrecht* (1989) 3.

NALGO (1988) *Conference Report* (London).

OECD (1991), *Employment Outlook* (Paris).

Offe, C., and Wiesenthal, H. (1985), 'Two Logics of Collective Action', in Offe, C. (ed.), *Disorganised Capitalism* (Cambridge: Polity Press).

Olea, M., and Rodriguez-Sanudo, F. (1987), 'Spain' in Blanpain, R. (ed.), *The International Encyclopedia of Labour Law and Industrial Relations* (Deventer, Netherlands: Kluwer).

Prior, J. (1986), *A Balance of Power* (London: Hamish Hamilton).

Purcell, J. (1991), 'The Rediscovery of the Management Prerogative: The Management of Labour Relations in the 1990s', *Oxford Review of Economic Policy* 7.

Redmond, M. (1991), 'Ireland', in Blanpain, R. (ed.), *The International Encyclopedia of Labour Law and Industrial Relations* (Deventer, Netherlands: Kluwer).

Salamon, M. (1987), *Industrial Relations: Theory & Practice* (Englewood Cliffs, NJ: Prentice-Hall).

Scheuer, S. (1992), 'Denmark: Return to Dencentralisation', in Ferner, A., and Hyman, R. (eds.), (1992).

Simpson, B. (1986), 'Trade Union Immunities', in Lewis, R. (ed.), *Labour Law in Britain* (Oxford: Blackwell).

—— (1989), 'The Summer of Discontent and the Law', *Industrial Law Journal* 18.

—— (1990), 'Recent Legislation: Code of Practice on Trade Union Ballots on Industrial Action', *Industrial Law Journal* 19.

—— (1991), 'The Employment Act 1990 in Context', *Modern Law Review* 54.

—— (1993), 'Strike Ballots, the Judiciary, Government Policy and Industrial Relations Practice', *Industrial Law Journal* 22.

Sisson, K. (1989), *Personnel Management in Britain* (Oxford: Blackwell).

Smith, P., and Morton, G. (1993), 'Union Exclusion and the Decollectivisation of Industrial Relations in Contemporary Britain', *British Journal of Industrial Relations* 13.

Steele, M. (1990), 'Changing the Rules; Pressures on Trade Union Constitutions', in Fosh, P. and Heery, E. (eds.), *Trade Unions and their Members* (Basingstoke, Macmillan).

Tebbit, N. (1988), *Upwardly Mobile* (London: Weidenfeld and Nicholson).

T&G/GMB (1992) 'Training for Britain's Economic Success' (London).

TGWU (1992a) 'One Union T&G' (London).

—— (1992b), *Report of the General Executive Council on the Klein Consultation* (London).

—— (1993), 'Focus for the Future' (London).

Thomas, D. (1986), 'The Hidden Negotiating Power of the Compulsory Ballot', *Financial Times*, 3 Jan.

Treu, T. (1988), 'Italy', *Bulletin of Comparative Labour Relations* 17.

—— (1991), 'Italy', in Blanpain, R., *The International Encyclopedia of Labour Law and Industrial Relations* (Deventer, Netherlands: Kluwer).

TUC (1983), *Hands up for Democracy* (London).

—— (1984), *The 1984 Trade Union Act: The TUC Response to the New Legislation* (London).

—— (1987), *Green Paper* Trade Unions and Their Members (London).

—— (1988), *Annual Report* (London).

Turner, H. A. (1962), *Trade Union Growth, Structure & Policy* (London: Allen & Unwin).

TURU (1989): Trade Union Research Unit, Ruskin College, 'Balloting before Industrial Action', Occasional Paper no. 100.

Undy, R., Ellis, V., McCarthy, W. E. J., and Halmos, A. M. (1981), *Change in Trade Unions* (London: Hutchinson).

Undy, R., and Martin, R. (1984), *Ballots and Trade Union Democracy* (Oxford: Blackwell).

Upchurch, M., and Donnelly, E. (1992), 'Research Note: Membership Patterns in USDAW 1980–1990', *Industrial Relations Journal* 23.

Urwin, H., and Murray, G. (1983), 'Democracy and Trade Unions', *Industrial Relations Journal* 14.

Valdes Dal-Re, F. (1988), 'Spain', *Bulletin of Comparative Labour Relations* 17.

Visser, J. (1992), 'The Netherlands: The End of an Era and the End of a System', in Ferner, A., and Hyman, R. (eds.), *Industrial Relations in the New Europe* (Oxford: Blackwell).

von Prondzynski, F. (1992), 'Ireland: Between Centralism and the Market', in Ferner, A., and Hyman, R. (eds.), *Industrial Relations in the New Europe* (Oxford: Blackwell).

Waddington, J. (1988), 'Trade Union Mergers: A Study of Trade Union Structural Dynamics', *British Journal of Industrial Relations* 26.

—— (1992), 'Trade Union Membership in Britain, 1980–87: Unemployment and Restructuring', *British Journal of Industrial Relations* 30.

Walsh, K. (1991), *Competitive Tendering for Local Authority Services: Initial Experiences* (London: HMSO).

Webb, P. (1992), *Trade Unions and the British Electorate* (Aldershot: Dartmouth).

Weber, M. (1978), *Economy and Society*, (ed.) Roth, G., and Wittich, C., 4th edn., 2 vols. (Berkeley, Calif.: University of California Press).

Wedderburn, Lord (1985), 'The New Industrial Laws in Great Britain', *Labour and Society* 10.

Wedderburn, Lord (1986), *The Worker and the Law* (Harmondsworth: Penguin).

Wedderburn, Lord (1988), 'United Kingdom', *Bulletin of Comparative Labour Relations* 17.

Wedderburn, Lord (1989), 'Freedom of Association and Philosophies of Labour Law', *Industrial Law Journal* 18.

Wilkinson, T. (1987), *Guide on Workplace Balloting* (London: Institute of Personnel Management).

Willetts, D. (1992), *Modern Conservatism* (Harmondsworth: Penguin).

Willman, P. (1989), 'The Logic of "Market-Share" Trade Unionism: Is Membership Decline Inevitable?', *Industrial Relations Journal* 20.

—— Morris, T., and Aston, B. (1993), *Union Business* (Cambridge: Cambridge University Press).

Wilson, A. (1986), 'The Debate over Labour Law: New Rights or New Responsibilities', in Coates, K. (ed.), *Fairness and Freedom* (Nottingham: Russell Press).

Young, H. (1989), *One of Us* (London: Macmillan).

INDEX